THE POLITICS OF INFORMAL JUSTICE

VOLUME 2

Comparative Studies

STUDIES ON LAW AND SOCIAL CONTROL

DONALD BLACK *Series Editor*

Center for Criminal Justice
Harvard Law School
Cambridge, Massachusetts 02138

THE POLITICS OF INFORMAL JUSTICE

VOLUME 2

Comparative Studies

Edited by

RICHARD L. ABEL

School of Law
University of California, Los Angeles
Los Angeles, California

ACADEMIC PRESS
A Subsidiary of Harcourt Brace Jovanovich, Publishers
New York   London   Toronto   Sydney   San Francisco

ACADEMIC PRESS, INC.
111 Fifth Avenue, New York, New York 10003

United Kingdom Edition published by
ACADEMIC PRESS, INC. (LONDON) LTD.
24/28 Oval Road, London NW1   7DX

Library of Congress Cataloging in Publication Data
Main entry under title:

The Politics of informal justice.

   (Studies on law and social control)
   Includes bibliographies and index.
   Contents: v. 1. The American experience--
v. 2. Comparative studies.
   1. Justice, Administration of. 2. Justice,
Administration of--United States. I. Abel,
Richard L. II. Series.
K559.P64   347   81-14920
ISBN 0-12-041502-X (v. 2)   342.7   AACR2

PRINTED IN THE UNITED STATES OF AMERICA

82 83 84 85   9 8 7 6 5 4 3 2 1

Contents

NONINDUSTRIAL SOCIETIES

II

THE DRIFT TOWARD FASCISM

4   UDO REIFNER

Individualistic and Collective Legalization: The Theory and Practice of Legal Advice for Workers in Prefascist Germany   81

III

LIBERAL CAPITALISM

IV

THE REVOLUTIONARY SITUATION

List of Contributors

Numbers in parentheses indicate the pages on which the authors' contributions begin.

Richard L. Abel (1), School of Law, University of California, Los Angeles, Los Angeles, California 90024

Marc Galanter (47), Law School, University of Wisconsin–Madison, Madison, Wisconsin 53706

Bryant Garth (183), School of Law, Indiana University, Bloomington, Indiana 47405

John Owen Haley (125), School of Law, University of Washington, Seattle, Washington 98105

Heleen F. P. Ietswaart (149), Service de Coordination de la Recherche, Ministère de la Justice, 75001 Paris, France

Allen Isaacman (281), Department of History, University of Minnesota, Minneapolis, Minnesota 55455

Barbara Isaacman (281), National Labor Relations Board, Region 18, Minneapolis, Minnesota 55401

Sally Engle Merry (17), Department of Anthropology, Wellesley College, Wellesley, Massachusetts 02181

Catherine S. Meschievitz (47), Law School, University of Wisconsin–Madison, Madison, Wisconsin 53706

Udo Reifner (81), School of Economics and Politics, Freie Universität Berlin, Berlin, Federal Republic of Germany

Boaventura de Sousa Santos (251), Faculdade de Economia, Universidade de Coimbra, Coimbra, Portugal

Jack Spence (215), Department of Political Science, University of Massachusetts–Boston, Boston, Massachusetts 02125

1

Introduction

RICHARD L. ABEL

Informal justice is a phenomenon of international provenance and rapidly growing significance. In the United States in recent years it has been the subject of several major national conferences, it has aroused the interest of the American Bar Association and the Department of Justice, and it has spawned alternative dispute institutions in more than 100 cities throughout the country. It has also been the focus of considerable experimentation and scholarship in both Europe and the Third World. The chapters in this book (and in the companion volume on *The American Experience*)[1] vividly demonstrate that examples of informal

[1] The idea for these volumes originated in a panel discussion at the second National Conference on Critical Legal Studies, held in Madison, Wisconsin, November 10–12, 1978, at which drafts of several of the essays were presented and in which the authors of others participated. CCLS is an organization of several hundred law teachers and students, legal workers, and social scientists committed to the exploration of the relationship between legal theory and practice and the struggle for the creation of a more humane and just society. It was founded in Madison in 1977 and since then has held conferences in Boston, San Francisco, Buffalo, and Minneapolis. Although most of the contributors to these volumes are members of CCLS, each chapter expresses the views of its author alone, and these volumes are not an official publication of the Conference.

1

justice can be found in every social formation, flying the banner of every political ideology: in precapitalist societies and contemporary Third World nations; under liberal capitalism, social democracy, and fascism (in both their historical and contemporary manifestations); and in socialist revolutions and established socialist regimes.

Any attempt at understanding informal justice obviously must begin with a conceptualization. Yet precise definition is difficult: The boundaries of the phenomenon are constantly shifting as new institutions are created or old ones recharacterized. The best I can do is suggest some of the relevant parameters. These are institutions of justice in the sense that they define, modify, and apply norms in the course of controlling conduct or handling conflict. Their informalism is less a positive ideal than a set of loosely associated aversions to characteristics attributed to formal justice. Thus informal justice is said to be unofficial (dissociated from state power), noncoercive (dependent on rhetoric rather than force), nonbureaucratic, decentralized, relatively undifferentiated, and nonprofessional; its substantive and procedural rules are imprecise, unwritten, demotic, flexible, ad hoc, and particularistic. No concrete informal legal institution will embody all these qualities, but each will exhibit some. How these variables are actually combined is an empirical question; which ones should be considered essential is a normative problem; both issues require analysis.

The chapters that follow situate contemporary experiments with informal justice (including those described in the companion volume) in a broad comparative and historical perspective. They emphasize that legal informalism is a capacious slogan—a flexible vessel into which almost any political content can be poured. Ietswaart, in particular, shows that the boundary separating both liberal and socialist notions of popular justice from the fascist reality of summary justice is uncomfortably permeable. The political meaning of informal justice can therefore be ascertained only within a specific historical context. In this introduction I will draw upon the chapters following to identify the common elements in four such settings: precapitalist social formations, fascism, the welfare state, and socialism. I will also consider variations within each category and pressures that tend to transform one type of informalism into another or push it in the direction of formalism.

The chapters by Merry and by Meschievitz and Galanter outline the characteristics of informal justice in precapitalist societies and thereby demonstrate why comparable institutions cannot be recreated under Western capitalism. Precapitalist legal informalism is embedded in and contingent upon a social structure in which: relationships are multiplex and continuous, the supporters of one disputant are bound to the other by crosscutting ties, there is little residential mobility, and reputation in the face-to-face community is highly valued and easily lost in the absence of privacy. Western capitalism not only lacks these qualities but also actively rejects them. Relationships are commodified and thus single purpose; bourgeois individualism values the ability to terminate them at will, to repudiate ascriptive loyalties, to move freely, and to enjoy the anonymity offered by mass society. It is not surprising, therefore, that when informal legal institutions are introduced into Western capitalist societies they do not help to preserve relationships (though they are often justified by invoking this goal) but rather serve to celebrate their termination. Furthermore, when such institutions are established or artificially resuscitated by the state, they are inevitably "rationalized" to meet the dictates of bureaucratic control and economic efficiency; in the process their jurisdiction is expanded, thereby undermining the social infrastructure of the institution—a closed network of multiplex relations that bourgeois society finds claustrophobic.

Precapitalist informalism also rests on the implicit threat of violence (natural and supernatural)—whether mobilized by the victim, the victim's supporters, or even the offender's own allies (who fear revenge). It is this threat that persuades the parties to submit to mediation, to accept a proposed solution, and to carry it out. The capitalist state, by contrast, claims to monopolize violence—this is one of its defining features. Indeed, its informal legal procedures may be particularly severe with parties who resort to private force to redress wrongs. In consequence, informal institutions under capitalism must rely on state coercion rather than private threats (although the former usually remains covert) in order to induce the parties to consent to their jurisdiction, agree to their recommendations, and comply with them. The mere existence of coercive alternatives to informal institutions inevitably colors the dispute process within the latter, in contemporary India as well as in the West. Their staff rely increasingly on coercion and seek to acquire more state authority. The institutions thus tend to criminalize civil disputes and to become a mechanism for state control rather than dispute settlement. Reliance on coercion, in turn, leads to the formalization of institutional procedures. Even minimal power corrupts.

Precapitalist and capitalist societies each display distinctive forms of equality and inequality that affect the operation of informal justice. Adversaries in precapitalist informal legal institutions often possess roughly equivalent resources of wealth, status, and power. The same may sometimes be true in certain confrontations within capitalist informal justice—primarily labor and commercial arbitration. In each instance informalism is valued for similar reasons—it is believed to produce a just result. But adversaries in precapitalist societies are often unequal, in which case the outcomes of informal processes inevitably reflect and reproduce those inequalities. The same, of course, is true under capitalism. The difference is not in what happens but in how it is valued. Many inequalities in precapitalist society are accepted by its members as legitimate, but inequality is troubling to most citizens of Western capitalist states and repugnant to many. Furthermore, the fundamental ideology of capitalism—liberal legalism—

proclaims "equal justice under law" and therefore cannot tolerate a legal process, formal or informal, in which outcomes *patently* turn on the relative power of the parties.

Precapitalist informal justice can function with rules that remain largely implicit, vague, and inarticulate because it can draw upon an underlying normative consensus grounded in tradition. Because Western capitalism is characterized by a high degree of normative dissensus and rapid change, norms must be imposed by informal institutions and often will seem unjust to one or both parties.

Third parties in precapitalist informal institutions occupy the role of intermediary because they already possess legitimate authority; few private citizens enjoy comparable authority under capitalism, and they are rarely chosen as mediators. Indeed, the capitalist state creates informal institutions precisely because it recognizes that the sources of authority within civil society have been severely eroded. The corollary of this difference in the prerequisites for the role is that acting as mediator in precapitalist society is an important means by which a person gains social status, political authority, and even wealth, whereas those chosen to mediate by the capitalist state garner no significant benefits. Because they function sporadically and serve large anonymous jurisdictions they do not even enhance their reputations. This is not accidental: The capitalist state seeks to undermine rather than encourage the emergence of any independent—and potentially competitive—base of authority. Mediators in precapitalist society are effective because they are familiar with the parties and the history of their dispute. The capitalist ideology of liberal legalism requires that mediators be ignorant; presumably they are therefore less capable of devising a satisfactory outcome.

Informal legal processes in precapitalist societies are very time-consuming: Although an initial audience can usually be obtained promptly, there may be frequent postponements, and each hearing will be lengthy and thorough. Capitalist informal legal institutions, by contrast, conduct short and superficial hearings (if these are longer than the routinized perfunctory procedures of formal courts). Mediators are rewarded by the state for the number of cases completed, not for the way in which they handle each one; parties invest less time and energy in resolving the dispute because they do not value their relationship as highly. Finally, precapitalist informal institutions provide concrete remedies—usually the transfer of something of value; part of that transfer is effectuated immediately, although the entire debt may never be paid. Capitalist informal institutions are necessarily powerless to compel the transfer of resources (or else they cease to be informal); they therefore strive, instead, to change behavior, a task for which they are poorly qualified.

It is not possible to use precapitalist informal legal institutions as a model for constructing informal justice under capitalism. The effort to do so is inevitably stillborn because it attempts to crossbreed distinct species—formality and informality—to produce offspring endowed with characteristics that are inherently contradictory. The evidence both from precapitalist societies that have sought to preserve or revive informal legal institutions after they have adopted formal courts and from capitalist societies that have recently introduced informal institutions is similar. Where the parties are relatively equal and bound together by strong enduring ties, they find the processes created or sponsored by the state too formal in comparison with two-party negotiation, mediation by kin, or perhaps professional therapy. Where the parties are unequal, whichever has the law on its side prefers to appeal to formal authority, seeking the enforcement of rights rather than conciliation. Thus disputants prefer true formality or true informality, not a hybrid. Either the quasi-informal institutions atrophy (as in India and also in Africa), surviving merely as ideology, or they resort to coercion both to generate a caseload and dispose of it. And just as coercion undermines the consent that is supposed to be the foundation of informal justice, so central control undermines the autonomy of local institutions. The upshot is that the state, in the name of informality, destroys indigenous, traditional informal justice and substitutes institutions that serve to extend central control, implement national programs, enhance the legitimacy of the official legal system by appearing to improve access, and undermine local community.

The examples of informal justice under fascism described in these chapters display striking commonalities even though they are situated in three different continents, separated in time by almost half a century, and embodied in institutions that appear quite disparate. Informalism in Japan between the wars was an attempt to restore a quasi-feudal social structure, threatened by the assertion of newly granted individual rights, by substituting conciliation for litigation. Legal aid in Germany during the same period was a means of defusing collective action by encouraging citizens to pursue individual rights in dependence upon lawyers (who, in turn, were subordinated to the National Socialist Party). In Argentina in recent years the military has appropriated forms of popular justice in its public accounts of the extermination of political opponents. But if fascist informalism tends toward an ideal type, it also exhibits disconcerting similarities with informal justice under other political regimes, notably welfare capitalism and socialism. This section will explore those similarities, as well as residual, but critical, differences.

Informalism was promoted in both Japan and Germany as a way of reducing conflict, avoiding litigation, and restoring social peace (arguments that are heard again today from American advocates of informalism). Yet in each case the actual result was an increase in conflict: In Japan, instances of conciliation multiplied, but the rate of litigation also rose; in Germany, the number of people using legal aid grew dramatically. Nevertheless, because these forms of conflict were highly individualized and could more readily be controlled by the state, they posed no real threat to social stability. Informalism was also justified as a means of reducing delay (again a claim often repeated in the United States). In Japan, however, cases referred to conciliation frequently took longer to resolve, and in Germany reliance on legal aid meant a delay in enforcing a right, one that might well be fatal if the lawyer concluded that the claim was untenable. Informalism appeared to expand the rights of the disadvantaged (another virtue arrogated by its contemporary proponents). It is true that Japanese legislation mandating conciliation sometimes improved the bargaining positions of debtors and agricultural tenant farmers and that German legal aid purported to implement Bismarckian social welfare legislation. Yet by giving the conciliator and the legal aid lawyer enormous discretion, informal processes actually diluted substantive rights. Indeed, informal institutions were often created precisely in order to avoid the difficult political choice between proponents and opponents of welfare rights—another means of institutionalizing the gap between law on the books and law in action.

In both countries, informalism was depicted as the embodiment of a higher good to which individual rights had to defer. In Japan, this was an idealized vision of a feudal society: Individual rights could not be allowed to commodify particularistic relationships; harmony was to be preserved through voluntary submission to hierarchical authority; the family was offered as a symbol of correct behavior and a model for dispute resolution. In Germany, individual interests had to be sacrificed for the sake of a society recovering from war and beset with severe economic problems; the goal was to restore the symbiotic relationship between state and capital that was seen as characterizing the late nineteenth century. But perhaps the most striking similarity between the two countries—and the most frightening because even it has echoes in the current movement toward informalism—was the transformation of a program, originally hailed as voluntary and facilitative, into a process that was compulsory and controlling. In Japan, conciliation at the option of the plaintiff was replaced by a mandatory procedure that increasingly resembled binding arbitration. In Germany, legal aid was placed under the control of the National Socialist Party, with the ultimate result that Jews, communists, and many other categories of people were totally denied legal rights.

If the fascist informalism of Germany and Japan has discomforting parallels with contemporary informal alternatives to courts under liberal capitalism, Argentinian summary justice displays equally disturbing analogies to forms of popular justice under socialism. In the latter two instances, the total behavior of both parties is relevant and subject to evaluation since they are being judged by their conformity to general principles rather than by their deviance from a fixed and limited number of rules. Indeed, it is not even behavior, however broadly defined, that is ultimately determinative but rather the essential qualities of the person being judged, whose behavior is only one datum among others. As a result, it is not particularly important to establish exactly what happened, or the consequences of the actor's behavior, i.e., causality is irrelevant. Informal justice in both cases is purposive, policy oriented, and therefore not bound by precedent or overly concerned with legality.

But if fascist summary justice and socialist popular justice share several important traits, in other ways the former is a caricature of the latter, a cruel parody in which a liberating form hides a hideously oppressive substance. Summary justice is imposed from above by an authoritarian state, not spontaneously generated from below by private citizens. It makes a pretense of public participation, but in fact the public is manipulated: It is depicted as helping the armed forces, and even its silence and passive resignation are interpreted as approval. Whereas popular justice is relatively undifferentiated from the society it serves, summary justice is highly differentiated—in terms of personnel, actions, weaponry, etc. This social distance is reflected in the discourse of summary justice, which is pompous and condescending, meaningful only as an exercise in the construction of symbols, not as a description of reality. Indeed, the army almost totally eschews ordinary modes of argumentation and persuasion, choosing to present its account of events as simply beyond question. Where popular justice views the parties as unique individuals who must be comprehended in their complex totality, the discourse of summary justice treats them as stereotyped exemplars of an anonymous, collective enemy. Where popular justice insists on procedural equality for all who appear before it, each of whom is entitled to make claims and offer arguments, the state monopolizes the discourse of summary justice and denies the accused any voice. Popular justice endows all citizens with a common humanity; summary justice imposes an absolute dichotomy between us and them. As a result, summary justice is uncompromising—the enemy is beyond redemption—where popular justice seeks to reconcile the parties and reintegrate both into the society. Summary justice is intensely moralistic. It seeks to present its actions as automatic, inexorable, unwilled—there is only one correct solution. Similarly, there is only one possible remedy—extermination, which cleanses society by purging it of foreign matter. Adjudication and execution are simultaneous. In popular justice, the outcome of every case is problematic, the remedies are varied and occupy the lower end of the spectrum of coerciveness, and their implementation is gradual and always subject to further discussion. Thus examination of summary justice serves the double purpose of alerting us to the dangers inherent in popular justice and highlighting the fundamental differences between the two phenomena.

If fascism represents a clear distortion of the ideals of informal justice, the welfare state endorses them, at least superficially. Formal law under liberal capitalism claims to offer all citizens equal protection against arbitrary state power. Yet experience quickly reveals the loopholes in that program. As Anatole France's famous aphorism reminds us, liberal legalism may protect against *state* power, but it does nothing to alter the distribution of private power, wealth, or status. Furthermore, it is not enough for the state merely to recognize rights when most citizens are incapable of asserting them. Welfare capitalism (and its political form, social democracy) seeks to answer both criticisms. First, it interposes protections against private power, i.e., capital. Second, it creates new systems to deliver rights (against both state and capital) to those who require protection. The provision of subsidized lawyers by private charity (including churches) and the state is one such mechanism. Another approach is to require the judge to play a more active role—as in nineteenth-century Europe, American small claims courts, and the Popular Audiences of Allende's Chile. A third is to appoint executive officials responsible for enforcing the law and equalizing the balance between powerful and powerless—contemporary regulatory agencies are an illustration.

Yet our success in using informal legal institutions to redress political, economic, and social inequalities has been mixed, at best. Informal institutions are said to be cheaper than their formal counterparts. This can permit the same level of state or charitable resources to deliver welfare rights to more people. But it also may mean that those rights are enforced less effectively in each instance, or that the state pockets any savings generated by the reduction in unit cost, spending the money elsewhere or choosing to lower taxes. Thus informalism can easily deteriorate from a mechanism for "making rights effective" into a process of diversion whose primary goal is to curtail state expenditures devoted to enforcing welfare rights.

State-sponsored legal services, like regulatory agencies, have also contributed greatly both to the expansion of welfare rights and to their implementation on a case-by-case basis. But lawyers who passionately champion the interests of capital may turn paternalistic when counseling and representing the powerless. Advocacy may degenerate into cooling out the grievant, as suggested by the history of legal aid in Germany and the United States. When the state grants legal rights and establishes means of enforcement—formal or informal—it inevitably undermines the efforts of the oppressed to help themselves, thereby fostering dependence. Because bourgeois legal rights are assigned to individuals, their pursuit encourages individualism and distracts from, or actually inhibits, collective action. All these trends are visible in the transformation of the workers' offices that accompanied the expansion of legal aid by the German state and churches in the early 1900s. As the workers' offices lost clients to legal aid, the former responded by focusing their limited resources on the assertion of individual rights, to the detriment of involvement in collective action. In order to do this they began to professionalize their staff, replacing workers elected by their peers with appointed paraprofessionals. Contemporary informal institutions for conflict resolution in Western Europe and North America encounter similar problems: In order to attract clients they must increasingly rely on a coercion that betrays the unique values of voluntary mediation and must simultaneously *reduce* access to formal legal institutions in order to enhance their own relative accessibility and attractiveness.

The dilemmas of informalism as a means of implementing welfare rights reflect the fundamental contradictions of liberal capitalism and are therefore incapable of resolution within its framework. The very sources of strength of the reform movement are ultimately its weakness. A major impetus for reform is what Garth calls "gap" politics: rhetorical invocation of the gap between the claims of liberal ideology and the reality of capitalist society, between the principle of equality and the persistence, even growth, of inequality, between the promises of substantive rights and their nullification in practice. "Gap" politics thus appears apolitical, an iteration of goals to which society is already committed rather than a call for radical change. But actual fulfillment of those goals would be extremely expensive and require major sacrifices. In the absence of an organized political base demanding such sacrifices, "gap" politics reduces to an empty repetition of tired promises that are renewed, only to be broken.

If informal justice cannot realize the ideals of welfare capitalism, it may play a significant, if limited, role in the transition to socialism. Under certain historical conditions the creation of institutions of popular justice may contribute to the transformation of the state from the top down: The Popular Audiences held by official judges in Allende's Chile are an example. Perhaps because the short-lived Allende regime controlled only one branch of the state apparatus—the executive—and was openly defied by a powerful and intransigent national bourgeoisie (while simultaneously being subverted by multinational corporations and the CIA), the experiment with Popular Audiences resembles welfare capitalism more than socialism. The Supreme Court required all inferior judges to hold special hearings intended to make justice more accessible to the working class and the poor. Most judges ignored the order, and others complied only in form, persisting in their usual procedures while designating certain hearings as Popular Audiences. Yet even those judges who supported the idea and whose courts were situated sufficiently close to working-class neighborhoods to permit meaningful access operated under considerable constraints. These additional duties were superimposed upon an already heavy caseload; both the dominant legal culture and the juridical reward structure assigned them a lower priority than the "regular" business of the court. Even with the greatest goodwill, judges could not overcome the social distance that separated them from the parties, which was a function of many intractable factors: dress, education, speech, the physical layout of the courtroom, etc. Hearings were brief and perfunctory, decisions were governed solely by legal principles, and judges quickly resorted to coercion rather than engage in the far more difficult and tedious process of mediation. Outcomes dealt only with the most superficial aspects of the controversy, usually by urging the parties to avoid each other. The judges saw the hearings primarily as an opportunity for the parties to blow off steam, but often they failed to perform even this function because only the complainant appeared. The Popular Audiences thus allowed the judiciary to: create the appearance of improved access to justice while courts actually remained inaccessible and delay increased; simulate informality; engage in subtle coercion while emphasizing the voluntary participation of the parties; and manipulate public participation. The parallels with contemporary experiments in the capitalist and social democratic nations of North America and Western Europe are clear.

But nineteenth-century Germany, Chile under Allende, the Portuguese revolution of 1974–1975, and the Mozambican war of liberation also exemplify attempts to create socialism from the bottom up through institutions of informal justice. These episodes have a good deal in common despite the fact that they occurred under totally different conditions—as part of a proletarian reaction against rapid industrialization and the rise of capitalism in Germany; in support of an elected socialist regime in Chile and therefore legitimated, but also confined, by the trappings of bourgeois legality; in reaction against a half century of fascist rule in Portugal; and in the course of an armed struggle against colonialism and capitalism in Mozambique—and despite the additional fact that they have had widely divergent outcomes—the first two were halted by fascist coups; the third is presently being reversed by an alliance of domestic and international capitalists and the leading capitalist nations; and the last is triumphant but threatened by the same forces, especially its racist southern neighbor.

In each case the institutions of popular justice were highly autonomous, neither dependent on nor controlled by the state—indeed, they were consciously oppositional. They financed themselves through contributions of time (and, to a lesser extent, money) that were initially voluntary, if they gradually became an obligation of membership in the collectivity. Their services were entirely free, in contrast to the prohibitively expensive formal justice of the state. Because those services were a gift by the collectivity to its members, both those who rendered the services and the parties who benefited from them agreed on the importance of directing their energies toward matters of general concern. Staff were wholly nonprofessional: in the workers' offices of Germany and the *campamentos* of Chile members performed judicial and executive roles for short terms and then relinquished them to others; the leaders of spontaneous resistance to state coercion in Portugal were completely undifferentiated from other participants in the struggle; members of the disciplinary committees in Mozambique, and later of the dynamizing groups, were popularly chosen from local residents. The institutions were partisan not neutral, strongly committed to change, a self-conscious expression of the political interests of oppressed groups: workers, peasants, urban squatters, women, etc. They served very small units whose members typically knew one another, often intimately. This knowledge and these intense relationships gave the institutions considerable authority.

Informal institutions that belong to a movement to create socialism from below are also distinguished by the problems they attack and the activities in which they engage. They are concerned with fundamental issues of social reconstruction rather than with idiosyncratic family conflicts or the inevitable irritants of daily life—the barking dogs and spite fences that preoccupy neighborhood justice under liberal capitalism (described in the companion volume). In handling interindividual problems they attempt to locate the causes, and thus the solutions, within the larger social framework—the struggle between labor and capital, unemployment, bourgeois property relations, inadequate housing, colonialism, sexism. When such institutions engage in conflict resolution they conduct lengthy hearings devoted to uncovering the roots of problems—unlike Oscar Wilde, they are willing to sacrifice their evenings for socialism. They develop an expanded repertoire of remedies, perhaps because they cannot fall back on the crutch of coercion. When, as in most of the instances described in the following chapters, these are institutions of the transitional period and thus only islands of socialism within a hostile capitalist environment, the ultimate sanction in the armament of social control is expulsion; in the one successful revolution— Mozambique—penal institutions seek to reintegrate offenders through a regime of work and academic, technical, and political education that employs a minimum of coercion, not to incapacitate or deter through lengthy imprisonment or execution.

But the resolution of individual cases is not the primary focus of informal legal institutions. Instead, they emphasize collective action: research that reveals the common features of disputes whose participants initially perceive, and present, them as personal and unique; education, publicity, and propaganda; the anticipation and prevention of future problems rather than redress of past injustices. At this stage in the struggle progressive forces avoid formal litigation, recognizing their political weaknesses and the fact that the judiciary is firmly in the hands of the bourgeoisie, but in any case litigation is eschewed as a highly individualistic form of political action. The emphasis on action that is collective and anticipatory compels the institution to shift from adjudication to legislation, even though it can impose new substantive norms only within the boundaries of the local community, at most, and even though these norms must be reconciled with tradition.

All of these challenges are fiercely opposed by the dominant classes and the state with all the means at their disposal, including the formal legal system. Thus one important manifestation of informal justice in the transition to socialism is the obstruction of formal justice—resisting a criminal prosecution, seizing the file in a civil action. Another (the obverse) is the demand for justice when the state refuses to act—conducting an investigation, marshaling evidence, insisting upon a trial. A further step in the struggle is the assertion of a competing jurisdiction—an alternative judiciary that repudiates the legitimacy of the state and pronounces its own verdicts, which often exculpate conduct that the bourgeois state had penalized and condemn behavior that it had excused. Finally, there is outright defiance of official substantive law and its coercive arm—the police—through strikes, the occupation of factories, and the seizure of urban dwellings and rural land. Because the political struggle continues even after the revolution has won a military victory, other informal legal institutions—vigilance groups—may be necessary to protect the revolution against physical and economic sabotage.

These case studies demonstrate that informal justice has an important, if limited, role to play in revolutionary struggles. It can proclaim symbolically the autonomy and competence of a group of workers or peasants or a community of urban squatters, and it can confer on those who participate in the struggle a sense of collective empowerment. It can provide a foretaste of socialist legality that gives meaning to the sacrifices demanded, as in the disciplinary committees in the liberated zones of Mozambique during the war of liberation and the dynamizing groups in the cities after it was won. But before such a victory, the assertion of a jurisdiction that competes with the still dominant capitalist state is constantly threatened—both directly (when the state uses its coercive power to overturn the decisions of informal institutions and to destroy the institutions themselves) and indirectly (when the state advertises its monopoly of legal coercion to entice grievants away from informal institutions). And even after the victory, socialist justice remains a focal point for critics of the regime, both internal and external. In addition, because the juridical occupies a subordinate position in every social formation, it must also play a secondary role within the struggle itself—a fact that is recognized both by the capitalist state and by those who are striving to overthrow it. For most German workers, the political functions of workers' offices quickly took second place to the fight for economic survival. In the *campamentos* of Chile, neighborhood courts attracted far less of the residents' energies than struggles over health and housing. And peasants in both Portugal and Mozambique were more interested in the reform of land tenure than the restructuring of legal institutions and processes. The capitalist state, for its part, can largely ignore challenges to its juridical authority. Popular action may paralyze the courts, but this by itself can no more destroy capitalism than can the occupation of universities by students. By the same token, though the bourgeoisie can also seek to undermine socialism by fleeing the country, thereby depriving it of all trained personnel—as in Mozambique—the new state can operate for a considerable period without a formal legal system.

Thus informal justice possesses serious limitations as a revolutionary strategy: It tends to create institutions that parallel formal justice rather than challenge it directly; at most they challenge the judiciary, not the legislature or executive; and they rarely touch the economic infrastructure. Informal justice can provide an important symbol of socialist legality, but the latter can triumph only as part of a much broader social, political, and economic movement.

Even when it does, the role of informalism remains problematic. The brief postrevolutionary period in Mozambique, together with the much longer experience of other socialist states (China, for instance, analyzed by Spitzer in the companion volume), strongly suggests that reformalization is inevitable, if the contents of bourgeois and of socialist law differ significantly. Mozambique has now adopted a written constitution, though one that emphasizes the collectivity as well as the individual, obligations as well as rights; it has nationalized the legal profession and sought to guarantee professional representation for all; it has drafted a new family code and reorganized its judicial system. Yet it has also retained important informal elements. The writing and rewriting of the family code has entailed a high level of political mobilization and vigorous public discussion. The new rural penal centers, which are intended to replace both the colonial prisons and the transitional reeducation centers, seek to reintegrate those incarcerated by minimizing coercion and by allowing them to live with their families, participate in self-governance, and devote substantial time to academic and political education. Such critical legal institutions as the labor commissions and the new court system also exhibit significant informal characteristics: They are staffed by a combination of lay persons and people with some legal training; they follow simplified procedures that obviate the need for lawyers; they encourage the public to attend and participate; and they invoke principles of socialism and sexual equality to modify substantive laws that have not yet been reformed. But Mozambique, like China, simultaneously reveals that the tension between informal popular justice and formal bureaucratized legality is not easily resolved: It has been difficult to involve women in the new legal institutions, and judges with legal training tend to dominate those without. The struggle for informal justice never ends.

I

Nonindustrial Societies

2

The Social Organization of Mediation in Nonindustrial Societies: Implications for Informal Community Justice in America *

SALLY ENGLE MERRY

INTRODUCTION

American courts are notorious for their failure to resolve minor, interpersonal disputes quickly, effectively, and in a way that satisfies the disputing parties. The increasing urbanism, transiency, and heterogenity of American society in the twentieth century has undermined informal dispute settlement mechanisms rooted in home, church, and community and increased the demand for other means of dealing with family, neighbor, and community disputes. However, many legal experts argue that the formality of the courts, their adherence to an adversary model, their strict rules of procedure, and their reliance on adjudication render them inappropriate for handling many kinds of interpersonal quarrels arising in ongoing social relationships (e.g., Danzig, 1973; Danzig and Lowy,

* Parts of this chapter were presented at the Society for Applied Anthropology, March 1979, and the American Society of Criminology, November 1979. I am grateful for the comments of Richard Abel, Donald Black, David Jacobson, Marguerite Robinson, Susan Silbey, and Barbara Yngvesson on earlier drafts of the chapter.

17

1975; Sander, 1976; Nader and Singer, 1976; American Bar Association, 1976; Cratsley, 1978). The American Bar Association, the U.S. Department of Justice, the American Arbitration Association, the Institute for Mediation and Conflict Resolution, and many community groups are experimenting with the use of mediation in community-based centers to resolve minor interpersonal disputes on the assumption that this will provide a more humane, responsive, and accessible form of justice (McGillis and Mullen, 1977; Sander, 1976; Bell, 1978). However, an examination of anthropological models of mediation suggests that community mediation in urban America, as these experiments are presently constituted, may provide a kind and quality of justice fundamentally different from that which their creators intended.

Every society develops a range of mechanisms for resolving disputes, some of which are informal, rooted in such local institutions as lineage, clan, religious association, or family, and some of which are more formal, coercive, and dependent on the political hierarchy. With the transition from small-scale, kinship-based societies to large, complex, urban social systems, disputants turn increasingly to formal rather than informal dispute resolution mechanisms. Community mediation, however, endeavors to turn the tide: to return control of certain kinds of disruptive and offensive behavior to local communities, where they can be managed through mediation, compromise, and restitution, enforced by community social sanctions and the desire of disputants to settle. It seeks to replace the formality of the court with the informality of the neighborhood, narrow considerations of legal principles with more general questions of morality and shared responsibility, win or lose outcomes with compromises, and penal sanctions of fine and imprisonment with compensation and informal social pressures. The introduction of neighborhood mediation, frequently termed citizen dispute resolution,[1] is thus part of a general movement toward delegaliza-

---

[1]Community dispute settlement centers are either court based or community based. Most of the programs that have been studied are closely connected to a court, receive referrals from court clerks and judges, and rely on the threat of judicial sanction to encourage mediation. Community-based models build on local community leaders to run the programs and to serve as mediators, and they eschew any connection with the courts either as a source of cases or as a sanction against recalcitrant disputants (see McGillis and Mullen, 1977: 163–173; Wahrhaftig, 1978). These centers endeavor to use community social pressure to induce compliance with agreements. Court-based mediation programs generally service a jurisdiction of several thousand to a few million residents: some serve an entire metropolitan area such as New York or Atlanta; community programs encompass smaller areas, with populations ranging from a few hundred to tens of thousands. Thus, the "neighborhood" in neighborhood justice centers appears to describe their informal process rather than the size of the catchment area.

Caseloads generally consist of minor interpersonal disputes, both civil and criminal. For example, the subject matter of referrals to the Boston Urban Court mediation program from September 1975 until April 1977 was 36 percent family disputes, 20 percent disputes between neighbors, 17 percent disputes between friends, and 10 percent landlord–tenant conflicts. Of those involving criminal

tion, toward removing dispute management from the courts on the premise that substantive justice is better served outside the formal procedures of the existing legal system (Abel, 1979).

The idea of mediation as an alternative mode of resolving disputes in American society draws on at least three sources: mediation in small-scale societies (especially Gibbs, 1963; Nader, 1969); peoples' courts in socialist societies (Cohen, 1966; Lubman, 1967; Berman, 1969; Cantor, 1974; Crockett and Gleicher, 1978); and labor and commercial arbitration in the United States (Mentschikoff, 1961; Fuller, 1971; Fisher, 1975; Getman, 1979). Danzig's influential article on alternative criminal justice systems, for example, draws on Gibbs's analysis (1963) of Liberian community moots in which disputes are fully aired, an audiences contributes opinions and evidence, and a mediator gradually leads the group toward a consensual solution (1973: 43). Fuller compares the process of labor arbitration to the widespread reciprocal exchange that maintains order among the Trobriand Islanders (Malinowski, 1926; Fuller, 1971). Wahrhaftig's community-based programs are inspired by Lowy's work on Ghanian moots (Lowy, 1978; Wahrhaftig, 1982). And the Florence Access-To-Justice Project (Cappelletti, 1978–1979) devotes an entire volume to the anthropological perspective (Koch, 1979). Clearly, the therapeutic and consensual nature of such forms of dispute resolution is attractive to a society increasingly critical of adversary adjudication and coercive sanctions. These proposed citizen dispute settlement centers appear to satisfy a happy conjunction of interests between those concerned with the quality and accessibility of justice available to the individual and those tackling problems of massive court congestion and mushrooming court costs.[2]

Yet the idea of a community center using informal procedures to dispense justice represents a turn toward a mode of dispute resolution that flourishes in

charges, half (52 percent) concerned some form of assault and battery (McGillis and Mullen, 1977: 97–98).

[2]Citizen dispute resolution programs provide an alternative to adjudication for minor civil and criminal complaints arising from domestic, neighborhood, family, merchant–consumer, and landlord–tenant disputes in which the parties know one another (Sander, 1976; McGillis and Mullen, 1977). Disputants air their grievances in an informal, personal, and supportive atmosphere in which a third party, usually a lay community member, simply mediates the dispute, facilitating the process by which the disputing parties collectively forge a mutually acceptable compromise solution or, in a few programs, agree to submit to arbitration. The mediation experience, ideally, is voluntary, noncoercive, more humane, and more closely tailored to the needs of individual disputants than is the court. The process is one of bargaining and negotiation, and the free-ranging discussion that fully explores feelings and perspectives usually lasts much longer than adjudication. Outcomes are generally compromises rather than zero-sum decisions and take into account the total relationship between the parties. Rules provide a framework for the discussion and are used by each side to justify its position, but they do not determine the outcome (Eisenberg, 1976; Moore, 1978). The process is not one of matching a problem to a rule but of establishing agreement between the parties about a fair or

very different social systems and legal cultures. Citizen dispute settlement centers are modeled after processes of mediation in horticultural and pastoral societies that generally consist of small, stable, close-knit, bounded settlements. A member must choose between bowing to group pressure or escaping from the local community and sacrificing much of his personal and political life and often his economic livelihood. He becomes accustomed to submitting to the informal social control of his peers. Furthermore, members of these societies share similar values, according to which disputes can be settled. The alternative of a formal coercive forum where disputes are decided with reference to state-imposed rules is often remote or nonexistent. Community mediation has been transplanted from this social context into a very different setting: the heterogeneous, transient, anonymous, and morally diverse American city whose citizens believe they possess legal rights that should be protected by the courts.

This chapter examines the social organization and process of mediation in small-scale pastoral and agricultural societies where it represents the predominant mode of settling disputes. The analysis suggests that we have idealized and misunderstood the process of mediation, focusing on its consensual and conciliatory qualities and ignoring the very important role of coercion and power (cf. Colson, 1974). Furthermore, we have uncritically transplanted the notion of mediation from small-scale societies, most of which lack courts, to complex, heterogeneous urban neighborhoods in a society with a highly differentiated legal culture. We need to consider the impact of these very substantial differences in social organization on the mediation process. Despite good analyses of the process of mediation (Gulliver, 1973, 1977; Felstiner and Williams, 1978), we lack a comprehensive analysis of the social context of nonindustrial societies within which mediation occurs (but see Felstiner, 1974). We have not analyzed the role of the mediators in relation to the disputants, the situations in which disputants choose mediation rather than feud, witchcraft, gossip, or adjudication, or simply tolerate a continuing state of conflict (Merry, 1979), or the extent to which power relationships enter into "mutually acceptable" settlements (but see Starr and Yngvesson, 1975). This chapter begins to examine the social organization and context of mediation in small-scale, politically unorganized societies and evalu-

---

just settlement, even if this deviates from existing rules. Settlements may even create new rules (Gulliver, 1973). The settlements are generally compensatory rather than penal, focusing on peacemaking and restitution rather than punishment (Koch, 1974: 31). They serve to reconcile the parties, diffuse hostility, and maintain relatively amicable and cooperative relationships. Mediation thus seems to be a more appropriate procedure than adjudication for resolving disrupted interpersonal relationships, since its central quality is "its capacity to reorient the parties toward each other, not by imposing rules on them, but by helping them to achieve a new and shared perception of their relationship, a perception that will redirect their attitudes and dispositions toward one another" (Fuller, 1971: 325).

ates the implications of these findings for the functioning of American community dispute settlement centers and the quality of justice they can provide.

MEDIATION IN SMALL-SCALE SOCIETIES

Mediation is an important mode of settling disputes in societies ranging from horticultural and pastoral peoples whose political institutions are coterminous with their kinship systems to peasant villages incorporated into nation-states. Although it is difficult to evaluate the "effectiveness" of mediation in these various settings, it is possible to examine the conditions under which disputants choose mediation rather than some other process. Disputants in societies of the first type turn to mediation as an alternative to violence, feud, or warfare; those in the second choose it in preference to violence or court. At one extreme are the peoples of highland New Guinea, for whom mediation only occasionally replaces vengeance (Koch, 1974; Meggitt, 1977). At the other are the peasant villagers of China, whose culture mandates mediation and who use it in virtually all disputes within the village despite the availability of a national court system, albeit one that is remote (Yang, 1945; Cohen, 1966; Lubman, 1967; Crockett and Gleicher, 1978).

This chapter examines the process and organization of mediation in the following societies, as well as those just mentioned: the Nuer (Sudanese pastoralists, Evans-Pritchard, 1940; Gruel, 1971; Haight, 1972); the Arusha and Ndendeuli (Tanzanian horticulturalists, Gulliver, 1963; 1969); the Tiv (Nigerian farmers, Bohannan, 1957); the Ifugao (Philippine agriculturalists, Barton, 1919; Hoebel, 1954); the Tonga (Zambian farmers, Colson; 1953); the Cheyenne (North American Indian hunters, Llewellyn and Hoebel, 1941); the Swat Pathan and Waigali (Southwest Asian farmers, Barth, 1959; Bailey, 1972; Jones, 1974); Sardinian shepherds (Ruffini, 1978); and peasant villagers in Liberia (Gibbs, 1963), Lebanon (Ayoub, 1965; Rothenberger, 1978; Witty, 1978), Zambia (Canter, 1978), Mexico (Collier, 1973; 1976), Taiwan (Gallin, 1966), Italy (Brögger, 1968), and Japan (Kawashima, 1973).

I will first describe mediation in four societies in detail and then extract from these and the other societies cited in the preceding paragraph some general features of mediation. The Nuer and Ifugao both lack centralized political organization and courts, whereas the Waigali of Afghanistan and the Zinacantecos of Mexico are peasant villagers incorporated into nation-states that outlaw the use of violence within the village and provide a judicial alternative. This analysis is inevitably tentative since I have not exhausted the ethnographic literature on mediation, yet the patterns that emerge are sufficiently consistent and represent such a wide geographical range that I feel they justify an effort to formulate a general model of the social organization of mediation in small-scale societies. Descriptions will be couched in the ethnographic present.

The Nuer

The Nuer are pastoral nomads, herding cattle across the barren flatlands of Ethiopia and the Sudan. Studied by Evans-Pritchard (1940) in the 1930s, soon after their final conquest by the British, the Nuer were still a proud and independent society of 200,000 individuals who recognized no central government and had neither courts nor formal political offices. Although Evans-Pritchard makes a few fleeting references to the use of government courts, his analysis assumes that Nuer society is still unaffected by the outside world (an assumption that may have been unwarranted, see Howell, 1954; Kuper, 1973). The political system is based on kinship, organized around an elaborate structure of lineages in which smaller segments are nested within larger, more inclusive segments. Lineage membership varies with the level of segmentation that is relevant to a particular situation.

The Nuer are contentious and fight frequently over issues such as cattle theft, cattle trespass, adultery, watering rights in the dry season, pasture rights, or borrowing without permission (1940: 151). A Nuer responds to any infringement of his rights by an immediate challenge to a duel, and children are taught early to settle disputes by fighting. Almost the only way Nuer achieve redress for wrongs is through force or the threat of force (*Ibid.*: 162).

In some situations, however, Nuer are willing to mediate disputes rather than pursue vengeance. The close male agnates of a murdered man are expected to avenge his death by killing the slayer or one of his agnates, but the aggrieved lineage can instead accept damages (bloodwealth) of about forty to fifty head of cattle. Disputants choose to mediate homicide disputes when they are close kin, when they or their kin live close together, or when marriage links the two kin groups. The existence of such crosscutting ties poses several problems if disputes are not settled. There is the constant danger of revenge if the villages of murderer and victim are close by or if agnates of the latter live in the village of the former. If members of the slayer's kin group eat or drink with, or even use the same utensils as, the dead man's kin group, the former believe they will die (*Ibid.*: 154). Consequently, the lineage of the slayer will quickly call in a mediator to arrange the payment of damages. If the disputants are only distantly related, however, and crosscutting ties are weak or nonexistent, they feel less need to submit to mediation since they have fewer social contacts (*Ibid.*: 157).

The Nuer have institutionalized the role of mediator in the leopard-skin chief. He has no secular, but only ritual powers (but see Howell, 1954: 28; Gruel, 1971; Haight, 1972). He can mediate a dispute only if the parties wish to settle and cannot prevent their recourse to violence if negotiations break down. His sole power is the ability to curse the intransigent disputant, who refuses to accept a reasonable settlement, with the threat that supernatural forces will aid his enemies if he continues to seek vengeance. Although Evans-Pritchard never witnessed a leopard-skin chief's curse, he saw the threat of a curse act as a deterrent (1940: 172). In homicide cases, the leopard-skin chief provides sanctuary to the slayer while bloodwealth negotiations progress so as to prevent the opposing kin group from taking vengeance in anger. The chief acts as a mediator between the two groups, assessing what the killer's lineage can pay and pressuring the victim's lineage to accept it. The mediator is expected to be impartial and belongs to neither of the disputing groups. The settlement he produces must be mutually acceptable and thus must take into account the status of the man killed—his social importance and position in the lineage structure— as well as the power of his kin group to extract damages (Howell, 1954: 60). Although the chief receives a small payment, it is unclear whether this must be spent in the ritual of reconciliation or belongs to him (see Gruel, 1971; Haight, 1972). The leopard-skin chief also mediates disputes concerning seizure of cows that are owed, adultery, or sexual relations with an unmarried woman, but tradition specifies damages for particular wrongs, and these can be collected only by force or the threat of force.

Mediation among the Nuer suggests a number of general characteristics of the process. First, the mediator is a respected and influential leader with expertise in settling disputes and some source of authority. Second, mediation occurs only when the disputants are linked to one another through a network of social relationships that renders a feud between their families disruptive and dangerous. Third, the mediator settles the dispute by negotiating an exchange of goods sanctioned by tradition: His role is to arrange the payment of damages. Fourth, the mediated settlement relies on coercion. Disputants are coerced both to negotiate and to accept the settlement recommended by the leopard-skin chief and lineage elders. The sanctions are public opinion, the threat of the chief's curse, and the real possibility of vengeance killings if the dispute cannot be resolved by payment of damages. Fifth, the settlement is not justified in terms of Western liberal notions of equality before the law but reflects the relative importance and strength of the disputants. Bloodwealth varies according to the status of the dead man. The leopard-skin chief, lacking a monopoly of force, only can arrange a settlement that both parties find mutually acceptable. Inevitably, such a settlement must reflect what the stronger is willing to concede and the weaker can successfully demand.

The Ifugao

The Ifugao are wet-rice farmers who own elaborate terraces climbing the steep hills around their small villages in the mountainous regions of the Philippines.

When studied in the early twentieth century by Barton, they had neither government nor courts, but they did have a highly institutionalized mediator role and an elaborate set of customs (Barton, 1919; Hoebel, 1954). At that time, the Ifugao were essentially unaffected by the colonial courts. Disputes commonly involve debt, breach of contract, adultery, slander, sorcery, murder, and other injuries against persons, property, and reputation. The plaintiff seeks a mediator, or *monkalun*, to assist him. The *monkalun*, however, is not an advocate for the plaintiff but represents the interests of the community at large in restoring peace and equilibrium (Barton, 1919: 94–95). He therefore must not be too closely related to either side.

The *monkalun* works as a go-between, shuttling back and forth between the disputing parties with messages and proposals he can reinterpret and elaborate. If one side appears intransigent, he adds dire warnings concerning the other side's readiness to abandon negotiations and fight, replete with descriptions of sharpened spears, talk of violence, and so forth. To maintain his honor, a defendant must initially resist any suggestion that he accept payment rather than exact vengeance, but the *monkalun* gradually pressures him to settle. If a deadlock occurs, the *monkalun* withdraws, leaving the plaintiff with the option of finding another *monkalun* or simply ambushing the defendant. If the defendant is generally thought to be unreasonable and stubborn in the case, public opinion will support such violence (*Ibid.*: 100).

The *monkalun* has no authority to make binding decisions, but he does wield considerable influence. He is a member of the highest stratum and has achieved the highest title through his wealth and genealogical connections.[3] A string of satisfactory settlements builds prestige as a mediator, attracts more cases, and provides fees in the form of pigs and other valuables. The opinions of the *monkalun* carry added weight because of his own reputation for violence and his social, economic, and political standing. An additional source of coercion is the threat of violence by the other side if negotiations fail. In Ifugao society, according to Barton, "the lance is back of every demand of importance, and sometimes it seems hungry" (1919: 94).

The *monkalun* negotiates payments, whose amount varies with the nature of the offense, the relative class position of plaintiff and defendant, the strength and geographical proximity of their kin groups, and their individual personalities and reputations (Barton, 1919: 61–69; Hoebel, 1954: 116–117). Higher strata both pay and receive higher damages. Offenses such as rape, adultery, slander, sor-

---

[3]The category to which he belongs is not a class, in the sociological sense, but a status in a society where individuals are born into unequal, ranked positions. In small-scale societies, such inequalities are often part of the kinship system but are also buttressed by differences in wealth and political power. Nevertheless, individuals of differing ranks are often interconnected through marriage, exchange, and coresidence. Such social inequalities are perceived as natural and basic to the social order.

cery, and even murder are seen not as crimes against society but as offenses against particular individuals, to be settled through payment of damages.

As with the Nuer, quarrels between residents of the same small valley are likely to end in mediation and settlement, whereas disputes between individuals who live farther away generally lead to violence and feud. In moderately remote areas, efforts at mediation are perfunctory, and in more distant locations no legal procedures are used at all.

Thus in this society, too, the mediator is an influential individual who enhances his position through his skill in that role. Individuals agree to mediate disputes and pay damages only where they are involved in ongoing social relationships with one another and have to deal with one another in the future. Those who are more distant eschew settlements. Mediators arrange the payment of damages, negotiating economic exchanges. Although the settlements must be mutually acceptable and are not imposed by the mediator, mediation itself is virtually compulsory since an individual risks the violence of his enraged adversary if he refuses to negotiate.

The Waigali

A third society, in the remote mountains of Afghanistan, relies on mediation as the predominant mode of handling disputes but has recently begun to submit some conflicts to the national courts. The process closely resembles that already described but has been influenced by the availability of courts.

The Waigali are herdsmen of goats and farmers of millet and maize who live in small villages in the valleys of the Hindu Kush, between Pakistan and Afghanistan. When studied by Jones in the 1960s, they retained considerable independence from the Afghan government by virtue of their location, but Afghan courts were available to disputants who chose to trek down the mountain to the nearby town and deal with officials of that alien cultural and linguistic world (Jones, 1974). Each of the nine villages occupying the Waigal Valley is politically autonomous, but they share cultural bonds and may cooperate or compete. Within each village, power is held by lineage elders who derive their authority from their wealth and family positions. In the absence of formal government and courts within the village the segmentary lineage system forms the backbone of the political structure.

Disputes occur over the theft of goats, trespass on pasture land, premature harvesting of walnuts or grapes, assault, extramarital sexual relations, and homicide. The Waigali are highly competitive over social status. They are quarrelsome and prompt to defend their rights, proud of ancestors who were warriors, and eager to appear fearless and decisive. Although they do not value reconciliation or compromise, villagers do endeavor to prevent conflicts within a village that divide and weaken it (*Ibid.*: 78). Disputes over serious offenses such as murder must be settled by either payment of damages or vengeance. When a dispute erupts within a village, it must be resolved quickly or violence and bloodshed will further split the village.

When such a dispute develops, the plaintiff usually appeals to a respected village elder to mediate. Those who regularly serve as mediators, *du-wrai*, include members of the landowning class and others with a reputation for being honest, forthright, skilled in formulating arguments, and clever in debate. Often they are also members of important lineages and have had many years of experience in village affairs. According to the Waigali, the most important trait is the ability to be objective: to focus on the problem, not the people (*Ibid.*: 62–66). The *du-wrai* are carefully selected in terms of their kin relationships to the disputants: They belong to the largest kin group of which both are members but to the subgroups of neither the plaintiff nor defendant. They are thus equally close to both parties. Since they are leaders of villages containing no more than 300 families, they are very familiar with the history of relationships between the disputants and with their families and personal reputations. The *du-wrai* have no power to enforce a legal decision.

The *du-wrai* function as go-betweens, visiting the house of the plaintiff and then that of the defendant, carrying messages back and forth and seeking to determine what will be mutually agreeable. At the same time, they gather evidence, present proposals, and even leave a "silent mediator" in each house as an informer to see what each side is really prepared to accept (*Ibid.*: 74–78). Like the Nuer, Waigali demand the maximum and do not want to acquiesce to a settlement too readily. Both sides are supposed to refrain from violence while the mediators are working, and they therefore conduct "round-the-clock" negotiations, some napping while others continue to shuttle from one party to the other, in order to forestall violence or a hardening of positions. Since each visit of the *du-wrai* demands lavish hospitality—meat, honey, and wheat bread (the most desirable foods), in an escalating pattern of competitive feasting—the costs to the disputants of continued negotiation quickly mount. Furthermore, uninterrupted negotiation is probably intended to wear down the disputants. If the *du-wrai* are unable to find a mutually acceptable settlement, they can threaten to call in more *du-wrai*, often from other villages, which has the double disadvantage of increasing the cost of hospitality and advertising to the larger society that the village is unable to maintain harmony.

The mediators deal with each side separately and caucus by themselves to formulate proposals, a strategy that seems effective because the disputants are really lineages and not individuals. The offender's kin group is collectively responsible for his debt, and the plaintiff's kin will all share the damages. If the particular offender or victim is intransigent, his own kinsmen may pressure him to compromise.

The settlement reached by the mediators takes into account both village norms and the status and relationships of the disputants. The *du-wrai* must consider previous conflicts, the total social personalities of the persons involved (including the importance of their lineages and their individual statuses), and the nature and extent of the affront (*Ibid.*: 78–82). An important man will hold out for higher damages, which both reflect and demonstrate his rank (*Ibid.*: 82).

Although disputants rarely turn to the Afghan courts, any case can be taken there directly. The availability of this alternative influences settlements even when it is not used. In one case, for example, the plaintiff wanted to kill the defendant but was deterred by the argument that a murder would involve the Afghan authorities, who impose long prison sentences (Jones, 1974: 83–91). Two kinds of cases are taken to the government court: those involving outsiders, such as Afghans, in disputes over the theft of goats, trespass on pasturage, homicide, debt, and boundaries; and those lodged by the subordinate social caste against the dominant, landowning caste. Roughly 10 percent of the villagers belong to a castelike social group with severely restricted rights, separate living quarters, segregated eating, and endogamy. Because the Afghan court does not accept the legitimacy of this subordinate status, its members frequently bring cases against their superordinates concerning land, property, and especially women, whom the landlords molest (*Ibid.*: 240). Knowing they will get no satisfaction within the village, whose mediators simply reflect existing social inequalities, they appeal to a court endowed with coercive power and a more egalitarian ideology. In this social setting, therefore, mediation tends to reinforce and perpetuate social inequalities, whereas adjudication exerts its authority to counteract them.[4]

Zinacantan

A fourth case suggests the role mediation plays in a peasant society with a more complex political organization that offers the alternatives of a state court and a local official with limited judicial authority.

Zinacantan is a Maya Indian community located high in the mountains of Chiapas in southern Mexico. The Zinacantecos are maize farmers, eking a poor living out of patches of land on steep mountain sides and increasingly working as migrant farmers in the lowland valleys. At the time of Collier's study in the 1960s, contact with the Mexican state was increasing, a few villagers spoke Spanish in addition to Tzotzil, and local leaders were learning about the power of the Mexican court located in a neighboring valley (Collier, 1973). Although

---

[4]Massell (1968; 1974) describes a similar situation in Soviet Central Asia, where the new Soviet government, anxious to restructure traditional Islamic societies, gave women legal rights of divorce, inheritance, child custody, political participation, and choice of marriage partner and created secular, Soviet courts to implement them. Women did make some use of these new options, although the short-term result was extensive social disruption rather than a simple improvement in the status of women.

Zinacantecos did not use the court frequently (only three to seven times a year), knowledge about it was widespread, and predictions about the action it would take significantly affected the settlements reached by local mediators.

Collier analyzes three levels of dispute settlement. First, leaders in each residential area, or hamlet, mediate disputes between neighbors and kinsmen who live within the hamlet and are involved in ongoing relationships, aiming at conciliation and compromise (*Ibid.*: 66–68). Second, cases can be taken to the town hall, where they are heard by the political leader of the village, the *presidente*, who has the power to make a decision enforced by a fine or up to three days in jail. In fact, the *presidente* also seeks to mediate disputes. Third, cases can be taken to the Mexican court, although this is expensive for both plaintiff and defendant, each of whom must hire a lawyer. The court imposes a zero-sum outcome that may include a steep fine or long jail sentence for the defendant, so that recourse to court is regarded as a serious step.

Mediators are hamlet elders, known for their wisdom, who have sufficient authority to persuade the defendant to appear. Some are politically powerful, and all enhance their reputations through successful mediation. Although they lack coercive power, they can encourage disputants to settle by threatening to send the case to the town hall court, which will consume additional time, expose them to the shame of a public hearing, and may lead to a fine or jail sentence (*Ibid.*: 26–28). A mediator may even threaten to take a case to the Mexican authorities.

Another potent form of pressure is the fear that anger in the heart of a dissatisfied disputant will call down the wrath of the ancestral gods and lead to the illness or death of his opponent. The mediator seeks to cool the anger in the heart of the plaintiff by satisfying his demands at the same time that he seeks to avoid infuriating the defendant with unreasonable requests for compensation. Since sickness is ever-present, it is common for a disputant or one of his kinsmen to fall ill after angering an adversary, thereby confirming this belief (*Ibid.*: 123–124). The mediator seeks to arrive at a settlement as quickly as possible, summoning the defendant as soon as a case is brought to him. Because settlement through compromise is paramount, the outcome does not necessarily uphold social norms. Thus here, as in the other societies described earlier in the chapter, mediation occurs between individuals whose ongoing relationship leads them to seek reconciliation, yet they are simultaneously coerced into settlements by the prestige of the mediator and the threat of sanctions, both secular and supernatural.

CHARACTERISTICS OF MEDIATION IN SMALL-SCALE SOCIETIES

These and the other case studies suggest some general features of process, social organization, and outcome in mediated settlements. Many of these features recur in Cuban Popular Tribunals (Berman, 1969; Cantor, 1974), Chinese Peoples' Mediation Committees (Lubman, 1967), Chilean neighborhood courts (Spence, 1978), and "courts" in American ethnic communities (Jaffee, 1972; Doo, 1973).[5]

The Process of Mediation

Mediation is prompt. Ideally, it occurs immediately after the incident, before the disputants have time to harden their positions or, as the Waigali say, before they can "think about their ancestors"—their pride and social positions. The process is time-consuming, taking hours or days, as long as is necessary to reach a settlement. Arusha disputes may be mediated for months (Gulliver, 1963). Negotiations are often conducted in public forums where neighbors and kinsmen can offer opinions and condemn the behavior of unreasonable disputants. Even when the mediator is a go-between who meets with the parties privately, the wider public often knows the nature of the discussions through its kin ties to both sides.

Mediators arrange the payment of damages. Their function is usually to negotiate an outcome that will satisfy both parties through an exchange of property, the demarcation of a new boundary line, or the rendering of a public apology; vague promises of improved behavior in the future are not sufficient. Injuries such as insult, adultery, assault, and even homicide are generally perceived as reparable through gifts of cattle, sheep, or other valuables in amounts specified by custom.[6]

The mediation process usually ends with immediate consummation of the

[5]Cuban Popular Tribunals, for example, serve 4000–5000 residents each, conduct informal public hearings within two months after the incident, focus on restitutive and rehabilitative settlements, award concrete damages, frequently give moral lectures and public admonitions, and disqualify a judge as biased only if he is a friend or enemy of the disputants, not just because he knows them. Judges are laymen, elected by the local residents, and receive three weeks of training in law (Berman, 1969; Cantor, 1974). Peoples' Mediation Committees in China were created in 1954 in each area or street in the city and in districts containing several villages in the countryside (Lubman, 1967). Mediators are elected by representatives of the residents and should be "politically upright." They mediate only when the parties agree. They also conduct propaganda and educate the people about national policies and laws. Urban mediators tend to be politically active housewives; in organizations and rural areas they are closely linked to the administration. Since they are part of the mechanism for constructing a socialist society, they operate within a clear moral system and often deliver harangues on moral virtue and new ways of thought. The mediators can invoke sanctions either through the police and other cadres in the urban neighborhoods or through work supervision in factories and communes (Ibid.: 1349). Individuals from peasant or worker backgrounds fare better than those whose families were bourgeois, reflecting communist values (Ibid.: 1346–1347).

[6]Schwartz and Miller (1964) conducted a cross-cultural examination of dispute settlement in fifty-one societies and found that mediation rarely or never occurred without some notion of damages.

agreement. When it is necessary to postpone the final settlement, for instance, while one disputant finds enough sheep, the assembly will often reconvene to observe the exchange (e.g., *ibid.*). In societies that lack written contracts, such an immediate exchange is the only guarantee of performance (*Ibid.*: 688). However, when debts are not paid promptly they often remain unsatisfied, offering fertile soil for future disputes. The last step in the mediation process is typically a ritual of reconciliation, whether drinking coffee together in a Lebanese village or a massive village feast financed by the loser as a public apology, as in prerevolutionary China (Yang, 1945).

The Social Organization of Mediation

Mediators are respected, influential community members with experience and acknowledged expertise in settling disputes. Successful settlements enhance their prestige and political prominence and often earn them some form of payment from the disputing parties. Among the Ifugao and Waigali, only titled members of the elite can become mediators, whereas among the Jalé, Zinacantecos, and Arusha individuals become mediators by virtue of their positions within the lineage system or kin network. Mediators often have special religious status, as in Nuer and Swat Pathan society. The reputation they earn for skillful negotiation, expertise in community norms and genealogies, and fairness and impartiality brings them more cases and political influence. Mediators are not outside authorities but informal leaders of kin groups, age grades, local hamlets, or other social grouping (e.g. Witty, 1978: 299). They are usually of higher social status than the disputants. Where disputes involve members of higher social strata, outsiders are often needed. In prerevolutionary China, for example, disputes between village leaders were mediated by gentry from neighboring villages (Yang, 1945: 185).[7]

Mediators represent the norms and values of their communties, often attaining their positions by virtue of their expertise in moral issues. They advocate a settlement that accords with commonly accepted notions of justice, couched in terms of custom, virtue, and fairness, and reflecting community judgments about appropriate behavior. To flout such a settlement is to defy the moral order of the community. Mediators often deliver moral lectures to one or both disputants. Finally, they are experts in village social relationships and genealogy, bringing to the conflict a vast store of knowledge about how individuals are expected to behave toward one another in general as well as about the reputations and social identities of the particular disputants. Mediators build upon their past

---

[7]Baumgartner notes a similar reluctance among judges in colonial New Haven to adjudicate cases involving their social equals (1978: 163–169).

experience with similar cases and their knowledge of local customs regarding such disputes, manipulating these rules to justify their opinions.

Mediators are generally neutral, but they are rarely disinterested; nor are they complete strangers to the disputants. Their impartiality is secured by crosscutting ties that link them to both sides. Waigali mediators, for example, have close ties to the lineages of both disputants but never belong to either. Jalé mediators have important exchange relationships with both sides (Koch, 1974: 140–141). A mediator's neutrality is also enhanced by his position as representative of an entire village or community or of an important component such as a lineage or age group. He may be an outsider, not intimately connected to either party, or an expert summoned because of his extensive knowledge of the substance of the dispute (Gulliver, 1977: 36–40). Like a labor arbitrator, he seeks settlements that seem fair to both sides in order to enhance his reputation and attract more cases (Fuller, 1971). But mediators are not always unbiased. If one side appears stubborn and unreasonable, the mediator may cast his weight on the other side in an effort to arrive at a settlement—a pattern observed among the Ifugao, the Zinacantecos, and the Swat Pathan.

Mediation is most likely to succeed between disputants whose various residential and kinship ties require them to deal with one another in the future. In other words, it is a phenomenon of communities. When social relationships are enduring, disputants need to find a settlement to continue to live together amicably. In societies without states and courts, the alternative to a mediated settlement is usually vengeance, which exposes the close kin of the offender to constant danger. Studies of such societies vividly document the role of the offender's kinsmen in pressing for payment of damages, particularly when these kinsmen have married into the victim's lineage (e.g., Colson, 1953; Evans-Pritchard, 1940; Gluckman, 1960).

Similarly, in peasant villages, where courts, as well as violence, offer alternatives to mediation, disputants agree to settle only when they belong to the same village or subgroup and feel the need to maintain amicable relationships. Several village studies indicate that members refrain from pressing their claims against covillagers in court for fear of disrupting important social relationships (e.g., Bohannan, 1957: 210; Yngvesson, 1976; Rothenberger, 1978; Witty, 1978: 307–311). Yet, where urbanization and social change break down this cohesion and mutual dependence, villagers seem more willing to use the courts (e.g., Ayoub, 1965; Gallin, 1966; Fried, 1966: 298; Kawashima, 1973: 73).

The Nature of Mediated Settlements

Mediated settlements are backed by coercion. Although the mediator lacks authority to impose a judgment, he is always able to exert influence and social pressure to persuade an intransigent party to accept some settlement and, often, to accept the settlement the mediator advocates. The community also exerts social pressure on disputants to settle and to abide by their agreement. Supernatural sanctions are often important as well.

Since mediators are usually powerful and influential, loss of their goodwill is itself a cause for concern. Some simply facilitate dyadic negotiations (e.g., Koch, 1974), whereas others practically adjudicate, backing their decisions with armed force. In the Swat valley in Pakistan, for example, saints serve as mediators by virtue of their religious positions but occasionally call on their followers to reinforce religious authority with military might (Barth, 1959; Bailey, 1972: 28ff.). One saint, for example, arrived at a negotiating session where the disputants had agreed to appear unarmed only to find one party and his armed followers about to massacre his unarmed opponent. The saint whistled, calling out his own armed men hiding behind the bushes, thus quickly shifting his position from mediator to arbitrator (Barth, 1959: 98–99). Similarly, the Ifugao *monkalun* acts as a go-between, but in the event of a failure to reach an agreement his reputation as a headhunter becomes salient, and he threatens violence against the stubborn party. A mediator's opinions are often backed by the economic and political power of his kin group.

The community itself exerts pressure to settle. Recalcitrant disputants become the objects of gossip and scandal. In Chinese villages they lose "face" for failing to behave in a reasonable, conciliatory manner (Yang, 1945). Swat Pathan who refuse to settle lose general support and gain a reputation for ungodliness (Barth, 1959: 98). Witchcraft and supernatural beliefs concerning illness also serve as a powerful incentive to restoring amicable relations. Zinacantecos believe that the anger in the heart of a dissatisfied party causes sickness in its object (Collier, 1973); those who refuse to act in a manner perceived as fair in a Chinese village open themselves to attacks by witchcraft (Yang, 1945).

One further form of coercion and social pressure is the need to maintain peaceful relations with the other party. Terminating relations may be damaging to political, economic, or kinship transactions; threats of violence or court action raise the specter of protracted, .ruinous litigation or a bloody feud. Insofar as they seek to avoid these disasters, disputing parties are coerced to settle. Nevertheless, in no case is a mediator's decision backed by institutionalized force, and parties are always free to reject mediation and face the consequences.

Mediated settlements between unequals are unequal. With few exceptions, a mediated settlement reflects the status inequalities between the disputants. Payments for homicide among the Sudanese Nuer and the Enga of New Guinea (Meggitt, 1977) depend on the social status of the dead man; Ifugao compensation varies according to the status of both plaintiff and defendant. The amount of damages a Waigali receives reflects his total social personality (Jones, 1974: 82). A Swat Pathan landlord who is pronounced loser in a conflict with a weaker adversary often simply refuses to abide by the agreement (Barth, 1959: 98). In prerevolutionary China, mediated settlements between families or individuals of equal prestige or wealth reflected community norms, but those between wealthy, educated families and the village poor often did not (Cohen, 1966: 1224) and were unjust (Yang, 1945: 242; see also Lubman, 1967: 1295).

Since a mediator lacks the ability to enforce his decisions, he must find an outcome both parties will accept. A mutually acceptable solution tends to be one in which the less powerful gives up more (Gulliver, 1963: 2–3; see also Ruffini, 1978: 236). The greater the power of the mediator, the more leverage he has to impose a solution that disregards the inequality of the parties. The judge, at least in theory, adjudicates the legal rights of the disputants; he does not weigh their total social personalities.

COMMUNITY MEDIATION PROGRAMS IN CONTEMPORARY AMERICA

This analysis of mediation in small-scale societies has important implications for the way that process will function in urban America and for the quality of justice it can provide. First, urban American mediation is more perfunctory, more delayed, and less concrete than mediation in small-scale societies. Hearings typically occur seven to eleven days after the incident is reported (McGillis and Mullen, 1977). This time lapse may mean that disputant positions have hardened.[8] A large portion of referrals are made by judges, in which cases the plaintiff has already decided against seeking a consensual settlement. Experiments with delaying the hearing for a three-week "cooling-off" period support the wisdom of rapid intervention since the number of disputants appearing for these hearings drops radically (*Ibid.*: 64). Negotiations and settlements are strictly private, so that community members can neither participate in the agreement nor pressure the parties to comply, except in a few community-based programs such as the San Francisco Community Boards. Hearings in American centers last a maximum of two and a half hours and often less (*Ibid.*: 163–173; Wahrhaftig, 1978). Although this is longer than many court trials, it does not approach the input of time and resources of mediation in small-scale societies.

Second, the enveloping social system of urban American neighborhoods is quite different from that of small-scale, nonindustrial societies. I argued earlier in the chapter that the efficacy of mediation depends on the existence of a cohesive, stable, morally integrated community whose powers of informal social

---

[8]A mediator in an African town, for example, found that hearings were more successful if held before the plaintiff made the decision to go to court, when his attitude became fixed and the justification for his case unquestionable (Harries–Jones, 1964: 36).

control can be harnessed to informally achieved settlements. Yet since American centers function in large metropolitan areas, the community pressures necessary to induce disputants to accept a compromise settlement are generally absent. Disputants are rarely embedded in a close, cohesive social system where they need to maintain cooperative relationships. Even when disputants come from the same neighborhood, unless they are integrated into a unitary social structure their conflicts in one relationship do not have repercussions for others. Further, they have the option of moving away from a conflict situation rather than settling it by compromise. This is probably a frequent pattern in American society (Felstiner, 1974), although it may carry a high cost (Danzig and Lowy, 1975).

My own study of an urban neighborhood suggests that avoidance, or moving away, is common but is usually chosen reluctantly after a long period of conflict and the exhaustion of other alternatives (Merry, 1979). Most of the disputes in this low-income, polyethnic housing project passed through a long phase of endurance, in which the disputants simply put up with barking dogs, dirty stairwells, minor thefts, and jealous, violent lovers while appealing to a variety of formal third parties—the management office, the police, and the courts. But few disputes were resolved by these third parties. Disputants rarely consulted neighborhood leaders. Efforts to mobilize community public opinion had little impact in this fragmented, diverse community whose social networks were largely restricted to each ethnic group (Merry, 1980, 1981). Disputants tended to rely on violence as an alternative to formal third parties. In the long run, disputes eventually terminated only after one or both parties moved out of the project. Thus, in those segments of American society where the social structure is fragmented and the population mobile, the need to settle may be slight and the incentive to mediate and to compromise correspondingly reduced.

Nor are court-based versions of citizen dispute resolution programs organized in a way that could exploit existing patterns of informal social control. Most programs serve areas with several thousand to several million residents rather than the smaller social units whose residents may belong to a single social network. The mediator, although usually chosen from the "local community," is almost always required to be a stranger to the disputants in order to assure his impartiality. This means that he lacks the store of knowledge about personal histories and reputations and the nature of previous settlements in the local area that appears to be critical to the success of a mediator (see also Felstiner, 1974). The mediator is not a person of unusual prestige, moral stature, or influence in the neighborhood but simply a resident who has had a week of training in mediation and is paid a nominal sum to hear cases occasionally on evenings and weekends.

These mediators are also unable to operate in terms of a shared moral system. They are enjoined by mediation trainers not to make moral statements or judgments and are encouraged to seek a mutually acceptable outcome, regardless of their notions of relevant laws or norms (McGillis and Mullen, 1977; Felstiner and Williams, 1978)—although Eisenberg (1976) cogently argues that negotiation always has reference to norms. Since each center serves a large area, mediators must handle cases from a wide variety of neighborhoods with diverse norms and values. They cannot assume that they share the value system of the disputants or that the disputants themselves agree on normative standards. Nor can they be familiar with the outcomes of similar disputes settled in the disputants' neighborhoods, which could serve as precedents. Public opinion cannot reinforce a decision reached in a private session attended only by mediators and disputants. Private hearings cannot serve as arenas to raise broader issues affecting entire neighborhoods, as Wahrhaftig observed occurring in a public hearing held by the community-based San Francisco Community Boards (Wahrhaftig, 1982). Agreements are not solemnized with the kind of public ritual that in nonindustrial societies frequently serves to solidify the commitment of the parties to support the agreement and secure public approval.

Citizen dispute resolution programs may be most effective in disputes between parties involved in an ongoing relationship they wish to preserve. Although most centers purport to deal exclusively with conflicts in "ongoing social relationships," this phrase conceals an important distinction between relationships with a long past that are terminating and those with a short history but expectations of a long future (Jacobson, 1971). The latter is the critical variable for mediation. The willingness of a tenant to compromise with his landlord may be far greater when he plans to stay in his apartment for another ten years than that of a tenant who has been there ten years but is planning to move the following week. Similarly, a domestic conflict in which both parties wish to preserve the relationship demands different treatment from one in which they are trying to establish the terms of their separation. Where separating parties share custody of a child, however, their relations will inevitably endure, and mediation can again be appropriate. Mediators are more likely to function successfully in disputes where both parties have an incentive to settle than in those where both wish only to win.

Further, mediation depends on a community fabric that links disputants in enduring relationships important to both and provides a shared set of values within which the dispute can be discussed. In the United States, urban ethnic enclaves often possess these qualities (Whyte, 1945; Gans, 1962; Doo, 1973). Programs in these social settings may be able to marshal informal sanctions behind their actions by selecting influential and morally respected individuals as mediators and making hearings public.

A third implication of this cross-cultural survey of mediation is that the process may be more appropriate for concrete disputes that can be settled by a simple exchange of property than for complex, emotion-laden interpersonal hostilities arising out of tangled webs of insult and rivalry, abuse and counterabuse, love and hatred. Resolution of the latter often involves vague promises of changed behavior or avoidance (Felstiner and Williams, 1978). It is this kind of dispute for which mediation is advocated and that judges, prosecutors, and the police feel least able to handle (see, e.g., Black, 1980). Yet there are indications that such cases are most resistant to long-term resolution through mediation, whereas the former result in outcomes that are easier to monitor and more likely to be viewed by disputants as satisfactory over the long run. An extensive questionnaire survey of users of five Florida citizen dispute resolution programs indicated that complainants who sought disengagement, payment or return of money or property, or control of animals were more often satisfied with the process than those who sought relief in domestic and child welfare cases, repair or service of property, maintenance of property, or alteration of future behavior (Dispute Resolution Alternatives Committee [DRAC], n.d.: 50). Those disputes most likely to be perceived by complainants as resolved in the long run (six to twelve months after the hearing) were landlord–tenant, harassment, and recovery of money or property; domestic or child welfare and neighborhood cases were least likely to be so perceived (*Ibid.*: 54).[9] Ironically, the kinds of cases for which citizen dispute resolution is most often advocated thus seem resistant to mediation, whereas those in which it might be more effective are handled fairly effectively by adjudication. Programs may thus be more effective in relieving court congestion and shunting aside troublesome cases than in providing a more desirable process to those now poorly served in domestic and neighborhood disputes.

A fourth feature of mediation in small-scale societies, with critical implications for American programs, is the central role of coercion. Mediation in village and pastoral societies does not occur without coercion, but the latter takes the form of informal social pressures, fear of supernatural reprisals, and expectations of violence at the hands of the aggrieved party or the mediator, rather than that of state coercion. In American programs, the role of coercion is a recurring concern. Danzig's influential article (1973) on community moots proposed handling disputes without recourse to coercion in any form, but other scholars, as well as citizen dispute resolution program personnel, argue that dispute settlement without coercion is unworkable (e.g., Fisher, 1975). The staff and mediators of the Dade County Citizen Dispute Settlement Program, for example, see their program's "lack of teeth" as a major problem and suggest that they need subpoena power and legal enforcement of mediation agreements (Moriarty *et al.*, 1977: 79). A persistent problem for many citizen dispute resolution programs is the high proportion of "no-shows"—disputants who fail to appear for scheduled

[9]Rates of long-term resolution were higher in disputes where the complainant sought payment or return of money or property (69.8 percent), disengagement (67.2 percent), or maintenance of property (61.1 percent), than in those where complainants sought domestic or child welfare relief (30 percent), repair or service of property (33.3 percent), alteration of past behavior (41.9 percent), or control of animals (42.1 percent) (DRAC, n.d.: 56).

hearings. The Florida mediators would like greater legal authority to cope with this. Statistics from other programs suggest that rates of appearance vary with the coercive powers of the referral source. In Boston's Urban Court program, for example, referrals from the clerks (a less coercive agent) were withdrawn in 36 percent of the cases, whereas referrals from the bench and the prosecutor's office were withdrawn in only 23 percent (Snyder, 1978: 129–130). Similarly, a study of five Florida programs suggests that the rate of "no-shows" is far lower when cases are referred by criminal justice sources than when they derive from private individuals or agencies (DRAC, n.d.).

Moreover, the court is used to coerce disputants not only to mediate but also to settle and to abide by the outcome. In many programs, cases are continued by the court pending successful mediation so that disputants are negotiating in the shadow of the courthouse, aware that failure to agree will put them back before the judge. Mediators having difficulty persuading disputants to submit to mediation and reach an agreement threaten court action if the process stalls. The three federally funded neighborhood justice centers (NJCs) rely on the coercion implicit in referrals from police, prosecutors, or the court, which suggests that disputes not mediated will be adjudicated (Sheppard *et al.*, 1979: 56–57). Mediators in Boston's Urban Court frequently "remind" recalcitrant disputants that the case will be decided by the court if they cannot reach an agreement (Snyder, 1978: 120). Staff in the Atlanta Neighborhood Justice Center attempt to resolve disputes through threats of court action if the merchant or landlord refuses to agree to mediation or fails to settle.[10]

Thus there are pressures within the citizen dispute resolution movement to rely more heavily on the coercive powers of the court or to demand new coercive powers for mediators in order to compensate for the absence of informal pressures. This endangers one of the primary attractions of mediation—its less coercive, more consensual process. Furthermore, this trend raises the specter of quasi-judicial entities exercising coercive powers outside the courts, controlling citizens without the legal safeguards of due process and the adversary system (*Ibid.*: 146–153). Such entities might become a way of expanding state intervention into the daily lives of citizens without proper regard for their legal rights, as Nejelski (1976) has argued with respect to juvenile diversion programs.

There are indications that citizen dispute resolution programs are coping with the problem of coercion through a second strategy: by producing settlements to which both parties will agree and that appear to provide a solution, yet that are essentially meaningless and unenforceable. Since a frequent measure of the success of citizen dispute resolution programs is the proportion of hearings reaching an agreement, resort to low-quality settlements is difficult to measure or

[10]I am grateful to Pat Christian, a student intern in the center during the summer of 1979, for this observation.

evaluate. Felstiner and Williams (1978) provide examples of two disputes in which the settlements appear unlikely to forge a new basis for coexistence by the disputants. Mediation programs have been criticized for their inability to deal with the underlying sources of social conflict such as social inequality, poverty, unemployment, racism, or sexism. Even in domestic disputes, however, mediation without coercion may not always produce the kinds of settlements desired. A woman disputant testifying before a Senate Judiciary Committee hearing on mediation in Boston in early 1979, for example, said that she turned to the court because she really wanted "someone with authority to tell my husband to stop hitting me." A mutually acceptable settlement by a nondirective, noncoercive mediator would not offer her the protection she seeks. Consensus has an important role in dispute settlement, but it should not be confounded with the need to curtail offensive, destructive behavior.

In my research on patterns of disputing in an American urban neighborhood, I found that disputants frequently appeal to the court in interpersonal disputes but use it as a sanction rather than as a forum for settling disputes (Merry, 1979). It is predominantly those less capable of using violence, such as women and the elderly, who threaten or actually go to court, not because they expect to win an effective judgment (cases are often dismissed) but in order to equalize the balance. If this is the role courts are playing in domestic and neighbor disputes, mediation clearly can not provide an adequate substitute.

The criticism that mediation programs are generating meaningless settlements is supported by the facts that caseloads remain low although the programs appear to offer a much-needed service and that large numbers of cases apparently amenable to mediation continue to appear in courts. Many referrals fail to come to hearings, and the percentage of voluntary referrals is very small. In the first six months of operation, for example, the three neighborhood justice centers held 525 hearings, 86 per cent of which were declared resolved, yet this represents only 29 hearings per center per month, a surprisingly low number considering that each center serves a large metropolitan area (Sheppard et al., 1979: 35). Furthermore, only 16 percent of these cases were voluntary referrals (Ibid.: 34). In a study of five Florida programs, only 7 percent of the cases were "walk-ins" (DRAC, n.d.: 16). Half the cases referred to the NJCs did not lead to any resolution, moreover, since either the parties withdrew the case, the respondent failed to appear, or the complainant made no further contact with the center (Sheppard et al., 1979: 34). The Los Angeles Neighborhood Justice Center, which relies almost exclusively on voluntary referrals, held an average of eight hearings a month (Ibid.: 44), despite what the director characterized as energetic and widespread media promotion and community contact efforts.[11] In one mediation center in operation since November 1975, 600 cases had been referred

---

[11]Personal communication.

by early 1978, with 60 percent from the court; approximately 360 were mediated (Felstiner and Williams, 1978). Another study of the same center reports that 438 sessions occurred in the first two years (Snyder, 1978: 130). This accomplishment is dwarfed by the fact that the local district court in this community of 225,000 handles 12,000 cases a year, although about half are motor vehicle law violations (Felstiner and Williams, 1978) and others may be actions by creditors or the police rather than interpersonal disputes. Perhaps this low level of use simply represents public inertia or ignorance about these programs, but it is also possible that disputants perceive them as ineffective or inappropriate forums for dispute resolution and take their conflicts elsewhere.

Mediation may provide an effective tool for dispute resolution, however, if its capacities and processes are more carefully understood and its use more circumscribed. It seems most appropriate for those disputes in which both parties wish to maintain their relationship. This desire provides an incentive to settle, to seek peace rather than victory. Neighbors quarreling over a common boundary or separating spouses settling child custody, for example, must find ways of living together, and this need to settle is itself a form of pressure to agree.

The observed inequality of mediated settlements in small-scale societies raises troubling questions about the quality of justice in American mediation centers. The impact of mediation may be quite different, depending on whether the dispute is between equals or unequals. Mediated settlements perpetuate differences in social status—a characteristic with very different implications in nonindustrial ranked societies and industrialized class societies that embrace an egalitarian ideology. Conflicts between equals and between unequals both fall under the rubric of "ongoing social relationships" and may therefore be considered appropriate for mediation. Yet there are significant differences between disputes among relative equals, such as neighbors or local small merchants and regular customers, and those between relative unequals, such as a violent husband and an abused wife or a large merchant and a consumer. In disputes between unequals, the weaker party may turn to a third party to equalize the balance and seek an equitable resolution, as the powerless Cheyenne turns to an important chief (Llewellyn and Hoebel, 1941). To be effective, the third party must possess sufficient power to equalize the balance between the disputants. Unless mediation centers address this problem or decide to deal only with disputes between equals, they risk serving the weaker parties poorly by accommodating their demands with inadequate compensation while inhibiting their appeal to courts where they could, at least in theory, demand a legally just settlement (cf. Silbey, 1979; see also Nader and Singer, 1976: 311; Getman, 1979). Of course, considerable research suggests that courts also serve to perpetuate inequalities (e.g. Galanter, 1974; Starr and Yngvesson, 1975; Mather, 1979).

There are some indications that disputes between unequals could become a significant proportion of the mediation caseload, although we lack information on this point from functioning programs. In the first six months of operation, the neighborhood justice centers found that almost half of their respondents were representatives of corporations or public and private organizations but that only 5 percent of complainants were (Sheppard *et al.*, 1979: 47). In two reports on Florida programs, respondents reported satisfaction with the mediation process more often than complainants, although these studies did not tabulate the proportion of corporate representatives (Moriarty *et al.*, 1977: 36–40; DRAC, n.d.: 33). Thus, we must ask whether mediation serves the weaker parties better than the courts do or simply perpetuates inequalities, as it does in small-scale societies. A mode of dispute resolution whose outcomes clearly reflect the economic and political inequalities of American society may ultimately be unacceptable in a polity based on legal, if not social, equality.

CONCLUSIONS

Existing versions of mediation, particularly those programs closely connected to courts, seem to function quite differently from mediation in nonindustrial societies. These programs do not rely on informal social controls rooted in the local community. In heterogeneous urban neighborhoods where the social fabric of community is loosely woven, mediation programs turn to the threat of the court to achieve settlement. Since one inspiration for mediation was dissatisfaction with penal sanctions in interpersonal disputes, their reappearance through the back door represents a return to a mode of sanctioning that has already been judged inadequate. If disputants are impelled to try to mediation before they can use the court, mediation centers may become meaningless at best and, at worst, another hurdle between the citizen and his day in court.

On the other hand, mediation has tremendous potential if it can be built on existing community structures (where these exist) rather than appended to the legal system; if it is restricted to disputes between relative equals, and if it is used only in future-oriented disputes where the parties feel a need to settle. It offers hope for resolving disputes arising from faulty communication and misunderstanding, those in which both parties wish to avoid the criminal penalties of the court, and those where an agreement involves a specific exchange rather than long-term promises of improved behavior.

Perhaps a mediation program that endeavored to build on existing social structures and mobilized informal social pressures through public hearings and the use of influential community leaders as mediators within small areas knit together through interlocking social relationships could achieve effective dispute resolution without recourse to the sanctions of the state.[12] But in some settings,

[12]These suggestions imply a proliferation of small-scale, localized centers for mediating disputes, yet this need not add to the cost. In fact, a program that grafted dispute settlement functions onto existing social service centers, community groups, and religious institutions might prove less expen-

the social structure may be too diffuse and the population too transient to allow mediation to function as it does in the anthropological prototype. Mediation cannot serve as a panacea for the problems that plague the courts; nor can it, alone, reverse the trend toward the dissolution of the cohesive local community in American society.

Societies must always choose some course between the conflicting goals of order and liberty. The cumbersome, formalistic procedures of due process serve, at least ideally, to protect liberty and to preserve the rule of law against state oppression. However, the price of these procedural safeguards for the protection of individual freedom may be a certain level of disorder, of disruption or rule breaking that goes unpunished, and inefficiency in the processing of cases. The social changes of twentieth-century America have gradually loosened community control over behavior, allowing greater liberty to nonconforming, disruptive, and deviant individuals. With the dissolution of informal social controls, the perceived increase in disorder has led to heightened demands that the court restore order even in the domain of neighborhood and family conflicts (e.g. Black, 1971; 1973). From this perspective the citizen dispute resolution movement is an anomaly: It seeks to return control over nonacceptable behavior to the local community without sacrificing the greater measure of personal liberty and autonomy that the very breakdown in informal social controls have provided. Informal control mechanisms in small-scale societies produce order at the expense of individual freedom, particularly for individuals of lower rank or power. It is particularly instructive that those American settings in which mediation occurs naturally are also those where members and powerful leaders exert considerable control over their fellows (see Yaffee, 1972; Doo, 1973). If Americans are unwilling to return to a social world in which their actions can be judged and condemned by neighbors and fellow workers, mediation programs will be unable to function.

The alternative is to create institutions that appear to grant communities control over behavior yet that in reality simply provide a forum for handling disputes outside the protections of due process (Snyder, 1978; Hofrichter, 1982). We still know too little about what mediation programs will do, but they contain the possibility of increasing state control over individual behavior outside the rule of law, of enhancing order at the expense of liberty.

An uncritical adoption of mediation could undermine social justice in other ways as well. Mediation could become a new mode of social control by local elites over deviant behavior (Hofrichter, 1982). As Silbey (1979) and Hofrichter (1977) argue, mediation might become a means for containing and deflecting grievances that spring from tensions in society itself, thus meeting individual

---

sive than the creation of wholly new programs. Furthermore, such a pattern might increase the flow of cases to the mediation center, thus avoiding the substantial intake costs now required in most programs.

demands without affecting the underlying normative order of society. The public demand for condemnation and punishment of deviant behavior may also be deflected. Mediation experiments offer the promise of more humane and just ways of resolving interpersonal disputes. But is this what they provide?

REFERENCES

Abel, R. L. (1979) "Delegalization: A Critical Review of Its Ideology, Manifestations, and Social Consequences," in E. Blankenburg, E. Klausa, and H. Rottleuthner (eds.) *Alternative Rechtsformen und Alternativen zum Recht.* Opladen: Westdeutscher Verlag (Jahrbuch für Rechtssoziologie und Rechtstheorie, band VI).

American Bar Association (1976) *Report of the Pound Conference Follow-Up Task Force.* Chicago: American Bar Foundation.

Ayoub, Victor F. (1965) "Conflict Resolution and Social Reorganization in a Lebanese Village," 24 *Human Organization* 11.

Bailey, F. G. (1972) "Conceptual Systems in the Study of Politics," in R. Antoun and I. Harick (eds.) *Rural Politics and Social Change in the Middle East.* Bloomington: Indiana University Press.

Barth, Frederik (1959) *Political Leadership among the Swat Pathans.* London: London School of Economics (Monograph No. 19).

Barton, R. F. (1919) *Ifugao Law,* reprinted, 1969. Berkeley: University of California Press (University of California Publications in American Archeology and Ethnology No. 15).

Baumgartner, M. P. (1978) "Law and Social Status in Colonial New Haven, 1639–1665," 1 *Research in Law and Sociology* 153.

Bell, Griffin (1978) "The Pound Conference Follow-Up: A Response from the United States Department of Justice," 76 *Federal Rules Decisions* 320.

Berman, Jesse (1969) "The Cuban Popular Tribunals," 69 *Columbia Law Review* 1317.

Black, Donald J. (1971) "The Social Organization of Arrest," 23 *Stanford Law Review* 1087.

——— (1973) "The Boundaries of Legal Sociology," in D. Black and M. Mileski (eds.) *The Social Organization of Law.* New York: Seminar Press.

——— (1976) *The Behavior of Law.* New York: Academic Press.

——— (1980) *The Social Organization of the Police.* New York: Academic Press.

Bohannan, Paul (1957) *Justice and Judgement among the Tiv.* London: Oxford University Press.

Brögger, Jan (1968) "Conflict Resolution and the Role of the Bandit in Peasant Society," 41 *Anthropological Quarterly* 228.

Canter, Richard S. (1978) "Dispute Settlement and Dispute Processing in Zambia: Individual Choice versus Societal Constraints," in Nader and Todd (1978).

Cantor, R. (1974) "Law without Lawyers: Cuba's Popular Tribunals," 4 *Juris Doctor* 24.

Cappelletti, M. (gen. ed.) (1978–1979) *The Florence Access-To-Justice Project,* 4 vols. Milan: Giuffrè; and Alphen aan den Rijn: Sijthoff and Noordhoff.

Cohen, J. A. (1966) "Chinese Mediation on the Eve of Modernization," 54 *California Law Review* 1201.

Collier, Jane (1973) *Law and Social Change among the Zinacantan.* Palo Alto, Calif.: Stanford University Press.

——— (1976) "Political Leadership and Legal Change in Zinacantan," 11 *Law & Society Review* 131.

Colson, E. (1953) "Social Control and Vengeance in Plateau Tonga Society," 23 *Africa* 199.

——— (1974) *Tradition and Contract: The Problem of Order.* Chicago: Aldine.

Cratsley, John C. (1978) "Community Courts: Offering Alternative Dispute Resolution within the Judicial System," 3 *Vermont Law Review* 1.

Crockett, George W. and Morris Gleicher (1978) "Teaching Criminals a Lesson: A Report on Justice in China," 61 *Judicature* 278.

Danzig, R. (1973) "Toward the Creation of a Complementary, Decentralized System of Criminal Justice," 26 *Stanford Law Review* 1.

Danzig, R. and M. Lowy (1975) "Everyday Disputes and Mediation in the United States: A Reply to Professor Felstiner," 9 *Law & Society Review* 675.

Dispute Resolution Alternatives Committee (DRAC) (n.d.) *The Citizen Dispute Settlement Process in Florida: A Study of Five Programs*. Florida: Office of the State Court Administrator.

Doo, Leigh-Wai (1973) "Dispute Settlement in Chinese-American Communities," 21 *American Journal of Comparative Law* 627.

Eisenberg, Melvin A. (1976) "Private Ordering through Negotiation: Dispute Settlement and Rule Making," 89 *Harvard Law Review* 637.

Evans-Pritchard, E. E. (1940) *The Nuer*. London: Oxford University Press.

Felstiner, William F. (1974) "Influences of Social Organization on Dispute Processing," 9 *Law & Society Review* 63.

Felstiner, William F. and Lynne Williams (1978) "Mediation as an Alternative to Criminal Prosecution: Ideology and Limitations," 2 *Law and Human Behavior* 223.

Fisher, E. (1975) "Community Courts: An Alternative to Conventional Criminal Adjudication," 24 *American University Law Review* 1253.

Fried, Morton (1966) "Some Political Aspects of Clanship in a Modern Chinese City," in M. Swartz, V. Turner, and A. Tuden (eds.) *Political Anthropology*. Chicago: Aldine.

Fuller, Lon (1960) "Adjudication and the Rule of Law," *Proceedings of the American Society of International Law* 1.

——— (1971) "Mediation: Its Forms and Functions," 44 *Southern California Law Review* 305.

Galanter, Marc (1974) "Why the 'Haves' Come Out Ahead: Speculations on the Limits of Legal Change," 9 *Law & Society Review* 95.

Gallin, Bernard (1966) "Conflict Resolution in Changing Chinese Society: A Taiwanese Study," in M. Swartz, V. Turner, and A. Tuden (eds.) *Political Anthropology*. Chicago: Aldine.

Gans, Herbert (1962) *The Urban Villagers: Group and Class in the Life of Italian-Americans*. New York: Free Press.

Getman, Julius A. (1979) "Labor Arbitration and Dispute Resolution," 88 *Yale Law Journal* 916.

Gibbs, James L., Jr. (1963) "The Kpelle Moot," 33 *Africa* 1.

Gluckman, Max (1955) *The Judicial Process among the Barotse of Northern Rhodesia*. Manchester: Manchester University Press.

——— (1960) *Custom and Conflict in Africa*. Oxford: Blackwells.

Gruel, P. J. (1971) "The Leopard-Skin Chief: An Examination of Political Power among the Nuer," 73 *American Anthropologist* 1115.

Gulliver, P. H. (1963) *Social Control in an African Society*. Boston: Boston University Press.

——— (1969) "Dispute Settlement without Courts: The Ndendeuli of Southern Tanzania," in L. Nader (ed.) *Law in Culture and Society*. Chicago: Aldine.

——— (1973) "Negotiations as a Mode of Dispute Settlement: Towards a General Model," 7 *Law & Society Review* 667.

——— (1977) "On Mediators," in Ian Hamnet (ed.) *Social Anthropology and Law*. London: Academic Press (Association of Social Anthropologists Monograph No. 14).

Haight, B. (1972) "A Note on the Leopard-Skin Chief," 74 *American Anthropologist* 1313.

Harries-Jones, P. (1964) "Marital Disputes and the Process of Conciliation in a Copperbelt Town," 35 *Human Problems in British Central Africa* 29.

Hoebel, E. A. (1954) *The Law of Primitive Man: A Study in Comparative Legal Dynamics*. Cambridge, Mass.: Harvard University Press.

Hofrichter, Richard (1977) "Justice Centers Raise Basic Questions," [1977] *New Directions in Legal Services* 168.

———— (1982) "Neighborhood Justice and the Social Control Problems of American Capitalism: A Perspective," in R. Abel (ed.) *The Politics of Informal Justice*, vol. 1: *The American Experience.* New York: Academic Press.

Howell, P. P. (1954) *A Manual of Nuer Law.* London: Oxford University Press.

Jacobson, David (1971) "Mobility, Continuity, and Urban Social Organization," 6 *Man* 630.

Jones, Schuyler (1974) *Men of Influence in Nuristan: A Study of Social Control and Dispute Settlement in Waigal Valley, Afghanistan.* London: Seminar Press.

Kawashima, Takeyoshi (1973) "Dispute Settlement in Japan," in D. Black and M. Mileski (eds.) *The Social Organization of Law.* New York: Seminar Press.

Koch, Klaus-Friedrich (1974) *War and Peace in Jalémó: The Management of Conflict in Highland New Guinea.* Cambridge, Mass.: Harvard University Press.

———— (ed.) (1979) *Access to Justice*, vol. 4: *The Anthropological Perspective: Patterns of Conflict Management: Essays in the Ethnography of Law.* Milan: Giuffrè; and Alphen aan den Rijn: Sijthoff and Noordhoff.

Kuper, Adam (1973) *Anthropologists and Anthropology: The British School 1922–1972.* New York: Pica Press.

Llewellyn, K. N. and E. A. Hoebel (1941) *The Cheyenne Way: Conflict and Case Law in Primitive Jurisprudence.* Norman: University of Oklahoma Press.

Lowy, Michael (1978) "A Good Name Is Worth More than Money: Strategies of Court Use in Urban Ghana," in Nader and Todd (1978).

Lubman, Stanley (1967) "Mao and Mediation: Politics and Dispute Resolution in Communist China," 55 *California Law Review* 1284.

McGillis, Daniel and Joan Mullen (1977) *Neighborhood Justice Centers: An Analysis of Potential Models.* Washington, D.C.: U.S. Department of Justice.

Malinowski, B. (1926) *Crime and Custom in Savage Society.* Totowa, N.J.: Littlefield, Adams, and Co.

Massell, Gregory (1968) "Law as an Instrument of Revolutionary Change in a Traditional Milieu: The Case of Soviet Central Asia," 2 *Law & Society Review* 179.

———— (1974) *The Surrogate Proletariat: Moslem Women and Revolutionary Strategies in Central Asia.* Princeton, N.J.: Princeton University Press.

Mather, Lynn M. (1979) *Plea Bargaining or Trial? The Process of Criminal-Case Disposition.* Lexington, Mass.: Lexington Books.

Meggitt, Mervyn (1977) *Blood Is Their Argument: Warfare among the Mae Enga Tribesmen of the New Guinea Highlands.* Palo Alto, Calif.: Mayfield.

Mentschikoff, S. (1961) "Commercial Arbitration," 61 *Columbia Law Review* 846.

Merry, Sally Engle (1979) "Going to Court: Strategies of Dispute Management in an American Urban Neighborhood," 13 *Law & Society Review* 4.

———— (1980) "The Social Organization of Strangers: Racial Integration in an Urban Neighborhood," 39 *Human Organization* 59–69.

———— (1981) *Urban Danger: Life in a Neighborhood of Strangers.* Philadelphia, Penn.: Temple University Press.

Mileski, Maureen (1971) "Courtroom Encounters: An Observation Study of a Lower Criminal Court," 5 *Law & Society Review* 473.

Moore, Sally Falk (1978) *Law as Process: An Anthropological Approach.* London: Routledge and Kegan Paul.

Moriarty, William F., Jr., Thomas L. Norris, and Luis Salas (1977) *Evaluation: Dade County Citizen Dispute Settlement Program.* Miami, Fla.: Dade County Criminal Justice Planning Unit.

Nader, Laura (1969) "Styles of Court Procedure: To Make the Balance," in L. Nader (ed.) *Law in Culture and Society.* Chicago: Aldine.

Nader, Laura and L. Singer (1976) "Dispute Resolution in the Future: What Are the Choices?" 51 *California State Bar Journal* 281.

Nader, Laura and Harry F. Todd, Jr. (eds.) (1978) *The Disputing Process—Law in Ten Societies.* New York: Columbia University Press.

Nejelski, Paul (1976) "Diversion: The Promise and the Danger," 22 *Crime and Delinquency* 393.

Rothenberger, John E. (1978) "The Social Dynamics of Dispute Settlement in a Sunni Muslim Village in Lebanon," in Nader and Todd (1978).

Ruffini, Julio L. (1978) "Disputing over Livestock in Sardinia," in Nader and Todd (1978).

Sander, Frank (1976) "Varieties of Dispute Processing," 70 *Federal Rules Decisions* 111.

Schwartz, R. D. and J. C. Miller (1964) "Legal Evolution and Societal Complexity," 70 *American Journal of Sociology* 159.

Sheppard, David I., Janice A. Roehl, and Royer F. Cook (1979) *Neighborhood Justice Centers Field Test: Interim Evaluation Report.* Washington, D.C.: U.S. Department of Justice.

Silbey, Susan (1979) "A Phenomenological Approach to the Study of Public Regulation." Presented at the Eastern Sociological Society Meetings, New York.

Snyder, Frederick E. (1978) "Crime and Community Mediation—The Boston Experience: A Preliminary Report on the Dorchester Urban Court Program," 1978 *Wisconsin Law Review* 101.

Spence, Jack (1982) "Institutionalizing Neighborhood Courts: Two Chilean Experiences," in R. Abel (ed.) *The Politics of Informal Justice*, vol. 2: *Comparative Studies*. New York: Academic Press.

Starr, J. and B. Yngvesson (1975) "Scarcity and Disputing: Zeroing-in on Compromise Decisions," 2 *American Ethnologist* 533.

Wahrhaftig, Paul (ed.) (1978) *The Citizen Dispute Resolution Organizer's Handbook.* Pittsburgh: Grassroots Citizen Dispute Resolution Clearinghouse.

———— (1979) *The Mooter.* Pittsburgh: Grassroots Citizen Dispute Resolution Clearinghouse.

———— (1982) "An Overview of Community-Oriented Citizen Dispute Resolution Programs in the United States," in R. Abel (ed.) *The Politics of Informal Justice*, vol. 1: *The American Experience*. New York: Academic Press.

Whyte, William Foote (1945) *Street Corner Society.* Chicago: University of Chicago Press.

Witty, Cathie J. (1978) "Disputing Issues in Shehaam, a Multireligious Village in Lebanon," in Nader and Todd (1978).

Yang, Martin C. (1945) *A Chinese Village: Taitou, Shantung Province.* New York: Columbia University Press.

Yaffe, James (1972) So Sue Me! The Story of a Community Court. New York: Saturday Review Press.

Yngvesson, Barbara (1976) "Responses to Grievance Behavior: Extended Cases in a Fishing Community," 3 *American Ethnologist* 353.

3

In Search of Nyaya Panchayats: The Politics of a Moribund Institution *

CATHERINE S. MESCHIEVITZ
MARC GALANTER

INTRODUCTION

India's massive attempt to provide access to justice for its rural population through the promotion of *Nyaya Panchayats* (village courts; hereafter NP)[1] is both theoretically provocative and practically important. Yet it remains largely unexamined empirically and virtually unknown outside India.

Completing a process of judicial reform started under colonial rule, India's post-Independence Constitution directed states to establish local self-government

*This essay is based in part on articles by Baxi and Galanter (1979) and Meschievitz (1979). An earlier version was read at the 1980 Joint Meeting of the Law and Society Association and the ISA Research Committee on Sociology of Law, Madison, Wisconsin, June 5–9. The first author's fieldwork in India was supported by a grant from the University of California Berkeley Professional Studies Program in 1977–1978. The authors would like to thank Richard Abel, Robert Hayden, and John Paul for their helpful comments and Upendra Baxi for many insights into the subject.

[1]On terminology: *Panchayati Raj* ('the regime of panchayats'—hereafter PR) refers to the policy of promoting elective village panchayats as units of local self-government. The judicial branch of these are *nyaya* (Sanskrit for 'logic' or 'justice') or in some states *adalati* (Persian for 'court') *panchayats*.

47

and to separate judicial and executive functions at the village level. Some states created NP intended to combine the virtues of traditional legal institutions (accessibility, informality, economy of time and money, and familiarity of legal norms) with those of the state legal system (impartiality, uniformity of law and procedures, and legitimacy). On the one hand, NP were to be integral parts of the state judicial service; on the other, they were to assist *Gaon Panchayats* (village level administrative bodies) in administering village affairs and educating people about the new democratic order. Despite evidence that NP have atrophied since their modest success in the late 1940s and fail to inspire the confidence of either the educated elite or the illiterate masses (Purwar, 1956; 1960; Khera, 1962; Retzlaff, 1962; Bhalerao and Singh, 1965; Tinker, 1967; Madan, 1969; Baxi, 1976a; Baxi and Galanter 1979), these multiple and often conflicting goals have been reiterated in recent discussions, most of which prescribe NP as the panacea for India's rural legal problems (India, Ministry of Law, Justice and Company Affairs, 1962; Singhvi, 1970; Singh, 1974; Naidu, 1977; Kushawaha, 1977; India, Ministry of Agriculture and Irrigation, 1978).

This chapter examines NP today in the state of Uttar Pradesh (UP) and offers a tentative explanation for the persistent loyalty they inspire despite their visible failure. Based on a study of previous reports of NP structure and authority and the first author's brief field study of two NP in Bharatpur Tahsil, Biswa District in 1978,[2] this chapter demonstrates their political nature, reveals the penetration of social and political inequality into NP structure and process, and situates NP within a pattern of disputing common among Indian legal institutions.

HISTORICAL BACKGROUND

India has a strong tradition of adjudication at the village level. The term *panchayat* literally means the 'coming together of five persons,' hence, the meeting, council, or court of five or more members of a village or caste[3] who assembled to judge disputes or determine group policy. Overlapping jurisdictions allowed caste *panchayats*, ad hoc village *panchayats*, and similar councils of trade guilds and artisan groups to entertain disputes involving their members.[4] Each convened informally or, more often, formally to hear complaints.

---

[2]All proper names for cities, villages, district, and people have been changed. The district is the major administrative unit within the Indian states and is divided into smaller units called *tahsils* (sometimes *taluks*). Within each *tahsil* are police *thanas* ('stations') and development *blocks*, which are not necessarily congruent.

[3]On caste, see note 11, following, and accompanying text.

[4]Louis Dumont (1970) has distinguished between types of traditional panchayats and suggests that earlier commentators confused "village *panchayats*" with locally dominant caste *panchayats*. An ad

After listening to all the available information and exposing the underlying issues, the *panchayat* would negotiate a solution acquiesced in by all participants.

Panchayats applied customary rules of behavior and forged a new consensus as local practices and understandings changed. Although some decisions might be enforced by the ruler, or king, who ideally held his own *durbar* (court), popular consensus secured obedience to most.[5] *Dharmasástra* (Hindu) and *Shar'ia* (Muslim) classical texts influenced but did not displace local law, and throughout most of Indian history there was no direct or centralized systematic control over law in the villages, where most people lived.

Throughout the nineteenth century, as English procedural and substantive law, the personal laws of Hindus and Muslims,[6] and custom mutually influenced one another in the courts of the Indian Empire, a new legal system gradually evolved. Many local *panchayats* lost authority, litigation in courts spiraled, and the legal profession became a central participant in the social and political movements of the late nineteenth and early twentieth centuries. Despite lingering criticism of foreign ideas, British and Indian elements had become blended into a distinctive Anglo-Indian system of laws and institutions (Cohn, 1965; Galanter, 1972; 1978). The post-Independence Constitution of 1950 maintained this system more or less intact, adding a layer of constitutionalism based in part on American and Australian models that gave lawyers and judges a mandate to use law and the courts to assist in the reformation of Indian society, making them promoters of radical change as well as custodians of the legal status quo. At a popular level the fusion of indigenous and imported legal forms is seen in the attachment most Indians display to both traditional dispute institutions and state legal institutions. With an ambivalence that may be typical of actors in highly pluralistic legal systems, Indians use every available forum to promote their interests regardless of any theoretical inconsistency (Khare, 1972; Galanter 1972; 1978; Kidder, 1977).

---

hoc village *panchayat*, made up of members of the locally dominant caste, heard intercaste disputes and serious village crimes, as well as cases among its own members. Other caste *panchayats* remained operative for their own intracaste disputes. Caste *panchayats* still resolve disputes in UP and other parts of India (Mehta, 1971; Moore, 1978; Hayden, 1980).

[5]On Indian legal tradition prior to the British, see Derrett (1964; 1968), Lingat (1973); on the survival of these traditions today, see Cohn (1959; 1961; 1965), Hitchcock (1960), Srinivas (1962), Nicholas and Mukhopadyay (1962), Rudolph and Rudolph (1965; 1969), Galanter (1968; 1972).

[6]By 1802 a comprehensive court system covered much of the subcontinent under British East India Company control. Care was taken to guarantee that in cases involving inheritance, succession, marriage, caste, and religious institutions and usages the personal laws of Hindus and Muslims would be applied. Nevertheless, on many topics, English common law and procedure became dominant; see Galanter (1968).

DECENTRALIZATION AND PANCHAYATI RAJ

Efforts to decentralize and reorganize local self-government using the institutional form of *panchayats*, which had been stymied in earlier decades, recurred in the 1880s.[7] In line with findings of government reports,[8] Indian governments created simple judicial tribunals called panchayat *adalati* to hear cases worth twenty rupees or less. Unlike the adalati in most parts of the Indian Empire, those in UP (then called the United Provinces) consisted of local leaders selected by the district magistrate on the nomination of *tahsil* officers. *Adalati* were originally created within a village, but when they failed to elicit popular support and participation their jurisdiction was enlarged to encompass several villages and a larger population. The *adalati* of UP were more active than most. In 1925 some 4772 *adalati* disposed of 122,760 cases (an average of 25.7 cases per *adalati* per year). But subsequent years saw a rapid decline, from 91,476 cases in 1931, to 85,339 in 1936, to 67,233 in 1937 (decided by 4180 *adalati*, for an average of 16 cases per *adalati* per year) (Tinker, 1967). Continuing reconsideration of local government schemes—a UP local government study in 1928 (United Provinces, 1928) and the Kher Committee Report of 1939 (United Provinces, 1940)—led to the enactment of the UP Panchayati Raj Act (No. 26) of 1947. It was the first piece of state legislation on the issue after Independence and, with substantial amendments, remains in force today (Saxena, 1972).

Most states now have a three-tier system of Panchayati Raj (PR).[9] In UP the adult men and women of each village (dubbed for electoral purposes the *Gaon*

[7]In South India, fourteen years after the introduction of British East India Company courts in rural areas (the *moffusil*), problems of large caseloads, high costs, corruption among court personnel, and exploitation by the growing class of Indian *vakils* (lawyers) troubled company administrators. In 1816 Thomas Munro created new village *panchayats* in which the headman presided over a council of village officials, following the traditional model. Munro felt that the administration of justice "may be improved" by employing Indians who "for ages have been in the constant habit of administering justice in their villages," represent "natural superiors," and possess a "knowledge of the people and their concerns" (Madras, 1857–1859). Unfortunately, although the headmen sometimes were traditional arbiters, they were not the only people performing that role. Consequently, the panchayats never got the support for which Munro had hoped, and by the 1850s village panchayats in the entire Madras Presidency handled less than fifty cases a year (Beaglehole, 1966). In North India Charles Metcalf tried a similar experiment in the United Provinces, with much the same results (Panigrahi, 1968).

[8]In addition to resolutions of the governor-general in council (Lord Mayo of 14 December 1870 and Lord Ripon of 30 September 1881 and 18 May 1882, India House mss.), see India, Home Government (1909); India, Government of India (1919).

[9]UP legislation actually preceded Constitutional Directives to organize village panchayats (Article 40) and to separate the judiciary and the executive at the village level (Article 50). By 1959 the Central Government's Balwantray Mehta Committee Report (India [Republic], Committee on Democratic Decentralization, 1958) urged all states to adopt the Panchayati Raj system. In 1961 the UP legislature amended their system slightly to correspond to the national model, in the Kshetra Samiti and Zillah Parishad Act (Saxena, 1972).

Sabha, or village assembly) elect representatives to the *Gaon Panchayat* (GP). Members of the GP then elect two of their members to represent the GP on the second tier, the *Panchayat Samiti* (PS), which serves one development block. In like fashion, each PS nominates a member to represent it on the district body, called the *Zillah Parishad.* Officers in the State Department of *Panchayati Raj* select members of the state legislature, state cooperatives, urban organizations, and Scheduled Castes and Scheduled Tribes to serve on the *Zillah Parishad* (see Figure 3.1).

Although it is theoretically a village institution, in practice a GP often encompasses one to five villages and 250–3000 people. In UP the head of the GP is called the *Pradhan* and the leader of the PS the *Promulkh.* Members of each body elect the head by secret ballot. The fourth component of PR are the Nyaya Panchayats. Each of five to ten GP selects two members to serve as *panchas*

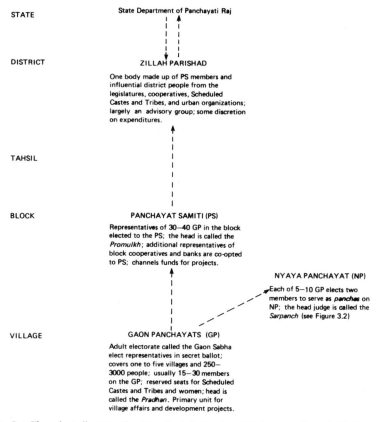

Figure 3.1 Flow chart illustrates the Uttar Pradesh Panchayati Raj system (From India [Republic], Ministry of Food, Agriculture and Cooperation, 1977).

(judges) on the NP. The ten to twenty *panchas* then choose a *Sarpanch* (head judge). Those elected as *panchas*, relinquish their seats on the GP. As Figure 3.1 reveals, then, NP lie between the village and the block levels (Saxena, 1972).[10]

Studies of PR show that though it has attempted to be responsive to the needs of the rural people it has generally failed to induce structural change in existing village power systems (Haldipur, 1974; Reddy, 1977; India, Ministry of Agriculture, and Irrigation 1978). It confronts three main problems:

1. An absence of broad local leadership and general popular support, dominance by local elites, and lack of interest among others in the electoral process (Dube, 1965; Kantowsky 1970; India, Ministry of Agriculture and Irrigation, 1978).
2. Inadequate financial support, little for the GP and PS to do, and confusion over the roles of elected *panchayat* members and block officials, which stimulates competition for favors and gaps in accountability and responsibility (India, Ministry of Law, Justice, and Company Affairs, 1978; Hardgrave, 1980)
3. Factionalism (also called *bundism*) in villages, along caste lines. Caste in India is the system of corporate groups (*jatis*), associated with different degrees of purity and pollution. Each group has its own rules of endogamy and exogamy and traditional occupations (Dumont, 1970; Tyler, 1973; cf. Marriott and Inden, 1974).[11] Charismatic leaders of caste groups compete in panchayat elections and work out a balance of power with lesser competing groups (Singh, 1974; Hardgrave, 1980).

As will be shown in the following discussion, all three problems beset NP operations as well.

NYAYA PANCHAYATS IN BHARATPUR

Bharatpur Tahsil lies some 130 kilometers northeast of Lucknow, the capital of UP. It is in Biswa District, one of fifty-seven administrative units in the state and part of a less developed region in UP. Literacy rates are low, and the

[10]A report lists 57 Zillah Parishads, 875 Panchayat Samitis, 72,848 Gaon Panchayats, and 8791 NP in UP (India, Ministry of Food, Agriculture and Cooperation, 1977). Different states have slightly different PR structures, which may include many more villages and people in the lowest tier. The names of the tiers vary from state to state; this chapter uses those current in UP.
[11]In the classical Hindu scheme of society there are four *varnas*, or overarching estates (often referred to as "castes"): Brahmins (priests and learned), Kshatriya (warriors, rulers), Vaishya (agriculturalists, merchants), and Sudras (servants). *Jatis* are associated with one or another *varna*, although there is sometimes conflict about *varna* identity. At the bottom, or beneath the *varnas*, are the "untouchabes" (officially, Scheduled Castes), a cluster of *jatis* with the lowest status. Although daily behavior is based on the interaction of *jatis*, notions of *varna* retain significance.

proportion of people dependent on agriculture for their livelihood is high.[12] In 1978 two sugar factories provided outside employment, but most villagers relied on their respective *thakurs*, or landlords, for their wages, in cash and in kind.

Bharatpur is part of what used to be the Princely State of Bharatpur, in which the raja and his chosen *taluqdars* and *zamindars* (large landholders) controlled vast estates and collected land revenues for the raja. A system of patronage and power allowed local *zamindars* to dominate villages and caste *panchayats* and helped create prescriptive usages that are still influential (Blunt, 1912; Metcalf, 1964; 1978; Stokes, 1978). Contemporary landlords (60 percent of whom are Rajputs[13]) enjoy tremendous deference from the people living and working on their lands. Many have opposed any bureaucratic change likely to weaken existing patterns of social and political control and continually compete with one another over economic and political resources (Brass, 1966). Kantowsky (1970) goes so far as to call the existing patterns of PR and development in parts of eastern UP a "Thakur Raj." Bharatpur commentators were critical of the local landlords for impeding decentralization efforts, a sentiment echoed in government reports that described state legislators as reluctant to pass decentralization measures for fear of alienating their more influential constituents (Brass, 1966; India, Ministry of Agriculture and Irrigation, 1978).

Administrative and judicial operations follow the territorial subdivisions of the state (see Figure 3.2).[14] Biswa is the district headquarters and seat of the district civil and sessions court and the district magistrate. The district officer of PR also has his office in Biswa. It is about seventy kilometers, or a one-to-three-hour bus ride, from Biswa to Bharatpur, head of Bharatpur Tahsil and a town of 25,000 people. The courts of the judicial magistrate, the subdivisional munsif, and the subdistrict magistrate are in Bharatpur; the first hears all original criminal cases for four police

[12]In 1971, Biswa District had a population of 2,302,029 people, 2814 inhabited villages, and less than ten towns and cities. Bharatpur Block encompasses 134 villages and 116,000 people; Dhanabad Block, 108 villages and 110,069 people. The average literacy rate is 14 percent (India, Bureau of the Census, 1971; Y.S. Singh, 1976).

[13]*Rajput* means a "prince" or son of a king. It is used to denote not an endogamous caste group (*jati*) but the members of a dispersed caste category united by a claim to a common attributional rank and a common lifestyle (Metcalf, 1978).

[14]The UP judicial system is divided into three classes: the UP Civil Service (Judicial Branch), the UP Higher Judicial Service, and the UP Civil Service (Administrative Branch). The first consists of munsifs and civil judges, the second of civil and sessions judges. Judicial magistrates and subdistrict magistrates are part of the third branch and hear cases under the Indian Penal Code and the Criminal Procedure Code respectively. The district judge sits as the civil judge while hearing civil cases and as sessions judge while hearing criminal cases. Below the district judge lie munsifs at each tahsil, empowered to hear cases of Rs. 2000 to Rs. 5000. Civil judges are special judges assigned to cases by the district judge and can hear original cases, revisions, and appeals. Appeals from a munsif thus can go to either the civil or district judge, both of whom sit in the district town. A civil judge or the tahsil munsif can sit as the judge of small causes court in each tahsil. Magistrates are of three grades, whose powers are defined by the Criminal Procedure Code (Zaheer and Gupta, 1970).

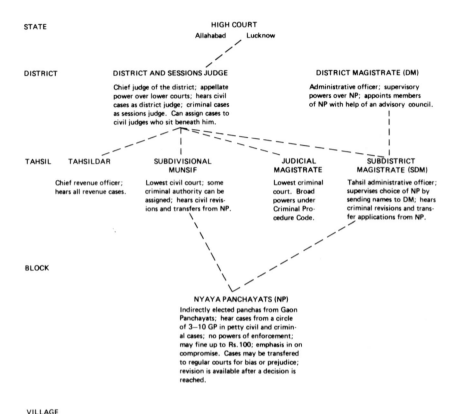

Figure 3.2. Flow chart illustrates the Uttar Pradesh Court system (From Zaheer and Gupta, 1970: 15).

thanas and the second all original civil cases for the *tahsil* and remaining criminal cases for two more police *thanas*. The subdistrict magistrate is in charge of maintaining law and order in the *tahsil*, often hears small criminal cases and now accepts NP revision applications.[15]

Observations were limited to two NP in Bharatpur Tahsil, Chanpur and Purannagar NP. Chanpur lies in Bharatpur Block four kilometers outside the city

[15]Prior to 1974 all subdistrict magistrates were "first class" magistrates, but a new Criminal Procedure Code reduced them to executive magistrates (who lacked criminal jurisdiction). There was confusion about who was to receive revision applications. The subdistrict magistrate of Bharatpur regained first class powers under an amendment to the code in 1976, but during the intervening two years no one accepted any revisions. Revision is the right of a high court or proper authority to call for the record of any cases decided by a court subordinate to it and from which no appeal lies. If the high court feels that the subordinate court misused a power, lacked power, or failed to use a power, it can

proper toward Lucknow. Ten GP send two members each to create Chanpur NP. Purannagar lies in neighboring Dhanabad Block (within Bharatpur Tahsil) twenty-three kilometers northeast of the city. Seven GP send two of their members to create Purrannagar NP. The jurisdiction of each NP is quite large and both NP are located close to the city of Bharatpur. Anyone within either jurisdiction who wishes to use the lowest state-sponsored courts, the munsifs and magistrates, must travel to Bharatpur.

A hybrid form of the informant system was used to collect data and record observations of people in Bharatpur about the two NP and to observe NP processes. During a two-month stay in the area it was possible to meet and speak at length with current *sarpanchas* of both NP, former *sarpanchas*, current and former *panchas*, and recent disputants. Locating participants in earlier NP cases proved harder than had been anticipated. A professor of political science at a local college in Bharatpur and his graduate assistant, both experienced in field research on local government institutions, assisted in the interviews and observations, translated records, and acted as interpreters during conversations. All GP and *pradhans* of Purannagar NP circle and many in Chanpur NP circle were visited and interviewed.

As the title of this chapter suggests, one has to search to find an actual NP meeting. Two occurred during the two months of Fieldwork and an offer to schedule a third for the benefit of the project was rejected. Although such infrequency might have been due to the busy spring harvest, meetings are generally haphazard and rare. Despite its spatial and temporal limitations, this study offers information about NP operations otherwise absent in the literature[16] and suggests avenues for future research.

IDEOLOGICAL AND STRUCTURAL DIMENSIONS OF NYAYA PANCHAYATS OPERATIONS

Panchayat Ideology

Previous studies, notably Baxi and Galanter (1979), have high-lighted the ideological confusion surrounding NP in UP and in other parts of India. Three

---

remand the case for further consideration, dismiss the case, or decide the case on the merits (All India Reports, 1968: Sec. 115).

[16]Previous studies on NP in UP focused on caseloads (Robbins, 1962; Kantowsky, 1968) or structure and policy (Singhvi, 1970; Pillai, 1977). While fieldwork was in progress, the first book-length study of NP was published (Kushawaha, 1977). He offers a favorable evaluation of NP, but his data demonstrate dwindling caseloads, protracted dispositions, inadequate financial and administrative support, lack of insulation from village politics, and general apathy.

separate roles and associated goals have been, and still are being, urged for NP: as an arm of the state judicial service, a branch of the community development program, and, lastly, a modified version of the traditional *panchayat*. As part of the state judicial system, NP (separated from *panchayats* exercising administrative authority in accordance with Directive Principle, Article 50 of the 1950 Constitution) (Tinker, 1967; Saxena, 1972) were to displace existing indigenous institutions—whether based on caste, village, or other groupings (see Baxi, 1976b)—and carry state power and a constitutionalist vision of India into the rural areas. Alternately, NP were to assist in the reformation of rural society by providing practical experience in handling village affairs and educating the general public about their privileges and obligations in an independent India. The skills and experiences of traditional village leaders were to be channeled into new elective bodies, and NP were also to involve those unaccustomed to asserting themselves in local arenas. Lastly, NP were to serve symbolically and practically as informal, accessible *panchayats* and to adopt many of the traits of traditional panchayats to buttress this role.

Reports on India's legal system and the administration of justice have reiterated the government's devotion to the *panchayat* and reflect what can best be called the dominance of the "*panchayat* ideology." Both the National Report on Juridicare (India, Ministry of Law, Justice and Company Affairs, 1978) and the Ashok Mehta Committee Report on PR (India, Ministry of Agriculture and Irrigation, 1978) note a decline in current NP systems in UP and other Indian states but support its retention and recommend smaller bodies, larger budgets, and slightly enhanced jurisdiction (see p. 69, following). However, in the intervening years no state has adopted these recommendations or otherwise altered NP, although some have abolished them altogether.[17] Scholarly resistance to the notion of the failure of NP[18] also supports the concept of a *panchayat* ideology, i.e., a belief in the efficacy of the *panchayat* in resolving disputes in rural areas in the face of strongly inconsistent evidence. This ideology is one component of the politics of rural justice in India. It offers a set of formulas by

[17]Maharashtra abolished NP in August 1975, and pending cases were transferred to regular civil and criminal courts (India, Ministry of Food, Agriculture and Cooperation, 1977). The state of Rajasthan also abolished NP, and *up samitis* (standing benches of each GP) now handle most petty disputes. Some were reported working in early 1978 (Moore, 1978). One official source lists ten states (including UP) where NP were in operation as of 1976 (India, Ministry of Food, Agriculture and Cooperation, 1977; see also India, Ministry of Agriculture and Irrigation, 1978).

[18]An earlier version of this chapter was presented to an audience of experts on the Indian legal system. Critical response from Indians present took two forms: Some accepted the data on the diminished operations of NP and urged a closer analysis of the current political roles of *sarpanchas*, suggesting that the roles they do play (although inconsistent with their official roles) make the NP a "vital" institution and therefore not moribund; others refused to accept that the data on NP in UP (or elsewhere) showed they were in fact failing.

which to portray social reality; it enables politicians and legal policymakers to appeal for public support without promising action. The *panchayat* ideology is one that politicians and legal policymakers can safely support without having to implement an effective NP system (much less committing them to use such a system themselves) (cf. Irschick, 1975; Torri, 1977; Kaufmann 1979).

Devotion to NP remains high in the Bharatpur region and reflects the numerous inconsistencies incorporated in the ideology of these institutions. Most people defended NP as being closer to their homes and cheaper to use than other courts and attacked local courts in Bharatpur for delays, expense, and bad decisions—but admitted they had never gone to either. Many *pradhans* asserted that no cases had ever left their villages for NP or regular state courts. Many villagers felt that NP were "formal" and insisted on deference from disputants. Current members of NP in Chanpur and Purannagar felt that increased authority would make the *panchayats* more effective but also feared that such changes would render the proceedings less comprehensible to both themselves and the parties. Some NP adherents thought that they ought to be maintained as long as they decided a single case that might otherwise be decided "unfairly" by the caste or ad hoc village *panchayats*, or not resolved at all. The only opposition came from the local legal profession and the judicial officers in Bharatpur, all of whom (except the subdistrict magistrate) wanted NP abolished.

Nyaya Panchayats Jurisdiction and Authority

NP have civil jurisdiction in pecuniary claims under Rs. 500 (about $60) (unless both parties agree to submit a larger matter) involving money due on contracts not affecting interests in immovable property, compensation for wrongfully taking or damaging property, and recovery of movable property. Criminal jurisdiction is more extensive and covers a substantial range of offenses under the Indian Penal Code (e.g., criminal negligence, trespass, nuisance, including water pollution, possession or use of false weights and measures, theft, misappropriation, intimidation, perjury, attempt to evade summons) and specialized statutes (e.g., Cattle Trespassing Act, Gambling Acts, Prevention of Juvenile Delinquency Act). The NP are authorized to levy fines up to Rs. 100, but they have no power to sentence offenders to imprisonment, even for failure to pay a fine. They also have the power to admonish in some cases and can compensate the victim out of the fines collected. The state government retains the power to enhance NP jurisdiction as well as diminish it if there is "admission of miscarriage of justice" (Pillai, 1977).

Two essential features of lay adjudication, simplicity of procedure and flexibility of functioning, are realized in the design of NP. They are not encumbered by the need to follow elaborate rules of civil and criminal procedure or the law of evidence. Complaints may be made orally or in writing; no legal representation is allowed, although in some civil matters parties may be represented by an "agent." Witnesses, if any, are examined on oath or solemn affirmation. After the parties present evidence and arguments informally they are asked to absent themselves; *panchas* confer among themselves and arrive at a decision, which is pronounced in open court. A judgment is written and signed (or thumbprinted) by the parties.

Despite these informal attributes, NP do differ from traditional dispute institutions in several significant respects (cf. Retzlaff, 1962; Dumont, 1970). Membership is fixed rather than flexible and based indirectly on popular election rather than social standing. NP constituencies are territorial units rather than functional or ascriptive groups. They decide by majority vote rather than consensus. They are required to follow statutory law. Because they are supported by the government, they can assess minor court fees, issue a summons, proceed *ex parte* in the case of a recalcitrant party, and execute decrees by attaching certain movable property; they are required to maintain records of evidence, judgments, and all panchayat transactions, and are subordinate to higher civil and criminal courts through the subdistrict magistrate; their decisions can be appealed in a few limited areas (India, Ministry of Law, Justice and Company Affairs, 1962; Saxena, 1972).

Resulting Structural Deficiencies

Several structural weaknesses, are apparent from the preceding descriptions taken together with data on NP in other parts of UP.

First, the system of constituting NP through a combination of election and nomination helps to render the public apathetic and fearful of official favoritism and increases factionalism in local *panchayat* elections. The "indirect" method authorizes the district magistrate to act on recommendations of lower officials and nominate influential persons from GP to serve on the NP benches. This can degenerate into a mechanical endorsement of untrustworthy suggestions by these officials (Robbins, 1962). At the same time eligible elites compete energetically for GP and NP positions. Moreover, infrequent elections (e.g., there have been no PR elections in UP since 1972, which was only the third since their inception) discourages public interest in the electoral process (India, Ministry of Law, Justice and Company Affairs, 1962; 1975; India, Ministry of Agriculture and Irrigation, 1978).

Second, the limited jurisdictional powers outlined earlier in the chapter reduce the effectiveness of NP decisions. Criminal cases of theft and misuse may not involve property worth more than Rs. 50; overlapping jurisdictions allow police to send cases cognizable by an NP to the *munsif* or judicial magistrate, and the latter readily accept applications to transfer cases from NP.[19] In Bharatpur, the *munsif* remarked that every NP decision has at least one procedural error, making every application for revision technically meritorious.

Lacking authority to send parties to jail, NP must rely on the police and the subdistrict magistrate to enforce their orders. Of the few fines levied in Chanpur and Purannagar NP, most were never collected. The former *sarpanch* of Chanpur told a story about his efforts to enforce a fine. Several men had been found guilty of a criminal offense and fined Rs. 100 each, but none was willing to comply with the judgment. They threatened the *sarpanch* and urged him to reverse the decision. After some days the *sarpanch* finally met with the guilty men and told them confidentially that if the fines were not paid the opposing party would surely seek revision and drag the case into the judicial magistrate's court. Once the case was there, the *sarpanch* argued, he could not predict what would happen. Within a few days each man paid a fine of Rs. 99, and the *sarpanch* had no further troubles with them.

Third, low budgets reduce NP activities considerably. Neither Chanpur nor Purannagar NP had permanent meeting places or permanent *chaprassis* (servants) to call witnesses and serve process. One operated from an empty storefront and the other from a vacant schoolroom near the local temple. Chanpur NP had a small record book of expenses and filing fees that was out of date; typical fees were one rupee for a summons and twenty-five paisa for filing a complaint. Such revenues did not allow the NP to build a large reserve and in 1978 the entire block of Bharatpur had Rs. 300 in its accounts for all seventeen NP.

Fourth, the low educational level of the *panchas* make it difficult for them to handle the procedural technicalities of NP operations. The sole requirement of a *panch* is that he or she be thirty years old and able to read and write Hindi in Devanagari script. Chanpur and Purannagar NP possessed unusually qualified *sarpanchas*—one was a B.A. graduate and law student in Lucknow, another was educated through the eighth grade, and an ex-*sarpanch* was an intermediate school teacher—but they seem to be the exceptions rather than the rule.[20] *Panchas* were all less well educated and spoke of other NP in the block whose *sarpanchas* were "drunks" and "malcontents." All expressed concern that the manuals, forms, and procedures provided for NP were too complicated for them to understand and said they left things to the *sarpanch* to decipher. None of the *sarpanchas* or *panchas* currently serving had ever been to the training sessions on

[19]A party to a dispute may apply for a transfer of his case to another NP in his block, or to the court of the judicial officer hearing the application. An application should be granted only in cases of local bias or fear of a prejudiced hearing by the original NP.

[20]A study of leaders of rural bodies in UP (Rangnath, 1971) discovered that in two areas of UP sarpanchas of the NP were more "literate" than heads of other bodies (e.g., GP). They also tended to be wealthier and of a higher caste. Rangnath attributed this to the social prestige such people conferred on the NP (but he had not studied NP operations).

NP offered by Biswa District PR officials in the past. Lack of PR funds limited the number of classes offered and *panchas* served, but most said they could not afford to take time off from work to attend in any case.

Fifth, even more confusing than the rules and regulations are the conflicting roles and duties that *sarpanchas* and *panchas* are supposed to fulfill. They are to be honest, upright, and impartial; sensitive to the needs of parties; responsive to the situation; energetic in obtaining information and declaring rights and wrongs; fair in reaching a suitable compromise; and forceful in levying and collecting a fine, with hardly any means to do so. They are judges but act only as a body. By accepting nomination to the NP they lose the power and prestige that goes with membership in the GP (which administers local development programs and is active in local politics) but confirm the power and position they already possess as local leaders. The rules they apply are a mixture of official law and local custom, which must be acceptable to a population that knows little about it. And all this is to be done without compensation.

Only those with time, money and local support are interested in filling the position just described. In Bharatpur, the *thakurs* seemed to dominate NP positions through their control of substantial landholdings and large political base (Kantowsky, 1970). All current and former *sarpanchas* revealed that others had urged them to run for NP positions, whereas people in the villages indicated that NP *sarpanchas* had been serving "for years." Competition is limited to opposing village factions, often amorphous and unstable, and the position of leaders depends on their success in suppressing internal opposition (cf. Beals and Siegel, 1966). Factions were already present in the villages prior to the introduction of electoral politics, but these have now come to play a major role in elections. One strategy is to create alliances and bargains across previously established lines (*Ibid*). A common result is a battle for position among a few contenders and their supporters. Most villagers do not view the NP as a representative but impartial body. The failure of NP in Bharatpur and elsewhere in UP must stem partially from the institutional structure that perpetuates traditional patterns of local dominance and offers little reason for confidence in its decisions.[21]

NYAYA PANCHAYATS IN ACTION: CASELOAD, PROCESS, POLITICS AND ALTERNATIVE FORUMS

The remainder of this chapter describes the activities of Chanpur and Purannagar NP during two months in the spring of 1978. As mentioned earlier, only

[21]Local differences among elites, dominant castes, and competing factions will alter patterns of control. Observations were limited to a small part of eastern UP, and much remains to be done in analyzing local electoral patterns, but we maintain the hypothesis that the structure of PR elections

two NP meetings were observed, simply because there were no others. Instead of describing a "typical" NP meeting, then, we analyze caseloads for UP and Bharatpur, describe NP processes, and explain the politics of the institution and its relationship to other dispute forums. Several cases collected during fieldwork are appended and will be used illustratively.

Caseload

NP in UP and in Bharatpur are moribund today, caseloads having declined from a state high of 1,914,098 cases in 1949–1950 to a paltry 17,782 in 1972 (see Table 3.1). The 8297 NP functioning in 1972 heard an average of 2.1 cases, whereas in 1950–1951 the 8543 NP heard an average of 59.3 cases. More recently, 16,035 new cases were reported filed in 7131 NP in 1976–1977 (an average of 2.2 cases a year) (Uttar Pradesh, 1977)—a statistic that may be misleading since the 1972 figures in that source are higher than those quoted earlier.[22] This trend is confirmed by other regional studies in UP (Kushawaha, 1977; cf. Kantowsky, 1968) and contrasts sharply with the steady rise in civil litigation in UP district courts until 1969 and the dramatic rise in criminal cases (see Table 3.2). The High Courts Arrears Committee of India reported that over 500,000 appellate cases were pending in all state high courts, 100,000 in Allahabad alone (Special Correspondent, 1977).

Inadequate though they may be, statistics derived from district, block, and tahsil PR offices amplify this sorry picture of NP for Biswa and Bharatpur. In 1976–1977 Biswa District NP decided a total of 1136 cases; in 1975–1976 Dhanabad Block NP reportedly decided a mere 23. When a similar inquiry was made of the Bharatpur Block PR officer, he produced statistical forms showing "no cases" in any NP between 1976 and 1978.

Available records of Chanpur and Purannagar NP appeared adequate but, after

---

and of NP will contribute to the persistence of existing patterns of dominance (see Kantowsky, 1970; Y. S. Singh, 1976; V. P. Singh, 1976).   _

[22]It is difficult to assess the accuracy of state and local records encountered in this project. A purely statistical study appeared doomed from the beginning because records were either unavailable, inconsistent, or incomplete. Published reports such as the *Report on the Administration of Justice in Uttar Pradesh* (Uttar Pradesh, 1961–1873) rely on data sent from district PR offices and yet are inconsistent with other published state reports (Uttar Pradesh, 1975–1977). State and district reports, in turn, rely on block reports and reports of panchayat secretaries, but visits to block offices and observations of record-keeping practices turned suspicions into positive distrust. Block officials revealed that the panchayat secretaries (who never attended NP meetings in Chanpur or Purannagar) fill in their monthly reports late, using figures that are questionable if not fabricated. Officials said the only way to know how many cases NP were really handling was to go to each NP, talk to the sarpanch, and see the records they might have on hand.

TABLE 3.1

Workload of Nyaya Panchayats in Uttar Pradesh, 1950–1972

Year	Number of NP	Civil		Criminal		Total filings	Filings per NP	Source
		Filed	Pending	Filed	Pending			
1950–1951[a]	8543					633,502	59.3	Purwar, 1960: 202
1951–1952	8543					123,363	14.4	Ibid.
1952–1953	8543					302,548	35.4	Ibid.
1953–1954	8543					347,790	40.7	Ibid.
1954–1955	8543					371,519	43.4	Ibid.
1955–1956	8543					105,376	12.3	Ibid.
1960	8583	82,321	—	—	—	—	—	1961: 6, 45
1961	8662	53,523	22,744	37,584	20,852	91,107	10.51	1961: 6, 45
1962	8662	49,164	22,275	32,579	18,384	81,743	9.43	1962: 6, 51
1963	8700	93,994	25,350	71,792	17,059	165,786	19.05	1963: 7, 57
1964	8626	83,627	19,684	55,873	15,424	139,500	16.17	1964: 6, 54
1965	8687	55,000	11,898	36,904	11,451	91,904	10.57	1965: 7, 46
1966	8680	35,362	19,498	31,854	8059	67,216	7.74	1966: 8, 47
1967	—	—	—	—	—	—	—	—
1968	8580	—	—	—	—	—	—	1969: 7
1969	8333	22,600	4025	15,671	2780	38,271	4.33	1969: 7, 53
1970	8727	22,912	4766	12,953	4293	35,865	4.10	1970: 8, 65
1971	8459	20,002	4274	10,376	2307	30,378	3.6	1971: 10, 88
1972	8297	10,502	3812	7280	2074	17,782	2.1	1972: 6, 44

SOURCES: Purwar (1960) and UP Law Ministry Reports (1961–1972) as indicated.

[a] Year runs from January 1, 1950, to March 31, 1951; thereafter each year begins at March 31 of the year. Filing rate is prorated for twelve months.

closer scrutiny, gaps and questionable entries emerged. Both incumbent *sarpan-chas* had the records of their NP only for their own brief terms; earlier records supposedly had been sent to the district PR officer in Biswa. One kept an attendance book for *panchas*, but it was simply concocted to reassure PR person-nel that all *panchas* had attended NP meetings (when they had not). The other current *sarpanch* did not maintain such a book because he was not willing to fabricate it, and *panchas* would not come anyway.

Chanpur and Purannagar NP records reveal a higher average caseload than the total UP figures suggest. Chanpur NP had decided nine civil cases over a nine-month period and had five additional cases pending in May 1978. Twenty-seven criminal cases had been filed during an overlapping fourteen-month period, two of which had resulted in fines (never collected). Those cases whose subject was described concerned small debts, claims to land, and assaults.

Purannagar NP had heard seventeen civil cases over a twenty-seven-month period, most of which involved debts. All had been "compromised," but the content of these compromises had not been recorded. Forty-six criminal cases had come to this NP during an overlapping twenty-six-month period: eleven resulted in fines, six had been dismissed, and the remainder were compromised. Most involved threats of violence, encroachment, cattle theft, destruction of property, and "unauthorized influence." Party names were recorded in the Purannagar records, and several recurred: e.g., a woman named Purana ("old lady") appeared in ten recorded cases and was involved in yet another in spring 1978 (see Appendix, Case 3).

Former *sarpanchas* revealed that caseloads of both NP had been much higher in previous decades and that, even today, these were reputed to be higher than other NP in the blocks of Bharatpur and Dhanabad. The larger number of NP criminal cases corresponds to an overall increase in criminal litigation in Bharatpur courts during this period. Criminal prosecutions in the judicial magistrate's court nearly doubled in two years between 1976 and 1978 and the criminal caseload of the munsif's court rose steadily over a five-year period. The Biswa District judge saw his sessions trials more than double and his criminal cases increase more than fourfold between 1971 and 1977. Revisions of NP cases did decline, despite the popular notion that they are virtually automatic. The subdistrict magistrate of Bharatpur heard no revisions in 1978, and the *munsif* had accepted only one in 1977. UP High Court records revealed no NP revisions or appeals from decisions to transfer NP cases since the late 1960s.

TABLE 3.2
Civil and Criminal Cases in State Courts in Uttar Pradesh, 1960–1972

Year	Civil cases[a]	Criminal cases (number of accused)	Source
1960	74,958	—	1961: 41
1961	75,174	760,704	1961: 8, 41
1962	71,912	789,670	1962: 8, 47
1963	71,068	845,982	1963: 10, 53
1964	71,371	879,687	1964: 9, 51
1965	81,908	895,859	1965: 9, 43
1966	85,114	873,023	1966: 10, 43
1967	—	—	—
1968	88,762	—	1969: 11, 49
1969	91,859	1,001,249	1969: 11, 49
1970	86,749	1,037,896	1970: 12–13, 60
1971	84,310	1,137,280	1971: 16–17
1972	85,483	1,315,510	1972: 10, 41

SOURCE: UP Law Ministry Reports (1961–1972).

[a] This includes paid subdivisional tribunals (courts of munsifs), small cause courts, district courts, and chief courts of the districts.

Process

Staffed by lay persons, NP are to promote simplicity and flexibility in adjudication. They must apply state substantive law but need not follow all the rules of the Civil and Criminal Procedure Codes, although they do have a regulation book, the *Nyaya Panchayat Nidoshika*. There are no pleadings, and lawyers cannot appear. Decisions are to be reached in open meetings after evidence is received and witnesses examined under oath. These aspects of NP authority and procedure, and those outlined earlier, reveal the constant tension between informality and formality.

Observation of NP in the Bharatpur region revealed that their actual operations do not correspond to the statutory requirements. Rules are followed or ignored as the *sarpanch* chooses. NP meetings are irregular, quorums usually are not met, and *panchas* and parties at NP meetings exhibit considerable confusion. The *sarpanchas* of Chanpur and Purannagar NP, for example, acknowledged procedural inconsistencies; the latter (here called VVS) heard evidence in one case when it first came before the NP but in another asked the parties to return the following month to begin testimony (cf. Appendix, Case 4 and Miscellaneous Cases).

Both *sarpanchas* admitted accepting and trying to resolve disputes before filing them as NP cases. VVS later contradicted himself by saying he filed every complaint with the NP and only then tried to settle the matter. He felt the threat of a protracted NP case would discourage frivolous complaints. The *sarpanch* of Chanpur NP (here called APM) told me of his two most memorable "cases" (see Appendix, Cases 1 and 2), which were not NP cases but attempts at informal decision making by the *sarpanch* alone.

The procedure in cases that are filed does not conform to statutes or rules. In one case VVS referred to the NP handbook but then fined a party for failing to appear—a power he does not have. Both VVS and APM have made independent inquiries into cases instead of creating the required "on the spot" commissions.[23] The list of procedural inconsistencies could be extended, but most involve *sarpanchas* exceeding their authority. The *panchas* deferred to VVS and APM and felt it right to do so. The NP is thus a body of men, dominated by the *sarpanch*, that handles disputes without regard to applicable rules and yet appears to villagers as formal and incomprehensible.

The emphasis of Chanpur and Purannagar NP did seem to be on compromise and reconciliation. Although the substance of these compromises was not re-

---

[23]Either party can request an "on the spot" commission of three people to look into any matter disputed, and the NP can order one on its own initiative. In one case before VVS the parties nominated members, and he appointed them to the commission. "Secret inquiries" are forbidden (*Daulat Ram v. Panchayat Adalat*, All India Reports 1954 All. 306).

corded and was not elicited from the two NP, cases did appear "compromised" on the books. Villagers and urban dwellers who supported NP admired the stress on compromise. Yet behind this ideal of compromise lies the coercive power of the *sarpanch*. VVS said that once he filed a case he tried to "force" a compromise. In one NP meeting he delayed hearing a case in order to induce the parties to compromise and threatened to send it to the magistrate if a solution were not forthcoming (see Appendix, Miscellaneous Cases). In another, he accelerated a hearing to achieve the same goal (see Appendix, Case 4). He liked to portray himself as a man who could enforce his decisions whether people liked them or not (cf. Hitchcock, 1960). Given the mild sanctions and weak enforcement powers of NP, it is not surprising that a *sarpanch* would have to rely on such tactics, but it is unlikely that those who wrote the NP legislation intended to encourage such a process.

NP are not only inconsistent and somewhat arbitrary but also slow. Cases last for months and even years. Of the cases recorded in Purannagar, nineteen took more than six months, thirteen more than a year, and seven were two years old and still unresolved at the end of fieldwork. Some of those who were critical of the NP said they took as long as regular courts and left even the successful petitioner in a worse position: with a decision that could not be enforced.

The declining use of NP is related to a low level of knowledge about the institution. Many villagers did not know who the *sarpanch* was, or where and how often the NP met. Villagers of Purannagar villages knew VVS not as the *sarpanch* but as the big *thakur* of the area. Most urban informants knew of NP and divided between support and disgust with their perceived ineffectiveness.

The dominant role of the *sarpanch* is now clear. Through an often capricious use of his power and position he can, and usually does, dictate the course of the NP. A closer look at the sarpanchas of Chanpur and Purannagar NP helps explain this phenomenon. VVS, about forty-five years old, was a thakur of the village of Seranpur in Dhanabad Tahsil. He controlled most of the land in his village and had arranged to elect a Muslim follower as *pradhan* of the Seranpur GP, thereby placating a substantial but less powerful faction in the village and giving VVS the lead in all village affairs. VVS had been *sahayak sarpanch* (assistant head judge) for twelve years before becoming *sarpanch*. He was an unassuming man, quiet, personable, conscientious in his job as *sarpanch*, and self-confident of his position in the region.

APM of Chanpur, in his mid-thirties, was equally self-assured, not just because of his local landholdings but also because of his contacts with police, the judiciary, Congress party politicians, and the outside world. His father had been very wealthy and had served on a previous NP. Sincere in his role as *sarpanch* and eager to mediate problems outside the NP context, he nevertheless admitted manipulating the system to his own advantage. Both men had trails of supplicants following them wherever they went. Finally, both clearly enjoyed the prestige that the title of sarpanch seemed to carry (as a respected leader and "judge").

Politics

The preceding descriptions of NP in Bharatpur indicate that *sarpanchas* tend to be traditional leaders—men who operate from bases of local respect, wealth, and familiarity with the people and their problems. In eastern UP they tend to be *thakurs* (cf. Hitchcock, 1960; Kantowsky, 1970). New elites have sometimes been successful in gaining control over GP (Mehta, 1971; Singh, 1974; Chakravarti, 1975), but there are few such victories in eastern UP. Those who acquire the position have manipulated people, resources, and information. As one UP village leader said nearly two decades ago: "Power is something you can't see. . . . It does not rest on a title like Pradhan or head judge. The power a man has rests in the support others know he has in the village" (Hitchcock, 1960: 255).

A thorough analysis of the caste basis of factions and of the regional power structure is required before any definitive conclusions can be drawn about the sources of NP power in Bharatpur. But the brief period of fieldwork did indicate that power is not broadly shared. The closer one is to the village, the more likely it is that caste will be an important factor in factions and power politics (Mason, 1967; Mehta, 1971).[24] In Bharatpur people defined *thakur* as "lord" and said they looked upon these *thakur* landlords as their lords. Existing factions become embroiled in local elections and compete for positions on GP. In parts of UP, middle and lower castes have recently assumed control over GP (Singh, 1976) but rarely over NP.

Factions influence both NP and GP elections. In Purannagar an ex-sarpanch told me how he, a Muslim, had been ousted from his position on the NP by an opposing faction of Hindus. VVS told of a similar threat that he had overcome by coopting his Muslim rivals into his faction. Factions generate conflict and often bring cases to an NP or cause them to be transferred from an NP to another state-sponsored court. The *munsif* in Bharatpur said faction was the greatest problem he addressed in applications for transfer from the NP. He usually accepts all such requests on grounds of bias or prejudice. Faction lay behind the prolonged dispute in Chanpur (see Appendix, Case 2), where several brothers

---

[24]Opinion is divided on whether "class," as opposed to caste, is an important factor in local factions. It is impossible to define class solely in economic terms because class in India is still intimately involved in the distribution of resources and thus power (V. P. Singh, 1976). If we define class as an aggregate of persons who stand in a similar position with respect to some form of power, privilege, or prestige, there are signs that power in rural areas has shifted and is located in broader political and economic structures (Beteille, 1974).

challenged their neighbors over a plot of land. Cases listed as assault and un-authorized influence in the Purannagar records were explained as family fac-tional fights in which litigation was initiated for the purpose of harassment.

Factionalism, ignorance, and local politics thus combine with other problems to reduce access to NP below the goal set by its original advocates (India, Minis-try of Law, Justice and Company Affairs, 1962; 1978). Although the NP are geographically less remote than the state courts in Bharatpur, the long distances between villages and NP headquarters discourage villagers from lodging com-plaints. Delays and postponements mean repeated trips to NP every month, perhaps just to find out that it is not meeting. Records of Chanpur and Puran-nagar reveal that three or four villages account for most of the NP cases; those villages are closer to the seat of the NP and thus are the home ground of the *sarpanch*. High material costs are reinforced by the high social costs of going to NP. Those who complain to the NP damage their public image and reduce their social standing. *Pradhans* and villagers criticized those "litigious" and "bad" people who go to NP and felt those people were insulting the village.

Alternative Forums

Caste, faction, stratification, and local politics militate against the use of NP as a forum for airing and settling disputes. For most people the forums with social utility (Feeley, 1976; see Kidder, 1973) are customary unofficial caste pan-chayats, traditional village leaders, or the regular state courts. Traditional caste panchayats (Mehta, 1971; Mathur, 1976; Moore, 1978), ad hoc meetings of the GP (Chakravarti, 1975), and charismatic *lok adalats* (people's courts) (Baxi, 1976b) operate in UP and elsewhere in northern India because they have com-bined resources, authority, and leadership in ways that are more acceptable and useful to the general population.

This analysis of the attractiveness of different forums was confirmed by fieldwork in Bharatpur. Most people do not and would not take a dispute outside their villages for resolution, preferring to go to their *pradhan* or another (caste) elder for assistance. Only where they distrusted the *pradhan* would they turn to the NP. Local *pradhans* estimated that three-quarters of all disputes are heard and resolved within the village. They counseled against going to the courts or NP but did not prevent anyone who was insistent. No caste *panchayats* or GP meetings were observed in Bharatpur in the spring of 1978, and therefore we cannot comment on the sources of *pradhan* power in arbitrating village disputes. But it is widely known that cases involving family matters, sexual excursions, marital arrangements, and commensality never leave the village (cf. Mathur, 1976; Hayden, 1980). Factional fights over customary rights, usages, and re-sources within a caste are invariably handled by a caste forum first. Only when the *pradhan* and other leading figures cannot control the factional eruption does a case reach the NP docket. Debt and assault cases in Purannagar NP expressed factional strife within a few villages, and the same parties frequently reappeared in the cases recorded in Purannagar during the period studied. A *pradhan* from another Purannagar village said the only case from his locality that went to the NP involved two men from opposite factions who would not accept his suggested solution.

It is noteworthy that, in a few villages in Bharatpur, Scheduled Castes were involved in litigation in the regular state courts more often than were other caste groups and were also more active in GP affairs (although absent from NP benches). These groups have seemed to turn to outside sources of support. Large numbers of lawyers (often called *vakils*[25]) broadcast legal advice and information to villages with high percentages of Scheduled Castes and encourage them to seek justice from regular courts, where the outcome, apparently, is more likely to be favorable (cf. Mathur, 1976).

CONCLUSION: NYAYA PANCHAYATS AND THE PATTERN OF DISPUTING IN RURAL INDIA

These tentative conclusions about NP structure and process can be located within a picture of litigation and disputing in rural India. Litigation can be seen as a process of negotiation in an ever-changing environment (Kidder, 1974a; 1974b). Long-term relationships produce repetitive conflicts, large and small, that lead to petty quarrels. Single disputes can be resolved, but the underlying conflict endures. The choice of the forum used in any given dispute indicates to the other party the rules that must be followed *in that dispute* but does not preclude the use of another forum with different rules at another time. In this setting, litigation allows people to vent frustrations while maintaining their relationships. It permits change (albeit slow) for people bound within restrictive social settings.

NP constitute an alternative forum blending old and new values and norms. Even if they could never fulfill all the conflicting goals that inspired them, NP could still offer disputants another outlet. Unfortunately, NP have not become an integral element of the pattern of disputing in rural India. What was to be a neutral, unbiased body of local leaders helping to negotiate and mediate petty disputes has either become a stronghold of landed elites and dominant castes or, in other localities, been stillborn. NP are perceived by villagers as alien institu-

---

[25]*Vakil* means 'go between' and refers to those trained in the law, originally by apprenticeship, more recently by training in law colleges. Today *vakil* and lawyer are synonymous in the countryside; city lawyers refer to themselves as advocates.

tions and therefore are used no more than the regular courts. Indeed, they have manifested the worst attributes of traditional and more modern legal institutions. Those with access to the state courts gain little by returning to the rural setting and using NP. Those without such resources must assess their opportunities within the village before challenging the dominant faction by going to the NP. Considerations of village social structure and economic resources circumscribe the value of the NP, making it useful only to those in a minority faction who have some claim upon the elected sarpanch but lack the means to go directly to the state courts. The decline in caseloads suggests that people originally used NP as an alternative forum but have since found them less satisfactory. Increases in regular court use, on the other hand, indicate that these institutions remain viable and suggest that those who are willing and able to abandon local institutions will bypass NP and go to the state courts. Furthermore, continued evidence of caste *panchayat* activity indicates that most people in rural settings prefer them as the method of resolving disputes.

Nonetheless, the steady decline in the use of NP is paralleled by a persistent belief in its value in solving rural legal problems. Those with limited means liked the idea of the NP as an alternative forum even if they had no immediate intention of going there. Educated people disliked the NP and said it served no good purpose, but even they did not recommend that it be abolished. Thus, the *panchayat* ideology persists in the face of evidence that they are not the first or even the second choice of disputants, have declining caseloads, and combine many of the least attractive traits of the old and new legal institutions.

Recent blue ribbon government inquiries into PR and the national and state legal systems in India (India, Ministry of Agriculture and Irrigation, 1978; India, Ministry of Law, Justice and Company Affairs, 1978) have recommended that NP be maintained and improved. After exhaustive hearings, the Ashok Mehta committee to investigate PR (India, Ministry of Agriculture and Irrigation, 1978) echoed the findings of the National Report on Juridicare (India, 1978) and suggested that each NP be reduced in size to three members. Two would be chosen by the present process but would serve away from their homes and landholdings. The third *panch* would be chosen from a body of retired judges willing to act in this capacity. The reports noted the inevitable influence of local politics on NP operations and hoped that planners could devise ways to channel this political energy into more constructive paths, but they offered no guidelines in this direction.

Although these recent proposals retain the *panchayat* symbolism, they view NP more as efficient mechanisms for delivering official justice than as revivals of indigenous legal institutions (Galanter, 1978). NP are commended as antidotes to popular alienation from official courts, as well as for their cheap, expeditious, and conciliatory process. But the recommendation that they be staffed by retired judges and lay members with rudimentary legal training indicates that they are no

longer commended as an embodiment of traditional values. Would reformed, re-
structured NP present an attractive alternative to state courts or village bodies? NP
would remain outside the villages; *panchas* would become strangers; powers
would not be enhanced. If the NP were impartial, they might be preferable to
more partisan local bodies, but their weak powers of enforcement and limited
jurisdiction would militate against their use. Given the choice between informal
village forums, formal external tribunals, and those that occupy a middle
ground, disputants have thus far chosen the extremes. One reason may be that
invocation of a formal government court does not commit a party to pursuing its
procedures to the bitter end. Indeed, litigation may provide opportunities and
devices for bargaining and mediation superior to those afforded in less formal
settings (Kidder, 1973; 1974b).

   This small field study of NP in Bharatpur in eastern UP agrees with earlier
analyses of their structure and of aggregate data in concluding that NP are
institutionally weak and moribund. Similar findings in other states (see India,
Ministry of Agriculture and Irrigation, 1978) suggest that the concept of a middle
tier of *panchayat* courts needs to be reconsidered. Most people have never used a
NP and probably never will. Three-quarters of all the disputes that arise in
villages remain there and are resolved by caste *panchayats*, GP, or ad hoc village
panchayats. The *panchayat* often is a useful and viable institution, but its success
depends on its structure and the source of its authority. Symbolically valued by
planners and theorists, NP are nonetheless little used today in most parts of rural
UP (and India). The persistence of the *panchayat* ideology in the face of clear
evidence of the moribund state of the institution exposes the failure of scholars as
well as policymakers to address the nature of disputes and law in rural India.

APPENDIX

Case 1

SUNDAR V. RAM KARAN: THE CASE OF THE PUKKA-KACCHA HOUSE (CHANPUR NP)

   Sunder of Bhadadurpur village sold a plot of land to Ram Karan of Bishunipur
for Rs. 300. They did not register the transaction (as they should have) but did
execute a written instrument. Ram Karan proceeded to erect a brick (*pukka*,
meaning 'solid' and of good quality) and mud (*kaccha*, meaning 'weak' and of
poor quality) house on the land and planned to establish a flour mill on the
premises. Pukka houses are a sign of wealth in villages; it is unusual to see *pukka*
and *kaccha* together. For reasons known only to Ram Karan, he changed his

mind and expressed a desire to sell the land. Sunder insisted that Ram Karan sell it back to him and offered to return the Rs. 300 in exchange for the contract of sale. By this time the total value of the land with the house and improvements was nearly Rs. 3000. Ram Karan returned the instrument, but Sunder refused to return the Rs. 300 or to let Ram Karan remove his bricks from the land.

Ram Karan went to APM as *sarpanch* of the NP to complain and seek advice. APM decided he could not act officially since the dispute involved the transfer of immovable property. He advised Ram Karan to go to court to recover his bricks and money, but Ram refused, saying he was "too poor." At Ram Karan's request, APM tried to negotiate with Sunder on the issue. As a result Sunder promised APM he would let Ram Karan take the bricks back but would not return the money. Later he refused to relinquish the bricks as well.

APM then wrote to the subdistrict magistrate and to the subinspector of police to report Sunder's activities and alleged that he had reneged on an agreement. No action was taken against Sunder. There was no NP decision to enforce. APM's effort at informal negotiation and compromise failed since Sunder kept everything—land, money, and bricks.

Case 2

RAM MONARE V. RAM DULARE: THE CASE OF THE
BARGAINING BROTHERS (CHANPUR NP)

Ram Monare and Ram Dulare owned adjacent plots of land in a village, the former as representative of his four brothers as well. A gully lay between the two plots, and when the brothers bought plots nearby, this gully was sought by both parties. Ram Dulare wanted to block the gully and use it as his own, but Ram Monare naturally opposed this move. Ram Dulare then asked APM as *sarpanch* to declare the gully his property. APM tried to reach a compromise. He persuaded the brothers to give a portion of the gully to Ram Dulare in exchange for a piece of land adjacent to Ram Monare's plot that belonged to Ram Dulare. Both men seemed satisfied.

But later others in the village felt that Ram Monare should fight this further and urged him to sue Ram Dulare in the regular courts. Ram Monare refused to do so, whereupon the instigators went to Ram Dulare and urged *him* to sue Ram Monare. He was easily persuaded that he deserved something more and demanded not just the portion of the gully he had accepted but also that a dhobi (washerman) be allowed to work on the land given to Ram Monare. The same persons (aided by a local advocate) convinced Ram Dulare that neither the NP nor APM acting on his own had authority to transfer land. Ram Dulare thus reasoned (correctly) that the previous agreement had no legal force.

Ram Dulare went to the court of the *munsif*, stated that the first settlement was no longer acceptable, and presented his new demands. The complaint was filed, and the suit was still in progress when the first author left Chanpur. Ram Dulare died before the hearings began, and APM asserted that the tension of the court case had certainly contributed to his early demise.

The complaint alleged that APM had imposed a decision that favored Ram Monare and that exceeded his authority. Ram Dulare had never agreed to it and asked to be legally relieved of the obligation. Ram Monare filed an answer and countercomplaint claiming that the agreement had been coerced by APM, that there was no written agreement between the two men, and that Ram Monare was unhappy with the entire behavior of APM.

The *munsif* said he understood that "the NP" undertook the case in ignorance of, not in disobedience to, the rule against dealing with immovable property. The absence of an order sheet indicated to the *munsif* that the decision had been entirely informal and had no legal significance except as evidence of party intent. But since the parties did not acquiesce in the decision, he agreed to accept the case but gave as his real reason the failure of the parties to submit a dispute over immovable property to the courts. He granted the son of Ram Dulare standing to sue in his father's place and set a date to hear the oral arguments of the lawyers. (Subsequent inquiries indicated that *munsif* had been transferred and the case postponed. No word has been received on its disposition.)

Case 3

PURANA V. CHINOO AND OTHERS (PURANNAGAR NP)

Purana is an old, wizened woman who had been a petitioner in an earlier case already decided by the NP the previous year. She asserted that Chinoo had constructed a building that encroached on her land in the village of Gairahwa. Chinoo had earlier argreed to remove the building as part of a compromise suggested by the NP. Purana wanted Chinoo to remove the structure now and charged that he had threatened her with bodily harm if she took the dispute to the NP again. Throughout this presentation Purana was crouching in typical northern Indian style, until VVS became irritated by what he construed as her insolence and ordered her to stand.

VVS commented on her story and told Chinoo he might have to put up bond to guarantee he would not harm Purana. Chinoo became angry and challenged VVS to create an "on the spot" commission to see the alleged encroachment for what it was worth. If VVS agreed to a commission, Chinoo said he would be willing to put up the bond.

VVS discussed the story with the other *panchas* and they decided (or rather,

VVS did) to take the bond issue up next time. Chinoo repeated out loud to no one in particular that they all would abide by a decision of the *sarpanch* and *panchas* and the *pradhan*. A few questions were put to the others in Chinoo's party, one of whom charged that Purana herself was the real encroacher. Purana was said to have agreed to an *up-pradhan* (assistant *pradhan*) compromise to vacate the land on which she was supposedly encroaching. VVS heard all this and told Purana to come to the next month's meeting with witnesses to support her story.

Case 4

BHAGALU V. KALATHNATHU (PURANNAGAR NP)

Bhagalu complained to VVS and the NP that Kalathnathu owed him over Rs. 1500 in accumulated debts and asked the NP to order payment in full. This was the first complaint by Bhagalu, and everyone listened intently. Kalathnathu showed VVS a debt agreement and admitted a debt to Bhagalu but asserted that a portion of the debt had been paid back (the exact amount he could not recall). He wanted the NP to determine what he owed Bhagalu, taking into consideration the partial payment. He said he was poor and could not hope to pay Rs. 1500. Others attending the NP entered the discussion and declared that Kalathnathu was a party in other debt litigation that was depleting his finances. VVS told both men to bring witnesses to the following month's meeting, but after an argument erupted over the amount of the debt VVS became very angry and told them they had to reach a compromise by then.

MISCELLANEOUS CASES (PURANNAGAR NP)

In one case two plaintiffs and three defendants came forward and greatly angered VVS when they told him they had not reached an agreement as ordered. They spoke loudly and stood in a manner that irritated VVS; he refused to allow them to squat on the floor but insisted they stand in front of him as they spoke. VVS then asked them to name four people from their villages they would respect as mediators. The men agreed, and VVS said he would speak to the men to get a compromise by next month.

In a second case begun that day, the parties paid their twenty-five paise np fee and were told to return next month to present their stories. In another, the defending party had not shown up, and VVS entered a fine of Rs. 10 pursuant to "Sec. 174" of the NP manual (beyond his authority). This was a penalty for not appearing and did not affect the merits of the case.

The fourth case was an old one, and VVS mentioned that it had been some time since he had asked the subdistrict magistrate to compel the parties to appear in response to his summons. The magistrate had not done this but told VVS to send the case to his court. VVS told the parties who were present to go and reach a compromise by next month or he *would* send it to the subdistrict magistrate.

REFERENCES

Unpublished Materials

India, Governor-General Minutes in Council. Resolutions of Mayo on 14 December 1870 and Lord Ripon on 30 September 1881 and 18 May 1882. India Office.
Uttar Pradesh, High Court (1972–1976) Litigation Statistics from the Office of Registrar.
Uttar Pradesh, Law Ministry (1961–1972) Annual Reports.
Uttar Pradesh Vidyan Sabha (1976–1977) Litigation Statistics from the Monitoring Cell for Lower Courts.
District, tahsil, block, and NP records from Biswa region.

Published Materials

All India Reports (1968) *Code of Civil Procedure with Commentary*. Nagdur: D. V. Chitaley
Bastedo, T. G. (1969) *The Judiciary in Bihar: An Administrative Study*. Ph.D. Dissertation, Department of Political Science, Duke University.
Baxi, U. (1976a) "Access, Development and Distributive Justice: Access Problems for the Rural Populations," 18 *Journal of the Indian Law Institute* 375.
———— (1976b) "From Tarkar to Karar: The Lok Adalat at Rangpur—A Preliminary Study," 10(1) *Journal of Constitutional and Parliamentary Studies* 52.
Baxi, U. and M. Galanter (1979) "Panchayat Justice: An Indian Experiment in Legal Access," in M. Cappelletti and B. Garth (eds.) *Access to Justice*, vol. 3: *Emerging Issues and Perspectives*. Milan: Guiffrè; Alphen aan den Rijn: Sijthoff and Noordhoff.
Beaglehole, T. H. (1966) *Thomas Munro and the Development of Administrative Policy in Madras, 1792–1818: The Origins of the Munro System*. Cambridge: Cambridge University Press.
Beals, A. R. and B. S. Siegel (1966) *Divisiveness and Social Conflict: An Anthropological Approach*. Stanford, Calif.: Stanford University Press.
Beteille, A. (1974) *Studies in Agrarian Social Structure*. Delhi: Oxford University Press.
Bhalerao, M. M. and R. D. Singh (1965) "Nyaya Panchayats in Varanasi," *Kurukshetra* (April).
Blunt, E. A. H. (1912) "United Provinces of Agra and Oudh," in *Census of India 1911*, vol. 25, p. 1. Allahabad: Government Press.
Brass, P. (1966) *Factional Politics in an Indian State*. Bombay: Oxford University Press.
Chakravarti, A. (1975) *Contradiction and Change: Emerging Patterns of Authority in a Rajasthan Village*. Delhi: Oxford University Press.
Cohn, B. S. (1959) "Some Notes on Law and Change in North India," 8 *Economic Development and Cultural Change* 79.
———— (1961) "From Indian Status to British Contract," 21 *Journal of Economic History* 613.
———— (1965) "Anthropological Notes on Disputes and Law," in L. Nader (ed.) *The Ethnography of Law*, 67(6) (pt. 2) *American Anthropologist* 82 (special issue).

Derrett, J. D. M. (1964) "Law and the Social Order in India before the Muhammadan Conquest," 7 *Journal of Economic and Social History of the Orient* 73.

_____ (1968) *Religion, Law and the State in India.* New York: Free Press.

Dube, L. (1965) "Studies in Leadership in Village India," in *Emerging Patterns of Rural Leadership in Southern Asia.* International Round Table Conference on Emerging Patterns of Rural Leadership in Southern Asia. Hyderabad: National Institute of Community Development.

Dumont, L. (1970) *Homo Hierarchicus: The Caste System and Its Implications.* London: Paladin.

Feeley, M. M. (1976) "The Concept of Laws in Social Science: A Critique and Notes on an Expanded View," 10 *Law & Society Review* 497.

Galanter, M. (1968) "The Displacement of Traditional Law in Modern India," 24 *Journal of Social Issues* 65.

_____ (1972) "The Aborted Restoration of 'Indigenous Law' in India," 14 *Comparative Studies of Society and History* 53.

_____ (1978) "Indian Law as an Indigenous Conceptual System," 32 *Social Science Research Council Items* 42.

Haldipur, R. L. (1974) "Sociology of Community Development and Panchayati Raj," 2 *Contributions to Indian Sociology* 30.

Hardgrave, R. (1980) *India: Government and Politics in a Developing Nation,* 3d ed. New York: Harcourt Brace Jovanovich.

Hayden, R. M. (1980) "Excommunication as Everyday Event and Ultimate Sanction: The Nature of Caste Suspension in India." Presented at Joint Meeting of the Law and Society Association and the ISA Research Committee on Sociology of Law, Madison, Wisconsin (June 5-8).

Hitchcock, J. (1960) "Surat Singh, Head Judge," in J. Casagrande (ed.) *In the Company of Men: 20 Portraits by Anthropologists.* New York: Harper.

India, Home Government (1909) *Royal Commission upon Decentralization in India,* vol. 1: *Report;* vol. 2: *Minutes of Evidence.* London.

India, Government of India, (1919) *Montague-Chelmsford Reforms.* Delhi.

India (Republic), Bureau of Census (1971) *Census of India.* Delhi.

India (Republic), Committee on Democratic Decentralization (1958) *Report of the Balwantray Mehta Committee on Democratic Decentralization.* New Delhi.

India (Republic), Indian Council of Social Science Research (1975) *Status of Women in India: A Synopsis of the Report of the National Committee on the Status of Women (1971-74).* New Delhi.

India (Republic), Ministry of Agriculture and Irrigation (1978) *Report of the Committee on Panchayati Raj Institutions.* New Delhi.

India (Republic), Ministry of Food, Agriculture and Cooperation (1977) *Panchayati Raj at a Glance* (1975-1976). New Delhi.

India (Republic), Ministry of Law, Justice and Company Affairs (1962) *Report of the Study Team on Nyaya Panchayats.* New Delhi.

_____ (1974-1977) *Annual Reports.* New Delhi.

_____ (1978) *Report on National Juridicare: Equal Justice, Social Justice.* New Delhi.

Irschick, E. (1975) "Interpretation of Indian Political Development," 34 *Journal of Asian Studies* 461.

Jain, S. C. (1967) *Community Development and Panchayati Raj.* Bombay: Allied Publishers.

Kantowsky, Detlef (1968) "Indische Laiengerichte, Die Nyaya Panchayats in Uttar Pradesh," 1 *Verfassung und Recht in Ubersee* 140.

_____ (1970) *Dorfentwicklund und Dorfdemokratie in Indien.* Bielefeld: Berdtsmann Universitäts Verlag.

Kaufmann, M. (1979) "India's Power Struggles Are Distinctly Indian." *New York Times* (July 8) Sec. E, p. 4.

Khare, R. S. (1972) "Indigenous Culture and Lawyer's Law in India," 1 *Comparative Studies in Society and History* 71.

Khera, S. S. (1962) "District Administration Panchayat as Courts of Justice," 8 *Indian Journal of Public Administration* 161.

Kidder, R. (1973) "Courts and Conflict in an Indian City: A Study of Legal Impact," 11 *Journal of Commonwealth Political Studies* 121.

——— (1974a) "Litigation as a Strategy for Personal Mobility: The Case of Urban Caste Association Leaders," 33 *Journal of Asian Studies* 177.

——— (1974b) "Formal Litigation and Professional Insecurity: Legal Entrepreneurship in South India," 9 *Law & Society Review* 11.

——— (1977) "Western Law in India: External Law and Local Response," 47 *Sociological Inquiry* 155.

Kushawaha, R. (1977) *Working of Nyaya Panchayats in India: A Case Study of Varanasi District.* New Delhi: Young Asia.

Lingat, R. (1973) *The Classical Law of India,* trans., J. D. M. Derrett. Berkeley: University of California Press.

Madan, T. (1969) *Changing Patterns of Rural Administration in Uttar Pradesh.* Bombay: All India Institute of Local Self-Government.

Maddick, H. (1970) *Panchayati Raj: A Study in Rural Local Government.* London: Orient Longman.

Madras (Presidency) (1857–1859) *Reports on the Administration of Civil Justice, 1857–1859.* Madras.

Marriott, M. and R. Inden (1974) "Caste Systems," *Encyclopaedia Britannica* 3:982–991. Chicago: William Benton.

Mason, P. (ed.) (1967) *India and Ceylon: Unity and Diversity.* New York: Oxford University Press.

Mathur, M. B. (1976) *Uttar Pradesh.* New Delhi: National Book Trust.

Mathur, M. V., I. Narain, and V. M. Sinha (1966) *Panchayati Raj in Rajasthan: A Case Study in Jaipur District.* New Delhi: Impex India.

Mehta, S. (1971) *Social Conflicts in a Village Community.* Delhi: S. Chand.

Meschievitz, C. S. (1979) "Whither Nyaya Panchayats: An Evaluation of an Experimental Dispute Processing Institution in Rural India," MS, University of Wisconsin Law School, Madison.

Metcalf, T. (1964) *The Aftermath of Revolt: India 1857–1870.* Princeton, N.J.: Princeton University Press.

——— (1978) *Land, Landlords and Rajas in India.* Berkeley: University of California Press.

Moore, E. (1978) "My Experiences with Justice in a North Indian Village," Ms., Berkeley Professional Studies Program in India, New Delhi.

Naidu, D. S. (1977) "A Case for Establishment of Nyaya Panchayats in Andhra Pradesh," 68 *Quarterly Journal of the Local Self-Government Institute—Bombay* 373.

Nicholas, R. and T. Mukhopadyay. (1962) "Politics and Law in Two West Bengal Villages," 11 *Bulletin of the Anthropological Survey of India* 15.

Panigrahi, D. N. (1968) *Charles Metcalf in India: Ideas and Administrtion 1806-35.* Delhi: Munshiram Manoharlal.

Pillai, K. N. C. (1977) "Criminal Jurisdiction of Nyaya Panchayats," 19 *Journal of the Indian Law Institute* 438.

Purwar, V. (1956) "An Apology for N.P.," *Quarterly Journal of Local Self-Government Bombay* (October).

Purwar, V. L. (1960) *Panchayats in Uttar Pradesh.* Luckinow: Universal Book Depot.

Rajasthan (1967) *Panchayati Raj in Rajasthan.* Jaipur.

——— (1973) *Report of the Committee on Panchayati Raj.* Jaipur.

Rangnath, V. (1971) *The Changing Pattern of Rural Leadership in Uttar Pradesh*. New Delhi: Indian Academy of Social Sciences.

Reddy, G. R. (ed.) (1977) *Patterns of Panchayati Raj in India*. Delhi: Macmillan.

Retzlaff, R. (1962) *Village Government in India: A Case Study*. Bombay: Asia.

Robbins, R. S. (1962) "India: Judicial Panchayats in Uttar Pradesh," 2 *American Journal of Comparative Law* 239.

Rudolph, L. and S. H. Rudolph (1965) "Barristers and Brahmins in India: Legal Cultures and Social Change," 8 *Comparative Studies in Society and History* 24.

_____ (1969) *The Modernity of Tradition*. Chicago: University of Chicago Press.

Saxena, R. C. (1972) *Commentaries on the U.P. Panchayati Raj Act 1947*, 4th ed. Lucknow: Eastern Book Co.

Singh, K. (1974) *Rural Democracy X-Rayed*. Ghaziabad: Vimal Prasad.

Singh, V. P. (1976) *Caste, Class and Democracy: Changes in a Stratification System*. Cambridge, Mass.: Schenkman.

Singh, Y. S. (1976) "Inter-Regional Disparities: A Case Study of Uttar Pradesh," 56 *Indian Journal of Economics* 443.

Singhvi, G. C. (1970) "Criminal Jurisdiction of Nyaya Panchayats." *Kurukshetra* 3 (November 16).

Special Correspondent (1977) "A Programme for Civil Liberties," 12 *Economic and Political Weekly* 570.

Srinivas, M. N. (1962) "The Study of Disputes in an Indian Village," in M. Srinivas (ed.) *Caste in Modern India and Other Essays*. Bombay: Asia.

Stokes, E. (1978) *The Peasant and the Raj*. Cambridge: Cambridge University Press.

Tinker, H. (1967) *Foundations of Local Self-Government in India*. New Delhi: Lalvani.

Torri, M. (1977) "Social System and Ideology in South India," 12 *Economic and Political Weekly* 1144.

Tyler, S. (1973) *India: An Anthropological Perspective*. Pacific Palisades: Goodyear.

United Provinces (1928) *Report on the Working of the System of Government of United Provinces of Agra and Ouch Allahabad*.

_____ (1940) *Committee on Local Self-Government (Kher Committee) Report*. Lucknow.

Uttar Pradesh (1975) *Nyaya Panchayat Nidoshika*. Lucknow.

_____ (1961–1973) *Report on the Administration of Justice in UP*. Lucknow.

Uttar Pradesh, Director of Panchayati Raj (1975–1977) *Annual Report*. Lucknow.

Zaheer, M. and J. Gupta (1970) *The Organization of the Government of Uttar Pradesh*. Delhi: S. Chand.

II

The Drift toward Fascism

4

Individualistic and Collective Legalization: The Theory and Practice of Legal Advice for Workers in Prefascist Germany

UDO REIFNER

TOWARD A THEORY OF LEGALIZATION IN ANTAGONISTIC SOCIETIES

Legal institutions for the underprivileged, especially legal aid programs, are analyzed by some as a means of supressing and disarming the working class (Paschukanis, 1966; Erd, 1978; Hofrichter, 1982) and by others as a contribution to social justice (Halpern, 1980; Trubek *et al.*, 1980). On the political right some see bureaucratization and tutelage endangering individual freedom, whereas others claim they enhance the public welfare by ensuring social peace. In his analysis of the different currents underlying the movement for delegalization Abel (1979) has already shown that the distinction between right and left political orientations does not help to answer the question whether legalization is progressive or reactionary.

My research into the legal institutions of workers in prefascist Germany seeks to demonstrate that the apparent ambiguity of the politics of legalization is a result of excluding from the analysis two essential dimensions: history and class struggle. Legalization does not exist in the abstract. As a technique for ordering

THE POLITICS OF INFORMAL JUSTICE
Volume 2

social relations in conformity with fundamental power relationships, it appears empirically in specific *historical* forms defined by how the *ruling classes* interact and exercize their power over the dominated classes. Therefore, we first have to analyze the form of legalization, i.e., the forms taken by such segments as law, legal institutions, professions, procedures, and ideology, which define every step in the process of legalization, from the making of a legal rule (promulgation), through its communication to the people (legal education), and its concretization in a special problem (legal advice), to its application (legal decision) and enforcement (legal sanction).

In a capitalist society not only the law itself but also every segment and every step in the legalization process is dominated by the bourgeois form of action deriving from the commodity form (see Paschukanis, 1966; Balbus, 1977). But the two other forms of class society, feudalism and socialism, have their own forms of legalization, a fact to which Marx did not pay sufficient attention.[1]

Just as the individualistic and private form of liberal bourgeois legalization was already present in historical periods in which feudal status law predominated (see Maine, 1969), so the collective form of proletarian legalization is present in capitalist society in the guise of the working class and its forms of action. But this insight—that just as socialism is created in and by capitalism, so collective forms of legalization are born in and by our individualistic legal system—is not enough to explain the totality of contemporary forms of legalization. We have to take into account that monopoly capitalism also develops new legal forms in order to counteract the increasing threat of the working class and to adapt legalization to the "new goals of the technostructure" (see Galbraith, 1968). This new, authoritarian variant of individualistic legalization we shall call "administrative legalization" (see Kamenka and Tay, 1975) because, in contrast with liberal autonomous forms (see Nonet and Selznick, 1978), it renounces equality, certainty, and formality in order to create legally sanctioned means for direct political intervention (see Fraenkel, 1974).

For our analysis of legal aid institutions in late capitalism we shall distinguish three main forms of legalization in terms of the underlying class interests and historical conditions of their realization:

1. The liberal form of legalization defined by the commodity form (*individualistic autonomous legalization*)
2. The socialist response to liberal rights—the dialectically developed contradiction of the content and form of individualistic law into its social and collective materialization (*collective legalization*)

---

[1]Perhaps with the elimination of classes under communism law and legalization will become superfluous and disappear. But this certainly will not occur with the overthrow of capitalism, as Paschukanis argued in his early works (cf. 1966 and 1972). Only the bourgeois form of law will disappear under socialism, and all speculations about law and communism have little scientific value until we understand the proletarian form of legalization.

3. What may almost be called the feudalistic reply of late monopoly capitalism, which legalizes collective social goals in an individualistic administrative legal "form" that contains the threat of delegalized social interests and delegalized repression in a dual state (*individualistic administrative legalization*)

Legalization in bourgeois society is primarily individualistic, an expression of the needs of capital. The individualistic autonomous form makes the ideals of bourgeois law—freedom, equality, and security—logically compatible with the despotism of free enterprise, with differences between rich and poor, and with total insecurity concerning the satisfaction of social interests. This individualistic autonomous form of legalization is formal, isolating, egoistic, ideologically ahistorical, disregardful of class, grounded on the exchange value of commodities, compensatory, and unidimensional. To the working class, the advantage of this form of legalization over feudal status law lies in its formal generality, equality, and certainty. Even if freedom of contract gives owners uncontrolled power to dispose of their property, bourgeois legality at least restricts arbitrary and unpredictable *state* intervention for ends other than those defined by law or the contracting individuals.

Because the individualistic form is based on a fictitious individual—the legal person—the generally shared values of bourgeois law can only be realized socially, i.e., adapted to the social individual in collective forms of legalization. This collective legalization subscribes to the content of bourgeois law. Just as the individualistic legal form developed the converse of its own content, so the individualistic reflection of social reality has to be turned upside down. Individualistic law with its formal protections is the direct and necessary predecessor of collective law. It is necessary as long as and to the extent that the individual worker is not fully conscious of its collective power and needs protection from the individualistic power of corporate entities. The working class therefore develops collective legalization by asking for full application of and respect for individual rights, which they can secure only collectively.

Collective legalization starts from the collectivity of interests, i.e., from the real individuals—"the ensemble of social relations" (Marx, 1969c: 534)—whose needs and lives are defined as a part of the collective. It is social, aggregate, historical, based on the use value of commodities, class conscious, preventive, scientific, and multidimensional. It has two functions:

1. Protecting and defining the collectivity in its relations with the external world by establishing its borders (interclass legalization)
2. Defining the inner structure of the collectivity (intraclass legalization)
   a. by the democratic distribution of collective resources for the satisfaction of individual needs
   b. by the requirements for individual behavior that derive from the external environments, i.e., whether a collectivity is under attack and thus

needs a more hierarchical structure or whether it is part of a more general collectivity so that external and internal relations are harmonious

Marx described this ambiguous nature of legal forms under changing social conditions.

The bourgeoisie had a true insight into the fact that all the weapons which it had forged against feudalism turned their points against itself, that all the means of education which it had produced rebelled against its own civilization, that all the gods which it had created had fallen away from it. It understood that all the so-called bourgeois liberties and organs of progress attacked and menaced its class rule and its social foundation and its political summit simultaneously, and had therefore become "socialistic" [1963: 66].

The bourgeoisie therefore developed policies that led to the responsive form of administrative legalization. This form denies all class antagonism, appeals to general standards of harmony and public welfare, and pretends to focus on equity by emphasizing the unique circumstances of every case. Administrative legalization thus seeks to appease social unrest. Its legal functions—orienting state intervention, ordering expectations, and rendering predictable the outcomes of activities—are greatly reduced. Its ordering functions are limited to asserting general goals of public and individual welfare. What is left is the legitimation of state intervention. Compared with other forms of legalization, it legitimates virtually any administrative action or inaction. This return to uncontrolled state action makes administrative legalization a form of delegalization, a reversion to unrestricted political power.

Delegalization also characterizes the repressive version of administrative "legalization." Although repressive law constrains the behavior of the oppressed, it delegalizes civil liberties, thereby legitimating the unrestricted power of the ruling class and the state apparatus. It delegalizes social relations by freeing power from the formal controls of autonomous law.

Figure 4.1 seeks to present, in summary form, a set of analytic tools for understanding legalization in late capitalism.

Our empirical study is focused on two historical models of legal aid, administrative and proletarian, which took quite distinct forms at the beginning of monopoly capitalism in Germany in 1900. Both can be seen as responses to the crisis of liberal autonomous legalization, which was embodied in a system of legal aid best described as the traditional "service delivery model" in which legal services are supplied by attorneys organized in liberal professions. Whereas proletarian legal aid took the form of "collective self-help," administrative legal aid was manifest in a model of "legal welfare" that later developed into fascist "legal care." Before elaborating these models, on the basis of annual reports, essays, and official statistics, a few remarks about the social and economic background

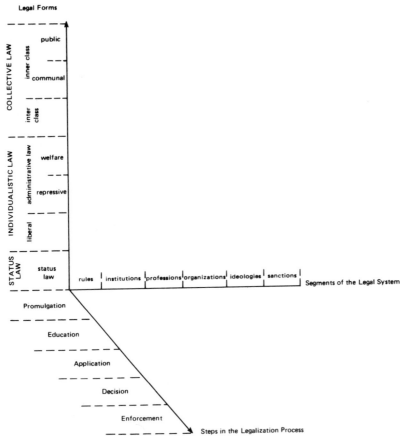

Figure 4.1. Diagram presents a model for the analysis of legalization.

may help us to see connections among the various steps of the legalization process and between legal and other socioeconomic developments.

THE HISTORICAL CONDITIONS OF LEGAL ADVICE IN PREFASCIST GERMANY

The second half of the nineteenth century in Germany was characterized by a relatively late but highly effective and rapid industrialization. This *Vergesellschaftung* of industry produced a new working class consisting mostly of former farmers or their children who could no longer live on a rural income. From 1870 to 1913 the German population grew from 40 to 67 million. At the same time the proletariat increased from 4.7 million to 10.8 million (Mottek *et al.*, 1974: 55).

For the working class, this national wealth brought poverty and insecurity. For example, in one coal-mining district between 1900 and 1906 the average annual fluctuation in the worker population was about 70 percent (Kuczynski, 1967: 314). The cost of living rose from 100 in 1900 to 130 in 1913 while the wage index oscillated a few points around 100 (*Ibid.*: 330). This favored the development of the subjective condition of *Vergesellschaftung*—collectivity. In 1863 the *Allgemeine Deutsche Arbeiterverein* (General Association of German Workers) was founded, although only two German states allowed workers the right to join an association (Deppe *et al.*, 1977: 23).

In 1871 the Bismarck government proclaimed the German Reich: four years later the General Association of German Workers and the Social Democratic Workers' Party amalgamated to form the Socialist Workers' Party of Germany. In 1878 parliament passed a law against the public menace (*gemeingefährlich*) of socialist aspirations, forbidding "all associations that aim to change the form of the state and society by Social-democratic, Socialist or Communist means" (Anti-Socialist Law, §1, October 21, reprinted in Blanke *et al.*, 1975: 66ff.).

The effects of this repression were quite the opposite of what was expected. Reformist and Socialist fractions in the workers' movement allied, and the union reorganized along industrial lines (the unionization of the German metalworkers in 1884 is an outstanding example), radicalized politically, and grew in membership. By attempting this radical suppression of the working class, the alliance of monopolistic bourgeosie, big landowners, and imperialistic militarists had destroyed much of the reformist hope for a neutral democratic state. Within a fifteen-month period in 1889–1890, 394,440 workers participated in 1131 strikes, demonstrating that despite police suppression the working class could develop its own forms of action and its own institutions.

Until 1870 the legal system had only one meaning for the working class— repression. The autonomous law granted the worker only one act of formalized freedom, the right to sign a contract in which he sold his imagined freedom. Engels expressed the actual relationship between law and working class in Germany when he stated:

> The whole of the civilised society is the state which is in all classical periods without exception the state of the ruling class remaining always essentially a machinery of suppressing the oppressed and exploited class . . . and when the barbarians hardly made a difference between rights and duties civilisation makes its difference and contradiction obvious also for the most stupid assigning nearly all rights to one class and all duties to the other [1976].

This relationship changed when the workers developed collective disobedience to individual contracts—the strike—and politically challenged the notion of parliament as a committee of independent individuals by forming political parties. The answer of the bourgeois state was repressive administrative legislation—the Anti-Socialist Law—which reenforced the repressive weight of the legal system that had been reduced by collective self-help. After five years of suppressing, banishing, imprisoning, and dismissing class-conscious workers, the Bismarck administration turned to responsive forms of legalization. In 1883 it passed the Illness Insurance Law, in 1884 the Accident Insurance Law for industrial workers, and in 1889 the Insurance Law for retired and handicapped people. With these laws, which the Social Democratic party did not support, the state replaced some important internal functions of the unions (Neumann, 1942: 468) and transformed the principle underlying individual support from solidarity to mutuality and the form of distribution from democratic participation to individualistic rights.

These activities on the rule-making level were complemented by a reform of the litigation system. When the Anti-Socialist Law was repealed in 1890 in the wake of one of the biggest strikes in the mines of Rhineland-Westphalia, the Reichstag created special labor courts for industrial workers. According to the claims of the government, the law would serve "the promulgation of peace between entrepreneurs and workers," which would "diminish the given social contradictions" (Michel, 1978: 48). These special courts, which could be established by cities, were intended to make the legal system accessible in much the same way that small claims courts do: fees were reduced to 30 RM (about $15), legal counsel was excluded, appeal was made more difficult, there was no revision, and procedure was shortened by making it largely oral (*Ibid.*).

All the debates about these new forms of legalization were framed in terms of an ideology that emphasized the responsibility of the law to respond to important social issues, the value of introducing informal procedures and laymen into legal counseling and the litigation process, and the need to combine rights with social welfare, court decisions with administrative activities. Its supporters constantly warned that otherwise working-class hatred of the state and of bourgeois ideals would lead to revolution (see Bernstein, 1910: 12; Ehrlich, 1967: 61; Neumann, 1957).

The working class was not prepared to deal with this new posture of the state apparatus toward its interests. There was no theory about how to use the law and legal institutions because nobody had foreseen that they might be available to the workers. Many socialists and trade unionists confounded the Marxist criticism of legal reformism with anarchist or liberal ideals of stateless society. Because both anarchism and liberalism were unattractive to the masses, who primarily wished to improve their living standard regardless of the method, the only plausible legal ideology for the working class was reformism: If only we get something through the law, whether it is offered in an individualistic or collective form, it is a step toward socialism. The Social Democratic party, in their Erfurt program, consequently demanded "free legal aid" and abolition of court fees. But in their daily practice the unions developed legal action much more dialectically than did the left theory of that period (Martiny, 1975: 159).

THE WORKERS' OFFICES

The first union response to the new legislation was to create commissions on social policy to study the pros and cons of the insurance laws, discuss them in union assemblies (Soudek, 1902: 15) and monitor their application (Müller, 1904: 15). Because the four social security laws had 534 sections, and amendments were passed every year (Leipzig, 1904: 11), all drafted in the bureaucratic language of Prussian administration, workers crowded into the consultation hours of the union newspapers, which, until then, were the only agencies offering individual advice. When the editors were no longer able to cope with the quantity of inquiries or the difficulty of their contents, the union commissions on social policy established consultation hours. It was then that the Nuremberg Association of Unions decided to open the first "workers' office" (WO).

According to the agreement creating the association, the workers' office in Nuremberg was intended to

> become a center for the economic interests of the workers. It should fulfill the task of supporting the unions . . . supervising the full and exact application of the new workmen protection laws by making surveys about wages and working conditions. It should also assume responsibility for operating an employment agency and distribute money for travel by union officials [Müller, 1904: 19].

The inauguration of the Nuremberg office stimulated a nationwide debate about legal advice in the unions because many *Lokalorganisationen* (local unions that had refused to centralize or to join national organizations) and some local branches of the "free unions" (e.g., the Social Democratic Union), like the Leipzig "Kartell" (the association of all unions in Leipzig), rejected workers' offices because they "would smother the union in bureaucracy" (*Ibid.*: 20). In the "red kingdom" of Saxony (Morizet, 1903) it took eight years before a workers' office was founded in 1904.

The first report of the "General Commission of the [Free] Unions of Germany," published in 1901 when 167,363 workers had been advised by workers' offices, reproduced the ideological confusion that institution had caused.

> The workers' secretaries [the staff of the workers' offices] shall dedicate themselves to giving the most effective weapons to the workers to fight a hostile legal order. They do not have to rely on the mercy of the Minister of Justice. Their image is due solely to the proper force of the working class. Remembering this, they will dedicate all their strength to liberating the working class from the chains of an antiquated legal order [Umbreit, 1903: 408].

The legal order should be fought by using it. This contradiction was not theoretically solved by choosing either reformism or anarchism. Only the practice of the WOs could show whether the combination of collective union activities with an individualistic legal system that offered some minimal recognition of workers' rights would lead to either collective legalization or individualistic union activity.

But from the beginning the development of collective forms was hindered not only by judicial procedures that remained unchanged but also by the nature of the cases the WOs had to handle. The central questions of class relations (wages, job security, and union activity) had not been legalized but had rather been left to extralegal arrangements between the opposing parties. By 1911, one-fifth of the workers already derived most of their "rights" from another collective form of "law," the collective agreement. Until 1918 courts and tribunals refused to acknowledge that this new form of "law" could overrule individual contracts (Sinzheimer, 1915: 150). Therefore, all rights arising out of collective agreements had to be enforced by extralegal procedures, i.e., conflict commissions containing equal numbers of capitalists and workers, or by strikes and boycotts. Only minimum standards were established by law, and these were generally broken in factories where the workers had little influence.

The efforts of the workers' offices lay in areas where collective action was difficult to organize. From 1901 to 1920 labor contract disputes never exceeded 17 percent of the WO caseload; 30 percent of all legal advice concerned social security law and another 30 percent involved tenants' rights and installment sales contracts. The rest was distributed among administrative law (8–10 percent from 1901 to 1905, 15 percent from 1910 to 1920, and as much as 25 percent during the war in 1917), penal law (7 percent), and issues pertaining to the workers' movement (1.5 percent) (see Statistical Annex of the Korrespondenzblatt, 1921: 53; Annual reports in the Korrespondenzblatt, 1901–1919). What nevertheless fostered collective forms of legal aid in this first period was the extralegal collective experience of the secretaries, the strengthening of a solidary ideology in the period of suppression, and the inadequacy of the legal procedure even to protect the individualistic claims of the workers.

Toward Collective Legal Advice: The Workers Offices from 1894 to 1906

INSTITUTION AND PROFESSIONS

The WOs were organized as grass roots institutions with no dichotomy between counselors and clients. The first principle was that counselors and clients were all members of one Union Kartell. Within the Kartell there were special

WO associations, which could be joined by individuals or by unions (thereby conferring membership on their members). The WO association had four functions:

1. Its members financed the workers' office.
2. The staff of the office was elected and dismissed by vote of the members, either directly or indirectly.
3. The association had to supervise all activities of the staff, fixing their tasks and working conditions.
4. Membership in the association or in one of the associated unions entitled one to obtain legal aid from the WO.

In a plenary session of the association, either a board of directors was nominated and then chose counselors with union experience or the counselors were directly chosen by the assembly. Any complaints about the workers' office had to be addressed to the board of directors. If the complainant was dissatisfied with its decision, he could appeal to the plenary session of the association. Each year the supervisory board reported to the plenary session about the work of the secretaries, finances, and complaints. The selection process favored those with lengthy union membership, experience in union organization, and ability as an agitator, propagandist, and leader. Most were leaders of smaller unions that lacked the money to employ full-time officials, such as the president of the Hatters' Union in Altenburg (Müller, 1904: 26).

The diversity of tasks performed by the secretary helped to prevent rapid professionalization and bureaucratization of the WOs. But perhaps the most important institutional support for collectivity was the system of financing. There was no fee for legal advice. Only in the thirty-seven WOs that admitted nonunion members for publicity reasons in 1903 did the "free-riders" have to pay a small contribution (Brunner, 1904: 707). The WOs were financed exclusively by contributions from the members of the WO association. The unions gave a bond for these contributions and collected the money. In Nuremberg in 1894, 3500 workers paid no more than two Pfennig (approximately one cent) a week (Soudek, 1902: 14).

Instead of exchanging legal advice for money, as in the service delivery model, solidary financing constantly reminded the secretaries that every case was performed for the collectivity. In the beginning this kind of financing did even more to stimulate collective action by the secretaries because the contributions were more or less voluntary. Those workers who did not, at the moment, need individual advice had to be convinced that the WO's activity had also helped to improve their working conditions (Martiny, 1975: 163). If they failed to demonstrate such collective utility, i.e., to focus on preventive activities, the budget showed a decline. Only the Gotha WO in "red Saxony" received any state support—2000 RM a year (about $1000) until 1909, when the state terminated its grant because it lacked sufficient influence over the WO's policy (Korrespon-denzblatt, 1910: 31; Martiny, 1975: 170).

After 1906 the WOs became more centralized, holding annual conferences of workers secretaries and formulating recommendations for their work. For though the Nuremberg WO had been a model for many others (even one in Mas-sachusetts; see Soudek, 1902: 25), there was considerable variety in organization and structure, reflecting the character of the local union and the attitude of employers and state agencies.

ACTIVITIES OF THE WORKERS' OFFICES

Besides giving individual advice and providing representation before tribunals, the WOs surveyed working and housing conditions, followed the judgments of the courts, supervised the official factory inspector, gave speeches on social and legal issues in union assemblies, and wrote annual reports about their own work and about the activities of all the unions in the local Union Kartell.

The WOs were usually open to the public six days a week, mornings and afternoons. At first an average of about fifteen clients a day visited each WO (Martiny, 1975: 170). But in 1914 the Lübeck WO reported that its two sec-retaries saw a low of twenty-eight visitors on May 10 and a high of ninety-eight on January 3 (Lübeck, 1914: 5). The WO represented clients before the social security tribunals in less than 1 percent of its cases. More important was the duty to speak in union assemblies: the Stuttgart WO gave forty-seven such talks in a single year (Kampffmeyer, 1901: 405). Much time was consumed by surveys and investigations, which sometimes involved the distribution and evaluation of more than 10,000 questionnaires. The annual reports also played an important role. The Bremerhaven report tells us that two secretaries occasionally had to work more than a month to finish these reports, which could be a virtual guidebook to class conflict. In 1905 the Bremen WO spent 1983.50 RM to print the report, more than half of their annual budget (Bremerhaven, 1906: 1). It would not be an exaggeration to estimate that analysis, prevention, and prop-aganda took nearly as much time as legal counseling.

Scientific Analysis   The political necessity to investigate the true causes of the misery of the working class forced the WOs to employ scientific means. They had to question the principles of individualism, such as the neutrality of the state and its courts, the blindness of justice, equality before the law, the promise of security, and the ideology of torts, which attributes the causes of misfortune to individual fault and accident. Conscious of the class character of their work, the WOs developed an empirical sociology of law—perhaps the first in history—with hardly any interaction with the ruling scientific community. Single cases were taken as indicators of underlying collective problems, which were explored through questionnaires, personal interviews, observation, and statistics in order to explain the social context of legalized social interests. Although technically very imperfect, these studies substantiated Marx's belief in the scientific vocation of the working class as the first class in history in which class interest does not hinder but promotes scientific insight (see Marx, 1969: postscript to the second edition).

I can give only a few examples from the rich empirical work collected in the annual reports of WOs[2]. The Bremen WO distributed 6062 questionnaires concerning the working conditions of all industrial workers. In the same year they surveyed the working conditions of women in two Bremen factories that, they proved, the factory inspector had never visited (Soudek, 1902: 68). In Nuremberg, answers to 14,142 questionnaires revealed the social conditions (work and housing) of the bakery apprentices and other employees (Müller, 1904: 68). In Harburg (1903: 11) the WO encountered many cases in which workers burned their eyes. It therefore collected their protective glasses and questioned the workers about how they used them. The WO found that the glasses weighed 65 grams (2.3 ounces), greatly hampered vision, and were made of metal that cut into the worker's face; in short, they were impossible to wear. This survey helped to falsify the argument that the accidents had been the fault of the workers.

Empirical research was also used as a weapon against the collaboration of doctors and insurance companies with the enterpreneurs who paid them. In every report about social security cases we find complaints about the medical certificates that fixed the percentage of disability and thus determined the calculation of the benefit. The doctors used several stereotypical arguments to lower the benefit rate, such as "sham-patient," "malingerer," the contribution of a preexisting condition to a work-related injury, and especially the cynical claim that after a time the worker "got used" to his disability so that the benefit rate could be lowered.

The Leipzig WO (Leipzig, 1904: 17) asked all lay judges in the insurance tribunals to fill out a questionnaire for every medical certificate received. It found that five out of ninety-one physicians (6 percent) supplied half of all the certificates. Furthermore, there was a significant correlation between the number of certificates a doctor completed and how favorable those certificates were to the employer. The insurance companies exploited the competition among doctors who wanted to perform these profitable jobs. This was also the reason why doctors generally rejected the requests of unions for opinion on an individual accident prior to litigation. The standard response was always that they expected to be asked for a certificate by the insurance company in the forthcoming litigation. That those who paid the piper called the tune was underlined in one report by a description of the public functions of the medical professor employed most

[2]For a more detailed overview, see Mombert, 1905.

frequently, a quotation from a book in which he professed the goals of the insurance company, and a typical certificate written by him. The reports criticized judges for relying on medical expertise, reproducing demystifying quotations taken out of documents the WOs had obtained from their members in the course of rendering legal advice. The survey also sought to disabuse doctors of their belief that they could profit from this competition for the goodwill of the insurance companies: half were asked for only one certificate a year. The whole survey was repeated the following year and showed a slightly more equal distribution of certificates. Surveys thus functioned as weapons against "soft" corruption in the medical profession.

The Bremerhaven WO (Bremerhaven, 1906: 9) evaluated the social security system. First, it published official figures showing a significant reduction in the number of work-related injuries giving rise to accident benefits. Then it contrasted the increasing number of people entitled to benefits as a result of a fatal accident. The WO argued that it was implausible that fatal accidents had increased at the same time that minor accidents had declined. It seemed far more likely that the tribunals had become less sympathetic to small nonfatal work accidents. This interpretation was supported by analyzing five decisions of insurance tribunals concerning the loss of fingers. Each decision seems to have an idiosyncratic justification, but, read together, they disclose the arbitrariness of legal reasoning even to the layperson.

Most of the surveys are presented in the form of stories, but stories carefully selected out of a year's experience to reveal the basic structures of the problem—"where reality corresponds to its explanatory concepts" (Marx, 1969: vol. 1, p. 52). This method of legal education requires two steps—from reality to theoretical abstraction and back to reality—as shown in Figure 4.2. Because this form of presentation parallels the way in which members of the working class transmit their own experience—e.g., fairy tales, folk songs, and ballads—it is probably a much more effective means of collective legal education than the usual scientific presentation would be. Furthermore, it has the fascination of "true stories" that

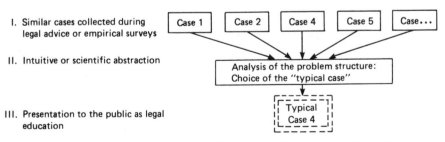

Figure 4.2. Diagram illustrates the structure of reasoning underlying the workers' offices survey results.

people may have heard before and with which they can identify. The Bremerhaven report (Bremerhaven, 1905: 36), for example, starts a story about a decision concerning family affairs with the phrase "For the use of all guardians and mothers of illegitimate children we want to take notice of the following case."

A summary of the ways in which these surveys were used shows that they served:

1. As a rhetorical resource in collective struggle
2. To evaluate individual legal advice
3. As evidence and argumentation in litigation and extrajudicial settlements
4. To enlighten union members about the causes of individual misfortune
5. To develope collective means to counteract the strategies of capital
6. To assess the effects of the struggle for social progress

As I will show later, these were the core of the preventive activities of the WOs.

Aggregate Social Explanation and Handling of the Cases   The new responsive laws differed from the autonomous form of liberal bourgeois law in that they reflected a concern for social issues. Illness, incapacity to work, hunger, and homelessness had become the subjects of labor law, installment credit law, and tenants law. Responsive law rejected the autonomous logic of exchange, in which illness was nothing more than a loss of labor power and an incapacity to fulfill the labor contract. But the new laws dealt with just a few social issues, reducing only the most inhuman consequences of neglecting human needs. The logic of the new laws remained welfare individualism: Illness, hunger, and homelessness remained individual problems that were alleviated by the mercy of the legislator.

The WOs tried to counteract this welfare individualism by broadening the issues in two ways: Their empirical surveys demonstrated the class character of an individual problem and showed the connection between different problems in the life of a worker and his family, as well as the source of those problems in the labor process.[3] Thus the class character of a problem was complemented by a demonstration of its human character.[4]

In Lübeck (1902: 55), for instance, the WO had to deal with many similar accidents caused by press machines in a particular factory. Under the accident insurance law it would have been sufficient to state whether these were "work

---

[3]Exploitation is not a moral category in Marxist theory. It merely reflects the fact that a worker, as a dependent salaried employee, is excluded from the decisions concerning the surplus value of his work product.

[4]This necessary alliance between socialism and humanism is theoretically developed by Sève (1972).

accidents" and the length of time and degree to which the worker was disabled. But the WO investigated the entire case. When it discovered that the machines did not comply with safety regulations it asked why the factory inspector had not, and could not have, seen it. According to the WO's report, the factory inspector earned only 1200 RM ($600) a year. He therefore performed his duties only part time. When he fell ill there was no substitute. So the WO report blamed not the factory inspector but rather the city of Lübeck, which showed so little concern for safety conditions in the factories and urged it to pay the factory inspector a higher salary in order to make his a full-time job. After investigating the immediate causes of the problem, the WO extended its inquiry to the social consequences. Women were unusually susceptible to this kind of accident, which the WO explained by their lack of the necessary concentration. Furthermore, injured women often were pregnant, which meant that they could not be anesthetized during treatment but had to either suffer the pain without narcotics or be permanently crippled. From its knowledge of worker psychology, the WO proposed that women be forbidden to operate these machines since a woman would never disclose her pregnancy before it was visible.

The "human dimensions" of the reported cases, the interrelationship of events in the lives of the workers, is emphasized by the headlines of the reports: "A long lasting case," "One pays out of practical reasons not on principles," "This is modern law," or, in the Bremerhaven report (1906: 15), "A worn-out man does not need the accident benefits." There are many reports describing the psychological impact of accidents, especially in cases where the worker lost a limb. One example is "The story of the suffering of an accident victim" in the Harburg report (1904: 26), in which we learn about a case lasting twelve years: the doctors and their certificates, the psychological background of a victim who has been labeled a sham patient, the statements of his comrades at work, and the influence of the accident on his family life.

The way in which the WOs handled child protection issues is equally significant. Individual advice was backed by surveys about the situation of children as well as contacts with children. On several Sundays the WO secretaries of Harburg went into town and counted the children they found working illegally in bakeries, restaurants, factories, etc. In Königsberg the WO organized weekend picnics for 300–500 children and mothers in order to gain the necessary contact and confidence.

The Bremerhaven WO (1906: 47) represented a child who had been placed illegally in a reformatory. The WO secretary visited the family and reformatory and spoke with the child and the officials. The child had been incarcerated "on moral grounds" because her mother had confessed the girl's sins to the priest, asking him for help, and he, in his obligatory statement, had disclosed these facts to the officials. The report then explains that the conditions under which workers' children and those of referents and judges grow up are hardly comparable. It is surely not accidental that the same report gives detailed information on how to leave the church in order to avoid paying church taxes.

The Lübeck report (1905: 33) gives a detailed, seven-page report about the case of a worker who was injured at work while cutting wood. He was initially found to be 30 percent disabled but then secured a significant increase through litigation. One year later the insurance company asked him to go back for reexamination at the hospital that had issued the certificate he had successfully attacked in court, which had called him a sham patient. When he refused to return, his benefit was again reduced. The WO then located another clinic in Königsberg and paid his travel. But the Königsberg clinic could not give a final opinion because the patient refused to stay for the required week of observation. He had been frightened by the bad reputation of this hospital. After this, he refused any further examination. The legal question was thus foreclosed—his complaint had to fail—but the WO continued its investigation. The secretary saw the worker at home and discovered the misery in which he was living. After his accident this man's wife supported the family. From then on she despised her husband as a useless sponger, treating him no better than a dog with whom she had to share a bed. It was the wife who had decided that an examination would only cost her money. The secretary tried to persuade the judge to consider these facts but failed and had to abandon the case. This, says the report, was the only instance in which the WO had to deny further representation. But from the perspective of the collectivity, the case served to reveal the social dimensions of a formal legal problem such as a failure of proof. Accident, worklessness, change in the family structure, family problems, and the loss of a merited benefit formed a vicious circle in which the real social problem was worklessness. In the Kiel report (1913: 14) the growing number of divorces is explained by "the unfavorable economic conditions that threaten family life."

The scope of legal advice was constantly broadened by the willingness of the WO to entertain all problems, not just those connected with work. Until fascism restricted the competence of union legal advice to labor and social security law, workers were also helped with consumer, housing, and penal law problems, which were treated in the context of the basic problem—being a dependent wageworker—and not as the isolated problems of individuals. Housing and work were already related by the fact that many workers lived in flats owned by their employers. And because the exploitation of consumers by unscrupulous business practices mostly affected workers, the connection between nominal and real income was also visible.

At first glance the family problems that presently play such a dominant role in public legal advice (see Reifner, 1978: 51) seem to have been excluded from the activity of the WOs as they do not appear in the statistics. But in fact family issues then were not seen as a special field like labor conflict and tenants' affairs.

Family problems appeared in the context of labor difficulties (unemployment, inadequate income), accidents (the case of the injured worker dominated by his wife), public law (child welfare), and juvenile delinquency. Social advice by the WOs was directed to the totality of the living conditions of the workers, relating isolated problems to the position of the worker in the process of production. Where this connection was not visible because the problems were perceived as private matters, the WOs were less active. Their activities proclaimed a moral view that sought to socialize (*vergesellschaften*) not only the consequences of the workers' problems but also the problems themselves. "If the worker would get *his law* from the bourgeoisie we would not need any legal advice centers. And since he does not get it a bourgeois legal advice center cannot help him" (Lübeck, 1905: 7).

Prevention as a Shelter for Collective Progress Individualistic legalization is focused on the compensation of injuries. Law is mobilized when someone's rights are violated, when conflict has already taken place. Because legal individualism asserts that any interest can be given a money value, an infringement is legally defined as the loss of a certain sum of money. Looking at the social causes of an invasion is therefore pointless under individualistic legalization. There is little likelihood that the same person will suffer a similar injury. Because both prevention and restitution are largely ignored, the individual case can be "solved" without any deeper insight into the problem. Only in collective forms of legal advice is preventive research rewarding. Then an individual infringement is viewed as just the first step in the violation of collective interests, an alarm for the members.

At least during their early years the WOs followed the principle that every injury was a lost battle in the class struggle. They did not seek to hide the fact that they could not restore a severed hand or leg or heal the injuries resulting from a lost job by securing a sum of money (e.g., Lübeck, 1902: 15). Instead, inspired by an ideology of prevention, they developed three kinds of collective activities: mobilizing public law for "private" collective interests, increasing public consciousness about "private" matters through critical information, and enforcing preventive rules through nonjudicial sanctions. To do this they had to break down three barriers erected by individualistic legalization: the wall between private and public law, the isolation of legal advice from the other steps in the legalization process, and the boundary between legalized and extralegal action.

Public Law Activities: At the end of the nineteenth century there were still many public intrusions into private matters, especially public laws used to suppress the working class, such as the antiassociation laws. On the other hand, there was no way to participate in administrative decisions or to force the courts to engage in public law activities.[5] The WOs therefore mobilized public law by political means. Public disclosure of administrative inertia and the threat of extralegal action if public law was not applied forced the state apparatus to act.

One of the most important preventive activities of the WOs was enforcement of factory inspection. In many areas the factory inspector was only a bureaucratic mechanism for channeling discontent with working conditions. In the face of the threat of a strike or public unrest, mobilizing the factory inspector was a cheap way to appease the workers. Without such pressure he collaborated closely with the entrepreneurs. As a public semilegalized institution for the defense of social interests (administrative welfare legalization), the factory inspector had a double effect: By legalizing only some of the goals of collective action it rendered illegal all self-help concerning safety at work; it thereby disarmed the working class without making longlasting concessions.

Individuals were effectively deterred from complaining to the factory inspector by disclosure of their names to the entrepreneur. In response, the WO developed the dialectics of an institution intended, more or less, as a means of social control. They took seriously the ideology of the institution—defense of the public interest—and "helped" them in their work. The Lübeck report had a special chapter evaluating the factory inspector's work each year. He therefore had only two choices: He could openly reject this help, thereby destroying the legitimating power of the institution and forcing the workers to return to self-help; or he could intervene more frequently in response to the information publicly provided to him.

Both responsive and repressive reactions to the WOs were reported. In Dortmund a policeman was sent to observe the counseling hours under the pretext of ensuring "that they are free of charge," for otherwise the WO would have been engaged in a trade requiring permission. The opposite is reported in Mannheim, where the factory inspector offered consultations in the rooms of the WO. In Leipzig the metalworkers ignored the factory inspector and continued to employ extralegal means of protest within the factories (Leipzig, 1906: 38). This stimulated the factory inspector to ask the WO about complaints. To channel social unrest, the state was even willing to use the WO to enforce public law, thereby expanding its public functions. The WO could legally undertake the tasks of the factory inspector, enjoying a semiofficial power to investigate complaints. This is an example where delegalization is an indirect but effective means to change the form of a given legalization.

Information: The secretaries were supposed to be "writers in social policy" (Müller, 1904: 32). They explained their work in the union journals, participated in the discussions of the committees on social policy, delivered speeches on

---

[5]There was nothing comparable to the contemporary class action, neighborhood action (*Nachbarklage*) in urban development, or the individual right to participate in a public action.

social issues in union assemblies, offered courses on law, and briefed the deputies of the Social Democratic party. But their most important mode of expression was the annual reports, which were intended to be "a history of the union—its development and struggles" (Leipzig, 1906: 7), "a manual for legal questions" (Bremerhaven, 1906: 1), "more than a mere enumeration of facts" (Lübeck, 1901: 6), "a source of critical enlightment on issues concerning the working class." Some examples may illustrate how these reports advanced sociolegal enlightment.

The Leipzig report (1904: 14) tells us that each victim of an occupational accident had the right to a second decision by the insurance company on the percentage of his disability. But the report advised workers not to use this "right" because no insurance company had ever changed its decision and the workers just wasted their time. The Harburg report described the legal aid scheme and the institutions that granted legal aid: Five were involved and the necessary paperwork was very complicated. Because most applications were denied the report concludes that it would be useless to apply for legal aid. The report notes an alternative system in Bremen, where all decisions are centralized in one institution, thereby rendering legal aid more accessible.

With their ongoing observation of the law in action, administrative activities, and the development of working and living conditions the WO provided the public with essential information. But critical information must be supplemented with organized power if it is to have consequences. Information and action had to be combined in a single institution.

Extralegal Collective Sanctions: Because the individualistic legal system only provided compensation for individual injuries there was no legal means to enforce the rights of the working class. This last step of the legalization process does not produce an ideology that could be developed dialectically into a form of collective legalization. Sanctions are the application of immediate state power through concrete individual decisions by state agents that specify the use of the repressive apparatus without any possible alternatives.

Bourgeois law could be interpreted collectively by the social application of its own ideals, legal education could be turned from propagating the law in the books to criticizing it in terms of the law in action, legal advice could be integrated into collective self-help, and even litigation can be used collectively, as "mass actions," "class actions," and "representative actions" have shown. But under a regime of individualistic legalization the state is the only legal subject, the only one who can exercise legal power. The only way to collectivize legal sanctions is to replace state power and to develop alternatives to law by liberating tamed social power. Delegalization thus became a means to change the form of legalization where the legal system was incapable of developing socially more adequate forms.

The Frankfurt WO secretary described the resources of the WOs: "Supported by the organized masses the WO is not powerless, not built on sand. With the backing of the unions it has mighty institutions of constraint! A close connection between unions and the WO is of basic importance for the effectiveness of the institution" (Kampffmeyer, 1901: 394). The basic sanction of the working class in a market system is the refusal to play the game, i.e., a strike in the realm of production, a boycott in the realm of reproduction. These direct sanctions are backed by indirect power exercised by the state apparatus, which may partly or totally be conquered by the working class. Politics and economics are closely related because strikes and boycotts may develop into political action. This threat also explains a great deal of legalization, which is a preventive measure by the ruling class that seeks to depoliticize economic issues by constraining them within legal forms.

There are only a few examples of such actions in the reports. This may partly be explained by the illegality of nonjudicial sanctions, whose publication would have represented a challenge to the public prosecutor. It is due, even more, to the fact that the WOs did not work in the center of class struggle; nor were they connected to single unions. But we still have some interesting hints. In Leipzig (Leipzig, 1906: 42) the WO had to deal with fraud in the building trade. When a house builder stopped paying the subcontractors, the latter did not pay the wages it owed its workers amd dismissed them. When the builder was liquid again construction would resume with other workers. Legal means took too much time and often led to unenforceable decisions. The Leipzig WO therefore promulgated the following "norms," which may be interpreted as collective law in interclass relations that instrumentalized the official legal system for collective purposes:

1. If you do not get your entire salary on payday, stop working at once (individual refusal).
2. Give immediate notice to the shop steward (making individual refusal a collective issue).
3. File a lawsuit against your employer (challenging the official legal system).
4. If the employer does not pay the judgment, the working place is off bounds for all construction workers until the debt is paid (developing individual action into collective action).

At the same time, the Social Democratic deputies in the Landtag were asked to draft a bill about this issue (mobilizing public law). The WO reports that these steps met with considerable success. The participation of nearly all construction workers rendered lawsuits practically unnecessary.

Litigation and nonjudicial sanctions were also combined in Bremerhaven. On August 3, 1910, about 1000 out of 8861 organized workers held a protest meeting against the jurisdiction of the Geestmünder Labor Tribunal and presented a resolution to its president asking that it favor the economically weaker parties (Bremerhaven, 1910: 26).

IDEOLOGY OF THE WORKERS' OFFICES

The ideology of the WO[6] was based on a distinction between the law of the people (*Volksrecht*) and the official law, comparable to Santos's distinction (1978) between Pasargada law and the Law of the Asphalt. The Lübeck report (1905: 41) employs the distinction between the "juridical legal view" and the "legal view (*Rechtsanschauung*) of the people." In the annual report of the "General Commission of the Free Unions of Germany" the editor distinguishes between "the legal order" and "law which is in accordance with the morals of the working class" and between the "law in the books" and "law." Another Lübeck report (1904: 60) places official "law" in quotation marks to signify "so-called law." But these distinctions did not lead to an anarchistic rejection of the entire legal system. The WOs rather tried to persuade the workers that the law they identified with their own morality was actually the prevailing law, which had just been misused by the ruling classes. The WOs wanted not an alternative law but a social application of the law. They laid claim to the legitimating power of the law, which forced them to develop the dialectics of bourgeois law.

In Bremerhaven (1910: 26) the union meeting called to protest the jurisdiction of the labor tribunal adopted a motion criticizing the uncertainty inherent in the individualized decision making of administrative justice. But in the same resolution it urged on the judges the social application of a liberal ideal of bourgeois law that would prevent a return from administrative to formal liberal justice. The tribunal should follow "the good old legal principle: 'In dubious cases you should decide in favor of the economically weaker party.'" No such principle ever existed in this form; it is the social application of a liberal principle in autonomous law that states: "in dubio pro libertate" or "in dubio pro reo." The law of the oppressed is thus seen as the correct application of the principles of the existing legal system. The bourgeoisie is violating its own law, mostly by false (unsocial) interpretations but also by new (administrative) statutes. "Apparent injustice pretends to legality because it has the power to violate the true law," declares the 1902 report (Umbreit, 1903: 401). The tendency toward lower benefits is explained by decisions "that have already given up the spirit of human interpretation of the law" (Bremerhaven, 1906: 10).

But the WOs knew that there was little chance to change the "law in action" through the available institutions. The law was used primarily to legitimate nonjudicial collective activities in interclass relations. A report about the convic-

---

[6]I am using *ideology* to mean a theory explaining and guiding practice, not a false reflection of reality, in the meaning of Marx and of Geiger (1964).

tion of a worker for picketing ends: "He served his time, he did not try the gods and appeal. He recognized that the court having jurisdiction over his case was the Hoppenstedt chamber. This was the only case [in this strike] in which blind justice got the chance to judge right and wrong" (Lübeck, 1905: 67).

The WOs felt intuitively that collective interests would be in the weakest position within a law suit.[7] In 1900 only 43,378 out of 4,279,727 RM in the budget of the central organization of the free unions (1 percent) was spent for legal protection (Soudek, 1902: 6). In 1903, 47,626 out of 205,906 requests for legal advice (23.1 percent) ended with a letter, and representation in court or tribunal is reported in only 1768 cases (.74 percent). In 1905 the proportion of cases litigated rose to 2.4 percent, and the absolute number increased fivefold, disclosing a tendency in union legal advice that I will deal with later in the chapter.

In order to avoid lawsuits the WOs did not apply communal intraclass standards of social peace to interclass conflict resolution. They denounced the variety of legal advice offices founded by ostensibly neutral welfare organizations:

> Whenever the defense of workers' interests against state and entrepreneurs is at stake a bourgeois legal advice office must fail. . . . It is just in these cases that they will seek to reconcile. But the worker does not want to hear about reconciliation. He wants to have *his rights and nothing else* [Lübeck, 1905: 7].

Mediation and arbitration were rejected for the individual worker. Only workers as an organized class were conceived to be strong enough to use these forms for disputes about the application of collective agreements.

Legal institutions were also avoided in interclass conflicts, but on substantive grounds, not strategic. Here official law was replaced by the morality of the working class, with the WO assuming the functions of a tribunal and using the threat of court procedures as a sanction (Santos, 1978). The WOs never applied a law that was contrary to their own convictions; on the other hand, they were prompt to support a legally unfounded claim using extralegal means when they found the claim morally convincing. One example that often recurs is support for illegitimate children. Conscious of the inhuman social conditions confronting the unmarried mother, the WOs tried to convince the father of the child to pay even when he was not legally obligated (Soudek, 1902: 32–33; Müller, 1906: 46).

The collective traces of the WO ideology can be summarized as follows: The WOs claimed that the law was their law. The working class was seen as the only class whose interests represented the ideals of bourgeois law. The

---

[7]This is an objection to Galanter's dichotomy (1974) between organizational ("repeat player") and individual ("one shot") litigants, for he equates collective associations with individualistically organized economic entities by means of the technical abstraction of "organization."

bourgeoisie, by contrast, misused the legal system through its power over juris-diction and legal interpretation (class justice) and its capacity to pervert the law by administrative statutes. So the realization of the law required partial, class-conscious, social advocacy that rejected the idea of reconciliation with opposing class interests. Law, justice, and morality were seen as a unity that had to be defended by collective means against formal and liberal logic as well as against administrative abuse.

The Reintegration of the Workers' Offices into Individualistic Legal Advice

Until now I have focused on the collective elements of the WOs. But it would be naive to think about the WOs as just collective self-help institutions. Even from the beginning individualistic forms of legalization competed with collective elements; between 1906 and 1910 the former assumed ever greater importance, destroying democratic structures and subverting preventive goals, class con-sciousness, and solidarity. Instead of surveys, propaganda, and extralegal activi-ties, the WOs concentrated on legal advice and judicial representation. As the judicial skills of the secretaries became more and more significant, democratic decisions were replaced by administrative procedures.

Individualization and depoliticization of collective issues became the personal interest of a new union professional, the legal aid officer, who was self-recruiting, expansive, and uncontrollable. In 1919 a WO secretary called for a general welfare office, financed by the state, that would integrate all existing legal advice centers (Peikert, 1919: 296). Another secretary asked that the WOs be officially authorized to function as arbitration councils. There was a recommendation that WO secretaries serve an apprenticeship, specialize in different legal areas, and receive higher pay (Peikert, 1919). The WOs emulated capitalist efficiency, judging their work in the terms of exchange value. Everything that could be counted was reported and put on the profit side of the ledger: number of visitors, number of problems, number of letters, instances of representation in courts and tribunals. To satisfy the single union branches they even distinguished clients according to their union membership and to the borough or village from which they came.

But the strongest evidence of their worth was the amount of money legaliza-tion itself secured in the form of compensation. Therefore, the statistics started to juxtapose the total amount of insurance benefits and damages against the costs of the WO. This figure, still shown in the reports of German unions today, purports to be the profit margin of the unions. To increase this figure the WO had to increase caseload, stress compensation at the expense of prevention, in short, concentrate on individualistic legal remedies in place of collective legalization.

This forced the secretaries to specialize, rationalize, and devote their energies to legal procedures.

Money and consent generated what appeared to be a purely technological mechanism. With an increase in caseload and the disappearance of democratic control this mechanism could develop into a bargain in which the working class sold its social human rights (not to be injured or dismissed, ill-treated or homeless and without the means for reproduction) for the few million marks represented by insurance benefits and damages.

PUBLIC LEGAL ADVICE CENTERS AND THE PEACE OF LAW MOVEMENT

When the workers' offices extended the influence of the unions and the Social Democratic party into the field of legalization, a wave of free legal advice centers spread over the country. Roman Catholic and Protestant churches, welfare organizations and Christian "non-strike unions," local authorities and chambers of commerce—all discovered within themselves sympathy for the poor worker who had just been able to escape the repression of the antisocialist laws. Although they all shared a fear of communism and socialism, by which they meant unions and the social democratic party ("A specter is haunting Europe"), the legal advice centers developed independently. Some offered to support the WOs financially if the latter would accept subordination (Frankfurt), some simply tried to collaborate with the WOs, and some consciously engaged in antiunion propaganda and cutthroat competition. All claimed to help the poor in order to prevent social unrest and the spread of revolutionary situations. They defined the single social problem as the distance between law and the poor. Barriers to law were proclaimed to be obstacles to justice that deprived the poor of their rights, but it may have been even more important that they reduced the effect of the legal system on the ideology, activity, and political behavior of the poor.

Two kinds of people worked in these centers: Some really believed in the law, misunderstanding the dialectical belief of the working class in a "misused law"; others, more powerful, saw free legal advice as a means of social control. Although they advocated greater accessibility of the legal system for the poor, their actual concern was to restore the accessibility of the poor to the influence of the ruling legal system. Both movements belonged to the "Association of Nonprofit and Impartial Legal Advice Centers," which stated that its goal was "to avoid unnecessary litigation by peaceful mediation" (Rules, 1911: 520). This association was only one part of a much broader legalization movement united by the ideology expressed in its self-styled name, the "Peace of Law Movement" (*Rechtsfriedensbewegung*). In accordance with this ideology, these organizations did not describe their activities in any detail: Each case was unique and not worth reporting. But what they did keep promoting in numerous publications was their ideology: Make peace of the law, with the law, and by the law, avoid conflicts and solve them peacefully.

The Establishment of Free Legal Advice Centers
for the Poor

When 226,260 persons came to the forty-eight workers' offices in the single year of 1906, the bourgeoisie recognized that legal aid for workers had to become part of the pacification policy. The former minister of trade, Möller, said in the Prussian parliament: "The propaganda activities through legal counseling administered by the Social Democratic party are exceedingly vast, exceedingly intensive and exceedingly effective and we would commit grave negligence if we would not satisfy this need in a different way" (Brunner, 1906: 401). With the support of the government, communities and nonprofit organizations instituted legal aid offices offering free legal advice to all citizens (Link, 1907: 173; Stranz, 1907: 576). In 1904 the Association of Nonprofit and Impartial Legal Advice Centers was founded. During the first years of its existence, until 1909, the association got more grants than it could spend (Link, 1920: 61).

In the legal advice centers laymen worked with public functionaries, especially those concerned with legal matters within the public administration or the courts. Legal advice was to be given objectively, without partisanship. The goal of counseling was to uphold the social peace and to avoid unnecessary litigation. Beginning in 1906, for instance, the legal advice center of the Office for Social Policy in Berlin was a member of the nonprofit Association for Legal Advice in Greater Berlin, which was subsidized by the state government, local authorities, and private associations. In 1906, 96 percent of its clients were employees and 4 percent entrepreneurs. Most of the inquiries concerned labor law (27 percent), social security law (15 percent), civil law (12 percent), family law (3 percent), and penal law (7 percent). The center gave oral advice in 3027 matters and written replies in 553 (Stranz, 1907: 576).

The movement grew rapidly: In 1908 there were 60 centers (Lutz, 1908: 8), in 1910 there were 261 providing advice in 521,480 matters (Reichsarbeitsblatt, 1911),[8] and by 1913 the 410 centers counseled clients in more than half a million instances (Link, 1920: 61). If the WO secretaries are included, there were in 1913 a total of 1143 free legal advice centers for the poor, which gave oral advice in 1,982,605 matters and written responses in 521,322 (Reichsar-

---

[8]For comparison, the free unions had 111 WO secretaries in 1910, which gave legal advice in 606,508 matters (Statistische Beilage des Korrespondenzblattes, 1921: 33).

beitsblatt, 1916). At the same time, there were only 1949 community courts and 12,297 attorneys (Reichsarbeitsblatt, 1913: 312). A very small body of social legislation had led to an immense apparatus for legalizing conflicts involving the working class.

The Ideological Justification of the Peace of Law Movement: The Legal Welfare

Industrial conflicts were integrated into the legal system not only by state and capital but also by the organizations of the working class itself. At first, such an integration had been resisted on both sides. From the perspective of bourgeois society and its legal science, which was based on Roman law, social interests were alien to a legal system that owed its virtues of rationality and security to the principle of exchange and the fact that legal interests could be dealt with only through money equivalents. The Civil Code of 1900 was almost the perfect expression of this legal understanding, relegating the interests of workers in employment, housing, and consumption to the liberty of contract and thus to the market (Menger, 1904).

On the other hand, the leaders of the working class rejected the dominant legal system as an expression of the will of the ruling class. Law was seen only as a means of repression. The Eisenach program of the Social Democratic party in 1891 demanded that rule making derive from the people as well through free litigation before judges elected by the people. The struggle of the working class was seen as a political struggle that had to lead to political rights. Both positions were increasingly modified under the influence of various pressures. In the peace of law movement, the two sides came to a temporary formal and ideological consensus.

WELFARE CAPITALISM AND "VOLKSRECHT" (PEOPLE'S LAW)

The bourgeoisie in Germany had realized very early that the uncontrolled power of a Manchester-style capitalism would produce dangerous growth in the workers movement. But there was no agreement within the legal profession about how the dispossessed classes could be reconciled with the state. The prevailing Romanistic tradition of jurisprudence looked upon the rights of workers as legal exemptions that should not disturb the legal system more than was necessary in order to stabilize it. But within the smaller Germanic law tradition there was a strain of anticapitalist criticism by conservatives (e.g., Ehrlich, 1967: 85, 169ff., 190ff.) longing for a restoration of feudalism and cooperativism that would alleviate the misery of the masses by holding state and capital responsible

for their welfare but would also exclude the cultureless masses from any participation in government. Subjective right and the principle of exchange confronted
the Volksrecht and the law of cooperation and corporation. Both theoretical
currents were the expression of the unique structure of the Prussian state, the
power of which was based partly on a feudal agrarian economy in East Prussia
and partly on a developed industry in other parts of the country. In this way the
two power groups unified in "the feudal bourgeoisie" (Neumann, 1977: 28, following C. Brinkmann), and formal and communal ideologies amalgamated
within the peace of law movement. This led to the following division of labor.
Lawyers should continue their independent and partisan work within the economy, but a new type of legal representation would be created for the lower
classes—legal welfare—that would be free but impartial and oriented to the
public welfare.

These legal advice centers were intended to "popularize the law, increase
public understanding of legislation, as well as mediate and prevent litigation"
(Dittenberger, 1911: 918). Legal advice centers were prohibited from representing
clients in court, except in the social security tribunals where unions also appeared (*Ibid.*). Thus the centers were, from the beginning, concerned with
extralegal conflict resolution intended to prevent a politicization of disputes.
Their task was "not political propaganda but legal advice and legal aid" (Die
Gemeinnützige Rechtsauskunft, 1919: 43). At the third annual meeting of the
Legal Advice Association, in 1913, the principal speaker called for abandonment
of "the old liberal individualistic view... legal advice centers have to nip conflicts in the bud. Their most important contribution to the maintenance of social
peace consists in disarming apparently unfair and futile demands" (Clauss, 1913:
894). Shortly after the First World War the director and founder of the Association of Nonprofit and Impartial Legal Advice Centers summarized their role as
follows:

> But the worse the disorder and confusion the more we have to lay the basis for reconstruction. . . .
> Nothing is more embittering than to be at legal disadvantage. Therefore, if we want to free the
> masses from bitterness, if we want to give them a feeling of responsibility toward the public, we
> first have to secure the legal position of the poor. . . . Differences in wealth and education will
> never be totally equalized, but differences in legal position can be compensated and must be
> compensated. This was true before the revolution and should be true even more now [Link, 1919:
> 71].

This revolution, however, had betrayed the demands of the working class by
reason of the cooperation of leading social democrats with the military leaders
(Neumann, 1977: 34ff.). Having proclaimed the republic, they viewed the revolution as finished. Law and order and a return to work once again became the
primary civic duty. Legal aid became even more important as a safety valve for
social unrest.

The legal advice centers have to work correctly and have a thorough understanding of the social conditions and needs of the poor; they should not be bureaucratic institutions, indifferently processing one case after another. There must be helpfulness, giving confidence to every visitor. Clients have to be treated politely and considerately [*Ibid.*: 72].

In 1920, about two weeks after the general strike of the unions succeeded in putting down the reactionary Kapp revolt and saving at least the form of democracy, the principal speech at the assembly of the legal aid association contained the following:

In our economy, which has been badly damaged by political turmoil and *continuous strikes*, all struggle and quarrels have to be avoided as much as possible. To heal the sick body of the people [*Volkskörper*] all disturbances and excitement should be fended off wherever they may come from. The public legal aid office can and shall participate in serving the peace of law and preventing trials and the inevitable struggle and agitation. They shall work toward social harmonization and the consolidation of the public sense of order. . . and thus create the urgent moral rebirth of the nation [Hüttner, 1920: 92].

Even after the revolution officials of the association gratefully remembered the support of the representatives of the former Prussian minister for commerce and trade (*Ibid.*: 90).

The peace of law movement increasingly developed into a mechanism for accommodating the interests of the socially underprivileged. This tendency was made all the more obvious by the ties between the public legal aid offices and the Association of German Banks and Bankers, which were acknowledged on the occasion of the twenty-fifth anniversary of the former. Corporate members of the legal aid association in 1931 included the association of German news publishers, a chamber of commerce, and the general creditors' association (Link, 1931: 5).

SOCIAL REFORMISM AND
THE IDEOLOGY OF PARTNERSHIP

The peace of law movement would not have been so successful had it not also received support within the social democratic movement. In 1906 the unions had characterized the new institutions of public legal aid as mechanisms "to perform anti-socialist and anti-union propaganda through the instrument of the state and the communities" (Brunner, 1906: 401) and had declined to found a legal advice center in cooperation with the city of Frankfurt because they wanted to have a "center to promote the class interests" (Soudek, 1902: 28). But in 1919 the same union urged that the WO and the legal aid office be combined in a general public "welfare office" (Peikert, 1919: 296). Some workers secretaries even accepted invitations to amalgamate with public legal aid offices (Sickel, 1931: 10).

Almost everywhere broad sectors of the bourgeoisie and the workers are cooperating in preserving law and order. . . .That raises the question whether, under these circumstances, the coexistence of the public legal aid office and the workers' office is still necessary. Insofar as the workers offices refrain from subsidiary political activities there are no obstacles to a merger with the public legal aid office [Link, 1919: 67; cf. Sickel, 1931].

The leaders of the Social Democratic party tried to legitimate their politics of legalization by generalizing it into a social peace politics. The enemy of democracy was seen not on the right, from where it later came, but on the left. Franz Neumann, then a union attorney, described this in retrospect from his American exile:

The class struggle should be replaced by cooperation among the classes—this was the goal of the constitution. Its essence was compromise between all social and political groups. With the help of political pluralism, which was hidden behind the form of parliamentary democracy, the antagonistic interests should be harmonized. This theory had its roots in the interpretation of German legal history by Otto von Gierke [a theoretican of communal law and corporation], which was mixed with a strange combination of reformist socialism (Proudhon) and the social dogma of neo-Thomism [1977: 32].

This politics was represented in the peace of law movement by Radbruch (later Social Democratic minister of justice), especially in his emphatic plea for mediation (1919a: 39ff.). He defined the central social problem of the era as the loss of respect for justice. He felt that Germans were "far too irritable and prone to litigate (*Ibid.*: 39). Litigation was often less concerned with solving conflict than with disputing about honor: "The judgment necessarily violates the honor of one party and adds to the hatred of his opponent, hatred of the state and its justice" (*Ibid.*: 41). For Radbruch, law represents the society as a whole; class antagonism either does not exist or cannot be expressed because it is too dangerous. Although he alludes to a national consciousness that is competitive and quarrelsome, he calls for a "national commonweal that asks us to keep the sword of justice in its sheath by means of a civil mediation procedure" (*Ibid.*: 42). The delegalization demanded by the conservative notion of legal welfare was seconded by Radbruch.

Because its task is not to realize the law but to make peace, the mediation procedure fulfills its goal when it leads to a settlement satisfying both parties to the litigation regardless of whether the proposed settlement is based on principles of positive law or on deviant conceptions of justice [*Ibid.*: 42].

Legal norms are replaced by "norms of life" (*Ibid.*). Radbruch (1919b: 95) praises the workers' secretaries as the predecessors of a new type of lawyer who serves both disputants. He is "situated above the parties. . . . He does not serve the legal norm, the will of the state, or an abstract idea but just the parties, the social classes to whom they belong and the whole society. Their ideal is not justice but welfare in the framework of justice" (*Ibid.*).

Radbruch extends a union tradition of dispute resolution in intraclass conflict to all conflicts. Transposing the morality of the workers movement to the relations of class struggle could not help but undermine the rights of workers, because the power of capital and its capacity to structure the legal situation outside the court could not be taken into account in the compromise. Neumann (1977: 34) has pointed out that this pluralistic concept must break down, sooner or later, if society is not harmonious but antagonistic. Ideologically, the peace of law movement responded to the real need of the workers for peace and calm after the world war and the world economic crisis. But peace was reduced to immobility in the face of the existing power structure. Pseudocommunal legalization suggested the unity of interests. All people should have an equal interest in legal security and legal peace. Contradictions within the law were disguised by the formal goals of maintaining peace. Legal advice could appear as an offer to mobilize public power on behalf of underprivileged individual interests, so that collective dispute appeared to be a superfluous detour. Atomized and integrated into a strange procedure, clients became the objects of a process aimed not at advancing their interests but at avoiding conflicts. Legal advice developed into a semblance of legalization that absorbed all those individual social problems that had always been the most important elements in collective mobilization. At the same time, clients were denied the weapon of strict formal civil rights that, under certain circumstances, could be used against their creators. The destruction of the legal consciousness among the underprivileged also allowed the ruling classes to preserve their own law. Notions like *Volksrecht*, "legal hygienics," and "national public weal" reflect this.

The disguised delegalization of workers' interests contrasted with the highly developed law governing economic relations, where partisan advocacy and litigation were available for commerce and industry. The foundations of "The Dual State" were already laid (see Fraenkel, 1974).

From the Peace of Law Movement to the "National Socialist Legal Care"

In the postscript to a report about the legal advice center in Hamburg, written by a high functionary of the ministry of justice of the German empire in 1924, we find a remarkable vision. The writer asks the judges to participate in the nonprofit public legal advice centers "in order to ensure that the need of the people for mediation will not lead to a new sort of special court movement that completely excludes judges and attorneys" (Volkmar, 1924: 952). The asserted "need for a helpful mediator to guide and advise" (*Ibid.*) was no more than the expression of powerlessness of the people following the complete legalization of social conflicts. The vision of special courts for special people and the exclusion of certain social groups from ordinary courts and attorneys, and even from the law, reflected the need of the ruling classes and were realized only ten years later for Jews, communists, and socialists.

At the end of the Weimar Republic public legal advice centers were still supported by the state. In a number of directives, law clerks, assistant judges, public functionaries, and judges were allowed to give legal advice. Most advice now concerned the areas where antagonistic social interests had previously been solved by social disputes, as labor relations and landlord–tenant controversies (see Herrfurth, 1927: 434). "If the state takes care for all these things, what then is the use of the unions? This was an often repeated question in Germany" (Neumann, 1977: 476). The unions had been ideologically as well as practically disarmed by their integration into a preemptive system of cooperation and mediation (*Ibid.*: 470ff.). In 1931 there was not a single offensive strike in Germany (*Ibid.*). Legal advice and legal counseling had thus become a substitute satisfaction for social needs.

Beginning in 1930 a successful effort was made to integrate the bar into the peace of law movement. The bar was then suffering a great economic crisis. The number of attorneys had risen from 12,729 in 1923 to 17,220. The profession was not able to provide work for all of them. New fields of activity had to be found. In 1930 the council of the German bar association opened talks with the legal aid association in order to reach an agreement about the participation of attorneys in the public legal advice centers (Jessen, 1931: 6). There were isolated warnings that the transformation of the attorney into an impartial representative of the general interest in legal welfare would threaten the function of the bar in society (Fischer, 1931). But the majority of the bar prevailed, represented in the talks by Jessen, a member of the general council and a National Socialist. The directive governing legal advice (see Grimm, 1932: 33–39), worked out together by the bar and the legal aid association, adopted the notion of "legal welfare" to guide lawyers: "It cannot be denied that legal welfare has always been part of legal work and therefore is in accordance with the essence of advocacy" (Jessen, 1932: 39). Jessen makes clear the reflection of the "Dual State" in the legal order of rich and poor when he distinguishes between "advocacy" and "legal welfare."

Each actual instance of advocacy starts from the idea of serving *one* party and is therefore governed by the relation of fidelity to a client; legal welfare activity does not recognize such a connection to a single person but aims to restore disturbed legal relations in order to protect the public from legal prejudice . . . [and] serve the state, the economy, and the public welfare [*Ibid.*].

Through legal welfare work, the rule of law, "which is threatened," would be protected (*Ibid.*: 39). The president of a labor court, a member of the council of the legal aid association, gave the following answer to the question whether a poor person should be given the same "partisan, individually working attorney" that the rich person can hire: "This would be an absurd exaggeration of the welfare state. . . .The legal welfare advisor should love the client who appears before him no more than any other person concerned with this affair, and certainly no more than his presumed opponent. . . .The client should be taken care of and not represented" (Kaufmann, 1932: 41). Legal welfare, with its peace and order ideology, was now seen to have been an important element of all advocacy all along: "The bar has long practiced legal welfare on a broad scale but invisibly, because it practiced mainly charitable welfare. . . . Therefore the organizational integration of the bar into the welfare apparatus is more or less new but not the task in itself" (Fischer, 1932: 42).

A new type of attorney was born—the "legal peace attorney"—whose goal was legal peace and not the representation of "the egoism of narrow-minded people who ask the attorney to represent their rights in the way *they* see them without concern for *the* law" (Klein, 1932: 43). "The attorney as an advocate of the law should be the welfare officer of *the* law. To be a legal peace attorney should be the highest professional ideal" (*Ibid.*). The right *of the client (sein Recht)* is now displaced by *the law (das Recht)*, which seeks "to replace the legal solution by something better, if necessary to prevent avoidable disputes" (*Ibid.: 44*). In this work the attorney "will make it clear that it is not important to be right and remain right . . . but that the proper rights should be found in upholding the real law of a lasting peace . . . The attorney of the peace thus becomes a genuine people's attorney (*Volksanwalt*)" (*Ibid.*).

This genuine attorney of the people and its underlying ideology were already a part of national–socialist revolution in the legal system which antedated 1933 (see Fraenkel, 1974: 97; Neumann, 1977: 71ff.). Jessen, well known in the peace of law movement before 1933, undertook to show its significance for National Socialism:

> We [the National Socialist Lawyers Association] are, on the one hand, in a position to take over many existing ideas and conceptions as well as many practical measures of former times and thus build up our house [the National Socialist society] on a broad foundation. On the other hand, the unchangeable fact is that national renewal implies a fundamental change of views" [1933: 125].

But in fact there were not so many new elements. Legal welfare was renamed "legal care"; the advisor should be objective and oriented to the public welfare. "We do not want to bring up a nation of grumblers and gripers; those who are stubborn or vexatious shall find no support for their blameworthy behavior" (*Ibid.: 126–127*). Legal care should have an educative function for the people and should be focused on legal peace activities. After most members of the bar had joined the Association of National-Socialist German Lawyers (BNSDJ) voluntarily or under only slight pressure (Reifner, 1976a: 708), the latter organized about two-thirds of all lawyers, or some 13,000 into the "Office for Legal Care of the German *Volk*" (Raeke, 1934: 126). All public legal care institutions were then handed over to the BNSDJ under the supervision of this office. With only a few exceptions, all other legal aid institutions were forbidden because it was feared that they could have goals other than legal peace and "service to the law"[9] (Raeke, 1936: 125).

It must have seemed like an insult to the Social Democratic members of the peace of law movement that their demand that legal advice center be legally recognized as official institutions for conciliatory proceedings under Code of Civil Procedure § 495a was achieved by the National-Socialist (NS) revolution, together with their demand for nationalization of all legal aid in a "public welfare office." By 1935 there were already 1323 legal care offices in Germany whose advisors were attorneys in the BNSDJ and whose directors were named by the minister of justice of the Reich. The offices had to document each case and report it to the law office of the Reich, thereby providing the NS state with a comprehensive system of political information. All demands against the party and the state or all demands by non-Aryans were excluded from legal help (Grein, 1937: 119).

Once the bar and many of the judges had been integrated into the NS system (see Neumann, 1977: 442, 657ff.; Reifner, 1981) the persecution of Jews, communists, socialists, democrats, and other opponents of the Third Reich could be intensified. First, all attorneys in the BNSDJ were threatened with exclusion from the party if they defended a Jew in court (Circular No. 38/35, in Mitteilungsblatt des BNSDJ, Annex to Deutsches Recht). The same sanction was provided for those who defended those who had been expelled from the party (Circular No. 39/35, *ibid.*). The new law added restrictions on admission to the bar. These laws concluded the ideological integration of the bar into the peace of law movement dominated by National Socialism. At the same time, they rewarded lawyers for their ideological conformity by creating the legal aid monopoly through the "law against abuse of legal advice." By excluding anyone else, even a judge, from giving legal advice, access to the legal system and the courts was placed firmly in the hands of the National Socialist Workers Party (NSDAP), which had no difficulty in controlling the corporately organized bar. The introduction to the "law of the bar" declares the result: The attorney is the "mandated independent representative and counselor in all legal affairs. . . . His profession is not business but service to the law" (Raeke, 1936: 1).

The leader of the BNSDJ interpreted this law as follows: "Admission to the bar creates the holy obligation . . . of always putting the welfare of the national community [*Volksgemeinschaft*] above that of the individual interest represented" (*Ibid.*). Access to the law had become a public grant, for which mere

[9]This is the title of an essay by the *Führer* of the BNSDJ (Raeke, 1936: 1).

legal need was not a sufficient condition. This new form of access to law had changed the law itself because "the pursuit of objectives directed against Party and State was a contradiction to the NS legal care" (Grein, 1937: 119). A great deal of conflict was absorbed by the 1.4 million annual legal consultations provided by the legal care institutions (*Ibid.*: 134). These problems were selected: in Berlin in 1934, 1252 out of 19,120 requests for legal advice were refused (*Ibid.*). And the remainder were handled in accordance with NS policy, which now represented "*the* law," order, peace, the community, the public weal, the "internal law," public welfare, *Volksrecht*, and all the other principles invoked to justify a special legal order for the poor.

The legal advice centers of the Association of National Socialist Lawyers (BNSDJ) were also the model for the numerically much more significant centers established by the National Socialist Labor Front, which replaced the workers' offices of the free unions. The declared purpose of these centers was to "further the national socialist ideal of the 'factory community' and help to strengthen the desire to preserve industrial peace through friendly settlement of disputes outside the labor tribunals" (Bulla, 1935: 158). In 1934, 400 such centers gave legal counsel in about 3 million matters (Grein, 1937: 134). They were the only avenue to a decision in labor disputes because the Labor Front not only appointed the lay judges of the labor tribunals (two of whom assisted each professional judge) but also had a monopoly over representation of workers in those tribunals (Labor Law § 11). These centers barred Jews and other non-Aryans, as well as "demands that were morally unfounded or not in accordance with National Socialist norms or the norms of the 'Honor of Work' [*Ehre der Arbeit*]" (Official Regulations for the Legal Advice Centers of the German Labor Front, § 5, reproduced in Schmieder, 1940: 39). In 1934, these centers gave legal advice in only 36.8 percent of the matters in which they were consulted, and the percentage dropped to 22.1 the following year. This shows that the legal care model in the legal advice centers for the poor developed much more successfully in the realm of industrial conflict once the workers had been disarmed of all other social weapons with which to advance their interests (Bulla, 1935: 158).

Administrative Forms of Legal Advice and the Threat of Delegalization and Deprivation of Social Interests

The public legal advice centers had developed a practical and ideological antithesis of the earlier workers' offices. A person had to go there alone and present his problem in the form of an isolated individual accident requiring social treatment. The counselor represented the objective legal order and the state. He pursued the official goal of making peace without regard to the social and political costs to the worker. The distance between client and counselor expressed the paternalistic superiority of the latter. He alone knew the law, but he did not disclose his wisdom to the client. Instead, he persuaded the client to accept mediation and arbitration procedures. The worker, atomized and isolated from the other workers, had to believe the counselor's estimate of his chances in the legal system. Because the office did not provide any other services, all they had to offer was social apathy and an ideology that would allow the client to endure his problems better. Consequently the public legal advice centers were staffed by judges and civil servants who were familiar with the ideology of neutrality and impartiality and had learned to view the law not through apprenticeship to an advocate, as an instrument in the process of interest enforcement, but in a university, where law is presented to students as an aesthetic system of logical combinations that has to be protected from lay criticism and "social dirt." Neutrality in class conflict thus meant accepting the inhumanity of capitalist individualism. The legal protections against exploitation once offered by the Bismarck administration to appease revolutionary currents in the working class were rendered inaccessible by interposing legal care institutions between them and a now powerless working class.

The peace of law movement thus created the conditions for a system of legal care within an authoritarian state that could become an alternative to the pursuit of rights by totally separating the pacifying function inherent in law from the legitimation of claims inherent in justice. The peace of law movement divorced law and interest and made the realization of law a matter of welfare and public care. The combination of law, peace, and health gave rise to a new pejorative vocabulary for the pursuit of rights as "unhealthy" and "unpeaceful." The legal norm as the leading imperative for administration and justice was replaced by higher functions of law such as peace, public weal, and community goals, as those were politically defined by the state administration.

The peace of law movement had offered the power of the state in support of individual interests and had thereby persuaded clients to abandon collective self-help. Once the workers had confidently entered the legal system by this gate without the protection of their organizations, the way forward was increasingly barred by "higher principles" and ideologies. The workers and other underprivileged groups had thus become doubly defenseless: first by their abandonment of collective forms of interest enforcement and second by their exclusion from the system of formal civil rights.

Let me summarize this development. The liberal legal system permits individualistic litigation suitable for zero-sum economic conflicts between capitalists. But this system was inaccessible to workers who wished to pursue their social interests. As the workers became partly organized they started to use this legal system collectively, causing it to change to some degree. This pressure was counteracted in two ways: first, by repressive laws against collective action, and second, by an administrative welfare system that opened the liberal legal system to the individual workers by providing tribunals, lowering court fees, and offering more rapid decisions. Because the workers' problems now had to be channeled into this narrow social aperture, free public legal advice centers were created to act as a funnel: large and welcoming at the top (through emphasis on the fact that it was free of charge, through publicity and public support, and through the use of high-status counselors, including judges, attorneys, and civil servants) but small and constricting where it led into the legal system. At first the unorganized workers took advantage of these institutions, thereby creating a social suction that drew the organized workers into it as well, deceived by the promise of easy enforcements of their interests without significant effort on their part. In order to compete with this administrative system, the workers' offices individualized their own legal activities, as I have already shown. Thus the legal activities of unions were weakened.

When state and capital succeeded in channeling most social demands into the forms of individualistic legalization by means of the legal advice institutions, the atomized workers were repeatedly filtered by invisible barriers as they sought to assert their rights. The denial of advocacy, the substitution of mediation and arbitration procedures, the emphasis on a peace ideology, public weal, and higher principles, deference to the will of the *Führer,* and the simple elimination of other sources of help directed social demands into the canal of apathy, returning them to the starting point where they could try again. After 1933 this form of "prelegalization" into a vicious circle of self-defeating activities finally robbed workers of all real legalization.

The tragedy of Social Democrats in this movement lay in their confidence in the social development of law (Sinzheimer, 1932: 164ff.) and in the democratic institutions of the state. Although the peace of law movement had always believed that abolishing the legal needs of the poor would help a good deal toward the pacification of the German nation (and, amazingly, continued to do so as late as 1936), those who really cared for the welfare of the poor lacked the skepticism toward the state that had warned the social movements of other nations not to surrender the use of collective weapons or the barriers of formal rights in exchange for the promise of individual welfare.

The development from social struggle to the struggle for the law, from legal aid through legal welfare to legal care, reveals an important danger inherent in every criticism of the dominant legal system that demands more social responsibility, more care for the poor, less formalism, less abstraction, less legalization—in short, that seeks an administrative form of legalization. If the organized power of the people concerned secures these changes within the legal system or if it is impossible to give these new substantive and procedural rights the same legal form as the principles of civil law, those sought to be helped are deprived of the last chance to change their living conditions and to escape the paternalism of total care and tutelage.

Law always depends on the social power of those whose interests it purports to protect. Ideologies that ignore this dependence by changing the rights *of* people into rights *for* people lead inevitably to deprivation of those rights. On the other hand, legal help that serves to organize the social power of the underprivileged—i.e., collective legal aid—will not only help the individual but also secure and extend the legal position of the collectivity. As long as there is no real chance for the poor to develop their own social power the formal principles of the civil law cannot be abandoned for the sake of a few welfare rights because the ruling power can always destroy social rights but not the basis of its own power, the civil law.

CONCLUSION

If law as coercive power, as tamed despotism (Hofmann, 1968: 1), will die one day, it will die only because it has attained its highest form. We therefore must develop legalization in accordance with the development (*Vergesellschaftung*) of society into higher and socially more adequate forms. Delegalization is meaningful only in the context of this development. It is always a step in the legalization process—either backwards to readapt social reality to antiquated legal forms or forward to develop higher forms of action that produce higher forms of legalization. In this development legalization is progressive if it tends to subordinate the legal person to the real person and his or her social needs.

The legal profession has a double task in this development. First, it must derive from the ideology of liberal legalism the forms of its social realization, thereby developing the ideal order of a future society as a basis for criticizing the present (Trubek, 1977: 556). Second, it has to adapt legalization to the needs of collective action, transforming legalization from a means of repressing collective needs and action into an instrument serving these needs and actions.

Collective legalization and the fight for individual liberal rights can never oppose each other. Because only a collective society and a collective legal system based on solidarity, prevention, and unity of interests can fulfill the functions that liberal subjective rights purport to perform (but do so only by creating a mystifying individualistic ideology)—namely, the promotion of liberty, equality, and security of real individuals—the rise of collectivity can never legitimate the abolition of individual rights. Legal advice is progressive in this context if it prevents individualization, supplies legal instruments for collective action, submits in practice to social action while ideologically guiding such action toward a new social order, is based on the social power of its clients, enhances this power, and tends to foster democratic institutions whose members govern collectively.

REFERENCES

Abel, R. (1979) "Delegalization—A Critical Review of Its Ideology, Manifestations, and Social Consequences," in E. Blankenburg, E. Klausa, and H. Rottleuthner (eds.) *Alternative Rechtsformen und Alternativen zum Recht*. Opladen: Westdeutscher Verlag (Jahrbuch für Rechtssoziologie und Rechtstheorie, Bd. 6).

Althusser, L. (1973) "Ideologie und Ideologische Staatsapparate," in L. Althusser, *Marxismus und Ideologie*. West Berlin: VSA (orig. publ. "Idéologie et appareils idéologiques d'Etat," *La Pensée*, No. 151, June 1970).

Balbus, I. (1977) "Commodity Form and Legal Form: An Essay on the 'Relative Autonomy' of the Law," 11 *Law & Society Review* 571.

Basso, L. (1973) "Die Rolle des Rechts in der Phase des Übergangs zum Sozialismus," 3 *Kritische Justiz* 313.

Bernstein, E. (1910) "Geschichte der Berliner Arbeiterbewegung," 1 *Correspondenzblatt der Generalkommission der Gewerkschaften Deutschlands* 31.

Black, D. (1976) *The Behavior of Law*. New York: Academic Press.

Blanke, Th., R. Erd, U. Mückenberger, and U. Stascheit (eds.) (1975) *Kollektives Arbeitsrecht— Quellentexte zur Geschichte des Arbeitsrechts in Deutschland*, vol. 1. Reinbeck: Rowohlt.

Blankenburg, E. and U. Reifner (1979) "Rechtshilfe als Teil eines Beratungssystems," in T. Rasehorn (ed.) *Rechtsberatung als Lebenshilfe*. Darmstadt/Neuwied: Luchterhand.

Blankenburg, E., R. Rogowski, and S. Schönholz (1978) "Phänomene der Verrechtlichung und ihre Folgen." West Berlin: Science Center, International Institute of Management (Discussion Paper dp/77–64).

Bremerhaven (1905, 1906, 1907, 1908) *Bericht des Arbeitersekretariats und des Gewerkschaftskartells für Bremerhaven und Umgegend. Geschäftsjahr 1905* 1906, 1907, 1908. Bremerhaven.

———— (1909, 1910, 1911, 1912, 1913) *Arbeitersekretariat und Gewerkschaftskartell für Bremerhaven und Umgegend—Geschäftsbericht für das Jahr 1909, 1910, 1911, 1912, 1913*. Bremerhaven.

Brunner, L. (1904) "Die deutschen Arbeitersekretariate im Jahre 1903," 42 *Correspondenzblatt der Generalkommission der Gewerkschaften Deutschlands* 699.

———— (1906) "Die deutschen Arbeitersekretariate im Jahre 1905" in 25 *Correspondenzblatt der Generalkommission der Gewerkschaften Deutschlands* 385.

Bulla (1935) "Ein Jahr Rechtsberatung der Deutschen Arbeitsfront," 6 *Deutsches Arbeitsrecht* 158.

Cappelletti, M., B. Garth, and N. Trocker (1976) "Access to Justice, Comparative General Report," 40 *Rabelszeitung* 669.

Carlin, J., J. Howard, and S. Messinger (1967) *Civil Justice and the Poor*. New York: Russell Sage Foundation.

Cerroni, U. (1974) *Marx und das moderne Recht*. Frankfurt: Fischer (orig. publ. *Marx e il diritto moderno*. Rome: Editori Riuniti, 1962).

Clauss, F. (1913) "Vierte Hauptversammlung des Verbandes der gemeinnützigen und umparteiischen Rechtsauskunftstellen," 20 *Deutsche Richterzeitung* 892.

Correspondenzblatt (1919) "Die Zukunft der Arbeitersekretariate," 48 *Correspondenzblatt der Generalkommission der Gewerkschaften Deutschlands* 553.

Deppe, F., G. Fülberth, H.-J. Harrer *et al.* (1977) *Geschichte der deutschen Gewerkschaftsbewegung*. Cologne: Pahl-Rugenstein.

Dittenberger (1911) "Bericht über die Tagung des Verbandes der deutschen gemeinnützigen und unparteiischen Rechtsauskunftsstellen," 19 *Juristische Wochenschrift* 918.

Edelman, B. (1973) *Le droit saisi par la photographie (Elément pour une théorie marxiste du droit)*. Paris: Maspero (trans. as *Ownership of the Image*. Boston: Routledge and Kegan Paul, 1979).

Ehrlich, E. (1967) *Grundlegung der Soziologie des Rechts*, 3d ed. Berlin: Dunker and Humblot (published in English as *Fundamental Principles of the Sociology of Law*. Cambridge, Mass.: Harvard University Press, 1936).

Engels, F. (1976) *Die Lage der arbeitenden Klassen in England*, in *Marx/Engels Werke*, vol. 2. Berlin (DDR): Dietz (orig. publ. 1845).

Engels, F. and K. Kautsky (1972) "Juristensozialismus," in Reich (ed.) *Marxistische und sozialistische Rechtstheorie*. Kronberg: Athenäum (orig. publ. 1890).

Engisch, K. (1968) *Einführung in das juristische Denken*, 4th ed. Stuttgart/Berlin/Cologne: Kohlhammer.

Erd, R. (1978) *Verrechtlichung industrieller Beziehungen*. Frankfurt on the Main: Campus.

Fischer (1931) "Die Entwicklung der Rechtsauskunftstellen," 16 *Recht und Leben, Wochenbeilage der Vossischen Zeitung* (April 16).

Fraenkel, E. (1932) "Die politische Bedeutung des Arbeitsrechts," reprinted in Ramm (ed.) *Arbeitsrecht und Politik*. Frankfurt on the Main: Luchterhand, 1976.

——— (1974) *Der Doppelstaat*. Frankfurt on the Main: EVA (orig. publ. as *The Dual State*, Chicago, 1940).

Fülberth, G. (1977) "Exkurs: Probleme der Gewerkschaften in der Theorie von Karl Marx und Friedrich Engels," in F. Deppe, G. Fülberth, H.-J. Harrer *et al. Geschichte der deutschen Gewerkschaftsbewegung*. Cologne: Pahl-Rugenstein.

Galanter, M. (1974) "Why the 'Haves' Come Out Ahead: Speculations on the Limits of Legal Change, 9 *Law & Society Review* 95.

——— (1976) "Delivering Legality: Some Proposals for the Direction of Research," 11 *Law & Society Review* 225.

——— (1979) "Legality and Its Discontents: Some Preliminary Notes on Current Theories of Legalization and Delegalization," in E. Blankenburg, E. Klausa, and H. Rottleuthner (eds.) *Alternative Rechtsformen und Alternativen zum Recht*. Opladen: Westdeutscher Verlag (Jahrbuch für Rechtssoziologie und Rechtstheorie, Bd. 6) 11.

Galbraith, J. K. (1968) *The New Industrial State*. New York: Signet.

Galtung, J. (1973) "Institutionalisierte Konfliktlösung," in Bühl (ed.) *Konflikt und Konfliktstrategie*, 2d ed. Munich: Numphenburger.

Geiger, Th. (1964) *Vorstudien zu einer Soziologie des Rechts*. Darmstadt/Neuwied: Luchterhand.

Gemeinnützige Rechtsauskunft, Die (1919) *Rechtsauskunftsstellen und Arbeitersekretariate*, Nr. 5, S. 43.

Grein, P. (1937) *Die unentgeltliche Rechtsberatung Minderbemittelter in Deutschland*. Berlin: Junker und Dünnhaupt.

Griffiths, J. (1977) "The Distribution of Legal Services in the Netherlands," 4 *British Journal of Law and Society* 260.

——— (1980) "A Comment on Research into 'Legal Needs,'" in E. Blankenburg (ed.) *Innovations in the Legal Services*. Konigstein: Verlag Anton Hein.

Grimm (1932) "Die Verhandlungen des Verbandes der Rechtsauskunftstellen mit dem Deutschen Anwaltverein über die Mitarbeit der Rechtsanwaltschaft bei der Rechtsfürsorge," 5/6 *Die Rechtsauskunft* 33.

Habermas, J. (1968) *Erkenntnis und Interesse*. Frankfurt on the Main: Suhrkamp.

Hahn, E. (1974) *Theoretische Probleme der marxistischen Soziologie*. Cologne: Pahl-Rugenstein.

Halpern, Ch. (1980) "Introduction: The Public Interest Law Movement in the USA," in E. Blankenburg (ed.) *Innovations in the Legal Services*. Konigstein: Verlag Anton Hein.

Handler, J. (1980) "Social Movements and the Legal System," in E. Blankenburg (ed.) *Innovations in the Legal Services*. Konigstein: Verlag Anton Hein.

Harburg (1903–1906; 1912) 1.–4., 10., 11. *Bericht des Arbeitersekretariats und Gewerkschaftskartells Harburg (Elbe)—unter Berücksichtigung der gewerkschaftlichen Entwicklung seit 1890 erstattet für das Jahr 1903, 1904, 1905, 1906, 1912, 1913*. Harburg: Verlag des Arbeitersekretariats.

Hartwich, H. H. (1970) *Sozialstaatspostulat und gesellschaftlicher status quo.* Cologne/Opladen: Westdeutscher Verlag.

Harvard Law Review (1976) "Developments in the Law—Class Actions," 89 *Harvard Law Review* 1319.

Henning, F.-W. (1974) *Das industrialisierte Deutschland 1914 bis 1972.* Paderborn: UTB Schöningh.

Herrfurth (1927) "Gemeinnützige Rechtsauskunft und Rechtspflege," 11 *Deutsche Richterzeitung* 433.

Hofmann, W. (1968) "Die Krise des Staates und des Rechts," 1 *Kritische Justiz* 1.

Hofrichter, R. (1982) "Neighborhood Justice and the Social Control Problems of American Capitalism: A Perspective," in R. L. Abel (ed.) *The Politics of Informal Justice,* vol. 1: *The American Experience.* New York: Academic Press.

Hüttner (1920) "Die gegenwärtige Lage der geneinnützigen Rechtsauskunft und des Verbandes der Rechtsauskunftsstellen" in 9/10 *Die Gemeinnützige Rechtsauskunft* 89.

Jessen (1931) "Rechtsauskunftsstellen und Anwaltschaft," 1 *Die Rechtsauskunft* 6.

⸻ (1932) "Rechtsfürsorge und Anwaltschaft," 5/6 *Die Rechtsauskunft* 39.

⸻ (1933) "Rechtsbetreuung der deutschen Anwaltschaft," 10/11 *Die Rechtsauskunft,* 125.

Kahn-Freund, O. (1932) "Der Funktionswandel des Arbeitsrechts," reprinted in T. Ramm (ed.) *Arbeitsrecht und Rechtssoziologie.* Frankfurt on the Main: EVA, 1976.

Kamenka, E. and A. S. Tay (1975) "Beyond Bourgeois Individualism: The Contemporary Crisis in Law and Legal Ideology," in E. Kamenka and R. Neale (eds.) *Feudalism, Capitalism and Beyond.* London: Edward Arnold.

Kampffmeyer, P. (1901) "Ein Wort über die deutschen Arbeitersekretariate" 16 *Archiv. soziale Gesetzgebung und Statistik* 393.

Kaufmann (1932) "Rechtsfürsorge und Armenanwalt," 5/6 *Die Rechtsauskunft* 40.

Kennedy, D. (1976) "Form and Substance in Private Law Adjudication," 89 *Harvard Law Review,* 1685.

Kiel (1901) *Arbeitersekretariat für Kiel und Umgegend: Bericht für das erste Geschäftsjahr (11. Juli bis 31. Dezember) und Kassenbericht.* Kiel: Selbstverlag des Arbeitersekretariats.

⸻ (1902, 1903 . . . 1910) *Zweiter, dritter . . . zehnter Jahresbericht des Arbeitersekretariats für Kiel und Umgegend Geschäftsjahr 1902, 1903 . . . 1910.* Kiel: Selbstverlag des Arbeitersekretariats.

⸻ (1911, 1912 . . . 1921) *Das Gewerkschaftsleben in Kiel im Jahre 1911, 1912, . . . 1921.* Kiel: Selbstverlag des Gewerkschaftskartells in Kiel.

Klein (1932) "Rechtsfriedensanwalt," 5/6 *Die Rechtsauskunft* 43.

Korrespondenzblatt der Generalkommission der Gewerkschaften Deutschlands (1890–1921). Berlin (published as Correspondenzblatt until 1919).

Kuczynski, J. (1967) *Die Geschichte der Lage der Arbeiter unter dem Kapitalismus.* Berlin (DDR): Akademie (Darstellung der Lage der Arbeiter in Deutschland von 1900 bis 1917/18, vol. 4).

Legien (1905) "Die deutschen Arbeitersekretariate im Jahre 1904," 22 *Correspondenzblatt der Generalkommission der Gewerkschaften Deutschlands* 345.

Leipzig (1904) *Erster Jahresbericht des Arbeitersekretariats Leipzig für das Jahr 1904.* Leipzig: Kommissionsverlag.

⸻ (1905, 1906) *Das Leipziger Arbeitersekretariat und die Leipziger Gewerkschaften im Jahre 1905/1906.* Leipzig: Kommissionsverlag.

Lenin, W. I. (1970) "Staat und Revolution," in: W. I. Lenin *Ausgewählte Werke,* vol. 2, 8th ed. Berlin (DDR): Dietz.

Link (1907) "Rechtskonsulenten und Rechtsauskunftsstellen," 9 *Die Arbeiterversorgung* 173 (March 20).

_____ (1919) "Die gemeinnützige Rechtsauskunft im neuen Deutschland," 8 *Die Gemein-nützige Rechtsauskunft* 71.

_____ (1920) "Geschäftsbericht des Verbandes der deutschen gemeinnützigen und unparteiischen Rechtsauskunftstellen über die Zeit vom 1 Oktober 1913 bis 32 März 1920," 6/7 *Die Gemein-nützige Rechtsauskunft* 61.

_____ (1931) "25 Jahre Verband der Rechtsauskunftstellen," 1 *Die Rechtsauskunft* 1.

Luhmann, N. (1974) *Rechtssystem und Rechtsdogmatik*. Stuttgart/Berlin/Cologne: Kohlhammer.

Lübeck (1901, 1902... 1915) *Erster, zweiter... 15. Jahres-Bericht des Arbeiter-Sekretariats in Lübeck*. Lübeck: Selbstverlag.

Lukaschewa, J. A. (1976) *Sozialistisches Rechtsbewußtsein und Gesetzlichkeit*. Berlin (DDR): Staatsverlag der DDR (orig. publ. Moscow, 1973).

Lutz (1908) "Schädigen die Rechtsauskunftsstellen für Minderbemittelte die Anwaltschaft in wirtschaftlicher Hinsicht?" 3 *Juristische Wochenschrift* 8.

Maine, H. S. (1969) "From Status to Contract," in V. Aubert (ed.) *Sociology of Law*. Harmondsworth: Penguin.

Marcuse, H. (1975) *Der eindimensionale Mensch*. Neuwied/Berlin: Luchterhand.

Martiny, M. (1975) "Die politische Bedeutung der gewerkschaftlichen Arbeiter-Sekretariate vor dem Ersten Weltkrieg," in H. O. Vetter (ed.) *Vom Sozialistengesetz zur Mitbestimmung, Zum 100. Geburtstag von Hans Böckler*. Cologne: Bund.

Marx, K. (1963) The Eighteenth Brumaire of Louis Bonaparte. New York: International Publishers.

_____ (1969) *Das Kapital—Kritik der politischen Ökonomie*, vols. 1 and 3. Berlin (DDR): Dietz.

_____ (1969a) "Einleitung zur Kritik der politischen Ökonomie," in *Marx/Engels Werke*, vol. 13, Berlin (DDR): Dietz.

_____ (1969b) "Zur Kritik der Hegelschen Rechtsphilosophie. Kritik des Hegelschen Staatsrechts," in *Marx/Engels Werke*, vol. 1. Berlin (DDR): Dietz.

_____ (1969c) "Thesen über Feuerbach," in *Marx/Engels Werke*, vol. 3. Berlin (DDR): Dietz.

Menger, A. (1904) *Das Bürgerliche Recht und die besitzlosen Volksklassen*, 3d ed. Tübingen: H. Laupp.

Miaille, M. (1976) *Une introduction critique au droit*. Paris: Maspero.

Michel, B. (1978) "Der Kampf der Gewerkschaften um die einheitliche Arbeitsgerichtsbarkeit," in K. Feser *et al.* (eds.) *Arbeitsgerichtsprotokolle*. Darmstadt/Neuwied: Luchterhand.

Mombert, P. (1905) "Neuere sozialstatistische Erhebungen deutscher Arbeiterverbände," 3 *Archiv für Sozialwissenschaft und Sozialpolitik* 248 (Neue Folge).

Monatsschau der Rechtsfürsorge (1933) "Kritik an anwaltschaftlichen Rechtsfürsorgestellen," 6 *Die Rechtsauskunft* 82.

Morizet (1903) *Les sécrétariats ouvrièrs en Allemagne*. Paris.

Morris, P. (1973) "A Sociological Approach to Research in Legal Services," in P. Morris, R. White, and P. Lewis (eds.) *Social Needs and Legal Action*. London: Martin Robertson.

Mottek, H., W. Becker, and A. Schröter (1974) *Wirtschaftsgeschichte Deutschlands—Ein Grundriβ*, vol. 3, Berlin (DDR): VEB Deutscher Verlag der Wissenschaften.

Mückenberger, W. (1975) Review of Wolfgang Däubler, *Das Grundrecht auf Mitbestimmung*, 1 *Kritische Justiz* 57.

Müller, A. (1904) *Arbeitersekretariate und Arbeiterversicherung in Deutschland*. Munich: Birk.

Nader, R. (1976) "Consumerism and Legal Services: The Merging of Movements," 11 *Law & Society Review* 247.

Negt, O. (1973) "Thesen zur marxistischen Rechtstheorie," 1 *Kritische Justiz* 1

Neumann, Franz (1957) The Change in the Function of Law in Modern Society, in *The Democratic and the Authoritarian State* (H. Marcuse ed.). New York: Macmillan.

_____ (1977) Behemoth: Struktur und Praxis des Nationalsozialismus 1933–1944. Cologne/

Frankfurt on the Main: EVA (published in English as Behemoth. New York: Octagon Books, 1963).

Nonet, Pz. and Pz. Selznick (1978) *Law and Society in Transition: Toward Responsive Law.* New York: Harper Colophon Books.

Paschukanis, E. B. (1966) *Allgemeine Rechtslehre und Marxismus.* Frankfurt on the Main: EVA. (orig. publ. 1926)

―――― (1972) "Für eine marxistische-leninistische Staats—und Rechtstheorie," in N. Reich (ed.) *Marxistische und sozialistische Rechtstheorie.* Frankfurt on the Main: Fischer Athenäum (orig. publ. 1931).

Peikert (1919) "Die Sozialisierung der Arbeitersekretariate," 26 *Correspondenzblatt der Generalkommission der Gewerkschaften Deutschlands* 295.

Raeke (1936) "Dienst am Recht," 1 *Juristische Wochenschrift* 1.

Radbruch (1919a) "Das Güteverfahren und das deutsche Rechtsgefühl," 5 *Die gemeinnützige Rechtauskunft* 39.

―――― (1919b) "Das Recht im sozialen Volksstaat," 10/11 *Die Gemeinnützige Rechtsauskunft* 95.

Reichsarbeitsblatt (1911, 1913, 1916) Die Rechtsberatung der minderbemittelten Volkskreise, Amtliche Statistik, Sonderbeilage.

Reifner, U. (1976) "Gewerkschaftliche Anwälte in Frankreich," 3 *Kritische Justiz* 258.

―――― (1976a) "Das System der Rechtsberatung in der Bundesrepublik Deutschland: Probleme und Tendenzen," 17 *Juristenzeitung* 504.

―――― (1978) "Zugangs und Erfolgsbarrieren in der Justiz." West Berlin: Science Center, International Institute of Management (Discussion Paper dp/78–97 2, 4 Demokratie umol Recht 1981)

―――― (1979) *Alternatives Wirtschaftsrecht—Am Beispiel: Verbraucherverschuldung.* Darmstadt/Neuwied: Luchterhand.

―――― (1980) "Legal Needs and Legalization—The Example of a Tenants' Rights Group in Berlin," in E. Blankenburg (ed.) *Innovations in the Legal Services.* Konigstein: Verlag Anton Hein.

―――― (ed). (1981) *Das faschistische Rechtssystems.* Frankfurt and New York: Campus.

Reifner, U. and I. Gorges (1979) "Alternativen der Rechtsberatung: Dienstleistung, Fürsorge und kollektive Selbsthilfe," in E. Blankenburg *et al.* (eds.) *Alternative Rechtsforem und Alternativen zum Recht.* Opladen: Westdeutscher Verlag (Jahrbuch für Rechtssoziologie und Rechtstheorie, Bd. 6).

Rottleuthner, H. *et al.* (1979) *Zwischenbericht zum Projekt "Probleme der Arbeitsgerichtsbarkeit."* Berlin (unpublished).

Rules for the Public Legal Advice Center (1911) 19 *Juristische Wochenschrift* 918.

Santos, Boaventura de Sousa (1978) "The Law of the Oppressed: The Construction and Reproduction of Legality in Pasargada," 12 *Law & Society Review* 5.

Schmieder, E. (1940) Die Rechtsberatung in der Deutschen Arbeitsfront. Dissertation, Universität Freiburg.

Schuyt, K., K. Groenendijk, and B. Sloot (1976) *De Weg naar het Recht.* Deventer: Kluwer.

Seifert, J. (1971) "Verrechtlichte Politik und die Dialektik der marxistischen Rechtstheorie," 2 *Kritische Justiz.*

Séve, L. (1972) *Marxismus und Theorie der Persönlichkeit.* Frankfurt on the Main: Marxistische Blätter (orig. publ. as *Marxisme et la théorie de la personalité.* Paris: Éditions Sociales, 1972).

Sickel (1931) "25 Jahre gemeinnützige Rechtsauskunft in Erfurt," 1 *Die Rechtsauskunft* 10.

Sinzheimer, H. (1915) "Der Tarifgedanke in Deutschland," reprinted in T. Ramm and O. Kahn-Freund (eds.) *Arbeitsrecht und Rechtssoziologie,* vol. 1. Frankfurt on the Main: EVA, 1976.

―――― (1932) "Das Weltbild des bürgerlichen Rechts," reprinted in T. Ramm and O. Kahn-Freund (eds.) *Arbeitsrecht und Rechtssoziologie: Gesammelte Aufsätze und Reden,* vol. 2. Frankfurt on the Main: EVA, 1976.

———— (1934) "Die Theorie der Rechtsquellen und das Arbeitsrecht," reprinted in T. Ramm and O. Kahn-Freud (eds.) *Arbeitsrecht und Rechtssoziologie*, vol. 2. Frankfurt on the Main: EVA, 1976.

Soudek, R. (1902) *Die deutschen Arbeitersekretariate*. Leipzig: Jäh & Schanke.

Statistische Beilage des Korrespondenzblattes (1921) "Die Arbeitersekretariate im Deutschen Reiche im Jahre 1920," 2 *Korrespondenzblatt des Algemeinen Deutschen Gewerkschaftsbundes* 330.

Stranz (1907) "Juristische Rundschau," 10 *Deutsche Juristenzeitung* 576.

Stucka, P. I. (1969) *Die revolutionäre Rolle von Recht und Staat*. Frankfurt on the Main: Suhrkamp.

Sykes, G. M. (1969) "The Legal Needs of the Poor in the City of Denver," 4 *Law & Society Review* 225.

Trubek, D. (1977) "Complexity and Contradiction in the Legal Order: Balbus and the Challenge of Critical Social Thought about Law," 11 *Law & Society Review* 529.

Trubek, D., L. Trubek, and J. Becker (1980) "Legal Services and Administrative State: From Public Interest Law to Public Advocacy," in E. Blankenburg (ed.) *Innovations in the Legal Services*. Konigstein: Verlag Anton Hein.

Turk, A. T. (1976) "Law as a Weapon in Social Conflict," 23 *Social Problems* 276.

Umbreit (1903) "Die deutschen Arbeitersekretariate im Jahre 1903," 26 *Correspondenzblatt der Generalkommission der Gewerkschaften Deutschlands* 401.

Unger, R. M. (1974) *Law in Modern Society—Toward a Criticism of Social Theory*. New York: Free Press.

Volkmar (1924) "Postface," 23/24 *Deutsche Juristenzeitung* 452.

Wagner, H. (1976) *Recht als Widerspiegelung und Handlungsinstrument*. Cologne: Pahl-Rugenstein.

Waldenburg (1915, 1916) Jahresbericht des Waldenburger Arbeitersekretariats der freien Gewerkschaften für das Jahr 1915, 1916. Waldenburg.

Weber, M. (1972) *Wirtschaft und Gesellschaft*. Tübingen: Mohr.

Zukunft der Arbeitersekretariate, Die (1919) 48 *Correspondenzblatt der Generalkommission der Gewerkschaften Deutschlands* 553.

5

The Politics of Informal Justice: The Japanese Experience, 1922-1942

JOHN OWEN HALEY

Between 1922 and 1942 the imperial Japanese government enacted a series of statutes providing for formal conciliation (*chōtei*) as a substitute for trials (*soshō*) in an increasing variety of civil disputes. The first was the Land Lease and House Lease Conciliation Law (No. 41, 1922). This was followed by the Farm Tenancy Conciliation Law (No. 18, 1924), the Labor Disputes Conciliation Law (No. 57, 1926), the Commercial Affairs Conciliation Law (No. 42, 1926), the Monetary Claims Temporary Conciliation Law (No. 26, 1932), the Agricultural Land Adjustment Law (No. 67, 1938), the Personal Status Conciliation Law (No. 11, 1939), the conciliation provisions appended to the Mining Law (No. 215, 1905, as amended by No. 23, 1939), the amendment of the Placer Mines Law (No. 13, 1909, as amended by No. 103, 1940), and finally, in 1942, the comprehensive conciliation measures of the Special Wartime Civil Affairs Law (No. 63, 1942).

In the debate surrounding these statutes, the justifications offered in their support and the criticisms leveled against them were specific and pointed. The proponents viewed litigation as both symptom and cause of a threatening process of social disintegration. Conciliation was thus conceived as a panacea by those who embraced what has aptly been described as the "collectivistic ethic" of the

125

prewar period (Dore and Ōuchi, 1971). Its critics, mostly lawyers, perceived that nothing less than the private law system and liberal legal order was at stake. The substitution of compromise for vindication of legal rights and the application of extralegal norms in lieu of the substantive provisions of the law made private law a meaningless appendage of the Japanese political and social order. In a real sense both were correct, and few episodes in modern Japanese legal history reveal as starkly the contrasts between the underlying assumptions of Western law and Japan's traditional ideology. The purpose of this chapter is to describe the debate and its background, to evaluate Japan's experience with conciliation during this period, and finally to suggest some conclusions and questions from the Japanese experience that seem especially relevant beyond Japan's borders.

THE IMPETUS TOWARD CONCILIATION

Rights versus Duties:
Western Law and the Japanese Tradition

At the end of World War I, Japan had concluded nearly three decades of experience with its Western-derived legal system. The institutional framework had been completed with the promulgation of the Meiji Constitution in 1889 and enactment of the Court Organization Law and Administrative Court Law in 1890. By 1898 the long process of drafting and legislating a comprehensive set of substantive and procedural codes had all but ended with the adoption of the last two books of the Civil Code (on relatives and succession). Japan had a well-trained career judiciary and procuracy as well as a rapidly growing practicing bar. Law faculties, especially that of Tokyo Imperial University, had become Japan's most prestigious educational establishments. Thus Japan's leaders could justifiably boast of success in adopting a new Western-based legal system.

Their achievement owed much, however, to the foundations on which it rested. Japan under Tokugawa rule (1603–1867) had developed a highly structured and sophisticated legal system that had much in common with the imported codes and courts (see Henderson, 1965). From registries to judicial methods, commercial practices to procedural forms, there were ample indigenous analogues to the legal institutions borrowed from the West. Thus, as described later in the chapter, departures from tradition in the substantive provisions of the imported codes and judicial institutions could be accommodated easily within the new system—but for one element.

Roman civilization bequeathed to the West a legal tradition that made private law central. The critical element of this tradition, and of private law itself, is the concept of legal rights. Roman law was primarily a system of rights defined as the claims of individuals to protection by specific procedures and remedies. Stripped to its essentials, the notion of a legal right in Western law expresses the capacity of the individual to activate and control the process of enforcing legal norms. Although we use the term more broadly—for instance, to define property—other terms such as *interests, estates,* or *entitlements* are more appropriate. The notion of a legal right is meaningful, therefore, only when it entitles the holder to legal protection upon demand. In a legal order such as that of Tokugawa Japan, in which those who exercise authority ultimately control the legal process, legal rights become irrelevant. This is not to say that property or other legally recognized interests are not protected or that relief for infringement or violation of legal norms is not forthcoming. It is possible, for example, to enforce contractual undertakings by invoking the simple injunction to honor one's promises, whose violation carries penalties, including remedial measures. Yet to the extent that the process for enforcing the penalty depends upon the discretion of a magistrate or other official, the parties may have duties—they do not enjoy rights. A party possesses private law rights only when the discretion of the magistrate is sufficiently limited that the party can require that relief be granted. Thus the Roman law maxim *ubi ius, ibi remedium* ("where there is a right, there is a remedy") is more than an aphorism. It expresses the crux of private law and the Western legal tradition. Few concepts, however, could have been as alien to traditional Japanese ideology.

By the mid-seventeenth century, the *Chu Hsi* Confucian doctrine disseminated by Japanese Neo-Confucian scholars had become the dominant intellectual force in Japan. It was especially attractive to the Tokugawa political regime as a rationalizing ideology that did not simply justify the existing feudal hierarchy but rendered it immutable as part of the static natural order. In this Neo-Confucian system all human ties could be reduced to the Five Relationships, three of which were familial: father and child, husband and wife, elder brother and younger. (The remaining two were sovereign and subject and friend and friend.) The moral imperatives of loyalty (*chū*) and filial piety (*kō*), for subject and child, and benevolence (*jō*) and righteousness (*reigi*), for sovereign and father, became the guiding ethical precepts for all hierarchial social and political relationships. The ultimate value was to approximate in human affairs the harmony (*wa*) and equilibrium found in nature. As expressed by Kumazawa Banzan:

> In heaven and earth, when the four seasons occur in accordance with the Four Virtues of Heaven, and the heavens and earth are properly positioned, all things grow. When man adheres to the qualities of benevolence, righteousness, propriety, and wisdom, and the Five Relationships are clearly upheld, then the family will be regulated, the state will be in order, and there will be peace in the world [Maruyama, 1974: 202].

Despite Neo-Confucian recognition of reciprocal obligations—for example, benevolence in return for loyalty—any notion of remedial rights was clearly antipathetic. The imperatives of loyalty and filial piety precluded any thought of asserting a claim as of right. Coerced conduct, by definition, could not constitute benevolence. Consequently, in giving formal expression to Neo-Confucian orthodoxy, positive Tokugawa law followed the Chinese *ritsūryō* format of criminal penalties and administrative regulations. Described in contemporary terms, it was a public law system in which legal norms were articulated in the form of duties and remedial protection was subject to the discretion of public authorities.

Although a money economy led to increasing litigation and a semblance of private law, such a Neo-Confucian order abhorred litigation and refused to recognize a legal right of access to the formal adjudicatory process (Henderson, 1965). Neo-Confucian ideology compelled the Tokugawa system to prohibit suits between those of different status and require that equals exhaust all means of compromise and conciliation before bringing suit. Even then the judge could enforce a compromise and chastise the litigants for failing to conduct themselves with proper decorum and to abide by Confucian precepts.

In this context, the primacy of private law in nineteenth-century Western legal systems and the consequent emphasis on justiciable rights meant that inherent in the modern Japanese legal order was a notion antithetical to its fundamental precepts. As a lifeless abstraction the idea of legal rights perhaps would have caused little concern, but their exercise in court was increasingly perceived as a significant threat to Japan's social and political order.

From the Civil Code Controversy to the
Rinji Hōsei Shingikai

Traditionalist concerns over the underlying notions of Western private law surfaced first in the final stages of the process of adopting a civil code. Controversy began almost immediately after the promulgation of the Civil Code of 1890, which had been guided to completion by the French scholar Gustav Boissonade. Two factions rapidly formed. One pressed for postponement and was led by members of the Law Scholars Society, almost all of whom had been educated at Tokyo University at a time when it was heavily influenced by English law. The other, which urged passage, was dominated by a French law faction educated at the Ministry of Justice Law School. Superficially, the issue might appear to have been which Western legal system—French or German—should prevail, not whether any Western law should serve as a model for Japan's civil law. The outcome of the debate was, in fact, the adoption of a second code, which was based in large part on the first draft of the German Civil Code and was later transformed into even more of a German product through academic gloss, even though it included provisions derived from English and French sources.

At a more profound level, the reaction to the 1890 code reflected early misgivings about the system of Western private law itself. As one might expect, opposition to the 1890 code focused on the Book of Persons, which contained the provisions most threatening to the familistic tradition and ideological underpinnings of the Meiji state. Hozumi Yatsuka, the ideological leader of the postponement faction, provided the opening salvo of the dispute with an essay entitled "The Civil Code Emerges and Loyalty and Filial Piety Are Destroyed." Asserting the need to redraft the code to conform with traditional values, he wrote: "Our country is a nation of ancestor worship, it is a land of the family system. Authority and law arise from the family. . . . To speak of the people, to speak of the nation, is to imply the family system" (Hozumi, 1891: 227).

Given reliance on the family as a means of conceptualizing the nature of the state, it is easy to understand why Hozumi and others regarded the modern legal definition of the family as inextricably tied to Japan's political order. In an earlier essay on patriotism (*aikokushin*) he had written that the Japanese state was a "family state" and racial group.

What unites a racial group is the authority of ancestors. The authority of ancestors does not lie in a promise among equals [i.e., the social contract], so the feeling of veneration is strong and the concept of obedience is profound. In the house [*ie*], the head of the house, representing the authority of the ancestors, exercises the patrimonial power over the family; in the nation, the emperor, representing the authority of the Sun Goddess [as mythological founder of Japan], exercises the sovereign power over the nation. Patrimonial power and sovereign power: both are powers whereby the emperor–father protects the children beloved of the ancestors [translated in Minear, 1970: 73].

Traditionalists won the debate. The first three books of Japan's existing Civil Code were redrafted and promulgated as Law No. 59 of 1896, and the books dealing with relatives and succession, taking somewhat longer, were completed in 1898 as Law No. 9. The result, however, was less the codification of actual family practices than the incorporation in fixed legal form of the traditional ideals of the *samurai* class. This was especially evident in the sweeping authority granted to the head of the greater family unit or house (*ie*), whose consent was now required by any house member for marriage, divorce, adoption, residence, and even transfer of property. The critical feature of these provisions, however, was not the legal principles they expressed but rather their formulation in Western terms as *legal rights* of the house head, who therefore was not subject to the restraints imposed by the reciprocal Confucian obligations of compassion and just conduct toward the "beloved" child or subject. Western law cast the concept of family, and thus the state, into a far more absolutist mold.

The consequences were predictable. Having been granted legal rights, people began to exercise them unrestrained by traditional ethics. The code had begun to live. As disputes occurred, Japanese courts quickly faced the issue of enforcing the new rights.

In an increasing variety of contexts, Japanese judges displayed their ingenuity in harmonizing novel legal norms with traditional customs and values. In disputes over changes of residence they restrained arbitrary exercise of the rights of the house head, borrowing the French doctrine of "abuse of rights." When house-head consent for registration precluded legal marriage, they found in contract theory a basis for offering some legal protection to the all-but-legal bride. The pattern was repeated outside of family law, where the consequence of casting traditional relationships in terms of rights produced harsh results for those who otherwise could at least have claimed the protection of Confucian moral admonitions of just conduct (Haley, 1978: 375).

Thus, by the end of World War I, it had become apparent to some that it was not the principles of Western private law that threatened traditional values. The courts could prevent unfettered exercise of legal rights and harmonize the new legal doctrines with traditional practices. But they could do so only in the context of litigation, a process that was itself subversive of the traditional moral order.

In June 1919 Japan's first party cabinet appointed a special commission to study and recommend reforms in the second Civil Code. The timing was not coincidental. Preservation of familistic values had long been the concern of those who, like Hozumi Yatsuka, linked the legal concept of family to the political order. The reinforcement of values of family and mutual interdependence and the corollary rejection of liberalism were increasingly viewed as ways of curbing the unwanted social consequences of industrialization. It was hoped that preserving what was essentially a Neo-Confucian orientation would reduce, if not eliminate, the social frictions and disintegrative effects of economic growth experienced in Europe (see Pyle, 1973; 1974). The collapse of the European political order, the spreading symptoms of impending social upheaval in Japan, such as the Rice Riots of 1918, and the menace perceived in the Russian Revolution instilled Japanese leaders with a sense of urgency.

The commission—formally titled the *Rinji Hōsei Shingikai* (the Ad Hoc Commission for the Study of Legal Institutions)—contained the elite of Japan's legal establishment. Its chairman was Japan's leading academic jurist, Hozumi Nobushige (Yatsuka's elder brother); its vice-chairman, Hiranuma Kiichirō, was then procurator general and subsequently justice minister, chief justice, Privy Council president, and prime minister. The other members included Tomii Masaaki, one of the principal drafters of the Civil Code; Okano Keijirō, another future justice minister, who had assisted in the drafting of the Commercial Code; Suzuki Kisaburō, minister of justice in the Kiyoura and Inukai cabinets; and Minobe Tatsukichi, who was to become the nation's leading administrative and constitutional law scholar. Nearly a third of the members were practicing lawyers heavily involved in party politics, including Hara Yoshimichi and Ogawa Heikichi, two of the few attorneys ever to hold the post of minister of justice, and Hanai Takuzō, the lawyer appointed to defend Kokoku Shūsui. Three other members were also to become ministers of justice; two, chief justice of the Great Court of Cassation; and two, president of the Privy Council. The staff included Hozumi Shigeto (Nobushige's eldest son and a professor of law at Tokyo Imperial University), Makino Eiichi (one of Japan's leading prewar legal scholars), as well as two future procurator generals and another future chief justice.

Prime Minister Hara Kei outlined the objectives of the commission at its opening meeting: to recommend changes in the Civil Code that would conform the law to Japan's "virtuous ways and beautiful customs" (*Asahi Shimbun*, July 17, 1919: 2). A second goal was to draft legislation creating a jury system that allowed public participation in the judicial branch of government. The twin goals were quite in keeping with the thrust of earlier reform proposals—to meet the crisis of stability by reinforcing traditional values while widening participation in the political process (Duus, 1968: 133–161).

Political divisions within the commission apparently prevented agreement over changing any of the substantive provisions of the Civil Code. But there was consensus about the desirability of conciliating family disputes. Thus the principal recommendation in the commission's final report in 1922 was the creation of a separate family court that would conciliate civil cases involving family matters. In the language of the report: "The existing systems in which family disputes are resolved by means of formal trials fails to maintain the beautiful customs of old" (Hozumi, 1931: 287). In other words, almost the only item on which the commission could agree was that litigation in family disputes threatened Japan's familist tradition. (They also recommended institution of the jury system.)

The actual number of family cases was quite low. As indicated in Table 5.1, there were never more than 93 actions per million persons per annum between 1898 and 1941. Yet the absolute number of cases had increased steadily since the turn of the century, and the litigation rate relative to population had peaked in 1919. Moreover, there were significant institutional restrictions on family cases. For example, only district courts (*chihō saibansho*) had trial jurisdiction in cases involving the family law provisions of the Civil Code. Since during most of this period there were only 51 district courts located in major cities, as compared with 281 more widely dispersed ward courts (*ku saibansho*), it was much less convenient to bring a family case than an ordinary civil action.

The Repeating Pattern

The effort to deal with family disputes followed a pattern that was repeated by nearly all the conciliation statutes. An outbreak of disputes viewed by Japanese leadership, especially the bureaucracy, as socially damaging produced attempts to ameliorate the causes through substantive legal reform. When this failed, as it generally did, formal conciliation was introduced. Although the Diet failed to

TABLE 5.1
New Civil Actions Involving Family Matters, 1898–1941

Year	Number of actions	Number of cases per 1 million persons
1898	1733	40.4
1899	3441	79.3
1900	3347	77.2
1909	3464	71.3
1910	3600	73.2
1911	3738	74.9
1912	3905	77.2
1913	3762	73.3
1914	3957	76.1
1915	3573	67.8
1916	4061	75.9
1917	4320	79.9
1918	4750	86.8
1919	5115	93
1920	5129	92.4
1921	5035	88.8
1922	5032	87.7
1923	4690	80.7
1924	4916	83.5
1925	5366	89.9
1926	5384	88.7
1927	5287	85.7
1928	5168	82.6
1929	5679	89.4
1930	4895	75.9
1931	4763	72.7
1932	5015	75.5
1933	5151	76.4
1934	5415	79.3
1935	6148	88.2
1936	6189	88.3
1937	6323	89.6
1938	5866	82.6
1939	5947	88.3
1940	6413	89.2
1941	6704	92.9

SOURCE: *Nihon Teikoku Shihōsho* (Ministry of Justice of the Empire of Japan), *Minji Tōkei Nenpō* (Report on civil case statistics), Tokyo, 1900, 1911–1941.

implement the 1922 recommendation for a family court, it did approve the Land Lease and House Lease Conciliation Law that year and the Farm Tenancy Conciliation Law in 1924. In both instances conciliation was viewed as a means of reducing social conflict exacerbated by a regime of private law.

By redefining leaseholds in terms of rights and duties, the Civil Code again eliminated the paternalistic familialism inherent in the traditional landlord–tenant relation, especially in rural areas, just as it had done in family law. As described by Ann Waswo in her perceptive study of rural tenancy disputes in the 1920s:

> Many tenant families in the Meiji era had farmed the land of the same landlord family for generations. In some cases, whether true in fact or not, the two families claimed a common ancestry, and their economic relationship was reinforced by kinship and religious ties. Even where kinship ties did not exist, the tenant was conscious of continuing a relationship with his landlord which his father and grandfather before him had initiated and which had provided his family's livelihood for a half-century or more. Born into and brought up in a status of dependency, he grew accustomed to hardship and to obeying the landlord's orders. Although he might occasionally feel that the treatment he received was unduly harsh, it did not occur to him to question the landlord's right to exercise whatever power he possessed [1974: 387].

The adoption of conciliation for landlord–tenant disputes fit the paradigm perfectly.

As Waswo explains later, the "right" to exercise power was tempered by the obligations that landlords owed their tenants and the community. This reciprocity provided the mutual self-interest that reinforced the traditional relationship. "Tenants accepted the wealth and power of landlords not only as part of the natural order of society, but also because both were useful in assuring their own survival and well-being" (*Ibid.*: 389).

In contrast, the Civil Code had converted the basic duties of tenants into enforceable rights of the landlord but did not give similar recognition to the latter's traditional social and moral obligations. Indeed, as redrafted after the postponement controversy, the code placed landlords in an even more favorable legal position. The 1896 code (which remains in effect today) changed the classification of a lease from a real right (*bukken*), as provided in the 1890 code, to an obligation (*saiken*). Although the code did recognize real rights in ground-rent arrangements in the form of superficies (*chijōken*) (articles 265–269) or emphyteusis (*eikosakuken*) (articles 270–279), these were insufficient to give full protection to tenants, who otherwise would have had what was, in effect, a perpetual lease. For one thing, each was subject to restrictions on duration that generally favored landlords. Ordinary leases were limited to a maximum of twenty years (article 604 [1]). An emphyteusis could run no longer than fifty years (article 278), and unless the term was provided by express agreement or custom, the landlord could appeal to the court to terminate a superficies after twenty, but before the expiration of fifty, years (article 268).

These provisions gave landlords the legal right to terminate many existing leases. Moreover, even where an existing lease was valid, if the landlord breached the lease and sold the property, the third-party purchaser apparently had the right to evict the tenant, the latter's only redress being a claim for damages against the landlord.

Japan's rapid industrialization soon produced the economic incentives for urban landlords to exercise these rights. The dramatic expansion of economic opportunities, especially during the period between the outbreak of the Russo-Japanese War and the end of World War I, resulted in a comparable growth in urban population. As the demand for housing in Japan's major cities outpaced supply and shortages became increasingly acute, prices and speculation rose precipitously (Watanabe, 1960: 177).

Industrialization also had disruptive effects on rural landlord–tenant relations. Since many rural landlords were among those attracted to the cities by the advantages of urban life, the number of absentee landlords increased, particularly in areas adjacent to the most prosperous urban centers, such as the Kinki region of southwestern Japan. Although their tenants, as a result, may actually have been better off economically, absentee landlords could not carry out the variety of paternalistic obligations they owed to their tenants and the village community and thereby lost some of their traditional status (Waswo, 1974: 397).

As landlords began to exercise their legal rights and abandon their traditional roles, the number of rural and urban tenancy disputes increased rapidly, both in court and out (Watanabe, 1960: 176.) In rural areas, for instance, the number of reported cases increased from 256 in 1918 to over 2700 in 1976 (Waswo, 1974: 374). The majority were in the Kinki region. The initial response to this outbreak of cases was to reform the code. The early attempts were directed at the urban situation, but they failed because of landlord opposition in the upper house of the Diet. The only reform approved prior to the 1920s was one article of the Law for the Protection of Buildings, enacted in 1909, which provided for registration of both ground-rent agreements and superficies in order to protect those who rented the land but owned the buildings against third-party claims. More significant reform was delayed until 1921, when the Land Lease Law and the House Lease Law were enacted. These statutes gave tenants in the major urban centers substantial protection through what amounted to rent control and a lifetime lease. Yet the Diet was actually just codifying case law, for Japanese judges had reached similar results in a long string of earlier decisions (see Hozumi, 1972).

The first statute to authorize formal conciliation in a civil case was passed the following year—the Land Lease and House Lease Conciliation Law of 1922. Like the Land Lease and House Lease laws themselves, it applied only to major urban areas. Conciliation was considered a critical adjunct to the substantive reforms. In presenting the bill to the Diet, the government noted, "Last year at the time the Imperial Diet approved the Land Lease and House Lease bills, hope was expressed in both the House of Representatives and House of Peers that a separate means for conciliation outside of formal judicial proceedings would be established for land lease and house leases" (*Saikō Saibansho*, ca. 1951: 21).

Tenant unrest in rural Japan caused greater alarm. As Waswo notes, "By the early 1920's a sense of crisis prevailed in official circles. Not only were tenancy disputes more numerous than industrial labor disputes; they revealed the existence of discontent in that very part of Japanese society, the rural villages, long regarded as the nation's ultimate guarantee of social stability" (1974: 374). This "sense of crisis" prompted various attempts at substantive reform, all of which failed. Yet the significant political actors agreed that resort to the formal legal process was not a suitable means for resolving rural tenancy disputes. Consequently, in 1924, the Diet approved the Farm Tenancy Conciliation Law. As explained by Nagashima Hatasu (one of the drafters), conciliation was essential in order to restore harmony and the spirit of sympathy and benevolence (*nasake*) to rural Japan (Nagashima, 1924).

Japan's new industrialists had long resisted the enactment of Western-style labor legislation, echoing the arguments of those who opposed family law changes that legal reform would subvert the traditional master–servant relationship:

> The situation is entirely different here from what it is in those countries where rights and obligations are set by law. To create laws hastily without realizing this fact would, in short, destroy our beautiful national customs and create a people who are cold-hearted and without feelings. If workers confront the factory managers with coldness, the factory managers will be unable to feel warmth. Ultimately the two will be in constant conflict over matters of wages and hours [quoted in Marshall, 1967: 60].

Business attempts to prevent labor reform were moderately successful, but rising levels of labor agitation and unrest following World War I demanded some response. In 1926 the Diet passed the Labor Disputes Conciliation Law, which provided for conciliation of industrial labor disputes by an administrative committee. Once again the pattern of prior statutes was repeated: Labor agitation and unrest produced a new process for resolving disputes rather than substantive changes in the conditions of workers.

The Broadening Scope of Conciliation

Each of the previous statutes had been passed in response to increasing litigation in peculiarly sensitive areas of Japanese social life. It was difficult to argue that conciliation satisfied special social needs in commercial disputes. Nonetheless, the government statement in support of the bill (drafted while Egi Chū, one of the original members of the *Rinji Hōsei Shingikai*, was justice minister), asserted that the law was designed to ensure "continuing harmony in future dealings between the parties" (*Saikō Saibansho*, ca. 1951: 34). Underlying this argument was the assumption of governmental responsibility for preserving cooperation in ongoing commercial transactions—a presage of things to come.

As those who championed collectivist values and rejected a liberal legal order increased in influence, conciliation was viewed with greater frequency as the preferred means for resolving every dispute. Consequently, by the end of the 1930s nearly all civil disputes had become subject to conciliation. The impetus toward conciliation thus culminated in 1942 with the Special Wartime Civil Affairs Law, which mandated conciliation of virtually any civil dispute and authorized judges to enter enforceable judgments without trial based on the conciliators' recommended settlement if the parties refused to accept it voluntarily (article 19[2]).

Under the early statutes, conciliation had been an optional alternative to litigation, one that a party had to choose. The Land Lease and House Lease Conciliation Law as originally enacted, for example, provided that trial proceedings would be stayed upon receipt of a petition for conciliation by one of the parties (article 5). The petition had to state the particulars of the dispute, and if it was inappropriate or the court deemed the petition frivolous, this was to be dismissed (article 3). By 1924 the Diet had amended the law to enable the judge to initiate conciliation on his own motion (article 4-2, Law No. 17). The Farm Tenancy Conciliation Law (No. 18, 1924) differed only slightly from the amended version of the preceding statutes in that it provided for conciliation of disputes that had not been filed as regular civil actions. Thus a petition for conciliation could be filed not only with the appropriate district court but also with the mayor of the town or village.

The next step was to remove the freedom of the parties to reject a recommendation by authorizing the conciliator to make a recommended settlement binding. Thus the 1932 Monetary Claims Temporary Conciliation Law provided in article 7 for "judgments in lieu of conciliation":

> If the court deems it proper, when conciliation is not reached in the conciliation committee [*chōtei i'nkai*], [the court] ex officio may render a judgment in lieu of conciliation, ordering modifications of interest rates, term, and other contractual relations after listening to the opinion of the conciliation committee, considering fairly the interest of both parties, and allowing for their resources, the nature of their business, amount of interest, fees, and payments made by the debtor, as well as the other circumstances.

The Agricultural Land Adjustment Law (No. 67, 1938) included a similar provision that made it possible to compel the parties to accept the settlement recommended by local farm tenancy conciliators (*kosakukan*) and judges (article 67). Comparable provisions for coercive conciliation were included in all subsequent conciliation statutes, to the point where the Special Wartime Civil Affairs Law gave all conciliation settlements the effect of enforceable final judgments, as previously noted.

The expansion of conciliation to cover all civil disputes and the progression toward coercive conciliation are critical factors in evaluating the motivation for these statutes. By the late 1930s the rejection of litigation as incompatible with collectivist values had become the principal explicit justification, but in the 1920s other explanations were voiced. Delays in litigation had become chronic, and some urged conciliation as a means of ensuring prompt justice. Hozumi Shigeto (1928), for example, praised the efficiency of conciliation in land and house lease cases. Disputes that had festered for two or three years now were resolved in a matter of weeks because lawyers had been eliminated. Yet in advocating a family court and conciliation of family disputes, Hozumi argued that the settlements would more accurately reflect Japanese morality. Conciliation was seen primarily as a corrective for social conflict, not as a speedier means for enforcing legal rights.

Indeed, from the first conciliation statute to the last, the central purpose of proponents was to ensure that dispute outcomes reflected Japanese morals rather than law. As stated in the government report in support of the Land Lease and House Lease Law, "Conciliation means resolution [of disputes] not by adjudication of the rights between the parties but rather in terms of their own morality and their particular circumstances" (Koga, 1977: 6). Similarly, a spokesman for the drafters of the Commercial Affairs Conciliation Law explained that in Japan, unlike other countries, even commercial disputes *should* be settled in terms of harmonious cooperation; a resolution based on human feelings (*ninjō*) and morality rather than law was the ultimate purpose of conciliation (*Ibid.*: 7). In other words, adjudication by law through an assertion of rights, whether by landlord or tenant, parent or child, businessman or worker, should be opposed as incompatible with a "moral" resolution. "The emphasis on harmony precluded the view of society as a balancing of conflicting self-interests. The demand for recognition of one's rights was itself unworthy. All should have the interests of the collectivity at heart" (Dore and Ōuchi, 1971: 203). The utility of conciliation in advancing a "moral" resolution for social conflicts was not just a matter of the outcome. As Henderson emphasizes in his seminal comparison of traditional and modern conciliation in Japan, the critical feature of the traditional process was its "didactic" quality: Conciliation provided an effective opportunity for officials to instruct the parties with respect to their moral and social obligations, not merely their legal duties (1965: 2–4). During the course of the proceedings, the judge or other conciliator could castigate one side of the controversy or both for failing to live up to traditional moral standards and still show his benevolence by recommending an equitable compromise.

THE CRITICS' RESPONSE

The proponents of conciliation spoke in the language of Japan's Neo-Confucian tradition, with all the claims to legitimacy it afforded. But not all agreed. Objections were raised, and the most vocal critics were lawyers. From the late 1920s through the mid-1930s, with some frequency, such widely read professional periodicals as *Hōsō Kōron* and *Hōritsu Shimbun* carried articles and comments critical of the trend toward more inclusive and more coercive conciliation. These seem to have reached a crescendo soon after the passage of the Monetary Claims Temporary Conciliation Law in 1932. Because the statute covered almost all actions to recover money owed, conciliation could no longer be viewed as a special response to exceptional disputes. As more than one observer noted, the temporary conciliation laws had become permanent (e.g., Matsuo, 1934: 2; Survey, 1934; 51; Narita, 1936; 3). By the end of the 1930s the political climate precluded open criticism. The trend had become irreversible and opposition futile.

No doubt the lawyer–critics were motivated in part by self-interest. Conciliation, as Hozumi Shigeto (1928) had remarked, reduced the need for legal representation. In fact, attorneys were actively discouraged from participating (Matsuo, 1934: 5). Whatever their motives, however, their arguments were sound, and they raised perceptive questions about the operation and effect of conciliation. Of course, not all lawyers were critical. Many supported formal conciliation, even arguing for its expansion (e.g., Ishibashi, 1930), but the majority of critics, or at least the most vocal, were lawyers.

The critics saw that conciliation did not just embody the Neo-Confucian ideals of the bureaucracy and other members of Japan's conservative elite. It also offered significant economic advantages to some. Conciliation compelled creditors to compromise their claims regardless of how legitimate or just they might be from a legal or moral perspective. The conciliation statutes, especially those authorizing conciliation in ordinary commercial and debtor–creditor cases, were thus criticized as debtor-relief measures (e.g., Azumamoto, 1932: 3; Miyoshi, 1934). It was estimated that in conciliated farm tenancy cases a 30 percent reduction of rent was common (Ladejinsky, 1937: 425). Similarly, conciliation of monetary claims was said to operate as a de facto reorganization of small and medium enterprises to rescue them from the burden of overindebtedness (e.g., Azumamoto, 1932: 3; Miyoshi, 1934: 7).

This does not mean that those who opposed conciliation were unsympathetic to the plight of persons struggling to maintain a decent livelihood in the midst of the Depression or to tenants and others in relatively weak bargaining positions who were pitted against overreaching landlords (e.g., Matsunaga, 1932: 7). Rather, they attacked what they saw as indiscriminate, across-the-board measures that relieved all debtors of responsibility for even their just debts (*Ibid.*:8) and argued that reform of substantive law was the proper way to protect the weak.

One answer to such criticism was that conciliators and judges were well placed to ferret out debtors who used conciliation improperly and would recommend a settlement that did not unduly disadvantage the creditor. Moreover, as noted earlier, conciliation was a "didactic" process in which the conciliators could be extremely severe in instructing the parties on how to conduct themselves in the future.

What troubled the lawyer–critics most deeply was the opportunity that conciliation measures provided for abuse. The commonest complaint was that defendants invoked the process as a procedural device for delay and obstruction; the statutes were being used to avoid debts, not to promote "harmony" (Miwa, 1935: 4). Apparently judges would entertain petitions for conciliation throughout the course of a regular action. Thus one lawyer complained that in landowner suits to vacate land and houses it was common for the defendant to petition for conciliation after the action was filed, in order to stay the proceedings, and that even after the conciliators had sent the case back to trial, the defendant would file another petition, causing great delay (Yamaguchi, 1934: 4). This, in turn, was said to lead to more frequent use of legal devices, such as notarial deeds (*kōnin shōsho*), that permitted creditors to collect debts without the need of a prior judgment (Kishii, 1935: 11).

Critics recognized that conciliation contradicted the underlying tenet of private law—the enforceability of legal rights. As one of the more vehement opponents described the process:

> The ideal of conciliation laws is to achieve in the particular circumstances of a dispute an harmonious resolution by reaching a mutual understanding and carrying this through by voluntary assent. The parties may not be family enemies or sibling opponents acting as though they are irreconcilable—fighting it out in court, a spark having set them off. In fact in most instances there is just a confrontation of economic interests and feelings. Even in these cases this ideal of resolving conflicts of interest is based on both sides yielding to a sense of morality, reconciling their feelings toward each other. And there is of course no objection to this . . . but it is a pipe dream. Reality is not so simple. Whatever is said, conciliators are laymen. They do not understand that the facts and circumstances of a dispute must be determined by a showing of evidence. Refusing to follow this reasoned approach in deciding how to settle disputes, they ignore the facts and reach a resolution with only one side, the creditor. . . . As a result the creditor's rights receive no protection [Matsuo, 1934: 7].

Inherent in conciliation was the notion that the legal rights of the parties must give way to the conciliators' sense of morality. Conciliation was simply a procedure in which the legal rights of all parties were compromised, and such denigration of rights was viewed as undermining the private law system and liberal legal order (e.g., Narita, 1936: 3).

Critics of the conciliation measures also attacked their constitutionality. The Meiji Constitution guaranteed the right of Japanese subjects to be tried by judges (article 24). Some argued that this applied to civil as well as criminal cases and noted that the conciliators were not necessarily judges (although judges partici-

pated in many cases) (e.g., K. Inomata in Survey, 1934: 52). Others maintained
that withdrawing protection from legal rights raised a constitutional question
(e.g., Matsuo, 1934: 7), but the absence of any constitutional provision specifically guaranteeing a right to trial in civil cases led most to reject the first argument (Survey, 1934). Indeed, Japan's leading constitutional law scholar, Minobe
Tatsukichi, replied to the cited bar association survey on conciliation: "I do not
believe it is unconstitutional" (*Ibid.*: 57). The guarantee of the right of access to
the courts in the postwar constitution thus had particular overtones for the
Japanese. The epilogue was the invalidation of the "judgment in lieu of conciliation" provisions of the Special Wartime Civil Affairs Law (No. 63, 1942) (see
Nomura v. *Yamahi*, 14 Minshū [Sup. Ct., G.B., July 6, 1960]).

AN APPRAISAL

The Effect of Prewar Conciliation

Both the proponents and critics of prewar conciliation correctly perceived the
role of litigation in Japan's modern legal system, if sometimes only dimly. As the
lawyer–critics were quick to point out, legal rights are meaningless unless enforced, and Western legal systems operate on this assumption. Yet, as explained
earlier, the process of enforcement was subversive of Japan's Neo-Confucian
tradition. The real issue, therefore, was not the value of conciliation as an
alternative to formal trials but rather whether Japan should continue to progress
in the direction of a liberal legal order. By the mid-1930s the answer was clear.
The military and civil bureaucratic elites chose cohesion over conflict, a collectivist ethic over liberal values. One cannot but be impressed by the endurance of the consequences of that decision in postwar Japan.

This chapter is not the appropriate place for a close analysis of the role of law
in modern Japan, but at least it can be posited here that the 1930s marked a
turning point. A glance at litigation rates in the prewar and postwar periods
reveals a marked difference (see Figure 5.1). There was, on average, nearly two
times as much litigation in the prewar period (Koga, 1976: 8; Haley, 1978: 368).
The postwar highs barely reach the prewar lows. The number of lawyers per
capita has also not returned to the prewar level. Nor has the political role of the
profession recovered its prewar vitality. In each election from 1890 through
1936 lawyers accounted for 15 to 25 percent of the Diet (Japan Statistical
Yearbook, 1924–1925; 1930; 1936). Today it is estimated that less than 5 percent
of the Diet are members of the bar.

Despite popular views to the contrary, Japanese society today seems considerably less free and open, in many respects, than it was in the early years of the

interwar period. There were, for example, no formal legal barriers to foreign investment until after World War II and no meaningful trade regulation until the late 1930s. Although the Japanese people continue to enjoy—or suffer—remarkable freedom from legal controls, they are governed by a vital set of social restraints. It is therefore tempting to see the introduction of conciliation as one source of this change, among many others. This was certainly the effect desired. Nonetheless, the evidence supports a contrary interpretation. However accurate proponents and opponents of conciliation may have been regarding the social costs and benefits of litigation, both erred in assessing the actual effects of conciliation.

It did not lead to a decline in the number of lawsuits, as was commonly assumed. In fact, the opposite was true. Every introduction of formal conciliation coincided with an increase in litigation. The effect of this alternative to trials, if unanticipated and certainly unintended, apparently was to bring more disputes into the formal process. There was a sudden decrease in the number of civil actions beginning in 1934 (see Figure 5.1). This was paralleled, in almost every category, by an equally dramatic decline in conciliation cases at about the same time (see Figures 5.2–5.5). Such statistics confound those who view conciliation as a means of dispute resolution preferred by Japanese in general as opposed to political elites (see, e.g., Kawashima, 1963: 55). They make sense, however, if examined from a litigant's point of view.

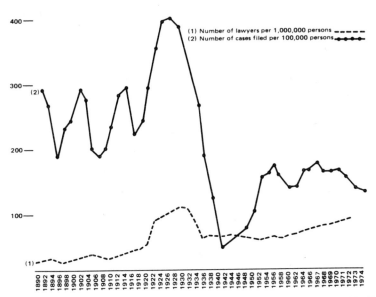

Figure 5.1. Graph shows new civil cases filed for final trial in district courts 1890–1941 (From Henderson and Haley, 1978: 721).

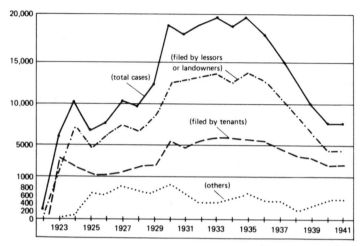

Figure 5.2. Graph shows new land lease and house lease conciliation cases filed 1922–1941 (From Nihon Teikoku Shihōsho, 1943).

In most instances lawsuits are a last resort, initiated only after negotiation, mediation, or both have failed to satisfy the parties to a dispute. As Hozumi Shigeto (1928) and others noted, the legal system in the 1920s had become increasingly incapable of providing the parties with meaningful relief. Delay was chronic. Despite a constantly growing volume of new cases, the government refused to increase the number of judges (see Table 5.2), although some supported this, including Makino Kikunosuke, member of the *Rinji Hōsei Shinjikai* and later chief justice (Makino, 1932: 175). Instead, in 1931, the government actually reduced the number of ward courts, the primary courts of first instance, though intense public pressure forced it to retract the decision and reactivate 62

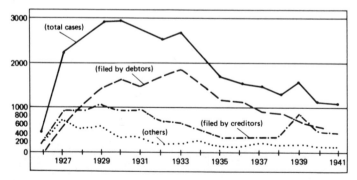

Figure 5.3. Graph shows new commercial affairs concilation cases filed 1926–1941 (From Nihon Teikoku Shihōsho, 1943).

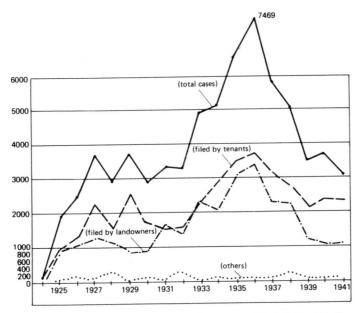

Figure 5.4. Graph shows new farm tenancy conciliation cases friled 1924-1941 (From Nihon Teikoku Shihōsho, 1943).

ward courts a year later (see *Kokumin Shimbun*, March 14, 1931: 7; *Asahi Shimbun*, March 30, 1932: 3). Yet conciliation had exactly the effect of increasing access, since laymen could be and were appointed as conciliators.

Perhaps it was true, as the critics charged, that conciliation demanded compromise, but half a loaf was better than none. Conciliation provided at least some remedy, if an imperfect one. Just as court delay during this period reduced the

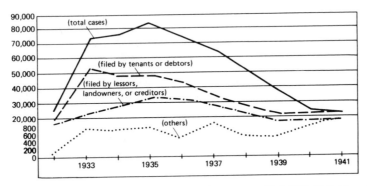

Figure 5.5. Graph shows new monetary claim conciliation cases filed 1932-1941 (From Nihon Teikoku Shihōsho, 1943).

TABLE 5.2
The Legal Profession in Japan, 1890–1973

Year	Judges	Public procurators	Private attorneys	Private attorneys per 1 million persons
1890	1531	481	1345	33.7
1892	1532	482	1423	35.1
1894	1221	383	1562	38.0
1896	1221	383	1578	37.6
1898	1244	473	1464	34.1
1900	1244	473	1590	36.3
1902	1208	363	1727	38.4
1904	1197	374	1908	41.4
1906	1179	379	2027	43.1
1908	1234	401	2006	42.7
1910	1125	390	2008	40.8
1912	1129	390	2036	40.3
1914	898	386	2256	43.4
1916	903	359	2665	49.8
1918	1004	478	2947	53.8
1920	1134	570	3082	55.6
1922	1150	578	3914	68.9
1924	1155	574	5485	94.0
1926	1121	564	5936	98.6
1928	1245	656	6304	101.5
1930	1249	657	6599	103.3
1932	1345	628	7055	107.1
1934	1370	648	7082	104.6
1936	1391	648	5776	87.6
1938	1470	686	4866	69.2
1940	1541	734	5498	70.7
1942	1581	625	5231	70.3
1944	1188	610	5174	70.1
1946	1232	668	5737	75.7
1948	1842[a]	1387	5992	74.8
1950	2261	1673	5862	70.5
1952	2323	1717	5872	69.9
1954	2327	1717	5942	69.7
1956	2327	1717	6040	69.9
1958	2347	1717	6235	70.4
1960	2367	1761	6439	70.2
1962	2450	1796	6740	71.3
1964	2475	1829	7108	73.9
1966	2518	1844	7687	73.2
1968	2525	1871	8016	80.4
1969	2580	1946	8580	84.6
1970	2605	1983	8868	86.2
1971	2619	2019	9167	88.2
1972	2681	2071	9483	90.2
1973	2688	2076	9921	92.0

SOURCE: *Nihon bengoshi rengōkai* (Japan federation of bar associations) *Shihō hakusho* (White paper in the legal system), pp. 102–103 (1974). (Number of private attorneys per 1 million persons added.)

[a] The figures after 1948 include the number of summary court judges and assistant procurators.

number of new cases being filed (Haley, 1978: 383–384), so conciliation stimulated litigation by providing an additional avenue of relief: A case could be filed and then referred to conciliation. To turn metaphor into analogy, as with most road improvements, the result was less to ease the flow than to increase the volume of traffic on both the highway and the subsidiary roads. In the end, therefore, both sides of the debate were wrong. Conciliation was not a panacea for social conflict. Nor was it the death knell of the legal system or the legal profession. Instead, it apparently provided a useful, if not wholly satisfactory, channel for legal relief.

The Lessons of Japan's Experience

Japan's prewar experience points to one conclusion that most litigants or practicing lawyers recognize as a matter of common sense. Litigation is primarily a means to enforce legal rights, not to resolve conflicts. People usually sue to compel others to meet legal obligations that they have refused to acknowledge or fulfill. In this respect, the critical characteristic of the legal order is the effectiveness of its sanctions and other means of coercion. The Japanese conciliation measures of the 1920s and 1930s illustrate the extent to which people will take advantage of any coercive mechanism offered even in a society whose values are antithetical to the formal legal process. That conciliation was used extensively, even though it was a less satisfactory means for enforcing legal rights than the ideal civil action, underscores the inadequacy of the legal process in Japan.

Many questions remain: What were the causes and consequences of this inadequacy? Why did litigation and the number of lawyers decline so abruptly in the mid 1930s? Why have the prewar and postwar periods differed so markedly? Does the inadequacy of the legal process inspire greater reliance on self-help—lawful and unlawful—and arrangements that avoid the need to resort to court? To what extent will the failure of a legal system to provide effective remedies lead to atrophy of the formal legal process, the development of extralegal alternatives, or compensating mechanisms? The answers will require further research and analysis.

REFERENCES

Statutes (in order cited in text)

Land Lease and House Lease Conciliation Law (*Shakuchi shakuya chōtei hō*), Law No. 41, 1922.
Farm Tenancy Conciliation Law (*Kosaku chōtei hō*), Law No. 18, 1924.
Labor Disputes Conciliation Law (*Rōdō sōgi chōtei hō*), Law No. 57, 1926.

Commercial Affairs Conciliation Law (*Shōji chōtei hō*), Law No. 42, 1926.
Monetary Claims Temporary Conciliation Law (*Kinsen saimu ringi chōtei hō*), Law No. 26, 1932.
Agricultural Land Adjustment Law (*Nōchi chōsei hō*), Law No. 67, 1938.
Personal Status Conciliation Law (*Jinji chōtei hō*), Law No. 11, 1939.
Mining Law (*Kōgyō hō*), Law No. 215, 1905.
Mining Law Partial Amendment Law (*Kōgyō hō chū kaisei hōritsu*), Law No. 23, 1939.
Placer Mines Law (*Sakō hō*). Law. No. 13, 1909.
Placer Mines Law Partial Amendment Law (*Sakō hō chū kaisei hōritsu*), Law. No. 103, 1940.
Special Wartime Civil Affairs Law (*Senji minji tokubetsu hō*), Law No. 63, 1942.
Constitution of the Empire of Japan (*Nihon teikoku kempō*), February 11, 1889.
Court Organization Law (*Saibansho hō*), Law No. 6, 1890.
Administrative Court Law (*Gyōsei saiban hō*), Law No. 48, 1890.
Civil Code [old] (*Mimpō*), Law No. 28, 1890.
Civil Code (*Mimpō*), Law No. 59, 1896, Law No. 9, 1898.
Land Lease Law (*Shakuchi hō*), Law No. 49, 1921.
House Lease Law (*Shakuya hō*), Law No. 50, 1921.
Law for the Protection of Buildings (*Tatemono no hōgō ni kansuru hōritsu*), Law No. 40, 1909.

Materials in Japanese:

Adachi, M. (1959) in *Nihon Kindaihō hattatsu shi* 7, pp. 38–86.
Azumamoto, K. (1932) in *Hōritsu Shimbun* (no. 3471), pp. 3–5.
Etō, Y. (1972) in Toshitani (ed.) "*Hō to Saiban*," pp. 178–182.
Horie, S. (1934) In *Hōritsu Shimbun* (No. 3642) pp. 5–6.
Hozumi, S. (1928) in *Tōkyō Asahi Shimbun*, January 12, 13, 14, 15, 16, 17, 18, all at p. 2.
———. (1931) In *Gendai Hōgaku Zenshū* 38, pp. 227–290.
Hozumi, Y. (1891) in Hoshino (ed.) "*Mimpōten ronsoshi*" (History of the civil code dispute), pp. 227–232.
Ishibashi, S. (1930) in *Hōritsu Shimbun* (no. 3140), p. 3.
Ishibayashi, S. (1930) in *Hōritsu Shimbun* (no. 3101), p. 3.
Iwano, J. (1931) in *Hōritsu Shimbun* (no. 3248), p. 3.
Kawagoe, R. (1934) in *Hōritsu Shimbun* (no. 3752), p. 30.
Kawashima, T. (1967) "*Nihonjin no hōishiki*" (Legal consciousness of Japanese). Tokyo: Iwanami.
Koga, S. (1977) in *Hanrei Taimuzu* (special issue no. 3), pp. 4–21.
Kishii, T. (1935) In *Hōsō Kōron* (bi, 413), pp. 45–47.
Kubota, H. (1935) In *Hōsō Kōron* (no. 414), pp. 45–47.
Makino, K. (1932) "*Makino Kikunosuke kaikoroku*" (Autobiography). Tokyo.
Matsunaga, K. (1931) in *Hōritsu Shimbun* (no. 3269), p. 19.
——— (1932) in *Hōritsu Shimbun* (no. 3365), p. 7–8.
Matsuo, K. (1934) in *Hōsō Kōron* (no. 408), pp. 2–7.
——— (1935) in *Hōsō Kōron* (no. 416), pp. 2–6.
Miwa, Y. (1935) in *Hōritsu Shimbun* (no. 3886), pp. 4–5.
Miyoshi, M. (1934) in *Hōsō Kōron* (no. 407), pp. 7–12.
Mizabuchi, K. (1932) in *Hōritsu Shimbun* (no. 3461), pp. 3–4; (no. 3462), pp. 3–4.
Nagashima, H. (1924) "*Kosaku chōtei hō kōwa*" (Discussion of Farm Tenancy Conciliation Law). Tokyo: Shimizu.
Nara, S. (1928). "*Kosaku hōan no gensei hihan*" (Severe criticism of the Farm Tenancy bill). Tokyo: Sōbunkaku.

Narita, A. (1936) in *Hōritsu Shimbun* (no. 4066), p. 3.

Survey (1934) in *Hōsō Kōron* (no. 408), pp. 51–63.

Nihon Teikoku Shihōsho (Ministry of Justice of the Empire of Japan) (1943) *Dai 67 Minji Tōkei Nenpō* (67th annual report on civil statistics). Tokyo.

Saikō Saibansho (Supreme Court), (ca. 1951) *"Wagakuni ni okeru chōtei seido no enkaku"* (Development of conciliation in our country). Tokyo.

Watanabe, Y. (1960) *"Tochi tatemono no hōritsu seidō"* (Legal system for land and buildings). Tokyp: University of Tokyo.

Yamaguchi, K. (1934) in *Hōritsu Shimbun* (no. 3628), p. 4.

Yoshino, S. (1935) in *Hōritsu Shimbun* (no. 3878) pp. 20–21; (no. 3879), pp. 19–21.

Materials in English

Dore, R. P. and T. Ōuchi (1971) "Rural Origins of Japanese Fascism," in J. W. Morley (ed.) *Dilemmas of Growth in Prewar Japan*. Princeton, N.J.: Princeton University Press.

Duus, P. (1968) *Party Rivalry and Political Change in Taishō Japan*. Cambridge, Mass.: Harvard University Press.

Haley, J. O. (1978) "The Myth of the Reluctant Litigant," 4 *Journal of Japanese Studies* 359.

Henderson, D. F. (1965) *Conciliation and Japanese Law: Tokugawa and Modern*, 2 vols. Seattle: University of Washington Press.

Henderson, D. F. and J. O. Haley (1978) *Law and the Legal Process in Japan*. Seattle: University of Washington School of Law.

Hozumi, T. (1972) "The Structure and Function of the 'Interpretation' of Juristic Acts, Part II," 5 *Law in Japan* 132.

Japan Statistical Yearbook (1924–1925, 1930, 1936). Tokyo.

Kawashima, T. (1963) "Dispute Resolution in Contemporary Japan," in A. T. von Mehren (ed.) *Law in Japan: The Legal Order in a Changing Society*. Cambridge, Mass.: Harvard University Press.

——— (1967) "The Status of the Individual in the Notion of Law, Right, and Social Order in Japan," in C. A. Moore (ed.) *The Japanese Mind*. Honolulu: University of Hawaii Press.

Ladejinsky, W. (1937) "Farm Tenancy and Japanese Agriculture," 1 *Foreign Agriculture* 425.

Marshall, B. K. (1967) *Capitalism and Nationalism in Prewar Japan*. Palo Alto, Calif.: Stanford University Press.

Maruyama, M. (1974) *Studies in the Intellectual History of Tokugawa Japan*. Princeton, N.J.: Princeton University Press.

Minear, R. H. (1970) *Japanese Tradition and Western Law: Emperor, State, and Law in the Thought of Hozumi Yatsuka*. Cambridge, Mass.: Harvard University Press.

Najita, T. (1967) *Hara Kei and the Politics of Compromise*. Cambridge, Mass.: Harvard University Press.

Pyle, K. B. (1973) "The Technology of Japanese Nationalism: The Local Improvement Movement 1900–1918," 33 *Journal of Asian Studies* 51.

——— (1974) "Advantages of Followership: German Economics and Japanese Bureaucrats, 1890–1925," 1 *Journal of Japanese Studies* 127.

Rabinowitz, R. W. (1968) 10 *Transactions of the Asiatic Society of Japan* (3rd ser.) 7.

Waswo, A. (1974) "The Origins of Tenant Unrest," in B. S. Silberman and H. D. Harootunian (eds.) *Japan in Crisis*. Princeton, N.J.: Princeton University Press.

⑥

The Discourse of Summary Justice and the Discourse of Popular Justice: An Analysis of Legal Rhetoric in Argentina *

HELEEN F. P. IETSWAART

For Emilio F. Mignone, in his tireless struggle for human rights

INTRODUCTION

This chapter analyzes the discourse employed to describe interaction between urban guerrillas and the armed forces in Argentina, in particular, incidents of confrontation in the streets. The texts on which it is based are mostly press reports of official communiqués concerning such incidents between March and November 1977.[1] I am concerned here only with the linguistic characteristics of the texts. Although these texts have a history, and perhaps a future, those have not been taken into account. That this type of text virtually disappeared from the press by the end of 1977 makes that a convenient terminal point.

---

*The final text of this chapter has greatly benefited from detailed criticism and commentary by Werner Ackermann and Richard L. Abel. However, the author alone is responsible for its contents and conclusions.

[1]My analysis is based entirely on publications in the Buenos Aires daily newspapers *La Opinión*, complemented with those in *La Nación* on Mondays, that being the day on which *La Opinión* was not published. There were 91 texts concerning confrontations in that period; of these, 71 are complete transcripts of the communiqués, and 20 are condensed or abbreviated versions that nevertheless

149

The texts concerned have a simple descriptive form: On their face they provide information; they tell a story, often in considerable detail. They refer to an actual geographical space and sometimes to people who exist or existed. But one should not confuse the published texts with real events resembling the picture those words evoke. In Argentina in 1977 there is no reason to assume that the events described actually happened at the time and place mentioned (not infrequently an identifiable street corner). Yet confrontations like those described surely did take place throughout this period. So we have, on the one hand, a social reality of violent interaction between political groups, the day-to-day details of which are not known, and, on the other, a corpus of verbal references to part[2] of that interaction, namely, violent confrontations in streets and around private dwellings involving casualties on one side or both and sometimes arrests. Though there is no one-to-one relation between particular incidents and texts, the latter, as a corpus, represents an attempt "verbally [to] appropriate the social reality" concerned.[3] In view of the extreme dissociation between social and verbal reality, I propose to consider the latter as a series of stories having first and foremost a relation to one another, though I will also consider the relation of the entire corpus to the broader political discourse.

Although the texts have a superficial descriptive form of the type "now here is another story about . . . ," I will argue that there is a deeper linguistic structure that strongly resembles the discourse of popular justice. Indeed, the texts may be considered an extreme form, a caricature, of popular justice discourse. But if they are distortions of the form, they nevertheless show that the form is free and allows such extreme applications—anybody may adapt it to any purpose.

---

contain the essential elements. During the same nine months the press reported 50 incidents of violence attributed explicitly to "subversives," such as bomb explosions and assassinations. The latter accounts frequently have much the same form and style as the texts describing confrontations and have been used as an additional source of data. These two categories, taken together, provide 141 texts for the period. Although the style of the texts remained the same, instances of "subversion" appeared with decreasing frequency in each of the three trimesters: March–May, 81; June–August, 38; and September–November, 22. There were 32 trials of alleged subversives throughout the period, distributed across trimesters: 6, 18, 8. Other related press reports include the follow-up of confrontations, supplying the names of those killed; homage paid to martyrs in the security forces; suicides of subversives while in detention or when apprehended; discoveries of caches of explosives, arms, printing presses, etc.; incidental arrests; information about activities of Argentine subversives abroad; plans and tactics of subversion in general; and subversives who gave themselves up to the police. There were 53 such items in *La Opinión* during this period. Journalists exercised greater control over this latter category, both in quantity and in quality.

[2]There are no official accounts of another important aspect of the interaction between the factions—the arrest by plainclothesmen of numerous citizens and their subsequent disappearance.

[3]See Burton and Carlen (1979). Their work on official discourse, legal and otherwise, which came to my attention after this chapter was written, is quite congenial to my own views and analysis, and I have adopted some of their terminology. On official discourse concerning the political enemy, see also Finlay *et al.* (1967).

In order to illustrate the degree to which the discourse of "summary justice"—as I will call it—may be likened to the discourse of popular justice, I will first develop a model of popular justice, an ideal type in the Weberian sense, briefly contrasting the latter with a model of formal justice. In constructing these models I will distinguish institutional and functional aspects from the discourse as such. Next I will outline the institutions and functions of summary justice, before turning to the discourse associated with it. In the latter analysis I propose to demonstrate the affinity of the "deep structure" of the discourse with that of popular justice discourse.

Yet that is not all there is to it. The specific textual elements, which are situated in a concrete historical context, may be better understood with reference to the contemporaneous political discourse about "subversion" in general. This more abstract discourse contains the categories that are represented by more or less standard signs in the individual texts. The relation between the two levels is analogous to that between legislative discourse and the discourse of the administration of justice (in a broad sense).

TWO MODELS OF
THE ADMINISTRATION OF JUSTICE

One of the most distinctive characteristics of law is that it puts something between the individual and the social environment, between the individual and his (theoretical) behavioral alternatives. To be sure, law is only one of the various systems that limit behavioral possibilities. Law claims to do this with respect to the entire community, i.e., it pertains to the most inclusive level of community organization to which individuals and groups involuntarily belong. Although I do not want to preclude later consideration of certain instances of tribal legal systems, I will limit the present analysis to the law of the nation-state.

Civil society is the most fundamental realm of social relations. Other forms of social organization, in particular the state, derive their substance, the subject matter of their activities, and even their historical *raison d'être* from the social relations of civil society, particularly those of competition and conflict. Admittedly, one may discern relations and activities at the level of the state that are apparently independent of what goes on in civil society because the various levels of societal organization inevitably develop a certain autonomy, but even those derive ultimately from civil society. Legal discourse may be considered one such level.

It is possible to imagine the existence of civil society without the state (indeed, there are numerous examples) but not the reverse. The actors of civil society, conceived as social groups, pursue objectives, defined at the level of civil society, through the mechanisms of the state. In that sense the relations of civil society are mediated by the state. The degree of mediation varies along a continuum; we may say that social relations are more mediated to the extent that the issues concerned are more abstract.[4]

Law is a typical form of mediation. One face of law is institutional. Law, as the representative of the "community," interposes institutions between social events and their authoritative evaluation. The other face of law is a belief system about the *proper* order of things. As such, it places norms—prohibitions, suggestions, incentives, obligations—between the individual and behavioral alternatives, thus imposing an (exclusive) world view, a set of ideas, categories and prescriptions that order "reality."

The more formal the legal system, the more marked the institutional intervention and the more distinct the resulting discourse. On the one hand, law may constitute something *between* the parties in a dispute, something that acts on behalf of the "community"; on the other, the "community" may have a quarrel with its individual members or groups. In formal systems this leads to the distinction between civil and criminal law. In criminal cases the community's institutions not only produce the controversy but also undertake to "resolve" it. The more formal the legal system, the greater the difference between the treatment of civil and criminal controversies and the more distinct the discourse of each.

Legal institutions, then, produce different types of discourse, among other things. I will limit myself here to an analysis of the legal discourse of the administration of justice. I suggest that there is variation in the degree of mediation (distance) between a social event and its authoritative evaluation in the name of the community—the administration of justice—and that the legal discourse employed will vary accordingly. This is, in the present context, the purpose of distinguishing types of administration of justice: to identify and characterize different types of legal discourse.

The degree of mediation between the social event (hereafter, "the event") and its evaluation and (possible) authoritative resolution has three main dimensions: time, space, and social location. Of these, the aspect of social location, or distance, requires some elaboration.[5] The major dimensions of social distance are differentiation and specialization. Differentiation refers to the existence of a legal sphere separate from both the community at large and other public offices. This is closely related to specialization, which refers to the various ways in which judges are distinguished from other members of the community in terms of

---

[4]Let me illustrate this with a labor law example. Before labor legislation was introduced, mediation by the state in labor–management relations was limited to ad hoc intervention in strikes, through the use of physical force. By comparison, a legally approved system of labor relations is mediation at a higher level of generality. Similarly, the controversies between different sectors of civil society about the type of economic system the country will have occur at a relatively high level of generality (in legislative debates).

[5]In what follows I rely heavily on Abel (1973) and Felstiner (1971; 1974).

occupation, age, sex, and social class. A fully specialized judiciary performs its job full time, and the office is characterized by a high degree of specialized knowledge and a distinctive language and mode of reasoning. Furthermore, the separation of the legal sphere is often expressed by its embodiment in a fixed, centralized location and may be symbolized by the use of robes, wigs, and courtroom arrangement, such as the physical division of the audience (the public) from the participants and, to a lesser extent, of the latter from the judges.

Where the principle of separation of powers is fully elaborated the distance between civil society and those who exercise the judicial function is greater than where the executive itself judges. I see a separate judiciary as a delegation by the executive of certain administrative tasks; once established over time, it may lead to a limited autonomy, but this is always subject to revocation.

On the basis of these distinctions it is possible to develop two models, or ideal types, that constitute the end points of a scale measuring the degree to which the administration of justice is mediated. Formal administration of justice largely coincides with Weber's concept of rationalized justice, in both its procedural and its substantive aspects. The least formal, or most immediate, administration of justice ("charismatic justice" and "Khadi justice"[6]) are defined by Weber rather negatively, i.e., as lacking certain characteristics of fully rationalized justice.[7]

Immediate justice may be usefully, even if not exhaustively, illustrated by instances of "popular justice."[8] This concept combines forms of the administration of justice that differ considerably in nature and origin. Some represent conscious attempts by an effective nation-state[9] to reduce the formality of existing institutions: popular justice in contemporary Cuba and Eastern Europe is

[6]The concepts correspond to Weber's two nonrational "types of domination": charismatic and traditional (patriarchalism) (see Rheinstein, 1967: 336–337).

[7]See Rheinstein, 1967: esp. Chs. 7–11, 14. Consider, for instance, the following sentence: "*Honoratiores* administration is an avocational undertaking, and for that reason it is normally slower, less bound by rules, more amorphous and hence less exact, and it is less unified . . . it is less continuous." This is opposed to the "precision, speed, consistency, availability of records, continuity, possibility of secrecy, unity, rigorous coordination" of a fully rationalized system of administration of justice (*Ibid.*: 349).

[8]There is an extensive literature on popular justice, most of which concerns comrades' courts in the Soviet Union and other Eastern European countries and the popular tribunals in Cuba, but some of which deals with developing countries such as China, Mexico, and Brazil. Here I will mention only the most important writings: Taras (1959); Podgórecki (1962); Berman (1963); Berman and Spindler (1963); Nader and Metzger (1963); Feiffer (1964: 111–129); Nader (1964a; 1964b; 1969); Cohn (1966; 1967); Eckhoff (1966); Lubman (1967); Berman (1969); Hammer (1969); Cuellar *et al.* (1971); Santos (1973; 1977); Spence (1982); and Blet *et al.* (1970). The model of formal justice relies on Weber's conceptualization and on my own knowledge of various Western legal systems. On popular justice generally, see Tiruchelvam (1978); see also Abel (1979).

[9] This term is employed to exclude nations in which the distinction between civil society and the state is nonexistent or insignificant so that the tensions between the two levels, typical of Western political culture, are largely absent.

best understood in this historical perspective. Popular justice always aims to democratize the administration of justice, in the sense of increasing participation or involvement by more sectors of the population. This could be viewed as "handing back" to civil society a measure of the judicial function that has progressively been removed from the populace.

On the other hand, sectors of civil society may retain or take back part of the judicial function, temporarily or permanently.[10] If this occurs within an effective nation-state, the extent of popular justice will depend on the degree to which state institutions tolerate such alternative forms. It should be noted that the state is not necessarily threatened by such expressions of popular justice, especially if these develop in sectors of civil society that were never integrated in the state, such as the *favelas* in Rio de Janeiro (Santos, 1973; 1977) and their counterparts in other Latin American cities.[11]

The following account of popular justice attempts to integrate these quite diverse manifestations, which share a relatively low degree of mediation by state institutions and an emphasis on popular, especially lay, participation in the administration of justice. The model necessarily entails comparisons with, and opposition to, formal justice.

THE MODEL OF POPULAR JUSTICE

Institutional Features

In popular justice, the judicial function is exercised by institutions that are relatively undifferentiated from the community in which they operate. The community elects lay persons to all levels of judicial office. Because the job is relatively unspecialized—it is not a career, and officeholders continue to do their other, regular work as well—the turnover of personnel is relatively high, and a large proportion of the community has access to office. The job is not charac-

---

[10]Examples are the administration of justice in revolutionary, and thus quite temporary, situations (e.g., Iran in 1979) and by marginal groups within an otherwise effective state (e.g., Brazil) (see Santos, 1977), and also the various alternative institutions for the administration of justice in Western capitalist societies.

[11]The development of popular justice in certain *campamentos* in Chile during the Allende regime (Ietswaart, 1973; Spence, 1982) seems to exemplify an alternative form that appeared threatening to the existing state institutions because of the specific political context. In April 1972 leaders of one such *campamento* who also administered justice were indicted on charges of "usurpation of the judicial function." Although the charges were ultimately dropped (interview, October 1972), the case caused much excitement in judicial and wider legal circles and received extensive attention in the (right-wing) press.

terized by a high degree of specialized knowledge or the use of a distinctive language.

The judicial function is avowedly close to political office and public administration generally,[12] whereas this is denied in the official discourse of formal justice systems. Although the judicial office is permanent and differentiated in various ways, this separation does not take the physical form of a distinct, permanent location exclusively dedicated to judicial activities. Jurisdiction is frequently decentralized and coincides with geographical areas such as the neighborhood and other functional units such as the workplace or school. Thus, there tends to be a proliferation of physical locations used for both the administration of justice and other social activities. In this sense, the administration of justice is closer to the community it serves and accordingly more accessible than it normally is in more formal systems. Another aspect of this proximity to the community is the lack of a special uniform for the performance of the function—a characteristic of formal justice that symbolically expresses the impersonal nature of the judicial function, thus adding to the separateness of the office. Consequently, the institutionalization of popular justice reduces the distance between social "events" and their authoritative evaluation.

Functions

The declared functions of popular justice extend beyond dispute settlement and the official sanctioning of deviant behavior to include a proactive approach to problem situations, education (of both the offenders and the community) in the norms of society, and the implementation of general policies. In all this, popular justice is prospective rather than retrospective. Tribunal sessions are scheduled after work or between shifts so that community members may easily attend. Variety in the types of decisions and sanctions available to the judges facilitates the performance of these functions.[13]

By contrast, the official functions of formal justice are only two: dispute settlement and the sanctioning of deviance. The judicial function is limited to evaluating the facts by means of evidence presented by the parties, in terms of the "applicable legal norms," and deciding the case accordingly. In doing so, courts seek to develop a coherent and consistent body of legal thought, which, in turn, is

---

[12]This has been mentioned in descriptions of Cuba (Berman, 1969; Cantor, 1974) and Chile (Ietswaart, 1973; Cheetham et al., 1972; Spence, 1982).

[13]In Cuba, where popular justice was highly developed, the following sanctions were designed to respond to particular types of wrongdoings: public admonition, relocation (especially for neighbors who frequently quarrel), exclusion from a particular place (for youths who repeatedly make a nuisance of themselves in such places), house confinement while not at work or at school, or an order to repair damage (for torts) or to finish a particular level of education (see Berman, 1969; Cantor, 1974).

supposed to help make those social relations to which they apply increasingly orderly and thus predictable.

In popular justice, proceedings are relatively informal: the disputants make oral presentations, preferably without the intervention of legal representatives. The time span between the social event to be judged and such judgment (another aspect of distance) is relatively small. The audience typically consists of ordinary community members who are called upon to participate in the proceedings and frequently do so.

The distinction between civil and criminal cases hardly exists; all cases are "problems" to be resolved as satisfactorily as possible. Obviously, some cases will be considered more serious than others, and sanctions may vary accordingly,[14] but such distinctions refer to current policies and values rather than to legal categories. The community directly affects input into the proceedings. Individual members and groups are actively involved in bringing "problem cases" to the attention of the authorities, assist in the pretrial investigation of cases, attend tribunal sessions, where they may participate in the hearings (e.g., as character witnesses or sources of other information), and, finally, offer an audience for moral instruction and exhortation by tribunal members.

The Discourses of Popular and Formal Justice

The discourse of popular justice is most easily described by contrasting it with that of formal justice. Both discourses may then be related to the institutional and functional features just described.

If we first consider the themes of the discourse, we find that the subject matter of formal justice discourse is typically a specific instance of social behavior, relatively delimited in time and space; such behavior may or may not be characterized by some particular mental state attributed to the actor on the basis of other observable behavior. Evidence and the legal classification of "the" facts concern first the overt behavior and then the associated mental state. These are not necessarily treated separately; frequently they constitute an indivisible legal category (contract, crime). Judicial discourse thus abstracts, in a distinctive way, a fragment of social reality. Although the mental element is sometimes considered, the evaluation does not concern the "person" of the accused or the litigant,[15] i.e., the moral quality of their being as expressed in their behavior.

---

[14]In Cuba, as in marginal settlements in Chile (*campamentos*), the most severe sanction would be expulsion from the community. In Cuba this sanction is formalized as "relocation."

[15]Here we encounter an important tension between the values that govern the discourse. On the one hand, it must abstract from the person and judge only "behavior"; on the other, it must attribute such behavior to a responsible, rational person who can be found "guilty" of deviant behavior. Thus, the discourse must be concerned with establishing the existence of a mental element that is generally

The relatively large distance between the social event and the trial, as measured along the dimensions indicated earlier (time, space, and social location), has implications for the type of discourse. First, the people involved must be explicitly identified in the pretrial papers (police reports, indictment, pleadings) and again at the trial. Such knowledge commonly will not be shared by all involved, especially not by the judge(s). Second, a good deal of the discourse at the trial is concerned with "evidence" establishing the legal truth of the alleged events. This is done from the outset with a view to the legal categories deemed appropriate by the parties or prosecutor. Thus, although the classification of facts in terms of legal categories is presented as logically distinct and neatly separated from the preceding step (the establishment of those facts), the two may usefully be considered a single process. The need to classify the facts within one or another legal category (or none at all) determines the process of establishing those facts. Determining the facts, then, aims to arrive at a *legal* truth, at "establishing that relative truth which is attainable within the limits set by procedural acts of the parties" (Rheinstein, 1967: 227).

This conception of the proper subject matter of judicial discourse renders it highly autonomous, i.e., separate from other types of discourse. Popular justice discourse, on the other hand, is primarily characterized by its lack of autonomy; it is, instead, close to everyday common sense and moral discourse, and often to political discourse. Thus, it applies (a selection of) the various categories used in such other discourse, in easily recognizable form. In particular, its categories of deviant behavior are drawn from such other areas of discourse, without much abstraction or reformulation. It also invokes categories of specifically approved behavior. Compared with the discourse of formal justice, popular justice discourse abstracts a different part of social relations for purposes of official evaluation and judgment. The extreme of popular justice discourse is "considering the whole person," not just a particular aspect of behavior. An intermediate point is the application of broad categories of behavior, such as "hooliganism" and "loafing."[16] Although popular justice discourse does not always go to the extreme of considering the whole person, it tends to take account of a larger section of social reality than formal justice discourse, with respect to both the parties (aspects of personality, general social performance) and the people and circumstances surrounding them (family relations, work environment).

Popular justice discourse also applies a broader concept of "institutional deviance" than formal justice discourse, in the following sense. Because all cases

---

defined negatively: omission, negligence, carelessness, etc. This aspect of the discourse is declining in importance as strict liability spreads.

[16]In many Latin American countries there is a strong tendency to formulate offenses in ever broader terms, as vague as "being a threat to the security of the state." On the equally vague concept of "loafing" or "hooliganism" in Cuba, see Loney (1973).

are considered "problems" to be resolved, all people appearing before the tribunal are viewed as potential troublemakers, whether they are quarreling neighbors, parents who have lost control of their children, or workers allegedly pilfering from the factory store. By contrast, formal justice discourse does not characterize the substance of "civil litigation" as deviant behavior.[17]

The proximity between the social event and its evaluation, in both time and space, has several implications for the discourse of popular justice. There is normally little need to identify the accused, the litigants, or the other people involved (e.g., witnesses). They are known to all present, and both judges and public may well have heard of the dispute or the alleged wrongdoing. The situation is akin to someone being caught in the act and sanctioned then and there by his captors. This is clearly related to the treatment of evidence in the proceedings. There is little room for a flat denial of the accusations or the invocation of sophisticated legal categories to classify behavior. Accordingly, the discourse is not much concerned either with establishing what actually occurred or with characterizing it in terms of differentiated legal categories. The legal norms involved are generally nonproblematic, so that there is little verbal activity devoted to arguing their applicability or proper interpretation.[18] In fact, they may never even be mentioned.

This has implications for the use of the concept of causality. Let me start, once more, with the reference point of formal legal discourse. All legal discourse within the adjudicative form consists of a decision and its justification.[19] In formal justice discourse the decision is typically zero-sum (right–wrong; one wins, the other loses).[20] The whole discourse is oriented to attributing "the" act (or omission) to a person. Because of the necessity to attribute certain events to the action (or inaction) of a person (and not to more general social circumstances), the concept of causality must fit this reduced view of social reality. Thus it is said that particular behavior "caused" particular events as legally recognizable consequences and that certain events must have been reasonably "foreseeable" at the time of the alleged behavior in order to count, legally, as consequences.

In formal justice discourse the justification of the decision refers back to

[17]The fact that particular instances of litigation are considered troublesome by overburdened courts in formal justice systems is quite a different matter.

[18]Although "characterizing an act as within a certain legal category" is really one and the same process as "the proper interpretation of the legal norm," this is not acknowledged within the universe of formal legal discourse. There, typically, the former is said to pertain to the realm of "facts" and the latter to that of "norms."

[19]On this issue, and particularly the aspect of justification, see Wasserstrom (1961); see also Levi (1948); Burton and Carlen, (1979).

[20]There are exceptions, whose importance it is hard to evaluate. In the law of torts, the concept of comparative negligence may lead to a sharing of the accident costs. In contracts, the plaintiff may be found to have contributed to the loss resulting from breach if he has not mitigated his damages by immediately selling the goods to the best buyer.

previous legal discourse (both legislative and adjudicative); it rarely uses elements of nonlegal discourse. Such antecedent legal discourse is encapsulated in specific, preexisting rules, presented as impersonal and objective. Judges are supposed to avoid all reference to their own opinions. These preexisting rules (which may express general policies in *mediated* form) typically form part of a coherent, consistent, and more or less complete system of normative utterances. Rules, and the categories to which they refer, are ordered in a set of concepts, and the whole forms an impersonal normative universe—impersonal in the double sense that it is presented as though it were not man-made but rather an ever-present, objective existence and that it applies without regard to the person.

The discourse of popular justice relates events differently. It applies a broader concept of causality, in accordance with its broader "abstraction" from social reality. Attribution of both causality and responsibility (liability) are not necessarily limited to the alleged actor; a social group (work team, family, or neighbors), a general social deficiency (housing shortage), or a nonmaterial element such as "capitalist ideology" may be held causal and responsible.

I distinguished earlier in the chapter between the decision and its justification. In popular justice discourse, the decision is justified in terms of policy objectives and prevailing ideology—the system of values and beliefs generated by the dominant political culture. There is little or no reference to preexisting rules of law, and those that are invoked are nonproblematic and express well-known policies and values. This is related to another feature of popular justice discourse: Cases are treated as individual incidents, not as recurrent events. Accordingly, the discourse does not continuously refer back to itself in previous instances, either with respect to the facts ("we consider the facts of this case similar to the facts of such-and-such earlier case") or with respect to the justification for the decision ("we decide this way because that is how we have decided such cases before, according to a rule that says we should do so"). Thus, the discourses of popular justice tends to be prospective rather than retrospective.

Judges and witnesses may draw on their personal knowledge, especially that concerning relevant social relations, and may make statements such as: "That Jones is generally considered a troublemaker."· Members of the community present may also volunteer such information and opinions, thus contributing to the discourse. In the discourse of popular justice the "objectivity" associated with, indeed said to be guaranteed by, the "impartiality" of Weberian rational administration of justice is of little significance; on the contrary, a high value is placed on input from the judges and other participants *as members of the community.* [21] Because a major objective of the administration of popular justice is the

---

[21] In all modern Western systems for the administration of justice there seems to be eternal tension between the desire to achieve some degree of "objectivity" (distance) in adjudication and the desire to prevent extreme alienation of the administration of justice from the population it is supposed to serve. Judges ought somehow to be representative of their constituency but also disinterested in any particu-

"betterment" of the offender and the "improvement" of the social relations concerned (both of which evaluations must be defined by a particular society at a particular point in time) the discourse allows judges and other participants to display their personal knowledge and views.

The most salient features of the discourse of popular justice may be summarized as follows:

1. Its subject matter is the allegedly deviant behavior and a relatively large slice of the social environment, including the personalities of those directly involved, "the whole person."
2. Only a relatively small part of the discourse is concerned with identifying parties to the dispute, or ascertaining "the facts," or arguing about the content and application of legal norms; the emphasis is rather on defining the problem and determining the remedy. The discourse is prospective rather than retrospective.
3. It is cast in terms of categories drawn from the prevailing political and ordinary language, without much verbal mediation through legal categories.
4. The justification of the decision rarely refers to previous cases. It approximates pure casuistry, though this is limited by the fact that the justification is framed in other discourses, principally the political.
5. The concept of causality is broad and allows attribution of deviant behavior to people other than the offender or litigants and to social circumstances beyond the immediate control of any individual.
6. The discourse typically ends in a generalized formulation of approved and disapproved behaviors and attitudes, expressed in a moral discourse and related to statements of general goals presented as approved by the entire community or as simply beyond discussion.
7. Members of the community are deeply involved, both actively and passively.

THE MODEL OF SUMMARY JUSTICE: THE ARGENTINE CASE

What I have termed "summary justice" is an aspect of certain totalitarian states. Its development is a corollary of the explicit definition of a "political enemy number one" representing the highest degree of political deviance. Not

---

lar case. Legal systems strike the balance in different ways. Some have confidence in both the integrity and the social integration of appointed judges; others employ a jury or elect their judges.

all totalitarian states explicitly name a political enemy. Some limit themselves to defining social deviance; others may go as far as labeling ideological deviance. Yet all major political cultures implicitly define their political enemies—Nixon's "enemies list" is an example—some regimes are just more straightforward than others. The definition of "political crimes" is a threshold step in proclaiming the idea of political deviance.

Summary justice, then, deals with this "political enemy number one." Its declared objective is "the total elimination of the enemy."[22] Its major sanction is instant execution, the alternative being arrest. Certain sectors of the police and the armed forces specialize in this form of social control. These institutions have strategies for dealing with the enemy, some of which are more conspicuous than others. Visible strategies include street confrontations between urban guerrillas and the armed forces and the official discourse about such confrontations.[23] I suggest that the latter should be seen as a distinct element: Its function seems to be to convey an image of the enemy, i.e., a set of typical intentions, attitudes, and patterns of action. It consists of discrete narrative texts ostensibly describing day-to-day events in the struggle with the enemy. Taken together, these texts probably provide a plausible picture of the sort of street confrontations that transpire, but there is no reason to assume that the incident described in any given text actually took place at the time and place indicated. What we have here is a rather extreme form of *dissociation* between instances of social reality and their authoritative verbal descriptions. But it is important to point out that dissociation can be found in all legal discourse, if to a lesser extent. Analytically, it may be compared to the discourse associated with plea bargaining. There, the original accusation may accurately describe what the defendant did, and the guilty plea may represent a distortion. Or, the defendant may have been overcharged so that the original accusation was distorted, and the guilty plea may depict the behavior of the defendant more faithfully.

In summary justice the extreme dissociation between social reality and official discourse makes the latter a caricature, as I will try to show in analyzing the Argentine texts in the following sections.[24]

The discourse considered is contained in communiqués (most of which emanate from various quarters of the armed forces) describing confrontations and, to

---

[22]There are numerous official statements to this effect, see, e.g., Presidential Message of April 19, 1977 (*La Opinión*, April 20, 1977); Speech by General Viola, April 29, 1977 (*Ibid.*, April 30, 1977); Speech by General (R.) Villegas, April 23, 1977 (*Ibid.*, April 31, 1977); Speech by General Trimarco, June 9, 1977 (*Ibid.*, June 10, 1977); Speech by General Catuzzi, May 6, 1977 (*Ibid.*, May 7, 1977).

[23]See, e.g., Amnesty International (1976); see also Rouquié (1978) and the references included there.

[24]What follows is a first elaboration of the material, in broad terms. The data will be subject to a more detailed semiotic analysis, which will be presented in a separate paper.

a lesser extent, other violent incidents involving urban guerrillas. I shall deal first with the principal texts—those concerning confrontations—which typically consist of several parts: (*a*) introduction; (*b*) assertion that information from the public initiated the incident; (*c*) description of the confrontation itself in more or less detail, at the end of which one or more "subversive elements" are typically killed; (*d*) some statement about the identity, or more frequently the future identification, of the people involved; and (*e*) epilogue. Parts *b* and *e* are optional.

A complete text may serve as illustration:[25]

> The Command of Army Zone 1 informs the public that in the course of search operations that the Argentine Army is currently carrying out, a confrontation with subversive elements has taken place on the first of the current month, in which five subversive delinquents were slain. The incident referred to occurred today at 1:10 A.M. in Avalos street at the 300 block, in the area of Temperley, in which battle forces, after a short pursuit of an automobile that eluded a traffic control, caught up with the same, with the intention to identify them [*sic*], and they were unexpectedly received with gun fire. The aggression was immediately countered and subsequently it was found that three male and two female subversive delinquents had been killed, who apparently belong [sic] to the subversive gang montoneros.

> The confrontation mentioned has caused among our own ranks two officers wounded, one seriously.

> The Zone 1 Command wishes to point out that in this unremitting battle we are waging delinquent subversives will continue to perish until their complete extermination, so as to restore peace and tranquility to the inhabitants of the Fatherland [*La Opinión*, June 2, 1977].

The introduction—the first paragraph in this text—follows a standard form. It invariably contains the element of "informing the public" and summarizes the report. It should thus be considered an extended headline rather than part of the main text. At the same time, it sets the tone and introduces the theme—now the audience knows what the story will be about. It also establishes, verbally, the presence of the public. Time and location will often be precisely indicated, as in the example cited. The duration of the whole incident may also be specified, e.g., "after over three and a half hours of courageous perseverance of the forces of order."

The account may usefully be seen as a sequence of modules, arranged in a limited number of sets. I have identified three, differentiated in terms of the origin of the incident. Confrontation may follow: (*a*) systematic or sporadic control of cars in the street; (*b*) general or specific control of houses in an area; or

---

[25]All translations are mine. The original texts are generally characterized by a highly pompous and cumbersome style, a feature I have tried to retain in the translations, which explains their deliberate awkwardness. In addition, the originals not infrequently lack correct syntactic structures, an aspect I have also retained in most instances and indicated by the word *sic*. There are logical gaps and inconsistencies, which are also indicated by *sic*.

(*c*) systematic or incidental control of people in public places (such as streets or bars), e.g., a check of identity papers. During this phase of the incident there will be some "suspect behavior," which may either precede the control and indeed provoke it—e.g., a car speeding or a person walking in the street in a "suspect manner"—or occur during the control—during a checkup in a tearoom a young-ster hastily gets up and tries to leave, or a car in the line tries to get out and dodge the control. Sometimes it is clear that the behavior described is out of the ordinary, but on other occasions there is the mere assertion of "suspect be-havior." Two short examples may illustrate this point.

The Commander of the 2nd Army Corps "Lieutenant General Juan Sánchez" informs the public that today at approximately 1 A.M. forces of order moved along Avenida Godoy at block 5200, performing duties of security, when they observed the suspect movements of an automobile Citroen, without number plates, in which two male persons and one female could be discerned [*La Opinión*, May 22, 1977].

The Zone 1 Command informs the public that another victory has been gained over Marxist subversion, thanks to the spontaneous and valuable collaboration of the neighbors of the house [*sic*], who advised the forces of law about suspect happenings in a dwelling situated at 1151 Uriburu Street (Monte Grande), during the night of 23rd May [*Ibid.*, May 25, 1977].

Some texts impute motives to justify the label "suspect," e.g., people trying to paint subversive slogans on street walls (however, since all are killed in the incident it is hard to know what they were really doing). Alternatively, the element of "suspect behavior" may be omitted and the participants instead de-scribed as "young man/woman" or "young people," which, as we shall see, is equivalent to "suspect behavior."

Thus, from the outset, the normal, *legitimate* behavior of the authorities (invariably referred to as "the forces of order" or "the forces of law" or, less frequently, "the security forces") is contrasted with the "suspect," *illegitimate* behavior of the enemy. Where the element of "suspect behavior" is omitted the initial illegitimate behavior may be characterized as "disobeying the orders" to come out of the house or the car, to stop, to surrender, and the like, the latter again representing the legitimate behavior of the security forces. The text typi-cally emphasizes that such orders were ignored, and this is frequently where the violence starts: Instead of surrendering the subversives open fire—the ultimate act of aggression. The "forces of order" respond to such aggression, i.e., defend themselves, and in the same act proceed to "restore order." In the simple, one-line story this shoot-out ends with the killing of one or more subversive elements, whose gender is normally specified.

The car was ordered to stop so that its occupants might be identified and known, and the car was stopped. A male person alighted the same armed with a rifle with which he opened fire on the forces of order. The latter immediately returned the fire and a short but fierce shoot-out was

the result. Under these circumstances the delinquent was fatally wounded, and almost in-
stantly the engine caught fire and exploded, while the other male and the female person were still
inside the automobile [*Ibid.*, May 22, 1977].

The security forces will then enter the house or place or search the car(s) and
will encounter what could be called additional, or corroborative, evidence—
subversive literature, arms and ammunition, etc.

In the exchange of fire the occupants of the automobile were slain, being three men and a
woman. On the site of the incident the following objects were confiscated: a home-made machine
gun of 22 mm, a revolver 38 long, 2 pistols of 12 mm and approximately 500 pamphlets with the
letterhead "national liberation movement"—prt–erp [Partido Revolucionario de los Trabajores-
Ejercito Revolucionario del Pueblo] [*Ibid.*, July 6, 1977].

An optional element at this point is the discovery of "three children of tender
age" in "the house"—an element to which I will return later.

Near the end of the account, either after the death of the subversive elements
or after the search of the car or house, there will be some statement about the
identity of the people involved. Their identity is generally not only unknown but
also treated as unimportant, although their present anonymity is almost always
mentioned. The most common variation of this module of the story is "whose
identity will be investigated," and we are left with that. Other indications of the
irrelevance of the identities of members of the enemy forces are simple inconsistencies such as "whose identity is unknown except that he was high up in the
hierarchy," or "known as 'Pepe' (his body was mutilated beyond recognition by
the explosion)." If a body count is published later it may show similar inconsistencies.[26] But there is rarely any further press report of the identities of those
killed.[27]

Another type of incident (less frequent in the period under investigation than it
had been previously) starts with the "transportation of a prisoner" in a car. The
car stops at some point, and the prisoner escapes and flees. He may be killed
while fleeing, or he may "hide in a house," which would then initiate the house
sequence, or he may "get into a car," which would be followed by a race and a
final shoot-out.

The Command of Army Zone 4 informs [the public] that on the 2nd of March of the current year,
at about 22.00 hours, the following incident took place. While the forces of law transported the
delinquent subversive Alberto Braicovich (DNI 10.767.433) [Documento Nacional de Identidad,

[26]Such a body count will frequently include the age of the deceased, invariably between 18 and 35;
I discuss this further later in the chapter.

[27]The publication in the press of the names of those killed in specific "confrontations" was
generally considered to be a means of communicating to the enemy forces that the people mentioned
had died somehow, usually while in detention.

carried by all adults], belonging to the subversive gang self-named montoneros, who had been arrested earlier, one of the cars had to stop to change a tire. The prisoner, taking advantage of the circumstances described, managed to escape and fled quickly. He was ordered to stop several times, but as the orders were ignored the forces of order opened fire on him, being fatally wounded [sic]. The incident took place in the area of San Miguel (Buenos Aires) [Ibid., March 5, 1977].

Sometimes, though rarely, the prisoner flees and is lost.

The element of flight is rather frequent and may be found in every type of story, at any point. People may be said to flee from a car or street to a house, or vice versa, thus changing the sequence of the original story and producing a more complex combination of modules. The result of flight is not predictable (i.e., not standard): it may be successful or unsuccessful. It is the act of fleeing that has symbolic relevance.

The modules described in the preceding discussion may be combined only in certain ways, just as the vocabulary in which they are formulated is rather restricted. Because they are more or less separate, independent units, they are sometimes juxtaposed in an improbable fashion, and the sequence of modules may show gaps or inconsistencies. For example, the story may have centered entirely around a private dwelling, all the occupants of which were killed in the shooting and left unidentified, and then the text will state, "In the car, which was badly damaged, large quantities of subversive leaflets were found, as well as a number of small arms." Although this feature is relatively infrequent,[28] even its occasional appearance is an indicator of the "truthfulness" of the texts or, in the language of literary criticism, their verisimilitude and thus of their sign value. I suggest that because the verisimilitude of the texts as a whole is relatively low, attention should focus on other aspects, especially the sign value of the individual modules.

The description of the confrontation ends with an epilogue that varies in content. It may contain an expression of gratitude for the cooperation of the public in general, or may be addressed more specifically to the "neighbors" or "passers-by" (without whose assistance and orderly behavior the victory over the enemy could not have been won). It may include a lecture to the public on the nature of subversion and subversive activity or the responsibility of parents for the education of their children. It may also eulogize the security forces, emphasizing their sacrifice, courage, patriotism, and the like and referring to

---

[28]Gaps and jumps in the text are only one index of the verisimilitude of the discourse as a whole. Others are the casual treatment of the identity of the people involved (see text accompanying nn. 26–27) and, a more frequent feature, the reference to an unidentified man and an equally unidentified woman as a "couple" (who may have fled or been killed). The latter two features indicate the "privileged" vantage point of the producers of the discourse with respect to what is known (see Burton and Carlen, 1979: Ch. 5). Indeed, they seem not just the privileged but the exclusive possessors of knowledge; there is no invitation to share the view and conclusions of the speaker ("the court is satisfied"), but there is rather its mere imposition.

their sacred mission to eliminate subversion. And it may combine any number of these elements.

> The Commander of Army Zone 4 wishes to point out: (1) the important cooperation and assistance rendered by the public at all moments, in particular the act of informing about the suspect activities taking place in the house in Avellaneda, whose arrest [sic] made it possible, in large measure, for the forces of law to join forces with the citizenry in order to deal a heavy blow to Marxist interests through its local agents.... (3) The imperative need for the public to persevere in its battle position duly providing the information which allows to expose the activities and identity of the enemies of the fatherland [*Ibid.*, May 31, 1977].

> Once more these delinquents assert their objectives: indiscriminate murder. They have no respect nor affection for the people. Their only interest is in killing. Citizens, in the face of the agony of horror unleashed by these subversive elements, please do continue to cooperate in the effort to recuperate the country, assume this reponsibility in all seriousness and reject subversion. Defend the family and the community. The Nation sacrificed heroes and martyrs who have given their lives so as to defeat subversion. Do not allow such sacrifice to have been in vain [*Ibid.*, April 24, 1977]. [This is an account of an act of violence attributed to the "enemy" that falls short of being a confrontation.]

Other texts related to the discourse of summary justice can also be found in the press, usually on the same page as the accounts of confrontations. First there are reports about more or less violent incidents that fall short of being open clashes with the security forces. For example, an account describes a person walking down the street in a "suspect manner"; a security officer wants to verify what is going on, and suddenly there is an explosion that kills the terrorist who apparently carried a bomb. Or neighbors denounce "suspect happenings" in a house; the security forces arrive and instruct the occupants to leave the premises. There are long discussions inside, with shouts and strange sounds, and in the end it becomes evident that everyone in the house is dead, either killed or committed suicide. The module of "finding evidence" may be added to such incidents, as well as the optional modules previously described and some form of epilogue, as in the first of the following examples.

> The Command of Sub-zone 15 fulfills its duty of communicating to the citizenry that on the 1st of June 1977, at approximately 21.00 hours, members of this Command were able, through the valuable collaboration of the public, to locate a depository of explosives at 11600 (eleven thousand six hundred) Vertiz street, which belongs to a gang of Marxist subversive delinquents.

> As it would have been too dangerous to transport the large quantity of explosives to another part of town, it was found necessary to detonate them on the site, after evacuating the people from the area.

> Once more the gangs of Marxist subversive delinquents willfully endanger the life of defenseless human beings, implementing orders from fugitive leaders living abroad, the advocates of human rights which they violate themselves, who are unable to accept their defeat, but try to humiliate the Nation with such acts from their safe place outside the country [*Ibid.*, May 3, 1977].

> The Command of the 1st Army Corps informs the public that on Saturday, the 30th of April the following incident took place in the cinema "San Martín" in the area of Ramos Mejía

(province of Buenos Aires). A (female) delinquent subversive belonging to the Marxist gang montoneros was busy placing a bomb in the ladies' bathroom, when she was caught in the act by a number of visitors to the cinema.

The feelings of indignation caused by this act made the public try to lynch the subversive delinquent, but in the end they thought better of it and called the forces of law instead. Meanwhile, before the arrival of the police, the subversive delinquent swallowed a capsule of cyanide while she carried with her, and she died a few minutes later. . . .

The reaction of those present is quite eloquent: it expresses clearly their total condemnation of Marxist subversion which they reject wholeheartedly. The reaction of the subversive is equally evident: her fright in view of the indignation of the very same people who, she had been deceitfully told, she should represent [*Ibid.*, May 4, 1977].

In addition, there are miscellaneous reports of how young people get started on the road to subversion, how they are seduced and indoctrinated in foreign ways of thinking and adopt another life-style, leaving their families and engaging in underground activities. These stories generally emphasize the family (its suffering and also its responsibilities) and the fact that those people involved are young people.

Trials of "subversives" are also reported in the press. Accused are tried by either military tribunals or ordinary criminal courts. These reports are not comparable to the accounts of violent confrontations because they do not employ the same discourse but rather summarize the charges and the sanctions imposed. At the beginning of the period under consideration they emphasized the severity of the sanctions (headlines would read, "Harsh punishment for five terrorists"); later they stressed the leniency obtained by surrendering to the police and repenting.

Now that I have outlined the major features of the texts, it may be appropriate to justify why I consider them susceptible to analysis in terms of legal discourse, especially the discourse of the administration of justice, given that their content and political context seem to have remarkably little to do with law, let alone justice. My reason is that these texts form part of a broader political discourse whose principal purpose is legitimation. They combine elements of formal justice discourse (police reports in particular) with a broad aura of natural justice. The security forces are the mere agents of a natural order that imposes itself, frequently without human intervention.

The information about the death of the four extremists is contained in a communiqué issued late on Saturday evening by the 3rd Army Corps with Headquarters in Córdoba. The report points out that on Friday the 3rd, at 23.00 hours, military personnel belonging to the fifth Infantry Brigade performed a control on the roads leading to the province of Santiago del Estero. At a certain moment, an automobile crossed the inter-province boundary and was ordered to stop. The driver, nevertheless, increased the automobile's speed while his fellow passengers opened fire on the forces of law, who countered the aggression. Under these circumstances the automobile left the road, collided [*sic*] and caught fire. Later the [*sic*] four terrorists—two of whom females—were found to be dead. Only one of them—Ramón Ferreyro, alias "the Black"—was identified [*Ibid.*, June 7, 1977].

The continuous, relentless endeavors of the forces of law, in their on-going inquiry into the facts of subversive nature, have allowed to make it clear once more that those delinquents who had thought they could elude the weight [sic] of justice through lapse of time and clandestinity, such justice will inevitably reach them sooner or later [sic]. The present fact proves it [*Ibid.*, May 5, 1977].

Where human intervention remains necessary it takes the form of the administration of natural justice, in accordance with the proper formulas: presumption of innocence, evidence, identification of the accused, and the like. It is only necessary to translate the signs for each of these elements and determine how they relate to one another. The order of the elements in the formula is also important, and each system of adjudicative discourse develops its own rules for what is acceptable. The contradiction between the model to which the present texts implicitly refer (the national, ultimately Spanish, tradition of formal justice) and the form they actually take would seem to disqualify them from being considered instances of any discourse of the administration of justice, including that of popular justice, despite their similarities with the latter. But I suggest that the texts present a caricature of legal discourse, which should remind us how important it is to distinguish analytically between the discourse of justice and actual justice.

THE DISCOURSES OF SUMMARY JUSTICE AND POPULAR JUSTICE

When we compare the discourse of summary justice just described with the model of popular justice discourse previously elaborated, they appear to have a certain affinity, although the former sometimes takes extreme forms. I shall now analyze the discourse of summary justice, integrating the general political discourse about subversion with the accounts of specific incidents of confrontation. The general political discourse serves as the frame of reference for the discourse of summary justice.

Involvement of the Public

The public is very much present in the discourse of summary justice, in several ways. At the outset of each text it is addressed as a witness of the event to follow: "This is to inform the public." Members of the public denounce "suspect" people and situations, thus cooperating actively with the security forces in their central, and self-arrogated task, the total elimination of public enemy number one—subversion. Furthermore, the public is present in the background of each incident, behaving properly by obeying the orders of the security forces and assisting them whenever possible. The public understands its civic duties and is praised for this in the epilogue. It may also be the object of a lecture consisting of political and moral statements about good and bad people, proper and improper behavior. Thus the public is present everywhere, as neighbors, passers-by, parents, and other roles.

Significantly, the concluding exhortation of praise and admonition may address itself to the "citizenry" rather than to the more neutral "public." Because the phrase "the people" is so pervasive throughout the discourse, the use of the concept "citizen" at the end of the text inevitably affects to some extent the connotation of the earlier term. The implication of "citizenry" is obviously positive and associated with "us" as opposed to "them" (an opposition that structures the general political discourse about subversion, an aspect to be elaborated later in the chapter). Thus, at the outset of each text, the public is called on to identify with "us" in its assigned role as a witness.

The use of terms such as *citizen* constitutes an appeal to the totality of feelings associated with patriotism, loyalty, responsibility for the future of the country, the preservation of "Western civilization," etc. Because all the attributes of *us* and *them* are mutually exclusive, the phrase "this is to inform the public" implies that us equals citizenry equals good or, more elaborately, that the people are with us and the people are on the right side, and *you* (the reader) surely have no doubt about whom to identify with. Therefore the people, taken as a witness to the incident described in the text and later as an audience, cannot be anything but an approving witness and an applauding audience.

This points to a remarkable aspect of the discourse of summary justice, which distinguishes it sharply from that of formal justice, namely, the absolute absence of "the other": no opposing view is presented, the adversary has no voice. As such, the discourse is an extreme example of the "verbal appropriation of social reality." As we shall see later, the same is not true of the general discourse about subversion, where the views of the adversary are presented, and rejected, as they are in other justifying or legitimating discourse.

The cooperative, well-behaved citizen of the discourse is the only citizen whose existence is recognized. All behavior that falls short of positive cooperation is suspect. Thus the discourse creates a broad area of crime-by-association. Subversives are not limited to the active core of the urban guerrillas (montoneros and ERP—PRT) but include those who assist them, purposely or unwittingly, those who sympathize with subversive ideas or have done so in past, and even those who are simply indifferent, the passive spectators of the political arena.

In the general discourse about subversion an attempt is made to identify the "people" with the security forces, suggesting that they are really one and the same. This is most clearly expressed in speeches to young army recruits and to those who have just terminated their military service. Obviously, it is such people who do most of the actual fighting against subversion and suffer most of the casualties. Because military service is compulsory, conscripts may be considered a cross section of the population (although in fact some sectors are underrepresented). Accordingly, their entry or departure is taken as an opportunity to emphasize the unity of the people and the armed forces. That discourse is cast in terms of civic duty, participation in the patriotic mission of the armed forces to eliminate subversion and save the country and culture, sacrifice, courage, responsibility, martyrdom, and the like. Since military service constitutes the first time many of these young men have been separated from their families for any significant period, tribute is paid to the sacrifice and suffering of their relatives.[29] All these characteristics are typically associated with "us," and thus a strong link is established between the population at large and the security forces.

Now one may ask why a government as authoritarian as the post-1976 Argentine regime needs to employ so much talk about popular involvement in its political discourse, including accounts of the day-to-day struggle against subversion. Why does the authoritarian regime not just assume full responsibility for that struggle alone? Two elements may contribute to understanding why this appears to be a felt need. First, the regime, at least in its own view, is in a transitory stage. In the long run it will need some form of legitimation, some form of popular support, or at least an acceptance that goes beyond mere tolerance. This is recognized both in general political discourse and in the discourse of summary justice, where it takes a suggestive, descriptive form—the people are, the people do—not an explicit normative one—the people should be or should do. Second, and perhaps more obvious, the discourse is well within the Argentine tradition of political rhetoric. Whatever the degree of authoritarianism and repression, the rhetoric of official political discourse tends to be populist, like the style of government in several respects.

The Subject Matter of the Discourse: The Whole Person

The discourse of summary justice may be characterized as an extreme form of popular justice discourse with respect to its subject matter: the subversive (terrorist, subversive delinquent, etc). Being a subversive is treated by the discourse as a status that affects the whole person. It is essentially a life-style, a permanent mental state, determined by certain objectives, convictions, and values. Instances of actual behavior function as indicators of such objectives and of other aspects of the mental state. They are simply *signs* that the person described is a

---

[29]See, e.g., Speech by General Videla, April 25, 1977 (*La Opinión*, April 26, 1977). The importance of the element "family life" will be elaborated later in the chapter.

subversive. The behavior as such has hardly any other importance; it is *being* a subversive that is the crime, not doing anything.

The legal category in more formal systems of justice that comes closest to the concept of the subversive is that of treason. This "most heinous of crimes" inevitably involves the whole person; the minimum punishment is permanent loss of the rights of citizenship, and in many instances the death penalty is felt to be mandated. The social stigma attached to treason is also very strong and inclusive, affecting the whole person and forming a legitimate basis for presuming the existence of associated behavior and mental states, such as lack of loyalty to the group and the destruction of basic moral feelings (responsibility, honesty, reliability, respect for authority, and the like). It may not be coincidental that the concept of treason, the traitor, and the deserter plays an important role in the general discourse about subversion, where it appears to invoke recognizable legal discourse in the Western tradition, of which the Argentine system forms (or perhaps we should say formed) part.

The general discourse about subversion is complex and suffers from internal contradictions. It belongs to the larger body of political discourse, which may usefully be seen as primarily serving to legitimate. Such discourse is not a logical argument but rather is a number of paired signs, one of which the audience is invited to identify with and the other of which it is urged to reject as evil. The signs have simple connotations in terms of us–them and good–bad and refer, first, to characteristics of being, values, and objectives and, second, to behavior.

Some phrases describing the nature of subversion are highly abstract: "lacks all respect for the essence of Argentine being" and "intends to establish marxist totalitarianism in our country." But the discourse sometimes does descend to slightly more concrete levels so that it may provide guidelines for recognizing individual subversive elements and concrete subversive acts. If the audience is supposed to stay away from subversives and avoid being even their unwitting accomplices, it must be able to know one when it sees one. Therefore a whole series of characteristics are linguistically associated with the concept of subversion. The image presented to the public in the press is remarkably similar to the way in which the media portray other important types of deviance, such as drug use, in Western countries (Young, 1971).

Subversives are traitors who have placed themselves outside the law, outside the community. As public enemy number one, subversion must be eliminated; capital punishment is therefore the only appropriate sanction. In order not to be caught, subversives will frequently choose exile, fleeing the country like cowards. Otherwise they are in hiding, engaged not in honest work but in underground activities. Whether in exile or underground, they have lost their status as citizens; they are no longer Argentines. Furthermore, subversion is really a foreign product, a disease clandestinely introduced into the country, which infects the entire people and their culture. The deserter who has abandoned his community is associated with the individual who has rejected his family and lost all respect for family life, and with the subject who repudiates authority. Life in hiding is necessarily a life of dishonesty, even falsity; it is irregular in all senses.

At the level of behavior subversion is principally characterized by aggression, useless and arbitrary violence, the instigation of disorder, and even chaos. The enemy is always referred to as an abstraction, using nouns such as *subversion, subversive delinquency,* or at best as a group of "terrorists" or "subversive delinquents." Subversives are not individuals but members of a category.

If we look back at the texts described earlier, we may recognize a number of signs derived from the categories found in the general discourse about subversion. The entire discourse of summary justice is oriented toward identifying subversive elements. It does so by combining a number of acknowledged signs of that status. The people involved do not obey official orders (they reject authority); they flee, they hide in a house (they are cowards; they do not confront the security forces in open battle); they have no identity papers or counterfeit ones (falsity, dishonesty); they open fire at the security forces (aggression, attack); they carry bombs, firearms, and the like (violence, no respect for life); they even expose small children to all the risks of their life-style (no respect for life or the family); quite a few women are involved (no respect for the family or the proper order of things); they have leaflets and other forms of literature in their possession (they try to diffuse alien ideologies).

All these signs establish the status of the people involved; they "prove," in the terms of the discourse, that those people are "subversive elements"; their individual identity is therefore irrelevant. The people recognize them for what they are. It is then remarkable that the texts almost always refer to "identification," in the sense that either "the identity cannot be established," or "identification of the bodies will be pursued," or "those killed were so-and-so." The mere mention of the issue of identity is an (implicit) reference to a more formal legal discourse— that of criminal trials. This leads us to another aspect of the discourse that seems to have the same implicit reference, namely, evidence.

Evidence

Evidence is clearly considered important in the discourse of summary justice. Even in its more abbreviated forms it preserves an order for the presentation of elements that reflects their evidentiary value. The entire text is directed toward establishing the status of "subversive," but some of the elements, e.g., instances of specific behavior such as "disobeying official orders," have illegal connotations in themselves. The signs that indicate the status of "subversive" have already been mentioned: young person; suspect behavior (sometimes even suspect attitude); disobeying legitimate orders; opening fire; resisting the forces of order; fleeing; possessing firearms, bombs, and leaflets; possessing false identity papers; women participating in acts of violence. All but the last three are typically found in the text *before* the killing of the subversives. The possession of weapons, bombs, leaflets, and false identity papers, which would constitute more persuasive evidence, or at least a firmer basis for legitimate suspicion (in another discourse),[30] here are merely additional, though important, signs that come after the fact. They may seem superfluous, but because each text is a whole they function as elements of a style that increases the weight of previous elements.

Causality, Sanctions and Remedies, and Legal Norms

Let us now consider briefly the other elements of the discourse of the administration of justice in the context of the discourse of summary justice. "Causality" has lost all applicability. It is relevant only where consequential behavior is the subject matter of the discourse, i.e., where behavior and its consequences both are necessary and must be linked before either can be considered legally relevant. This mode of discourse is characteristic of highly formal systems of justice. As we have seen, the discourse of popular justice displays a diluted form of causality. But because the discourse of summary justice focuses on establishing the status of people, as an attribute of being, and treats concrete instances of behavior as merely incidental, there is no role for causality.

Whereas the discourse of popular justice is preoccupied with identifying the "proper remedy" that will "improve" the problem situation, the discourse of summary justice is little concerned with either remedies or sanctions. Its range of solutions is very limited; indeed, there is really only one: summary execution; only rarely is someone "captured."

The discourse of summary justice does not explicitly refer to legal norms. The Argentine regime was actually empowered to create such norms, and at the outset of the period under study (March 1976) the military junta did issue a number of instructions (*comunicados* or *bandos*) specifying the circumstances that would justify summary execution, which are typically those concrete behaviors mentioned in the discourse analyzed: shooting at a security officer, running when ordered to "stop," etc. Therefore, though these actions could have been justified in terms of legal norms, the discourse of summary justice does not do so, and this refusal is its distinctive characteristic. The principal justification for the ultimate act of execution remains implicit in the description of the relevant quality of being: subversion. And such implicit justification is framed in terms of general political discourse. The same lack of explicit justifica-

---

[30]Obviously, these may also be offenses in themselves.

tion also means that the discourse does not refer back to earlier cases. On these two points, especially the latter, the discourse of summary justice is closer to that of popular justice than to that of formal justice.

SUMMARY JUSTICE:
THE ARROGANCE OF DISCOURSE

The discourse of summary justice (viewed broadly so as to include the relevant parts of the general political discourse about subversion) is characterized by great pomposity, a highly standardized vocabulary and syntax, a low level of verisimilitude, and extreme condescension, indeed arrogance—a refusal to take its audience seriously. The relative lack of verisimilitude is one index of this arrogance.

Two major contradictions within the discourse may serve to illustrate this characterization. The first one concerns the origin and nature of the deviant behavior—subversion, terrorism—and the type of crime that is being punished. The discourse is consistently ambiguous about both. On the one hand, the texts assert that subversion is a foreign evil, an international conspiracy in which Argentina is presently one of the major battlegrounds. Argentine youths are corrupted by foreign ideologies introduced by agents who enter and leave the country clandestinely. On the other hand, they maintain that Argentine culture, the "essence of Argentine being," is being corrupted from inside, that some "disease" is eating it away, that the real fault is to be found within the basic cell of the community—the family—which has allowed this loss of values to contribute to the degeneration of the whole country. This contradiction within the analysis of the nature and source of "subversion" is closely linked with ideas concerning the nature of the crime. On the one hand, the texts describe the crime as purely political; those who engage in subversion are characterized as seeking to change the political and social order, to establish a different regime. On the other, the texts assert that it "has been proved [sic] that they are common criminals."[31] This contradiction is convenient, indeed necessary in order that the discourse may be credible at both the national and international levels. At the latter, the discourse emphasizes that Argentina is a principal victim of international political terrorism, performing its heroic duty by standing firm on the battle line. At the same time, the discourse endows Argentina with discretion to deal with the political enemy in its own way; national laws and policies apply, and national institutions need not defer to foreign criticism or control. The discourse as a

[31]Statement by Albano Eduardo Harguindeguy (minister of the interior) in a press conference of September 6, 1977 (*La Opinión*, September 7, 1977).

whole, in its extreme arrogance, makes no effort to resolve or obscure such contradictions.[32]

The second contradiction concerns the discursive role of the concept "the family." In the general discourse about subversion the family is a major value associated with "us" and one of the most important institutions "we" venerate, maintain, and protect. "They," on the other hand, have neither respect nor affection for the family. In fact, subversives have no family; they have abandoned it to live underground. In rejecting their families, they have lost their membership in the community and the nation. As traitors they are no longer citizens.

But this image of the solitary fugitive rarely occurs in the discourse of summary justice. Instead, the texts frequently refer to "a couple," "two married people," or "a man and his concubine,"[33] even to the point of sacrificing verisimilitude: "a couple" is said to have fled or to have been killed but not identified. The texts go on to describe a number of people, including children found living "in the house" in relationships that resemble the family. These concrete "descriptions" contrast sharply with the more abstract image of the family relations of subversives (or lack thereof) contained in the general discourse. Such ambiguity appears to be related to the role attributed to women in subversive activities. The whole phenomenon of subversion is rendered more perverse if women are implicated in it.[34] The more extreme images of subversives in the general discourse include stereotypes of sexual deviance such as "a preoccupation with sex," "indulging in pornography," and the like. In many texts the presence of women is specifically mentioned, subversion being totally contrary to "proper" female interests and activities. Caught in this contradiction, the discourse loses credibility and increases its arrogance.

These two illustrations of the arrogance of summary justice discourse may be generalized. The "privileged position of knowing" enjoyed by the producer of the discourse (see Burton and Carlen, 1979: 74ff.) takes such an extreme form that the producer employs concepts from different and incompatible universes without even attempting to integrate them. In formal justice discourse the privileged knowledge of the judge must be mediated through the testimony of witnesses and other evidence; in popular justice discourse such privileged knowing does not always need to be mediated—the personal knowledge of the judges is acceptable; in summary justice the producer of the discourse is by definition all-knowing and

[32]As such, it is less complex than the discourse intended to meet the legitimation needs created by the Irish civil war, or even those generated by ordinary police behavior, as analyzed by Burton and Carlen (1979).

[33]Concubinage, rather than marriage, is the prevailing form of union between adult men and women in certain sectors of the Argentine population.

[34]Women are generally punished more severely than men for many similar acts because they are held to a higher (i.e., double) standard; see, e.g., Simon (1975), Smart (1976), and Crites (1977).

needs no mediation at all. The producer simply knows that the people involved are "subversive delinquents," that two people he may never have seen are married, that the intention of a person walking in the street is to paint subversive slogans on the street walls, etc. There is no place for questioning or doubt, there is no need for evidence before such knowing is proclaimed.

CONCLUSION

The discourse of summary justice described in this chapter consists of a unique mixture of elements that resemble those found in other forms of legal discourse. It combines formalism and pomposity with shallow rhetoric and a low level of verisimilitude in a typical way that finds hardly any parallel, even in Latin American countries that are otherwise comparable, such as Brazil and Chile. Argentine official discourse liberally uses phrases such as "the essence of Argentine being," which would be wholly ridiculous and unacceptable elsewhere and render the discourse condescending and arrogant.

Its pomposity and stereotyped vocabulary and syntax are reminiscent of formal justice discourse, especially police reports. So are the preoccupation with the identity or identification of the people involved (although this is rather belated by the standards of other discourses) and the limited number of sanctions applied.

On the other hand, summary justice discourse may be likened to popular justice discourse on several grounds. First, "the public" pervades the discourse in a striking fashion that is typical of popular justice discourse. The people perform a number of crucial roles: they are approving witnesses to the events, they cooperate by informing the security forces about "suspect happenings" and generally assisting them, and they serve as the audience for a moral and political lecture about "subversion" and their role in the struggle against it.

Secondly, the subject matter of summary justice discourse is closer to that of popular justice discourse than it is to that of formal justice discourse. Formal justice discourse concerns social *behavior* and strictly limits the range of behavior to be considered (although it does allow mental states to play a subordinate role). Occasionally it goes further, for instance, when it makes the status of membership in a prohibited political party a crime that is evidenced merely by such a specific behavior as paying dues or attending meetings. But in formal justice discourse such status crimes are the exception rather than the rule.

Popular justice discourse tends to deal with a larger segment of social behavior, taking into account more elements of the surrounding environment. Thus it defines a "problem" in addition to, or instead of, an offense. It weighs more elements of the social status of the people involved. Summary justice discourse goes to the extreme of considering the person as a whole, reducing behavior to a mere indicator of the essential "being" of the person. It deals with the "subversive," a characterization that involves the total personality in a literal sense. It is also the "whole person" who is punished: the subversive is executed summarily. Summary justice discourse conceptualizes its subject in such an extreme fashion that it alienates itself from other forms of judicial discourse, and from legal discourse in general, to the point where it caricatures them.

Because of the way in which it defines its subject, the discourse of summary justice lacks several of the elements of judicial discourse. The concept of causality loses all meaning because there is no need to attribute social consequences to specific behavior; the latter is merely evidence of the status to be "proved." The discursive use of evidence has been turned inside out—the *behavior* is the major piece of evidence, and "corroborative evidence" (possession of arms, leaflets, etc.) may be presented after the sanction has been executed.

Thus we have reached the point where we must conclude that the discourse of summary justice is not like judicial discourse at all. It is arrogant, even autistic, in the sense of being so self-centered that it loses all contact with both its audience and its ostensible discursive opponent. Judicial discourse is essentially legitimating and seeks to convince. It sets up an opponent whom it subsequently defeats, observing certain discursive rules in doing so. When referring to facts it presents them as plausibilities, something an ordinary person would recognize as a possible social or psychological reality. It follows a logical order of argument. Summary justice discourse does nothing of the kind. It mixes elements drawn from, or acceptable in, judicial discourse in such a way that it loses the quality of legal discourse and becomes a caricature.

REFERENCES

Abel, Richard L. (1973) "A Comparative Theory of Dispute Institutions in Society," 8 *Law & Society Review* 217.

———— (1979) "Delegalization: A Critical Review of Its Ideology, Manifestations, and Social Consequences," 6 *Jahrbuch für Rechtssoziologie und Rechtstheorie* 27.

Amnesty International (1976) "Report on the Mission to Argentina, 6–15 November 1976." London: Amnesty International (mimeographed copy).

Bankowski, Zenon and Geoff Mungham (1979) "Law and Lay Participation," 1978 *European Yearbook in Law and Sociology* 17.

Berman, Harold J. (1963) *Justice in the USSR*, rev. ed. New York: Vintage.

Berman, Harold J. and J. W. Spindler (1963) "Soviet Comrades' Courts," 38 *George Washington Law Review* 842.

Berman, Jesse (1969) "The Cuban Popular Tribunals," 69 *Columbia Law Review* 1317.

Blet, R., M.-F. Gérard, M. Guémann, M. Miaille, F. Natali, N. Obrego, M. Sem, and E. Vieux (1979) *La justice en Chine: Des Cent fleurs aux cent codes* Paris: Maspero.

Burton, Frank and Pat Carlen (1979) *Official Discourse: On Discourse Analysis, Government Publications, Ideology and the State.* London: Routledge and Kegan Paul.

Cantor, Robert (1974) "New Laws for a New Society," 2 *Crime and Social Justice* 23.

Cheetham, Rosemond, Santiago Quevedo, Gaston Roja, Eder Seder, and Franz Vanderschueren

(1972) *Pobladores: Del legalismo a la justicia popular,* Santiago de Chile: Universidad Católica de Chile (CIDU).

Cohn, Bernard (1966) "Anthropological Notes on Disputes and Law in India," 67 *American Anthropologist* 82.

————— (1967) "Some Notes on Law and Change in North India," in P. Bohannan (ed.) *Law and Warfare.* Garden City, N.Y.: Natural History Press.

Crites, Laura (ed.) (1977) *The Female Offender: A Total Look at Women in the Criminal Justice System.* Lexington, Mass.: Lexington Books.

Cuellar, Oscar, Rosemond Cheetham, Santiago Quevedo, Jaime Rojas, and Franz Vanderschueren (1971) "Experiencias de justicia popular in poblaciones," 8 *Cuadernos de la realidad nacional* 153.

Eckhoff, Torstein (1966) "The Mediator and the Judge," reprinted in V. Aubert (ed.) *Sociology of Law.* London: Penguin (1969).

Feiffer, George (1964) *Justice in Moscow.* New York: Simon and Schuster.

Felstiner, William L. F. (1971) "Forms and Social Settings of Dispute Settlement." Working Paper No. 3, Program in Law and Modernization, Yale Law School.

————— (1974) "Influences of Social Organization on Dispute Processing," 9 *Law & Society Review* 63.

Finlay, David J., Ole R. Olsti, and Richard Fagan (1967) *Enemies in Politics.* Chicago: Rand McNally.

Hammer, S. (1969) "Law Enforcement and Social Control," 24 *Soviet Studies* 379.

Ietswaart, Heleen F. P. (1973) "Popular Courts in Chile," 30 *Guild Practitioner* 37.

Levi, Edward (1948) *An Introduction to Legal Reasoning.* Chicago: University of Chicago Press.

Loney, Martin (1973) "Social Control in Cuba," in Ian Taylor and Laurie Taylor (eds.) *Politics and Deviance.* London: Penguin.

Lubman, Stanley (1967) "Mao and Mediation: Politics and Dispute Resolution in Communist China," 55 *California Law Review* 1284.

Nader, Laura (1964a) "An Analysis of Zapotec Law Cases," 3 *Ethnology* 404.

————— (1964b) *Talea and Juquila: A Comparison of Zapotec Social Organization.* Berkeley: University of California Press (Publications in American Archaeology and Ethnology, vol. 48).

————— (1969) "Styles of Court Procedure: To Make the Balance," in L. Nader (ed.) *Law in Culture and Society.* Chicago: Aldine.

Nader, Laura and Duane Metzger (1963) "Conflict Resolution in Two Mexican Communities," 65 *American Anthropologist* 584.

Podgórecki, Adam (1962) "Attitudes to Workers' Courts," reprinted in V. Aubert (ed.) *Sociology of Law.* London: Penguin (1969).

Rheinstein, Max (1967) *Max Weber on Law in Economy and Society.* New York: Simon and Schuster.

Rouquié, Alain (1978) "L'Argentine du Général Videla: deux ans de Réorganisation Nationale (1976–1978)," 1978 *Problèmes d'Amérique Latine* 10.

Santos, Boaventura de Sousa (1973) "Law against Law." Working Paper No. 4, Program in Law and Modernization, Yale Law School.

————— (1977) "The Law of the Oppressed: The Construction and Reproduction of Legality in Pasargada," 12 *Law & Society Review* 5.

Simon, Rita James (1975) *Women and Crime.* Lexington, Mass.: Lexington Books.

Smart, Carol (1976) *Women, Crime and Criminology: A Feminist Critique.* Boston: Routledge & Kegan Paul.

Spence, Jack (1978) "Institutionalizing Neighborhood Courts: Two Chilean Experiences," in R. L. Abel (ed.) *The Politics of Informal Justice,* vol. 2: *Comparative Studies.* New York: Academic Press.

Taras, T. (1959) "Social Courts in the USSR," 14 *Soviet Studies* 398.

Tiruchelvam, Neelan (1978) "The Ideology of Popular Justice," in Charles E. Reason and Robert M. Rich (eds.) *The Sociology of Law*. Toronto: Butterworth.

Wasserstrom, Richard A. (1961) *The Judicial Decision: Toward a Theory of Legal Justification*. Stanford, Calif.: Stanford University Press.

de Wit, John (1978) "On the Facts and How to Use Them." Paper presented at the Sixth Conference of the European Group for the Study of Deviance and Social Control (Bremen/Steinkimmen).

Young, Jock (1971) "The Role of the Police as Amplifiers of Deviancy, Negotiators of Reality and Translators of Fantasy: Some Consequences of Our Present System of Drug Control as Seen in Notting Hill," in Stanley Cohen (ed.) *Images of Deviance*. London: Penguin.

III

Liberal Capitalism

7

The Movement toward Procedural Informalism in North America and Western Europe: A Critical Survey

BRYANT GARTH

One task of comparative legal scholarship is to relate seemingly isolated national developments to more pervasive social movements. Given basic similarities among advanced capitalist countries, particularly in their commitment to promoting economic growth and stability and to ameliorating the conditions of their disadvantaged populations, comparative study helps us to understand the direction in which these welfare states and their legal systems are likely to move. Procedural issues have recently assumed a central importance in welfare state programs, which are now facing a turning point in their development. Rights that promise a more egalitarian society have proliferated, but implementation has been limited. Yet even the existing level of welfare is expensive, raising the question whether to retreat from the promises or attempt to fulfill them. The interest in procedural informalism in a number of advanced capitalist countries in Western Europe and North America reflects these tensions in the welfare state.

It will be useful to begin by distinguishing between the substantive and procedural aspects of what is often termed legal formalism. This concept is most frequently identified with Weber's ideal type of formal legal rationality: law

183

THE POLITICS OF INFORMAL JUSTICE
Volume 2

Copyright © 1982 by Academic Press, Inc.
All rights of reproduction in any form reserved.
ISBN 0-12-041502-X

legitimated by reference to criteria intrinsic to a refined legal system (1954: 61–64). In addition to this formal legal rationality, however, Weber also referred to "juridical formalism," which I prefer to term procedural formalism. This formalism "guarantees the maximum freedom for the interested parties to represent their formal legal interests" (*Ibid.*: 226).

> Facts which are neither stipulated nor alleged and proved, and facts which remain undisclosed by the recognized methods of proof... do not exist as far as the judge is concerned, who aims at establishing only that relative truth which is attainable within the limits set by the procedural acts of the parties [*Ibid.*: 227].

Procedural formalism is thus characterized by passive judges, strict rules of evidence, and the use of legal counsel by both parties. These features no doubt can help judges to elaborate formally rational decisions, and there is a historical relationship between formal legal rationality and procedural formalism, but I think it is useful to keep these manifestations of legal formalism distinct.

My focus in this chapter is limited to what I consider the procedural aspects of Weber's legal formalism. There has been a decline in procedural formalism in welfare state societies for two reasons (cf. Unger, 1976; Luhmann, 1976; Charvet, 1976). First, law has increasingly become an instrument for social planning in modern Western welfare states. Political parties and interest groups work within the political system to seek reforms implemented by the state, and these reforms typically are embodied in new laws. Social change for the disadvantaged is sought through law (cf. Friedmann, 1959: 485–503; Friedman, 1977: 22–23; Savatier, 1977). It is therefore not surprising that the political significance of civil (and criminal) procedure—the means by which laws are or are not enforced— has been acknowledged more explicitly.[1] Procedural factors, together with the organization of courts and the legal profession, determine whether social programs and regulatory schemes achieve their ostensible goals (see Mayhew, 1975). Recent procedural innovations, such as the revived interest in informalism, illustrate increasing interest in pursuing substantive results through procedural reforms.

Pressures to abandon or at least supplement formal procedure have also accompanied the relatively recent recognition of a right of "access" or "equal access" to the courts. The postwar constitutions of the Federal Republic of Germany (see Article 19[4]) and Italy (Article 24) proclaim a right to sue in court; it is also embodied in the 1950 European Convention on Human Rights (Article 6). Other countries, including the United Kingdom and the United States, increasingly honor the principle of a right of access. The centrality of law in the

---

[1]Weber noted this more than half a century ago: "That capitalism could nevertheless make its way so well in England was largely because the court system and trial procedure amounted until well in the modern age to a denial of justice to the economically weaker groups" (1954: 353).

welfare state also argues for a right of access. Such a right may inhibit procedural informalism, but it also can stimulate procedural reform. For example, the European Court of Human Rights, which enforces the European Convention on Human Rights in the twenty-one countries that have ratified it, recently invalidated the system of legal aid in Ireland on the ground that it did not provide equal access to the courts for an indigent woman seeking a legal separation (European Court of Human Rights, Judgment of October 9, 1979, *Airey*). The court noted the relationship between rights to access, legal aid, court reform, informal procedures, and notions of substantive justice. It stated that the Convention is intended to guarantee not rights that are theoretical or illusory but rights that are practical and effective.... This is particularly so of the right of access to the courts" (slip opinion, p. 9). An effective right of access could be provided by the "institution of a legal aid scheme" *or* by "a simplification of procedure" (slip opinion, p. 12).

Several central characteristics of law in the welfare state, therefore, encourage procedural informalism in Europe and the United States. To understand the implications of this phenomenon, however, one must recognize that procedural informalism does not express a coherent institutional program. First, there have been significant differences in the timing of this decline in legal formalism, differences accounted for mainly by the early development of many welfare institutions in Western Europe. Second, the manifestations of the decline may be very different in countries that are otherwise comparable. Particular legal institutions produced by varying historical traditions provide different institutional settings for the movement away from procedural formalism. And third, assuming that there is a clear movement toward procedural informalism, it is not ideologically homogeneous. A decline in the requirement of procedural formality permits a variety of reforms. Informalism is a banner under which different persons and groups can pursue their own substantive ends. Opposing groups may advocate a common reform that each believes will advance its own interests, and they may even share the rhetoric of "access," but it is necessary to keep their actual objectives in sight. Much of this chapter will be devoted to classifying these objectives and highlighting their similarities and differences.

I will describe three approaches to procedural reform, each of which can be seen as part of a broad movement toward procedural informalism in the United States and other welfare states, particularly those of Western Europe. These approaches can be termed (*a*) "making rights effective," (*b*) "conciliation;" and (*c*) "diversion."[2] I will first trace the evolution of the institutions in which these

---

[2]My typology has some similarities to those employed by Galanter (1979), Johnson (1978), Nonet and Selznick (1978), and Unger (1976). Galanter distinguishes among "legalist," technocratic," and "communal." Johnson explains procedural informalism as justified by either "judicial overload," "access to justice," or "superior process" (1978: 173–179). For Nonet and Selznick the relevant

approaches are embodied, particularly where European and American developments have been significantly different. I will seek to ascertain the factors that contribute to or inhibit the ascendancy of each. I will then examine their interrelationship and assess, critically and comparatively, the potential and problems of procedural informalism. I will end with the inevitable question of where we should channel our energies if we are sympathetic to the reformist goals underlying welfare legislation and recent procedural innovations. The present dilemmas of the movement toward informalism inevitably reflect the crises of the welfare state.

"MAKING RIGHTS EFFECTIVE"

This approach to dispute processing takes the most optimistic view of law in the welfare state. Reform here can be seen as an effort to translate welfare rights created on behalf of the disadvantaged—including the right of access to courts—into effective rights (see generally Cappelletti and Garth, 1978). It is manifested in efforts to provide access to lawyers, administrative agencies, and dispute processing machinery for relatively disadvantaged persons, but I believe the real concern is with substantive rights rather than with the instrumental right of access. The principal method is to promote accessibility through changes in legal personnel and procedures, some of which foster informalism.

The development of this approach can be traced to the late-nineteenth- and early-twentieth-century precursors of the modern welfare state. Just as the welfare state antedates World War II, so this approach also has earlier roots. The Continental nineteenth-century codes of civil procedure, including the French Code of 1806, the Italian Code of 1865, and the German Code of 1877, expressed a philosophy of laissez-faire individualism. They emphasized procedural formalism and control by the parties over every aspect of the proceedings, even their pace (see Engelmann and Millar, 1927: 11–27; Cappelletti, 1971: 883–884; cf. Van Caenegem, 1973: 87–95). Legal aid to needy individuals was provided only as a matter of charity (Cappelletti *et al.*, 1975). This individualistic formalism was also evident in the United States, where neither federal nor state governments provided legal aid and "there was a strong movement to reduce the role and authority of the judge to that of mere umpire and to enlarge the sphere of the jury and the ability of the parties to play upon that body with a minimum of judicial interference" (James and Hazard, 1977: 6). But reform of civil procedure

---

distinctions are among "repressive," "autonomous," and "responsive" law. And Unger selects for analysis "customary law," "bureaucratic or regulatory law," and "autonomous law" (1976: 48–58). My model is probably closest to Johnson's, but I seek to make more explicit the political and substantive meanings of such concepts as "access" and "superior." I acknowledge that law in the welfare state is "purposive" but ask whose purpose substantive and procedural law reflects.

and legal aid began on the European continent earlier than it did in the United States.

A first major step was the Austrian Code of Civil Procedure of 1895. Influenced by a concern for social welfare, the code moved away from absolute party autonomy and toward an informalism that Homberger has characterized as "trial by colloquy" (1970: 24). Judges gained more control over the pace of the proceedings, and each judge became "a sort of informal collaborator" who could aid litigants unable to prosecute or defend their claims effectively (Ibid.: 25; see Code of Civil Procedure [ZPO] § 182). The judges' role, according to the code's draftsman, was to enforce the substantive law and settle conflicts in the interests of individuals and the public generally (see Cappelletti, 1971: 878). The courts were to become a social welfare institution (Wohlfahrtseinrichtung). Judges were assigned somewhat inconsistent functions: They were to attempt to bring the parties to an amicable settlement at any stage of the litigation, but at the same time such settlements were to conform to the law. Informalism was thought to be consistent with legal rights enforcement by active judges.

The Austrian code greatly influenced later revisions of other European (and some non-European) codes of civil procedure. It was soon followed by Weimar Germany, which, as others have noted, also anticipated many other developments in law and the welfare state (Unger, 1976). The reforms adopted by the Social Democratic government in 1924, which imposed on German judges the duties of their Austrian counterparts, clearly revealed a desire to reduce inequalities between the parties (see Kaplan et al., 1958: 1224) and exhibited "the tendency of a socialist government to strengthen the judicial authority" (Millar, 1924: 708). The powers of judges elsewhere in Europe were strengthened in succeeding years, and the active, relatively informal role of the judge is now well established in the European civil law countries, at least in principle (see Jolowicz, 1975; Perrot, 1977; Thery, 1978: 509–510).

The second influential precursor of the welfare rights approach was the legal aid reform in Weimar Germany, beginning in 1919. The state compensated private lawyers for representing indigents, thus creating the first of what are now termed "judicare" systems of legal aid (see Kaplan et al., 1958: 1469; Klauser and Riegert, 1971). At the same time, the Social Democratic government was active in the movement to provide free legal advice through public legal aid offices. Some ambiguities in these reforms will be discussed later in the chapter, but again it is notable that a concern with the enforcement of legal rights played an important part in this pre-fascist movement (see Reifner, 1982). That concern was also apparent in other German reforms of the period, such as the creation of specialized, less formal Labor Courts in 1926 (Ramm, 1971: 83–87; see also Bender and Strecker, 1978: 546). Thus legal aid reform, specialized administrative tribunals, and more active judges became key characteristics of Social Democratic reform on the Continent.

Administrative tribunals created in the United Kingdom in the early twentieth century reveal the same trend. The Liberal government deliberately entrusted the implementation of new social welfare laws, such as those providing old-age pensions, to tribunals rather than formal courts, and tribunals became increasingly important after World War II (see Robson, 1928; Street, 1968). Similarly, the Legal Aid and Advice Act of 1949, which gave England a judicare system, also antedated reforms in other common law jurisdictions.

These early efforts to restructure the legal profession and deformalize or bypass the regular courts in order to aid the disadvantaged set a pattern for later access reforms and resulted in lasting changes that anticipated and to a certain extent preempted the more recent movement. Nevertheless, developments since World War II and especially in the mid-1960s also expressed and greatly magnified this concern with the rights of the disadvantaged. New rights proliferated and procedures were changed, following a dynamic that can be called "gap politics."

With the maturation of the welfare state in the last ten to fifteen years, numerous enactments have sought to protect the underprivileged against the superior power and expertise of large governmental and private organizations. Examples include laws providing tenants with warranties of habitability, controlling rents, or guaranteeing security of tenure; consumer protection measures regulating contract terms, credit provisions, product standards, sales tactics, and debt collection; occupational safety standards; antidiscrimination laws; environmental protection measures; and schemes for urban planning. These laws and their earlier analogues embody a distinctively welfare state approach to social problems, in which social change is pursued through the creation of new rights. But if these laws are not enforced, or enforced only weakly, social change will be frustrated and the welfare state, which claims to offer a moderate, nonsocialist solution to poverty and inequality, will be seen as a failure. Those who favor the welfare state, which presumably includes those who enacted the laws promoting change, must respond to any perceived gap in the enforcement of these rights.

This gap has repeatedly been discovered since the mid-1960s. Important sociological studies of "legal needs," beginning in the United States (e.g., Carlin and Howard, 1965; Carlin et al., 1966), have shown that new legal rights have systematically been underenforced by both government and private individuals. The insufficiency of the public attorney general, the French *ministère public*, and their analogues has been well documented (see generally Cappelletti, 1975). Rehbinder, for example, wrote of the "environmental deficit" caused by weak public enforcement in the Federal Republic of Germany (1976: 374–375).

Isolated individuals rarely enforce their new rights, and they organize to do so even less frequently (see, e.g., Handler, 1978). Individuals tend to use the legal system only for divorce or to assert or defend "traditional" property rights (of course, they are also used *by* it as criminal defendants). The Dutch Ministry of Justice, for example, surveyed "the need for legal assistance, the way in which this need is or is not being met and the lacunae evident in this area" (Council of Europe, 1976: 9) and found that "lawyers serve individuals mostly in divorce cases; they do not to any great extent serve individuals in their conflicts with governments or organizations. On the contrary, lawyers serve corporate bodies and large organizations" (Schuyt et al., 1977: 112). Even when lawyers could secure payment under the judicare system (created in the Netherlands in 1957), they were not addressing the unmet need in nontraditional areas of the law. Similar conclusions have been reached in France (cf. Valétas, 1976), Germany (cf. Falke et al., 1979: 128–129, 134–136), Great Britain (see Abel-Smith et al., 1973; Morris et al., 1973), Australia (Cass and Sackville, 1975), Canada (e.g., Messier, 1975), and the United States (Curran, 1977).

Since lawyers—the usual agents for enforcing legal rights—do not handle the new rights, a serious gap has "appeared" between the welfare state laws on the books and everyday life. This gap endangers the claims of the welfare state and provides a powerful argument for making good on those claims, an argument that appears politically neutral. Gap politics thus provide the setting for the contemporary efforts to make rights effective.

Empirical studies have demonstrated the importance of institutions that (a) can reach individuals and persuade them to use lawyers and the legal system; and (b) can substitute for the failure of governmental and individual enforcement. The legal need studies have been closely related (as both cause and effect) to the development of government-funded neighborhood law firms for the poor capable of enforcing nontraditional rights. The spread of this institution from the United States (where the Office of Economic Opportunity Legal Services Program began in 1965) to Great Britain, the Netherlands, Canada, and Australia and, to a lesser extent, Belgium, France, and Norway, can be explained by the belief that neighborhood law firms, law centers, and law shops can satisfy legal needs that the private profession has failed to meet (see Garth, 1980).

Efforts to provide legal representation to enforce the rights of large unorganized groups of consumers, pollution victims, and the like have also led to the creation of innovative legal institutions (see, e.g., Cappelletti, 1976; Fisch, 1979; Trubek, 1979). Two notable European examples are the French "loi Royer" (Law of December 27, 1973, no. 73–1193, article 46 [1973], J.O. 14139) and the German Law on Standard Terms of Contract (Law of December 9, 1976, §§ 13, 18, 21 [1976], BGBl I 3317), both of which grant consumer organizations special standing to enforce rights created by the new laws.

The focus on rights and the gap in their enforcement has now led beyond institutions of legal representation to procedural informalism as a means of implementation (see generally Cappelletti and Garth, 1978). In the United States, such reforms were proposed as early as 1966 by Jean Cahn and Edgar Cahn, the intellectual founders of the neighborhood law firm movement (1966: 948–955). Reformers have sought to devise alternative procedures and extrajudicial institutions that can attract individuals and enable them to vindicate their rights without lawyers. Such reforms hope that individuals will gain expertise through the experience of using an alternative forum and be freed from dependence on lawyers and that this will overcome the limitations of the number of lawyers that realistically can be made available for these tasks. Typical examples of rights-conscious informalism include housing tribunals, consumer complaint mechanisms, and reformed small claims courts (see Ruhnka *et al.*, 1978).

A further justification for these new procedures and institutions is reduction of the caseloads handled by poverty lawyers. If certain routine legal needs can be met without lawyers, then neighborhood law firms can perform other functions. Roland Penner, a member of the governing board of the legal aid society in Manitoba, argues that poverty lawyers should concentrate on "community and group action, in which the legal and the political intertwine. . . One of the reasons for this is the very significant and welcome development in the many areas of mediation-type services (rentalsmen, consumer protection bureaus) and more informal mechanisms (small claims courts, welfare appeal boards)" (1977: 91). Neighborhood law firms and other institutions of advocacy can team up with informal procedures to expand and enforce the rights of the disadvantaged.

The recent emphasis on small claims courts, housing courts, and the like is more characteristic of advanced, Western common law countries, such as Australia, Canada, Great Britain, and the United States. A fundamental aim of common law deformalizers has been to make judges take a more active role in equalizing the abilities of the parties to engage in fact-finding and legal analysis (for Australia see, e.g., Taylor, 1979; for Great Britain see, e.g., Applebey, 1979; for the United States see, e.g., Johnson *et al.*, 1977: 90). In the civil law countries such as France and Germany, the approach has necessarily been somewhat different. Earlier European reforms of regular courts, especially those in Austria, France, Germany, and northern European countries such as Sweden, anticipated the trend toward informalism. Nevertheless, one can detect a further movement in recent years toward court reform and alternatives as ways of promoting enforcement of new substantive rights. These include the French decision to eliminate all court costs except attorney's fees (Law of December 30, 1977, no. 77–1468 [1977], J.O. 6359), which has removed a substantial barrier to litigation. Germany has recently provided alternative forums for certain consumer disputes (see e.g., Bender and Strecker, 1978: 563–564). But it is in Sweden, the most "advanced" welfare state within the civil law tradition, that devices for the enforcement of new rights are most striking and innovative. For example, after a 1962 governmental study revealed that "a proceeding in the court was not a feasible alternative for most consumers" (Eisenstein, 1979: 522), the government created a Consumer Ombudsman, a Market Court, a Public Complaints Board, and a simplified small claims procedure (see generally *ibid.*).

A number of complementary institutions have also been developed to advise and guide consumers.

It should not be assumed that any of these institutions is completely successful in enforcing rights, but they do represent an effort to harness the virtues of procedural informalism—accessibility, active decision makers, and a less inhibiting environment—to the movement to make rights effective.

An assessment of the staying power and potential of this movement requires an understanding of its sources of support. Certainly the increased power of minority groups and of consumer and environmental movements have contributed, but other forces may be more important. Much of the initiative to "make rights effective" comes from three sectors: relatively "nonpolitical" governmental agencies and bureaucracies; private, nonprofit charitable foundations concerned with social problems; and certain sectors of the legal profession. Gap politics appeals to technocratic reformers who respond to the sociological evidence of unmet legal need. The role of the Ford Foundation in the United States is unusually significant and well known (Ford Foundation, 1973; 1976; 1978), but other foundations, such as the Nuffield Foundation in Great Britain, have also been important (cf. Byles and Morris, 1977). These institutions and their allies in government seek solutions to social problems that can avoid political conflict (see generally Marris and Rein, 1972). The premise of their approach to new rights is that legislative enactment implies a political consensus that the rights should be enforced. Welfare state governments often share this premise, which is consistent with the view of the Commission of the European Communities in Brussels, expressed in such documents as the proposed Consumer Action Program (see, e.g., European Communities Commission, 1979), and with that of the Council of Europe, which oversees the large number of countries bound by the European Convention for the Protection of Human Rights (see Council of Europe, 1976; Furrer, 1979).

Ministries of Justice (and their analogues, like the Lord Chancellor's office in Great Britain, which is charged with responsibility for the legal system) also want to investigate deficiencies and create mechanisms to solve problems in law enforcement (cf. Zander, 1979). To a lesser extent, leaders and activists in the legal profession share this concern since the prestige and legitimacy of the profession depend on the legitimacy of the legal system (see Trubek, 1977a: 560–565; Tushnet, 1977). The Report of the Pound Conference Follow-up Task Force, organized by the American Bar Association and chaired by United States Attorney General Griffin Bell, illustrates this.

> The ultimate goal is to make it possible for our system to provide justice for all. Constitutional guarantees of human rights ring hollow if there is no forum available in fact for their vindication. Statutory rights become empty promises if adjudication is too long delayed to make them meaningful or the value of the claim is consumed by the expense of asserting it [American Bar Association, 1977: 167; see also Tate, 1979].

The influential Society of Labour Lawyers in Great Britain has expressed this sentiment in even stronger terms.

> A major function of the legal profession should be to assist people [to] obtain the social rights provided by law and to ensure that laws designed to reduce inequality and provide welfare benefits operate as effectively as possible. . . . We must help the many thousands of people who do not avail themselves of their rights [Society of Labour Lawyers, 1978: 1].

Of course, most members of the legal profession, and especially those in the lower ranks of the highly stratified American bar, are concerned first with their financial situation, and this may inhibit certain types of reforms. But the creation of consumer remedies does not reduce lawyers' business; indeed, their existence may allow a lawyer to satisfy a client with a referral and even persuade him to return with some fee-generating work (sse, e.g., Macaulay, 1979). The German legal profession, for example, has been very conservative about legal aid reform that could divert judicare business to government-funded staff lawyers, but the *Deutscher Juristentag*—the professional association of lawyers—has supported measures that give consumer organizations standing to enforce a 1976 law regulating contract terms (see Sandrock, 1978: 553).

Some segments of the legal profession thus promote reforms in order to enhance the legitimacy of the legal system and their own financial self-interest, whereas other agencies seek technical rationalization. If it is true that the movement for legal aid, public interest law, and procedural informalism stems largely from the three sources described, that will no doubt affect the possibilities of achieving social change by making rights effective.

An evaluation of the impact of that approach must await description of the other two, but several preliminary observations should be made. First, a serious commitment to the enforcement of the rights of the underprivileged could be expensive. It may be necessary to create new courts, to make old ones more accessible, and to train and pay high quality, sympathetic judges and paralegal assistants. Assuming that institutions can be designed to reach the disadvantaged, attract them into the legal system, and enforce their rights against relatively powerful private and public opponents, new resources will have to be committed, and such resources may not be forthcoming. In England, for example, the decision to handle small claims by arbitration rather than to create a network of small claims courts that might have been more effective was evidently governed by financial considerations (see Zander, 1978: 323–324).

Nor should we overlook the even greater expenses inherent in the rights themselves. More effective enforcement of social welfare rights will require additional government resources, and implementation of housing, consumer, environmental, and other legal regulations will impose further costs on many private interests. Because making rights effective—which can be seen as an expansion of the welfare state—is expensive, advocates of procedural informalism naturally turn to the second and third approaches—which may significantly curtail the explosion of rights generated by welfare state legislation.

CONCILIATION

Conciliation aims not to vindicate rights but rather to resolve disputes on terms acceptable to the parties. Conciliation is not necessarily inconsistent with making rights effective, since the agreed resolution can resemble the legally dictated outcome. But the ideology of the proponents of conciliation and its actual operation strongly suggest that it tends to undermine the enforcement of rights.

An understanding of European instances of conciliation again requires a brief historical discussion. Conciliation appears to have prospered at two distinct periods: in the aftermath of the French Revolution, when it reflected a distrust of the lawyers and judges of the *ancien régime*, and more recently, alongside the welfare state emphasis on accessibility and rights enforcement. It is useful to begin by describing the earlier manifestation, since its institutional legacy may influence present concerns.

One result of the hatred of judges expressed during the French Revolution was the creation of an alternative institution, the justice of the peace (*juge de paix*) by a decree of August 16–24, 1790 (see Garsonnet and Cézar-Bru, 1912, vol. 1:85; Engelmann and Millar, 1927: 751). The ideal of the new judge was described contemporaneously as

> [a] judge who does not think, who does not exist except for his citizens. Minors, the absent (*les absents*), those deprived of rights (*les interdits*) are the particular object of his solicitude; he is a father in the milieu of his children: he says a word, and the injustices are repaired, the divisions eliminated, the complaints stopped; his constant attention assures the goodness of all; he receives in turn the sweetest of rewards; he is everywhere cherished, everywhere respected [Garsonnet and Cézar-Bru, 1912, vol. 1: 87, quoting Faure].

Conciliation by justices of the peace prior to the institution of a lawsuit, originally a matter of custom, was legally sanctioned in 1838 and made obligatory in 1855 (see Thery, 1978: 510). But the number of successful conciliations steadily declined throughout the nineteenth century, until the requirement had "degenerated in the cities into a vain formality" (Garsonnet and Cézar-Bru, 1912, vol. 1: 87; see also *ibid.*, vol. 2: 258, 282, 692). Still, though the procedure was finally abolished in 1949 for cases before the *tribunal civil* (and in 1958 for cases before the *tribunal de grande instance*), it continues to apply to smaller cases before the *tribunal d'instance* (the former *juge de paix*).

Under the influence of the French justices of the peace, Prussia created the institution of the *Schiedsmann* (mediator) in 1808 (see Bierbrauer *et al.*, 1979:

42). The *Schiedsmänner* were members of the landed gentry who attempted to settle disputes amicably. The institution still survives in a number of German *Länder*, where *Schiedsmänner* are chosen by the local government. Each officeholder has jurisdiction to attempt conciliation in minor criminal and civil disputes. But the *Schiedsmann* has been a declining institution, whose caseload has decreased from 287,507 in 1880 to 38,021 in 1975 (*Ibid.*: 48).

This decline was briefly interrupted during the 1920s. In 1924, for the first time, criminal defendants were required to appear at the conciliation hearing, and this led "to a sudden rise in the rate of success" (*Ibid.*: 49). This upgrading of the *Schiedsmann* was one of several manifestations of conciliation in Weimar Germany (see Reifner, 1982). As Reifner has explained, the few "Public Legal Advice and Mediation Centers" (*Öffentliche Rechtsauskunft—und Vergleichsstelle:* ÖRA) in Germany today date from that period. These institutions, the most prominent of which is located in Hamburg, provide legal advice to the poor and attempt to mediate conflicts (see generally Falke *et al.*, 1979). Like the *Schiedsmänner*, they are also "conciliation agencies," empowered to conduct the conciliation required before the institution of a minor private criminal prosecution. Such efforts at conciliation, like those of the informal, active judges sanctioned by reform in the 1920s, can be consistent with making rights effective. Bender and Strecker, at least, consider the ÖRA the most successful institution in Germany for "explaining to people with low incomes and little business skill what their rights are and helping them enforce their rights" (1978: 557). This legal aid agency is the model for a national system of legal aid currently proposed by the Social Democratic Party (see Blankenburg and Reifner, 1979: 8).

Informal procedures in Germany, and to a lesser extent throughout Western Europe, provide a foundation for the expansion of conciliation (for Italy, see Cappelletti and Perillo, 1965: 68–69; see also Engelmann and Millar, 1927: 805–06). Unfortunately, it is difficult to determine how such institutions as active judges and the ÖRA operate in practice—whether they emphasize legal rights or amicable settlements. There is some evidence that the Stuttgart model of civil procedure, which was the basis for the recent procedural reform in the higher German first instance courts (*Landgerichte*) (Law of December 3, 1976, for the Simplification and Acceleration of Judicial Proceedings [1976], BGB1 I 3281), may be oriented toward judicially induced settlements (see Bender, 1979: 471). But we do not yet have enough information, and it is clear that there has been no revival of institutions such as the *Schiedsmann*.

Recent procedural innovations in the United States and France, however, clearly do stress conciliation.[3] This is the explicit mandate of the three experimental Neighborhood Justice Centers funded by the Department of Justice (see,

---

[3]Another relevant German institution is the system of resolving disputes between workers within an enterprise (*Betriebsjustiz*) (see Metzger-Pregizer, 1978).

e.g., Sheppard *et al.*, 1978) and of the Dispute Resolution Act of 1980 (Pub. L. 96–190), despite its zeal for "experimentation" (see generally Hearings, 1978). Of equal or greater significance are contemporary French reforms, especially the institution of the local *conciliateur* (see generally Faucher, 1978).

The French Ministry of Justice in early 1977 began an experiment in four of the ninety-four French départements. Local *conciliateurs* were appointed by the presidents of the relevant courts of appeal and instructed to try to bring parties to an amicable settlement. After a brief trial period, all these *conciliateurs* supported the extension of the institution throughout France, and the decree of March 20, 1978 (no. 78–381 [1978], J.O. 1265), carried this out (see Faucher, 1978: 631). Parties may voluntarily seek the services of a local *conciliateur* to resolve a wide variety of civil and minor criminal matters but not disputes between individuals and the government. *Conciliateurs* are readily accessible, usually in the town hall. They are respected individuals, retired judges, and other persons not holding elected office, who combine guarantees of competence and impartiality. They serve voluntarily, provide simple advice, hold informal hearings, and persuade parties to reach an agreement. A widely circulated pamphlet published by the Ministry of Justice states prominently, "If you are in conflict, the *conciliateur* may be useful for you" (Ministère de la Justice, 1978).

The sources of this emphasis on conciliation, which also characterize informal procedures in other countries, are again complex. Obviously much of the recent interest stems from hostility to legalism, lawyers, and more generally government bureaucracies and "overregulation." Recent elections in Europe and the United States confirm growing political opposition to government initiatives and regulations, which can translate into a hostility to the proliferation of law. There are outcries against "legal pollution" in the United States (Ehrlich, 1976) and "society's indigestion from legislative inflation" in France (Savatier, 1977) and an increasing conviction that formal justice is too expensive. An influential French article advocating local *médiateurs* suggested that adversary procedures may be less "satisfying" to many disputants, "who would have been able to find a better solution in equity in conciliation or arbitration" (Bartolomei, 1975: 300).

Some of the attractions of conciliation are advanced in an article expressing the ideology of Governor Jerry Brown of California. His legal affairs secretary sought to justify the administration's refusal to create more California state judgeships and then called for increased experimentation with legal processes in which the goal "is the prompt restoration of normal relations between the disputants as fast as possible. . . . The central concern is to discover what is proper and decent, not so much what is legal. A good, and therefore a right, solution is what the parties can agree on" (Kline, 1978: 18–19). Not only does the article criticize the expense, delay, and inaccessibility of formal legal processes but it actually disparages the goal of making rights effective. Enforcement of legal rights is replaced by a concern with what is "proper and decent," equated rather optimistically with

"what the parties can agree on." The article also makes cost a major consideration. Since conciliation can be conducted by relatively low-paid personnel without legal training, it can substitute for the more costly expansion of courts and
other rights-oriented institutions: "If for no other reason, economic realities
alone are forcing a consideration of such conciliatory approaches to dispute
resolution" (*Ibid.*: 17).

Another virtue of conciliation is that it is politically uncontroversial. Enforcing rights is bound to disturb many powerful interests; an approach that emphasizes low cost and social harmony is more easily marketed in the present
political climate. It is instructive that mainstream Democrats in the Carter and
Brown administrations are among the foremost advocates of conciliation. Conciliation has its conservative proponents, but it can also be seen as the dispute-
processing component of the "postliberal" agenda of reduced government spending, fewer social programs, containment of the rights explosion, and the creation
of a more harmonious, spiritual social order where "less is more." The postliberal ideology seeks to persuade disadvantaged groups, with whom it professes
sympathy, to act "reasonably" in moderating demands on government and
business. The neighborhood conciliator can perform the same function at the
local level.

The ideology of conciliation thus appears hostile to the goal of making rights
effective. It would be oversimplifying, however, to see these two approaches only
as alternatives. Conciliatory mechanisms do not prevent new laws and procedures from being implemented, and neighborhood conciliation may have little
to do with the conflicts between individuals and powerful organizations. A closer
look at conciliatory justice is required.

Many advocates of conciliation propose to mediate only certain disputes between or among *individuals* (cf. Danzig and Lowy, 1975). It is now common-
place to observe that conciliatory mechanisms are better suited to the preservation
of ongoing complex relationships than is adjudication. Given the breakdown
of such institutions as the family and the church, governmental conciliation
may serve a useful function. In minor criminal or quasi-criminal matters,
disputes among neighbors, or certain intrafamily conflicts, neighborhood conciliators may employ commonsense standards of behavior and, in the process,
build neighborhood unity and improve community life.[4] Some discussions of
Third World and socialist courts, for example, emphasize this role (cf. Santos,
1977; Kurczewski and Frieske, 1979). This view of neighborhood life may be
somewhat romantic in modern, mobile societies (see Felstiner, 1975), but there
is no harm in trying. Nevertheless, some words of caution are in order before we

---

[4]There may be problems if the local "conciliatory" organization proves in practice to be merely an
extension of the coercive apparatus of the state (see, e.g., Hofrichter, 1982). My emphasis in this
chapter, however, is mainly on "civil" rights and their enforcement.

seek to fit Neighborhood Justice Centers or *conciliateurs* or (*Schiedsmänner*) into that mold.

First, a question naturally arises as to whether community standards will be allowed to evolve. The French *conciliateurs*, for example, are beholden only to the judges who appoint them, not to the "community," and it is clear that communities have been given no real control over Neighborhood Justice Centers (see Sheppard *et al.*, 1978: 17–22). Substantial participation by disadvantaged groups may be even less likely once the justice centers pass the experimental stage and are subjected to political pressures by local powers. In addition, it does not appear that these conciliation mechanisms are limited to interpersonal conflict. Many disputes involving welfare rights—consumer, landlord–tenant, environmental, employer–employee—are also being handled by Neighborhood Justice Centers and *conciliateurs*. Early, fragmentary evidence on the *conciliateurs* indicates that neighborhood conflict was the most common kind of case but that they also dealt with numerous consumer, landlord–tenant, and debt collection matters (Ministère de la Justice, 1977:2). The Neighborhood Justice Centers are also handling more disputes between individuals and institutions than was originally anticipated. In the most innovative center, in Los Angeles, the "largest source of cases are self-referrals with landlord–tenant or consumer–merchant disputes" (Sheppard *et al.*, 1978: 53). It is at least doubtful that new, often technical laws and regulations will play the same role in these institutions that they do in the elaborate system of consumer protection found in Sweden. A brief discussion of how conciliators are likely to operate in practice can illuminate this problem (see generally Bierbrauer *et al.*, 1979).

The conciliator or mediator in modern societies tends to appeal to the common interests of both parties in coexisting and in avoiding costly, lengthy, and psychologically debilitating court procedures. Both a carrot and a stick are involved. The corporate litigant able to afford the costs of litigation and to tolerate delay will have little to fear from going to court. But for the poor individual, litigation may be a much more formidable undertaking if innovative informal procedures, legal aid, or simplified substantive rules do not allow the complainant to vindicate the right effectively. There is no doubt that such an individual has a much greater incentive to make concessions in order to secure a "conciliated" settlement.

We may also be dubious about what the carrot of coexistence means in practice. In a period of high unemployment, chronic housing shortages, and a market dominated by large corporations, the employer, landlord, or merchant may not care a great deal about ongoing relations with a particular individual. Moreover, even if the organization voluntarily submits to conciliation, there are serious questions about the outcome (aside from the differences in bargaining power already discussed). The capacity of "shared community standards" to determine a fair outcome should not be exaggerated. The conciliator must have some idea of what result would be fair, and in the absence of a clear community norm he or she will probably resort to some notion of the law (see Bierbrauer *et al.*, 1979; cf. Faucher, 1978: 632). Otherwise, the only basis for settlement is the raw power of the parties. The question, then, must be the accuracy of the conciliator's view of the law and who is likely to benefit from inaccuracy. Since only the organizational litigant will probably know its rights—from experience in previous controversies, information disseminated through trade associations, or the advice of company counsel—and it is doubtful that the community para-professional conciliators can acquire sufficient legal (or technical) knowledge about welfare state rights, one can predict a definite bias against the supposed beneficiaries of welfare state laws. Conciliation may lead to an "amicable settle-ment," but its implications may be grave for individuals with problems involving powerful organizations. A one-sided emphasis on conciliation—either through alternative institutions or in regular courts—clearly reinforces the status quo and makes rights ineffective.

DIVERSION

Diversion overlaps with the first two approaches but has a different emphasis—the problem of court congestion. Diversion means the processing of disputes outside of court by means of settlement, conciliation, or arbitration. It assumes that court congestion cannot or will not be relieved merely by increasing the number of courts and judges (see, e.g., Marcus, 1979).

In theory, diversion could help make rights effective or foster conciliation, or both. No-fault systems of accident compensation, for example, are designed in large measure to reduce court congestion, but they may also enhance the ability of many accident victims to obtain compensation. And obviously any reduction in court congestion makes the courts more accessible to cases that are not di-verted.

There is a strong tendency, however, for diversion to exhibit what I feel are the darker implications of conciliation. First, it may extrude too many cases and the wrong kinds. Advocates of welfare rights, especially in the United States, have depended on the courts to resolve constitutional and other public law issues, and courts have generally been more receptive than legislatures to the claims of diffuse interests and the politically weak (see Chayes, 1976; Cappelletti, 1976). Diversion may prevent such claims from reaching the courts, and the substitute may be inadequate. Many American supporters of diversion may actually be seeking such a result.

The typical method of reducing court congestion and expense in Western Europe and the United States is simply to channel more claims into the cheaper processes used to decide relatively small claims. Raising jurisdictional limits increases the number of claims that can be handled by quicker, less formal procedures, using less qualified judges, with limited rights to appeal, and (most important from a European perspective) by one-judge instead of three-judge courts (see generally Cappelletti and Garth, 1978: 70). But there are ceilings on how much the small claims jurisdiction can be enlarged, and governments concerned about cost and congestion are resorting to other devices.

In Western Europe, diversion primarily means further attenuation of the traditional right to trial by a three-judge panel in serious cases. In France, the jurisdiction of the one-judge *tribunal d'instance* is "constantly expanding" in order to facilitate "the gradual introduction into our judicial system of a single judge" and to reduce overcrowding in the *tribunal de grande instance* (Thery, 1978: 511). A decree of August 28, 1972 (no. 72–789), for example, gave the *tribunal d'instance* jurisdiction over all disputes involving residential and professional leases. Similarly, a law of July 10, 1970 (no. 70–613), permits the president of the *tribunal de grande instance* to refer cases to a single judge unless they involve the discipline of legal professionals or the status of persons. A party may, however, object within fifteen days and the case will be returned to the full panel.

Recent German developments reveal the same pattern. Section 348 of the Code of Civil Procedure was amended late in 1974 to provide that any civil case can be referred for decision to a single judge. The parties can challenge the reference only on the ground that the case is particularly difficult or has unique social importance. A law of June 14, 1976, modified section 621 of the Code of Civil Procedure to divert divorce and certain other family matters from three-judge regular courts to new, one-judge family courts (see Bender and Strecker, 1978: 541). Creation of the new courts was justified by the procedural advantage of resolving a number of related problems in a single hearing but the reform was also motivated by a desire to divert such claims from regular three-judge courts. This trend toward a single judge has enabled the Continental countries to cope with court congestion (cf. Vigoriti, 1978: 658–660).[5]

In the United States it has been necessary to take further steps. The Federal Magistrate Act of 1979 (Pub. L. 96–82, October 10, 1979), which permits parties to consent to trial by a United States magistrate, can be viewed in this light. Of particular importance, however, are experiments with compulsory arbitration in lieu of trial, in which a dissatisfied party can get a court trial de novo. In late 1978, for example, California enacted a law requiring arbitration by private attorneys in all claims for less than $15,000 filed in Superior Courts with ten or

---

[5]In England, the "Payment Into Court" Rule may accomplish a similar end by promoting settlements in personal injury actions, often on terms unfair to one of the litigants (see Zander, 1976). There is interest in the United States in adopting such a scheme (see Johnson *et al.*, 1977: 45, 94–95).

more judges (Cal. Code of Civ. Pro. §§ 1141.10 et seq.). Similarly, the United States Department of Justice has been experimenting in federal district courts in Connecticut, eastern Pennsylvania, and northern California with compulsory arbitration by panels of three lawyers in large categories of cases where the prayer for relief does not exceed $50,000 ($100,000 in some instances) (see, e.g., Local Rules of the United States District Court for the Northern District of California, Rule 500; U.S. Department of Justice, 1979). President Carter (1979) recommended that such arbitration schemes be extended throughout the federal district courts. Compulsory arbitration of claims involving relatively large amounts of money is not new in the United States (see, e.g., Rosenberg and Schubin, 1961), but in the last few years there has been a remarkable burst of enthusiasm for such reforms. The growing concern about limited public resources, visible in the movement toward conciliation, has also prompted compulsory arbitration programs.

The move toward arbitration in the United States parallels the growth of one-judge civil courts in Europe, and the results may be similar. Although proponents of arbitration argue that it increases access and therefore helps the disadvantaged, the primary goal of diversion clearly is not the enforcement of rights. Those who wish to make rights effective seek to *attract* people who otherwise would not request legal protection and to create mechanisms that minimize the ability of the "haves" to manipulate procedures to their own advantage; diversion measures success by reference to its impact on court congestion and expense. Furthermore, though I think it is important to distinguish conciliation and diversion, the recent emphases on single-judge courts and arbitration greatly blur the difference. When arbitrators seek to avoid appeals by encouraging compromise solutions to disputes, they are essentially engaging in conciliation (cf. Sarat, 1976: 353–354). One-judge courts in Western Europe, similarly, may be more likely than three-judge panels to employ their statutory powers to promote settlements that overlook legal rights. Participation by three judges in Continental systems, where judges have considerable responsibility for developing factual and legal arguments, may be essential to assure legally correct results.

This suggests a general problem with the diversion of cases to informal procedures whose primary virtue is their low cost. If they are not carefully designed to reach the disadvantaged and compensate for inequalities in resources and in the capacity to present a claim, informal procedures may turn into tools for the advantaged—especially organizational litigants. For example, a generally optimistic evaluation of American small claims courts made the following observation about the enforcement of consumer rights against businesses:

> We... asked every judge... how often federal consumer protection provisions... and state provisions such as the Uniform Consumer Credit Code (UCCC) were raised either affirmatively or as a defense in small claims trials. Surprisingly, very few of the judges said that consumer protection provisions ever came up in small claims court. While most of the judges had heard of

these provisions, generally they were not familiar enough with them to check consumer transactions for compliance [Ruhnka et al., 1978: 27].

This corroborates Rubinstein's criticism that in informal settings "technical rules" favoring individuals, such as laws enacted recently in the consumer and landlord–tenant area, may "be overlooked as irrelevant to the substance of the particular dispute" (1976: 81). This focus on court congestion and keeping costs down could have profound repercussions for the enforcement of welfare rights.

CONSTITUTIONALISM AND PROCEDURAL INFORMALISM

The three strands of the movement toward procedural informalism have important implications for law in the welfare state. But before we develop these further we must briefly consider a possible limitation. Constitutionalism in the United States and as it has developed in Western Europe since World War II poses certain obstacles to procedural informalism.

The role of written constitutions, supreme courts, and judicial review has grown rapidly not only in individual European countries, such as Italy, Germany, and to a lesser extent France, but also in transnational Europe through the 1950 European Convention for the Protection of Human Rights (see Cappelletti and Cohen, 1979). The constitutions of the Federal Republic of Germany and Italy, and the European Convention, all guarantee the right to sue *in court*. This right expresses a liberal reaction to the abuses of quasi-judicial organs controlled by the executive under the fascist regimes. As a result, it is now established constitutional doctrine that cases cannot be referred to nonjudicial bodies unless the parties are entitled to a de novo hearing in court (see *ibid*.: 232–249, 331–341; Vigoriti, 1978: 663–664). These constitutional rights channel reforms seeking to enlarge access toward schemes that increase legal assistance or reduce cost barriers to litigation, and this limits experimentation. Similar considerations are reflected in insisting on de novo review by a three-judge panel following a decision by a one-judge court and in making submission to institutions such as the *conciliateur* voluntary (although neither is constitutionally required).

There are comparable pressures in the United States, stemming partly from state and federal constitutional rights to counsel and trial by jury (though a former American Bar Association president has recommended a constitutional amendment; see Stanley, 1977). Recent applications of the due process clause of the Fourteenth Amendment to the "new property" (Reich, 1964) have also militated against procedural informalism. *Goldberg* v. *Kelly* (397 U.S. 254, 1970) specifically held that federal and state grants of welfare and housing cannot be withdrawn without a formal adversary hearing, and subsequent decisions encouraged the formalization of much informal decision making (see, e.g., Verkuil, 1975: 854). The result is a tendency toward voluntary submission to, or de novo review of, informal proceedings.

As a result, many informal procedures and institutions may simply fail (see, e.g., Perrot, 1976: 240). Litigants may not choose to invoke the procedures or abide by the results. Thus far, for example, the Neighborhood Justice Centers have had remarkably small caseloads, and even these have consisted largely of matters referred by the criminal process and therefore the product of coercion (see Sheppard et al., 1978). The decline of the German *Schiedsmann* may be instructive. Arbitration entails particular problems, since a relatively small percentage of appeals to regular courts can eliminate the savings from diversion. The recent flurry of activity may therefore have much less impact than supporters hope or opponents fear.

Nevertheless, there is reason to believe that informal procedures can overcome the difficulties posed by the constitutional protection of formality. First, voluntary consent to informal processes can be manipulated. Choice of process depends on such factors as the cost, accessibility, and speed of the regular courts, and these may leave many disputants with no real options. Second, many manifestations of procedural informalism may be situated within regualr courts, especially those handling small claims. Judicial activism, the promotion of settlements, relaxed rules of evidence, and measures to discourage attorney representation can greatly reduce the formalism of small claims procedures. Finally, constitutional doctrine may be flexible enough to accommodate new types of informal procedure. In the United States, for example, several arbitration plans penalize unsuccessful appeals and yet have survived constitutional challenge (see Johnson et al., 1977: 39–47; Cal. Code of Civ. Pro. § 1141.21). Similarly, the emphasis on formal due process found in *Goldberg* v. *Kelly* has been replaced by a greater tolerance for informal procedures (see Verkuil, 1975: 855–861). A similar evolution could occur in European countries bound by written constitutions, and the approach taken by the European Court on Human Rights in the *Airey* case suggests that informal procedures may be permitted to substitute for the right to counsel and an adversary proceeding. Thus, whether the movement toward procedural informalism is motivated by the enforcement of rights, conciliation, or diversion, constitutional interpretation may not significantly impede it.

PROCEDURAL INFORMALISM AND THE PROSPECTS FOR SOCIAL CHANGE IN THE WELFARE STATE

The consequences of procedural informalism for social change depend to a great extent on which of the three approaches is dominant, and this may not always be easy to determine. The approaches overlap considerably, and relatively subtle differences in the activities of legal professionals, courts, and extrajudicial machinery may have a critical impact on the enforcement, underenforcement, or nullification of the welfare state rights of the relatively disadvantaged. We do not know, for example, how active judges in Western Europe actually settle cases and whether they help the weak; nor do we know if the ÖRA model of legal advice makes rights effective or ineffective.

My primary objective, however, has been to show how informal procedures that purport to promote access can have very different political effects. Given the centrality of legal enforcement machinery to the welfare state programs ostensibly designed to help the "have-nots," the political impact of different procedures is obviously of vital social importance. The growth of funding for empirical research into the legal system reflects a recognition of that importance. The results of such research, whatever the perspective of the researcher, help policymakers shape legal reform to advance the desired political ends, which can be the social change achieved by implementing the new rights of the welfare state or social stability without change.

I suggested earlier in the chapter that the recent emphases on conciliation and diversion may reflect electoral opposition to the welfare state. If those electoral trends prove to be lasting, we can expect "reformers" to seek to harmonize the legal system with the ideology of diminished expectations. The history of efforts to make rights effective, moreover, suggests that legal developments have only a limited autonomy, and it will be difficult to resist those who wish to shape procedures toward other goals.

First, the most active proponents of welfare rights have focused on technical questions rather than political issues. Many reformers have assumed that the creation of new rights rests on a consensus that they should be enforced; indeed, that very apolitical assumption helped to generate a good deal of the momentum for change. This dynamic suggests that "the welfare state is developing step-by-step, reluctantly and involuntarily" (Offe, 1972: 485). But if the consensus shifts to an emphasis on the limits of public resources and the costs of regulation and of legal rights, the technocratic momentum may be lost.

Second, though certain sectors of the legal profession may continue to be concerned with substantive rights, the profession has tended to emphasize "access" (Tate, 1979) or at most the ideal of "let the tribunal fit the case" (see, e.g., Association of American Law Schools Proceedings, 1978: 166–190). Even if leaders of the profession continue to support access to "appropriate" dispute processing institutions, such institutions may turn out to be inconsistent with, or at least irrelevant to the enforcement of rights.

A third potential problem with the movement to make rights effective stems from ambiguity about both rights and the notion of access to dispute processing machinery. It takes little insight into the legislative process to realize that some of the support for new rights on behalf of the disadvantaged comes from those who know that those rights are likely to be of little real value to most people and thus will cause little change in the status quo. As Edelman has demonstrated, governments often face major public problems by offering "reassuring rhetoric and gestures more consistently than . . . effective action" (1977: 147). Rights are often created mainly for their symbolic value.

The enforcement of rights and the expansion of access may be supported for another, related reason. In 1978, for example, the British Labour lord chancellor made a speech strongly endorsing the "law enforcement" activities of the law centres. He explained his support in the following terms:

> We live at a time not just of social change but to an extent even of social instability particularly in some of our more deprived urban communities. . . . One of the elements in this situation is the disturbing alienation of people from the legal order and the hitherto accepted legal and administrative machinery. It is in just those communities that there are special needs for legal services. And it is just those services which, I believe, can restore people's confidence in the ability of law, the courts and the legal system to redress their grievances, to protect their lawful rights and to provide a framework for an ordered community [1978: 2–3].

Examples of such statements could easily be multiplied (see, e.g., Johnson, 1974: 169). As the lord chancellor's speech suggests, this concern for social control can lead to encouragement of rather aggressive measures for the enforcement of rights. It is also possible, however, for the social control functions to assume predominance. Access reforms will then focus less on access to rights and more on access by the state to potential dissidents.

The historical example of Germany, as described by Reifner, illustrates the way in which a concern for rights can be transformed into an insistence upon social peace and social control without regard to rights. The German trade unions in the early twentieth century began to utilize their legal aid institutions to enforce the rights created by Bismarckian reforms. Gradually the emphasis shifted away from rights and social change toward the socially integrative functions of legal assistance. By 1920, for example, "the leaders of the Social Democratic party [and the unions] tried to legitimate their politics of legalisation by extending it to a policy of social peace" (Blankenburg and Reifner, 1979B: 21). Soon thereafter the only goal was social peace, fostered through conciliation and nonadversary legal advice.

Legal aid and small claims courts in the United States, also initiated at the turn of the century, experienced a similar development. One stated purpose of these reforms was to enable the poor to enforce their legal rights. Another was the desire to assimilate immigrants into the legal system and minimize social unrest (see, e.g., Auerbach, 1976: 53–62). The dismal story of the failure of informal courts to help the poor is well known (see Yngvesson and Hennessey, 1975: 221–228). An ideology of social peace also came to dominate legal aid organizations. As Michael Grossberg has revealed, for example, the nationally acclaimed Boston Legal Aid Society "strayed from client advocacy" toward an emphasis on social peace. "A legal aid lawyer strove to work out an equitable solution for all concerned parties. . . . The society attempted to bring about a real understanding between people who are in the midst of a controversy with one another and established [sic] a lasting peace which is worth as much as all the money involved" (1978: 17).

These historical examples illustrate the fate of some of the precursors of the welfare state movement toward procedural informalism (for England, cf. Leat, 1975). They suggest that informalism tends to evolve away from a concern with rights, even if that motivated the original reform. The result of the proliferation of access reforms may be that the social control capabilities of the state are enhanced—the state seeks greater access to the poor and the disaffected to reduce their potential for social disruption—without any corresponding extension of rights. This possibility points to the fundamental dilemma of the movement toward procedural informalism viewed as a device to achieve the social change promised by the welfare state.

Procedural informalism may be designed to minimize the advantages of powerful organizations within the dispute resolution process and may even succeed in doing so to a certain extent. Moreover, such procedures are probably necessary if welfare rights are to be implemented. "A system designed to accommodate a conservative procedural model, premised on limited government and private allocation of societal resources, with a liberal political and economic model, contemplating active government distribution of societal resources, is plagued by frustrating contradiction" (Verkuil, 1975: 855). But a number of factors appear to divert procedural informalism from the enforcement of rights to other goals. That fate may not be inevitable, but historical and recent trends point to the same conclusion.

Informalism eliminates procedures that can have an impact on results independent of relative power relationships. Formalities create barriers, but they also provide a shield behind which it is possible to achieve a politically unpopular result. Informal procedures are more readily manipulated and therefore more subject to immediate political influence. Informal institutions, for example, can be captured by the powerful in the way that administrative agencies have been. Avoiding such capture probably requires the kind of effort that only relatively strong organizations can muster (see, e.g., Trubek, 1979).

This suggests that the enforcement of rights through informal procedures and institutions can succeed only if it overcomes the limitations inherent in the lack of a political constituency and builds organizations that will strengthen those who stand to benefit from those rights. There is evidence that rights can help in organizing disadvantaged groups (see Scheingold, 1974), and a number of activists in legal services (see, e.g., Wexler, 1970; Law Centres Working Group, 1978) and public interest law (e.g., Trubek, 1977b; Handler, 1978) have suggested that those movements can be used to build and strengthen rights-oriented organizations. If that is a realistic assessment in the prevailing political climate, then informal procedures may be useful, even essential, in maximizing the enforcement of rights. The welfare state may be forced to expand or abandon the rights it has promised. But if constituencies are not built, then procedural informalism, even when consistent with the enforcement of rights, is likely to resemble conciliation or diversion (see also Nader, 1979; Cover, 1979).

Legal reformers who wish to build on welfare state promises may have a difficult task. An extraordinary effort will be needed to shape the movement toward procedural informalism in a favorable direction. The success or failure of that effort will have a significant impact on how welfare state reforms affect the day-to-day lives of ordinary people. Problems remain in making rights effective. That approach perpetuates the paternalism inherent in the idea of "legal needs," which are defined from above by lawyers, sociologists, and social workers, among others. Furthermore, the categories of need assume the existence of such inherently unequal statuses as consumers, tenants, employees, and the "poor." The proliferation and enforcement of rights may ameliorate these statuses, but it obviously does not address more fundamental questions about their very existence. In the absence of a broad-based political movement going beyond the welfare state, therefore, we may be relying on professionally dominated activities that spread not only rights but also an acquiescence in "duties" that contribute to the perpetuation of unequal conditions (see, e.g., Offe, 1977; Piven and Cloward, 1977). This chapter cannot develop a critique of the welfare state from a perspective sympathetic to its ostensible goals, but we should recognize that the limits of the welfare state in both the United States and Western Europe are evident even in the most progressive of the movements for change through procedural reform.

REFERENCES

Abel-Smith, Brian, Michael Zander, and Rosaline Brooke (1973) *Legal Problems and the Citizen.* London: Heineman.

American Bar Association (1977) "Report of the Pound Conference Follow-up Task Force," 74 *Federal Rules Decisions* 59.

Applebey, George (1979) "Small Claims in England and Wales," in M. Cappelletti and J. Weisner (eds.) *Access to Justice. vol. 2: Promising Institutions.* Alphen aan den rijn: Sijthoff; Milan Giuffrè.

Association of American Law Schools Proceedings (1978) "Panel II: Let the Tribunal Fit the Case—Establishing Criteria for Channeling Matters into Dispute Resolution Mechanisms," 80 *Federal Rules Decisions* 166.

Auerbach, Jerold (1976) *Unequal Justice: Lawyers and Social Change in Modern America.* New York: Oxford University Press.

Bartolomei, Louis (1975) "Eléments pour une justice nouvelle," 1975 *Gazette du Palais Doctrine* 300.

Bender, Rolf (1979) "The Stuttgart Model," in M. Cappelletti and J. Weisner (eds.) *Access to Justice: Promising Institutions*. Alphen aan den rijn: Sijthoff; Milan: Giuffrè.

Bender, Rolf and Christoph Strecker (1978) "Access to Justice in the Federal Republic of Germany," in M. Cappelletti and B. Garth (eds.) *Access to Justice: A World Survey*. Alphen aan den rijn: Sijthoff; Milan: Giuffrè.

Bierbrauer, Günter, Josef Falke, and Klaus-Friedrich Koch (1979) "An Interdisciplinary Study of the *Schiedsmann* in the Federal Republic of Germany," in M. Cappelletti and J. Weisner (eds.) *Access to Justice: Promising Institutions*. Alphen aan den rijn: Sijthoff; Milan: Giuffrè.

Blankenburg, Erhard and Udo Reifner (1979) "Beyond Legal Representation: Dispute Processing, Non-Judicial Alternatives, and the 'Third Wave' in the Access to Justice Movement." Paper presented to the Colloquium on Access to Justice, Florence (October 15–18).

Byles, Anthea and Pauline Morris (1977) *Unmet Need: The Case of the Neighbourhood Law Centre*. London: Routledge and Kegan Paul.

Cahn, Edgar and Jean Cahn (1966) "What Price Justice? The Civilian Perspective Revisited," 41 *Notre Dame Lawyer* 927.

Cappelletti, Mauro (1971) "Social and Political Aspects of Civil Procedure—Reforms and Trends in Western and Eastern Europe," 69 *Michigan Law Review* 847.

_____ (1975) "Governmental and Private Advocates for the Public Interest in Civil Litigation: A Comparative Study," 73 *Michigan Law Review* 793.

_____ (1976) "Vindicating the Public Interest through the Courts: A Comparativist's Contribution," 25 *Buffalo Law Review* 643.

Cappelletti, Mauro and William Cohen (1979) *Comparative Constitutional Law*. Indianapolis, Ind.: Bobbs-Merrill.

Cappelletti, Mauro and Bryant Garth (eds.) (1978) *Access to Justice: A World Survey*. Alphen aan den rijn: Sijthoff; Milan: Giuffrè.

Cappelletti, Mauro, James Gordley, and Earl Johnson, Jr. (1975) *Toward Equal Justice*. Dobbs Ferry, N.Y.: Oceana; Milan: Giuffrè.

Cappelletti, Mauro and Joseph Perillo (1965) *Civil Procedure in Italy*. The Hague: Martinus Nijhoff.

Carlin, Jerome and Jan Howard (1965) "Legal Representation and Class Justice," 12 *U.C.L.A. Law Review* 381.

Carlin, Jerome, Jan Howard, and Sheldon Messinger (1966) "Civil Justice and the Poor," 1 *Law & Society Review* 9.

Carter, Jimmy (1979) "Reform of the Federal Civil Justice System," 1979 *United States Code Congressional and Administrative News* 388.

Cass, Michael and Ronald Sackville (1975) *Legal Needs of the Poor*. Canberra: Australian Government Printing Service.

Charvet, Dominique (1976) "Crise de la justice, crise de la loi, crise de l'état?" in N. Poulantzas (ed.) *La crise de l'état*. Paris: Presses Universitaires de France.

Chaynes, Abram (1976) "The Role of the Judge in Public Law Litigation," 89 *Harvard Law Review* 1281.

Council of Europe (1976) *Legal Services for Deprived Persons, Particularly in Urban Areas*. Strasbourg: Council of Europe.

Cover, Robert (1979) "Dispute Resolution: A Forward," 88 *Yale Law Journal* 910.

Curran, Barbara (1977) *The Legal Needs of the Public*. Chicago: American Bar Foundation.

Danzig, Richard and Michael Lowy (1975) "Everyday Disputes and Mediation in the United States: A Reply to Professor Felstiner," 9 *Law & Society Review* 675.

Edelman, Murray (1977) *Political Language: Words that Succeed and Policies that Fail*. New York: Academic Press.

Ehrlich, Thomas (1976) "Legal Pollution," *New York Times Magazine* 17 (February 8).

Eisenstein, Martin (1979) "The Swedish Public Complaints Board: Its Vital Role in a System of

Consumer Protection," in M. Cappelletti and J. Weisner (eds.) *Access to Justice: Promising Institutions*. Alphen aan den rijn: Sijthoff; Milan: Giuffrè.

Engelmann, Arthur and Robert Millar (1927) *A History of Continental Civil Procedure*. Boston: Little, Brown & Co.

European Communities Commission (1979) *Background Report, Positive Role for the Consumer: New Action Programme for Consumer Protection*. London: European Communities Commission.

Falke, Josef, Günter Bierbrauer, and Klaus-Friedrich Koch (1979) "Legal Advice and the Non-Judicial Settlement of Disputes: A Case Study of the Public Legal Advice and Mediation Center in the City of Hamburg," in M. Cappelletti and J. Weisner (eds.) *Access to Justice: Promising Institutions*. Alphen aan den rijn: Sijthoff; Milan: Giuffrè.

Faucher, B. (1978) "Reflexions sur les conciliateurs," 1978 *Gazette du Palais, Doctrine* 631.

Felstiner, William (1975) "Avoidance as Dispute Processing," 9 *Law & Society Review* 695.

Fisch, William (1979) "European Analogues to the Class Action: Group Action in France and Germany," 27 *American Journal of Comparative Law* 51.

Ford Foundation (1973) *The Public Interest Law Firm: New Voices for New Constituencies*. New York: Ford Foundation.

––––––– (1976) *Public Interest Law: Five Years Later*. New York: Ford Foundation

––––––– (1978) *New Approaches to Conflict Resolution*. New York: Ford Foundation.

Friedman, Lawrence (1977) "The Social and Political Context of the War on Poverty: An Overview," in R. Haveman (ed.) *A Decade of Federal Antipoverty Programs*. New York: Academic Press.

Friedmann, W. (1959) *Law in a Changing Society*. London: Stevens & Sons Ltd.

Furrer, Hans-Peter (1979) "Access to Justice: The Council of Europe Programme." Paper presented to the Colloquium on Access to Justice, Florence (October 15–18).

Galanter, Marc (1974) "Why the 'Haves' Come Out Ahead: Speculations on the Limits of Legal Change," 9 *Law & Society Review* 95.

––––––– (1979) "Legality and Its Discontents: A Preliminary Assessment of Current Theories of Legalization and Delegalization," in E. Blankenburg, E. Klausa, and H. Rottleuthner (eds.) *Alternative Rechtsformen und Alternativen zum Recht*. Opladen: Westdeutscher Verlag (Jahrbuch für Rechtssoziologie und Rechtstheorie, Bd. 6).

Garsonnet, E. and C. Cézar-Bru (1912) *Traité théorique et pratique de procédure civile et commerciale*. Paris: Librairie de la société du recueil général des lois et arrêts.

Garth, Bryant (1980) *Neighborhood Law Firms for the Poor: A Comparative Study of Recent Developments in Legal Aid and in the Legal Profession*. Alphen aan den rijn: Sijthoff.

Grossberg, Michael (1978) "Altruism and Professionalism: Boston and the Rise of Organized Legal Aid, 1900–1925," 1978 *Boston Bar Journal* 21 (May), 11 (June).

Handler, Joel (1978) *Social Movements and the Legal System*. New York: Academic Press.

Hearings before the Subcommittee on Courts, Civil Liberties, and the Administration of Justice of the Committee on the Judiciary, House of Representatives, 95th Cong., 2d Sess., on S. 957: Dispute Resolution Act (1978). Committee Print.

Hofrichter, Richard (1982) "Neighborhood Justice and the Social Control Problems of American Capitalism," in R. Abel (ed.) *The Politics of Informal Justice, vol. 2: The American Experience*. New York: Academic Press.

Homberger, Adolf (1970) "Functions of Orality in Austrian and American Civil Procedure," 20 *Buffalo Law Review* 9.

James, Fleming and Geoffrey Hazard (1977) *Civil Procedure*. Boston: Little, Brown & Co.

Johnson, Earl (1974) *Justice and Reform: The Formative Years of the OEO Legal Services Program*. New York: Russell Sage Foundation.

––––––– (1978) "Remarks," 80 *Federal Rules Decisions* 167.

Johnson, Earl, Valerie Kantor, and Elizabeth Schwartz (1977) *Outside the Courts: A Survey of Diversion Alternatives in Civil Cases.* Denver: National Center for State Courts.

Jolowicz, J. A. (1975) "The Active Role of the Judge in Civil Litigation," in M. Cappelletti and J. Jolowicz (eds.) *Public Interest Parties and the Active Role of the Judge in Civil Litigation.* Dobbs Ferry, N.Y.: Oceana; Milan: Giuffrè.

Kaplan, Benjamin, Arthur Von Mehren, and Rudolf Shaefer (1958) "Phases of German Civil Procedure," 71 *Harvard Law Review* 1193.

Klauser, Karl and Robert Riegert (1971) "Legal Assistance in the Federal Republic of Germany," 20 *Buffalo Law Review* 583.

Kline, J. Anthony (1978) "Law Reform and the Courts: More Power to the People or the Profession," 53 *California State Bar Journal* 14.

Kurczewski, Jacek and Kazimierz Frieske (1979) "The Social Conciliatory Commissions in Poland: A Case Study of Nonauthoritative and Conciliatory Dispute Resolution as an Approach to Access to Justice," in M. Cappelletti and J. Weisner (eds.) *Access to Justice: Promising Institutions.* Alphen aan den rijn: Sijthoff; Milan: Giuffrè.

Law Centres Working Group (1978) *Evidence to the Royal Commission on Legal Services.* Birmingham: Saltley Action Centre.

Leat, Diane (1975) "The Rise and Role of the Poor Man's Lawyer," 2 *British Journal of Law and Society* 166.

Lord Chancellor (1978) Speech to Law Centres Working Group Conference, Leeds University (September 22).

Luhmann, Niklas (1976) "The Legal Profession: Comments on the Situation in the Federal Republic," in D. MacCormick (ed.) *Lawyers in Their Social Setting.* Edinburgh: W. Green & Son, Ltd.

Macaulay, Stewart (1979) "Lawyers and Consumer Protection Laws," 14 *Law & Society Review* 115.

Marcus, Maria (1979) "Judicial Overload: The Reasons and the Remedies," 28 *Buffalo Law Review* 111.

Marris, Peter and Martin Rein (1972) *Dilemmas of Social Reform.* Hammondsworth: Penguin.

Mayhew, Leon (1975) "Institutions of Representation: Civil Justice and the Public," 9 *Law & Society Review* 401.

Messier, Camille (1975) *Les mains de la loi: Une problématique des besoins juridiques des économiquement faibles du Québec.* Montréal: Commission des services juridiques.

Metzger-Pregizer, Gerhard (1978) "Summary and Consequences for Criminal Policy," in W. Felstiner and A. Drew (eds.) *European Alternatives to Criminal Trials and Their Applicability in the United States.* Washington, D.C.: Law Enforcement Assistance Administration.

Millar, Robert (1924) "The Recent Reforms in German Civil Procedure," 10 *American Bar Association Journal* 703.

Ministère de la Justice (1977) "Conciliateurs," *La lettre de la Chancellerie* 2 (October 15).

――――― (1978) *Le conciliateur.* Paris: Ministère de la Justice.

Morris, Pauline, Jenni Cooper, and Anthea Byles (1973) "Public Attitudes to Problem Definition and Problem Solving: A Pilot Study," 3 *British Journal of Social Work* 301.

Nader, Laura (1979) "Disputing without the Force of Law," 88 *Yale Law Journal* 998.

Nonet, Phillipe and Philip Selznick (1978) *Law and Society in Transition: Toward Responsive Law.* New York: Harper & Row.

Offe, Claus (1972) "Advanced Capitalism and the Welfare State," 2 *Politics and Society* 479.

――――― (1977) *Lo Stato nel Capitalismo Maturo.* Milan: Etas Libri.

Penner, Roland (1977) "The Development of Community Legal Services in Canada: An Evaluation of Parkdale Community Legal Services in Toronto, Dalhousie Legal Aid Service in Halifax, and Community Legal Service, Inc., in Point St. Charles, Montreal." Unpublished.

Perrot, Roger (1976) "Les moyens judiciaires et parajudiciaires de la protection des consommateurs," 1976 *Gazette du Palais, Doctrine* 237.

———— (1977) "Le rôle du juge dans la société moderne," 1977 *Gazette du Palais, Doctrine* 91.

Piven, Frances Fox and Richard Cloward (1977) *Poor People's Movements: Why They Succeed, How They Fail.* New York: Pantheon.

Ramm, Thilo (1971) "Labor Courts and Grievance Settlement in West Germany," in B. Aaron (ed.) *Labor Courts and Grievance Settlement in Western Europe.* Berkeley: University of California Press.

Rehbinder, Eckard (1976) "Controlling the Environmental Enforcement Deficit: West Germany." *American Journal of Comparative Law* 24:373.

Reich, Charles (1964) "The New Property," 73 *Yale Law Journal* 733.

Reifner, Udo (1982) "Individualistic and Collective Legalization: The Theory and Practice of Legal Advice for Workers in Prefascist Germany," in R. Abel (ed.) *The Politics of Informal Justice,* vol. 2: *Comparative Studies.* New York: Academic Press.

Robson, William (1928) *Justice and Administrative Law.* London: Macmillan & Co.

Rosenberg, Maurice and Myra Schubin (1961) "Trial by Lawyers: Compulsory Arbitration of Small Claims in Pennsylvania," 74 *Harvard Law Review* 448.

Rubinstein, Leonard (1976) "Procedural Due Process and the Limits of the Adversary System," 11 *Harvard Civil Rights–Civil Liberties Law Review* 48.

Ruhnka, John, Steven Weller, and John Martin (1978) *Small Claims Courts: A National Examination.* Williamsburg, Va.: National Center for State Courts.

Sandrock, Otto (1978) "The Standard Terms Act 1976 of West Germany," 26 *American Journal of Comparative Law* 551.

Santos, Boaventura de Sousa (1977) "The Law of the Oppressed: The Construction and Reproduction of Legality in Pasargada," 12 *Law & Society Review* 5.

Sarat, Austin (1976) "Alternatives in Dispute Processing: Litigation in a Small Claims Court," 10 *Law & Society Review* 339.

Savatier, René (1977) "L'inflation législative et l'indigestion du corps social," 1977 *Recueil Dalloz Sirey, Chronique* 43.

Scheingold, Stuart (1974) *The Politics of Rights: Lawyers, Public Policy, and Political Change.* New Haven: Yale University Press.

Schuyt, Kees, Kees Gruenendijk, and Ben Sloot (1977) "Access to the Legal System and Legal Services Research," in B. Blegvad, C. Campbell, and K. Schuyt (eds.) *European Yearbook in Law and Sociology.* The Hague: Nijhoff.

Sheppard, David, Janice Roehl, and Royer Cook (1978) *National Evaluation of the Neighborhood Justice Centers Field Test: Interim Report.* Reston, Va.: Institute for Research.

Society of Labour Lawyers (1978) *Legal Services for All.* London: Fabian Society.

Stanley, Justin (1977) "The Resolution of Minor Disputes and the Seventh Amendment," 60 *Marquette Law Review* 963.

Street, Harry (1968) *Justice in the Welfare State.* London: Stevens & Sons.

Tate, Shepherd (1979) "Access to Justice," 65 *American Bar Association Journal* 904.

Taylor, G. D. S. (1979) "Special Procedures Governing Small Claims in Australia," in M. Cappelletti and J. Weisner (eds.) *Access to Justice: Promising Institutions.* Alphen aan den rijn: Sijthoff; Milan: Giuffrè.

Thery, Phillipe (1978) "Access to Justice in France," in M. Cappelletti and B. Garth (eds.) *Access to Justice: A World Survey.* Alphen aan den rijn: Sijthoff; Milan: Giuffrè.

Trubek, David (1977a) "Complexity and Contradiction in the Legal Order: Balbus and the Challenge of Critical Social Thought about Law," 11 *Law & Society Review* 529.

———— (1977b) "Review of Balancing the Scales of Justice: Financing Public Interest Law in America," 1977 *Wisconsin Law Review* 303.

———— (1979) "Public Advocacy: Administrative Government and the Representation of Diffuse Interests," in M. Cappelletti and B. Garth (eds.) *Access to Justice: Emerging Issues and Perspectives*. Alphen aan den rijn: Sijthoff; Milan: Giuffrè.

Tushnet, Mark (1977) "Perspectives on the Development of American Law: A Critical Review of Friedman's 'A History of American Law'," 1977 *Wisconsin Law Review* 81.

Unger, Roberto (1976) *Law in Modern Society*. New York: Free Press.

United States Department of Justice, Office for Improvements in the Administration of Justice (1979) "Preliminary Report on Court-Annexed Arbitration in Three Federal District Courts." Unpublished (January 19).

Valétas, M. (1976) *Aide judiciaire et accès à la justice*. Paris: CREDOC.

Van Caenegem, R. C. (1973) "History of European Civil Procedure," in 25 *International Encyclopedia of Comparative Law* Ch. 2.

Verkuil, Paul (1975) "The Ombudsman and the Limits of the Adversary Process," 75 *Columbia Law Review* 845.

Vigoriti, Vincenzo (1978) "Access to Justice in Italy," in M. Cappelletti and B. Garth (eds.) *Access to Justice: A World Survey*. Alphen aan den rijn: Sijthoff; Milan: Giuffrè.

Weber, Max (1954) *Max Weber on Law and Economy in Society*, ed. M. Rheinstein. Cambridge, Mass.: Harvard University Press.

Wexler, Stephen (1970) "Practicing Law for Poor People," 79 *Yale Law Journal* 1049.

Yngvesson, Barbara and Patricia Hennessey (1975) "Small Claims, Complex Disputes: A Review of the Small Claims Literature," 9 *Law & Society Review* 219.

Zander, Michael (1976) "Is the Payment-Into-Court Rule Worth Copying?" 40 *Rabels Zeitschrift* 750.

———— (1978) *Legal Services for the Community*. London: Maurice Temple Smith.

———— (1979) "Promoting Change in the Legal System," 42 *Modern Law Review* 489.

IV

The Revolutionary Situation

Institutionalizing Neighborhood Courts: Two Chilean Experiences

JACK SPENCE*

INTRODUCTION

Two general concerns animate interest in decentralizing urban courts or establishing neighborhood courts. Courts of modern urban commercial–industrial centers have highly specialized procedures necessitating professional advocates and caseloads dominated by disputes involving substantial material stakes or breaches of public order. These characteristics bar easy access to judicial services for those whose resources are modest or whose disputes are of lesser moment. Deprofessionalization, simplification, and decentralization can be seen as possible means of removing these barriers, though analyses of small claims courts suggest some limitations (Yngvesson and Hennessey, 1975). Decentralized courts can also be seen as efforts to replace urban anomic social relations with a

*From Spence, J., "Institutionalizing Neighborhood Courts: Two Chilean Experiences," Law & Society Review, 13, pp. 139–182. © Law and Society Association, 1978. Reprinted with permission. I wish to thank David Hunt, Igor Webb, Bob Wood, and Duncan Kennedy for their suggestions, Heleen Ietswaart for sharing her field observations on Popular Audiences, and the Foreign Area Fellowship Program for generous financial support.

215

greater sense of community and establish local level governance. They might permit peaceful face-to-face resolution of disputes and discourage damaging, anonymous retribution or lingering irresolution. Such courts might influence or be influenced by community norms and residents.[1]

The Allende period in Chile saw two urban judicial decentralization efforts speaking to these concerns. One emerged from the judiciary, under external political pressure, and was to feature professional judges holding weekly informal court sessions, without lawyers, for residents of working-class and poor neighborhoods within their jurisdictions. The other developed in a few highly organized, politically left, new squatter settlements (called *campamentos*) surrounding Santiago. Though particular structures varied, judges were lay people elected from the *campamento*. The following analysis compares an example of each of these two types.

The decentralized professional court and the lay courts of one *campamento* generated somewhat different caseloads, employed diverse methods of dispute processing, differed in ideological perspectives and goals (not necessarily articulated), and operated under distinct organizational constraints. Each achieved modest success; both encountered intractable problems hindering institutionalization. The analysis leading to these conclusions rests upon field research consisting largely of interviews with professional judges (participating and nonparticipating) and government and opposition leaders, direct observation of several dozen cases in the professional court, and (for the squatter settlement) extensive interviews with five informants who lived and worked within the squatter settlement.[2]

Law in a modern, capitalist state reflects the interplay between levels of class conflict and state structures and policies. The policies can serve to defend against increases in class conflict or to mediate intraclass relations, but developments in lawmaking institutions might also be the product of class conflict—in this case,

[1] For discussion of general urban decentralization strategies, see Kristol (1968), Kotler (1969), Altshuler (1970), O'Brien (1975), Yin and Yates (1975), and Yates (1976).

[2] The analysis also included interviews in a squatter settlement that did not contain its own unofficial court and was not within the jurisdiction of one of the professional Popular Audiences, to identify disputes and discover whether there was informal, regularized, third-party dispute processing, and interviews in an upper-class neighborhood exploring attitudes toward the idea of neighborhood courts. It has also benefited greatly from contemporary field research on the Popular Audiences by Heleen Ietswaart, and from surveys of squatter attitudes toward the system of justice and the idea of neighborhood courts performed by the Equipo Poblacional of the Central Interdisciplinario de Desarrollos Urbano y Regional, known as CIDU (see Cheetham *et al.*, 1972).

Political considerations and issues of local confidentiality prevented direct observation by outsiders, particularly United States researchers. Considerable anti-United States sentiment pervaded Chile during this period and was naturally strongest within left sectors. In addition, one found quite justifiable fears of CIA infiltration and a particular tradition in Chile of abusive research projects. For an account of the latter, see Horowitz (1967). For pertinent observations on nonnationals doing squatter settlement research, see Santos (1977: 8).

of social protest movements, themselves a result of contradictions within the capitalist economy or created by state policies (Useem, 1974; Epsing-Anderson et al., 1976). This framework does not deny the relevance within the traditional field of urban policies of local decisional analysis or analyses of decentralization strategies within local urban environments but seeks to place decision makers and strategy formation within a broader context.[3] In addition, this framework need not ignore the insights of the relationships of third-party dispute-processing styles and institutions to the character of social organization within the relevant community and to the types of disputes litigants choose to bring before them. Those relationships have been portrayed in numerous ethnographic studies usually exploring traditional, stable, self-contained cultures, or cultures gradually adapting to the presence of the legal outposts of a modern state.

But the present study does not see the types of dispute-processing institutions and their styles as outcomes only of local social organization and shared local values, or as the simple result of local residents choosing to take advantage of new options emanating from changing environmental pressures. The new legal institutions are seen as the result of direct challenges to traditional arrangements, which arose from changes in the level of class conflict and affected the priorities of national political structures, including political parties. The political developments gave rise to what Santos (1977), in his remarkable study of a Brazilian squatter settlement, refers to as legal pluralism, or the presence of legal modes and institutions somewhat independent of and distinct from the official dominant legality, though the political conditions in the Chilean case obviously differed from Brazil and resulted in distinct forms of legal pluralism. Specifically, the Chilean state in the late 1960s and early 1970s was not fascist, and that period was marked by increasingly high levels of class conflict and political mobilization. Neighborhood courts as a national political issue (among other issues) were spawned by the convergence of two political forces: an urban squatter land invasion movement, itself the product of the state's inability to resolve the inadequacies of the private housing market, and competition for power and policies among ideologically distinct national political parties, as well as state institutions such as the judiciary.

ORIGINS OF THE NEIGHBORHOOD COURTS

For a time in 1971 neighborhood courts became a Chilean political issue capturing national attention. The recently elected Allende Unidad Popular (UP) coalition government proposed a law to establish a nationwide system of elected, neighborhood, lay courts. The bill met such vociferous criticism in the

[3]For critiques of the reputational, decisional, and pluralist schools in urban political theory, and alternatives to those schools, see Katznelson (1976) and Castells (1977: 243–378).

opposition-controlled Congress that it was withdrawn. In political terms, the bill can be seen as part of a UP effort to gain the allegiance of thousands of uncommitted poor and working-class voters living in the many new (and not so new) squatter settlements surrounding Santiago. It was also an ideological attack on the existing judicial structure, which the UP regarded as biased against the working class.

In the previous decade the centrist Christian Democrats (DC), the left Communist party (CP), and the Socialist Party (SP) (the two leading parties of the UP) had each vied for the support of residents of poor neighborhoods. After the 1964 defeat of Allende by Eduardo Frei, the DC had the upper hand. Frei, with a more sympathic Congress than Allende was to have and with considerable financial support from the United States and international lending organizations, was able to launch education and housing programs that benefited, or promised to benefit, poor residents. However, as Frei's six-year term drew to a close, economic bottlenecks and financial problems severely hampered housing programs. Many people who had been promised homes (some of whom had even made numerous payments) or materials to construct their own homes failed to get them (Castells, 1974: 263; Pastrana and Threlfall, 1974: 35).

This failure, increasing central city land costs with attendant higher rents, and general economic stagnation in 1968–1970 led to an urban squatter settlement movement of organized land invasions. The CP, the SP, and the Left Revolutionary Movement (MIR), a party that viewed the electoral pursuit of socialism as a futile strategy, helped to organize more invasions. Squatter invasions increased from 11 in 1968 to 58 in 1969, and to 323 in 1970 (Castells, 1974: 271; Pastrana and Threlfall, 1974: 71). Frei and his multiclass-based party were in a bind. To repress the invasions by police power would weaken DC popularity among this growing and increasingly organized portion of the urban population, but to permit them would damage support among bourgeois classes frightened by the increase in mass illegality and the assault on private property. The tide was swinging toward the left, particularly when Frei had to endure intense political heat after police killed several people during a March 1969 squatter invasion in a southern city.

After Allende's victory in 1970, the UP proposed housing, health, and education programs, as well as neighborhood courts with jurisdiction over minor torts, crimes, and contractual disputes. These were aimed at squatter settlements and residentially based constituents. If the courts proved popular in the *campamentos*, the UP would benefit. Also, the DC feared that eligibility for judgeships under the UP bill (previous membership in labor or social institutions) would bias elections in favor of UP neighborhood candidates.[4] The DC's counter-

---

[4]Interviews with José Viera Gallo, Subsecretario del Ministerio de Justicia, and Ricardo Galvez, Relator de la Corte Suprema, October 1971.

proposal sought to cure the access problem and maintain what it saw to be the integrity of the judicial system by greatly expanding the number of professional judges.

The more explosive point of the UP bill centered on its critique of the existing judicial order. The left claimed that most poor people had no access to the judicial system. Some elements of the DC joined in this criticism, but they saw the solution not in lay courts but in expanding the number of professional judges. But to the UP (or at least those UP elements most in favor of the bill) such changes would not be sufficient because the professional judiciary was part of a legal order that systematically discriminated against the poor. "Legal" manipulations enabled rich landowners to absorb reservation lands from Indians in southern Chile, but theft of property by poor people, when apprehended, was sharply penalized (except in some cases of squatters, if they were well organized). The financial damage levied on a negligent wealthy auto driver (and almost all car owners in Chile were well-to-do) would be considerably greater if the victim were rich, given relative access to legal help, ability to prove damages, and bargaining power. The UP sought to change this legal order and saw creation of the neighborhood courts as one step in breaking bourgeois domination of judicial institutions (Novoa, 1964, 1965, 1972; *Chile Hoy,* October 6, 1972: 30, 32; Farias, 1972: 92; Cerroni, 1972: 85; de la Fuente Moreno, 1973: 77).

This critique kindled additional opposition to the proposal. Despite the limited jurisdictional power these courts were to have, the right opposition (centered in the National party) feared fulfillment of its prophecy that the left, once in power, would attempt to destroy the constitutional order (*El Mercurio,* Santiago, January 25, 1971: 23; January 27, 1971: 33; March 4, 1971: 3). Residents of upper-class neighborhoods expressed apprehension that, for example, their maids might bring a case against them in a neighborhood court.[5]

These objections might seem like overreactions or antileft propaganda. After all, the UP proposal was to pass through constitutional procedures, and it was hard to imagine the court of an upper-class neighborhood that would not be controlled by members of that class. But opposition did not stem just from fear of material losses through unsuccessful defenses in neighborhood courts. It also came from a real sense that the UP plan would upset the power balance based on status and deference to status. Allowing working-class lay people to be judges would undermine the legitimacy of professional judges. Even one maid forcing an employer to submit to a neighborhood court could become a celebrated case upsetting class-based patterns of deference. Granting institutional judicial power to working-class judges to levy even mild punishments would disturb power relations and create an unfortunate, or perhaps even disastrous, precedent.

[5]Interviews with seven families from Las Condes, a very well-to-do neighborhood in Santiago, November–December 1971.

Though the bill stalled in Congress and was later withdrawn by the UP, the debate surrounding it contained some of the same ideological currents as the two courts under study. Neither court was exactly what DC and UP sponsors had in mind, but each can be seen as a product of the class conflict and ideological differences that gave rise to the UP and DC proposals. The professional court experiment embodied an attempt to extend Chilean law and legal institutions to those without access to judicial services. The lay courts rejected the idea of professional judges, were established outside the legal system, and sought to delegitimize the judiciary. This latter effort entailed far more fundamental change and elicited both support and opposition from the diverse elements within the UP coalition.

OPERATION OF THE PROFESSIONAL NEIGHBORHOOD COURT

Judicial Participation

Following the demise of the neighborhood court bill, the Ministry of Justice requested the Supreme Court to order all judges below the Supreme Court to hold regular court sessions without lawyers in poor and working-class neighborhoods. Perhaps to avoid a propaganda coup by its left critics, the Supreme Court formally accepted the suggestion and issued instructions to courts to hold Popular Audiences, as they were to be called. But only three or four judges in the Santiago area actively participated in the program. None of them regularly left their courts and went out into individual neighborhoods within their jurisdictions. Those who did participate had courts located near working-class neighborhoods. Many other Santiago courts were housed in the central business district, although their jurisdictions included other areas of the city. Some centrally located judges announced on small signs in court hallways the hours of the Popular Audiences, but this was insufficient to generate a caseload. Other judges were candid about their lack of participation, stating that heavy caseloads prevented them from allocating time to the new program.[6] They did seem to have full schedules, but this explanation missed the purpose of the proposal—to shift judicial resources away from normal functions.

This low level of participation reflected the limited commitment of the Supreme Court. Though the president could appoint judges to the Supreme Court and lower courts, he could do so only from short lists of candidates selected by the Supreme Court for an appellate court and by an appellate court for lower

---

[6]Interviews with three nonparticipating Civil Court judges, November 1971.

courts. The Supreme Court had regulatory powers and could dismiss or reprimand judges in cases of malfeasance (Gil, 1966: 125). The widespread lack of compliance with the Supreme Court's Popular Audience memorandum reflected lack of enthusiasm for the program on the part of most judges (not surprisingly, given their normal caseloads and the professional status attached to them) as well as an informal understanding that the Supreme Court and the appellate courts under it also gave it low priority, at best.

The historically determined priorities of the judiciary, operating within a capitalist mode of production, gave attention to cases regulating relations between large economic organizations, disputes involving substantial material stakes between well-to-do individuals, or crimes threatening the social order— particularly the social order of the bourgeoisie. Professional status flowed from these priorities. Despite the best intentions of a few reform-minded judges, a substantial shift in priorities (amounting to one day per week for all judges) would not occur without substantial pressure from outside the judiciary. Nonetheless, judges hoping for promotion now had to estimate the effect of blatant nonparticipation on the UP-controlled Ministry of Justice. Putting up signs could give the appearance of participation and lay a foundation for the excuse that residents did not seem to want the service. Of the three judges actively participating in the program, one expressed high enthusiasm (and was also hoping for an appellate court appointment); another was unenthusiastic but strictly interpreted the Supreme Court communiqué as an order to be followed.[7] The last, my focal point, was somewhat enthusiastic and not obviously ambitious for immediate promotion.

Court Resources and Symbolic Access

Judges who did participate were expected to maintain their normal level of performance in their regular jurisdictions. Participation thus strained resources—a theme that pervades my analysis of the Popular Audiences of one court. Located several miles from Santiago's center, this jurisdiction included poor and working-class neighborhoods, relatively new *campamentos*, and some government-financed housing. The population of the area exceeded 100,000. In addition to stenographers and guards, the criminal court judge had an active staff of seven clerks, who were skilled paralegal workers. Under Chilean procedure the judge plays a much more active investigatory role than he does in common law practice. He examines witnesses and the accused, often without the presence of the attorney, and he can order the police to gather more evidence. His clerks also

[7]This conclusion is drawn from conversations in 1972 with Heleen Ietswaart, who observed Popular Audiences in mid-1972, and from her field notes.

play an active role in this process, taking depositions and formulating questions on behalf of the judge. On one occasion, for example, I observed a particularly incisive clerk reduce a tough-looking accused murderer to tears with her pressing questions.

The judge, however, almost never employed clerks in Popular Audiences. As will be shown, the effects of this sparing use of resources in the initial stages of dispute processing sheds light on the implicit goals and values of the Popular Audiences.

Early in the morning of the day appointed for Popular Audiences, disputants would begin lining up on rude benches in the hallway of the modest, concrete block, five-room court house. (The contrast with the more ornate, cavernous halls of justice in downtown Santiago was striking.) Those at the end of the line of some twenty to thirty people might wait several hours until their turn to appear before the judge's bench, a desk elevated on a small platform at the head of the building's largest room. This room also contained clerks' desks. During hearings, the clerks would be recording criminal case depositions or filling out forms on their typewriters. [8]

As the hearings unfolded, it became evident that many disputants would wait hours without having their disputes substantially processed. At least half the complainants came to court without the defendant. In these cases the judge could do little but hear the complaint and request that the defendant be brought the next time, or offer to issue a citation for his or her appearance. In other cases, the matter brought before the court had to be processed elsewhere (divorces, for example). The Popular Audiences could not preempt the special jurisdictions of other courts, except that in matters of "lesser import" the Popular Audiences regularly heard matters involving civil or criminal issues that were technically within another court's jurisdiction but usually ignored in the normal course of practice. In cases that had to be dealt with elsewhere, the Popular Audiences provided legal referrals. In over half the cases, disputants waited considerable time for a five-minute hearing resulting in a citation (often ineffective due to shortages of police services) or a referral.

The paradox of bureaucratically created delays in a reform designed to eliminate such barriers might be explained by the court's lack of organizational resources. Already stretched to the limit by its normal load of criminal cases, it could not spare skilled clerks to pass through the line of applicants at the beginning of the day, uncover the nature of each complaint, steer those with inappropriate business to the correct bureaucracy, and urge those without their oppo-

---

[8]The analysis of dispute processing in the Popular Audiences is based on observations of over ninety hearings, fifteen posthearing interviews with disputants, and multiple interviews with the judge, December 1971, February, March, and April, 1972, and supplemental conversations with and field notes of some three dozen hearings recorded by Ietswaart.

nents to bring in the defendant, perhaps with the assistance of a citation issued by the clerk. The mode of proceeding also wasted the court's resources by requiring the judge to spend additional hours dealing with cases in which the issue had not been joined. Since the judge was the most important figure in the court, it was paradoxical that his time contribution, as distinct from that of his staff, was less in criminal cases, regarded as the most important function of the court, than in Popular Audiences, where he acted virtually alone. Scarce organizational resources do not provide a complete answer for these delays. *Someone* was going to make the referral; it was a question of who should spare the time. Having the judge perform this bureaucratic response was a symbolic act—not one of substance.

The goal of the symbolic act was to convince the client that the *judiciary*, in its Popular Audiences, was not unresponsive to her or his needs. No claim or problem was too small to come before the patronal figure of the judge. This does not mean that the Popular Audiences were simply a sham public relations effort. Another subconscious function might have been to convince the judge, as well, that he was a judge "of the people" and that no problem was too humble for him to consider.

For this symbolic effort to produce a satisfied client, it was essential that the bureaucracy maintain client ignorance about its functions and respect for its hierarchy. If the client did not know that *anyone* in the court could provide a simple referral, she or he was more likely to be happy with the handling of her or his problem and awed by the judge's knowledge of the law and his "connections," and *less* likely to be annoyed about the unnecessary delay.

If judges were to be satisfied by the symbolic effort, they had to disregard efficiency and maintain a superior view of their role vis-à-vis clients. In this case, the judge might have viewed himself as giving a "gift" to those without normal access to the judicial system. This need not necessarily imply a condescending noblesse oblige, but it did require maintenance of a certain status hierarchy. The "gifts" were handed "down" by a judge superior in class, income, education, and, most important, power to an inferior disputant. But if the disputant were critical of the judge's service, or of the long delays, the symbolic act would lose its effect, and the service rendered by this official representative of the state would be depreciated.[9]

---

[9]The Popular Audiences in two other courts seem to have treated complainants who appeared without respondents or simply needed referrals in a somewhat different manner but one consistent with the image of judge as patron. In one court, all cases went to the judge, but he listened to the disputant at length even when the appropriate disposition was clearly a citation or referral. This judge was very impressed with the "unique" role of the Popular Audiences in conferring judicial attention upon the poor and outcast. Another judge used a clerk to screen the disputants and handle those needing a citation or referral, and the judge heard only those disputes that had been joined. This

Popular Audiences Disputes

Over two-thirds of the observed Popular Audience cases seen by this court involved disputes between family members or neighbors. Half the remainder were between people who seemed to have ongoing social ties—at work, as friends, or as neighborhood merchant and customer. The rest, as far as could be determined, had no social ties outside the activities leading to the dispute. As a general rule, disputes between neighbors and within families had been simmering for some time and seemed, on the basis of permitted testimony, to contain complicated ranges of claim and counterclaim, dispute and subdispute. That this should be true of the neighbor arguments probably reflected the lack of mobility and privacy and, at least in some *campamentos*, a more intense level of social interactions than that associated with, say, United States car-dominated urban neighborhoods in which people without ethnic ties live in apartments. Since no ethnographic study was attempted, it is difficult to make these generalizations. Nonetheless, studies of other squatter settlements, as well as my own search for regularized, informal, third-party dispute-processing agents in a ten-year-old neighborhood of squatter-settlement origin, suggested social organization involving residentially based (sometimes family-based) multiplex relations that were more extensive than those suggested by Felstiner (1974) in his model of a technologically complex, rich society and less extensive and frequent than those in his technologically simple, poor society.[10]

Property claims were not infrequent in the Popular Audiences. Separated couples often faced problems of one person holding property claimed by the other. There were observed cases involving real property (none involved boundary, foundation, or easement disputes), damage to a house, disputed occupancy, or rent payment. In almost every case between families and neighbors, property claims were complicated by charges of physical or mental injury. These abounded in great variety: pestering, too much noise, slander, contentiousness, ill-behaved children, general gossip, "hanging around," threats of slander, assault, battery, voyeurism, lack of respect. Often such charges would be the entire case. Cases between acquaintances from work, merchant and customer, or unrelated parties often concerned only property: debts, rent, evictions, or damaged goods.

The following examples give a more concrete sense of the variety of cases and help illustrate the dispute process in the Popular Audiences.

---

judge thought the Popular Audiences were worthless and held them only because she thought the Supreme Court required them—an interpretation not shared by her colleagues. These conclusions are drawn from the field notes of Heleen Ietswaart.

[10]The framework for analysis of dispute processing was developed in Spence (1971, 1973) and elaborated in Spence (1979). I owe an intellectual debt to the work of Richard Abel (1973).

CASE ONE

A man and a woman appear before the judge, the man looking somewhat sullen, the woman angry. The judge inquires what the court can do for them. The woman complains that the husband does not provide adequately for herself and their two children, drinks too much, and when drunk is abusive toward the children and herself. On occasion he has struck her and the children. The judge asks the man if he has hit his wife. He admits that he has but goes on to affirm in increasingly angry tones that he has only struck the children lightly for misbehaving and the wife, not because he was drunk, but because she berated him for not having enough money or called him lazy—things she has said publicly as well. She interjects that this is not so, that she has not ridiculed him publicly, and he heatedly claims she has told her relations of her disappointment in him. At this point the judge interrupts the lively argument and inquires, once again, if it is true that the husband has struck his wife. He reprimands the husband, informing him that there is no excuse for striking his wife and that it was a violation of the law. The judge says that if this assault and battery is repeated, he will see to it that the husband is prosecuted under the law. He asks the man if he understands, and the husband nods yes. The judge then urges the couple to try to live in tranquility and dismisses them.

CASE TWO

Two women appear before the judge. The first claims that the other's young children are ruining her property, that she is poor and cannot afford this kind of trouble. She explains that she keeps a few chickens in her yard and charges that the second woman's children have made a practice of letting the chickens out, chasing them, and throwing rocks at them (though she does not claim that they have been injured or lost). Moreover, she says, the children and their mother show her no respect: The children taunt her, and the mother, in addition to not stopping the children, makes fun of her "dirty yard" to neighbors, thereby sowing disrespect for her throughout the neighborhood. The second woman maintains that the woman's yard is dirty and a disgrace to the neighborhood and that the first has been spreading slanderous rumors that might threaten her marriage. The first interjects that this is a lie. At this point the judge cuts off testimony and begins to lecture the women on the importance to Chile of maintaining neighborly relations. He demands that they stop bothering each other and suggests that they might best accomplsih this by going out of their way to avoid one another.

CASE THREE

Two men take their turns for a hearing. One states that he has erected a small shack (presumably in a squatter settlement) but, for unstated reasons, has not occupied it. He has permitted the second man and his family to occupy it, charging them a monthly rent. The arrangement has gone on for over a year, but now he wants to rent the home to his brother and his brother's family. His complaint is that the second man refuses to move his family out. The second man claims that he and his family have no place to go, that they have treated the house well and paid the rent on time, and that this behavior should be enough to allow them to remain. He does not contest the ownership of the home or suggest that there has been a verbal or written agreement establishing the rental arrangement over a certain period. The judge explains to the second man that he must move out, since the house does not belong to him, that he can stay no longer than a month. But he suggests to the first man that he try to give the second as much time as possible to find another place to live.

Processing of disputes showed similar characteristics across dispute types. There were no formal boundaries to the kinds of claims or counterclaims that could be asserted, though some falling within the formal jurisdiction of another court (e.g., divorce) would be referred by the judge. There were no formal rules of evidence; both sides could present hearsay, direct observations, comments of dubious relevance to any of the claims, or conclusory statements without support. Nonetheless, an unstated time limit bounded the hearings. Almost all hearings ranged from five to ten minutes, with a few lasting fifteen (not counting the mid-hearing delays and interruptions). This time limit might have eliminated evidence and tended to restrict the scope of the claims. There were no trained third-party advocates, though sometimes a disputant would be accompanied by a friend who would help press the claim.

The judge cut off testimony for several reasons. He would seize upon an obvious "legal handle" that could be used as a basis for orders to the disputants. For example, in the argument between husband and wife, the latter's claim that the husband had beaten her, once admitted, became the main focus for the judge's handling of the case. One could argue that all aspects of the dispute were processed, if not resolved, but a sounder analysis would be that the boundaries of the processed dispute did not correspond to the real dispute (Santos, 1977: 25). Permitting testimony without recognizing it perhaps allowed disputants to "blow off steam," but the brevity of the proceedings limited this option. The decision clearly reflected the dictates of formal law, and other claims were either ignored, explored briefly to see whether they raised issues cognizable within Chilean law, or dismissed as beyond the competence of the judge.

It is less obvious in the landlord–tenant case that testimony had been cut off or that claims were being ignored, but the judge did not explore features of the case beyond those pertinent to Chilean property law. The outcome strictly adheres to that law, save in the judge's suggestion that the landlord be flexible in exercising his rights. Unfettered by the substance of Chilean law or time constraints, the judge might have pursued other inquiries to a more equitable solution. Using his broad investigatory powers, the judge might have inquired about the exact nature of the "landlord's" claims to the building and property. Was this a case of a squatter occupying another squatter's property? What were the actual needs and options of the plaintiff's brother and the current "tenant," given family size, salary, and employment? These questions are meant not to suggest that the judge's treatment of the case was unfair but only to indicate the boundaries surrounding the processed dispute and possible paths to different outcomes.

Two other modes of dispute processing appeared in cases involving property claims. In some, though the formal legal issue was clear, the evidence presented was not. Rather than searching for the "truth," the judge sometimes divided the contested property (when this could easily be done). If the evidence clearly favored the plaintiff, the judge might ease the terms of payment. These were compromise solutions, but they should be distinguished from compromises attained through lengthy mediation resulting in consensual agreements and from efforts to maintain tranquility in a local society with face-to-face relations by "making the balance." Here the dispute was quickly arbitrated, and the process was dictated primarily by the administrative needs of the court. The judge did not have time to pursue more detailed evidence in order to arrive at the "truth," and the court could not be burdened by plaintiffs returning with further allegations of repeated unpaid claims against the same defendant.

In cases without an obvious "legal handle," the judge cut off disputants if charge and countercharge threatened to "get out of hand." Otherwise, he would stop them after ten minutes and then, as in our second case, lecture them on proper familial or neighborly behavior. In these he often asserted that patriotic virtue demanded neighborliness and implored disputants to behave better or to ignore and avoid one another. Here the time boundaries, and other constraints discussed later in the chapter, precluded exploration of the roots of the disputes or the details of the multiplex relations that fostered it. A brief period of blowing off steam was permitted, but there was little effort to mediate. The lectures often stated a compromise position, but they were not always neutral. In husband–wife cases, the judge invariably took the side of the wife unless the husband charged infidelity and spent more energy imploring the husband to improve his behavior. When employing the "lecture method," the judge attempted to have both parties at least nod agreement to his invocation of harmonious relationships.

In cases without a "legal handle," the judge was presented with a real dilemma. It was difficult to find an arbitrated "legal" outcome. If a formal legal claim was wrapped up in the flurry of charge and countercharge (for example, defamation of character), it was difficult to resolve without complicated hearings. Yet the disputes were real, heavily charged with emotion, and often long-standing and complicated. The second case could not be mediated in fifteen minutes, though the judge's brief effort to get disputants to indicate agreement, if unlikely to restore harmony, was a beginning in that direction.[11] In short, though a hearing had been held and multiple claims presented (other elements of the dispute may well have been omitted entirely), only marginal progress was made toward dispute resolution. In fact, one might argue that though the judge heard the charges, the generality of his comments and decison did not really amount to processing the case.

Structural and ideological considerations defined the approach of the Popular Audiences to dispute processing. Operating within a relatively informal procedural framework without lawyers, written petitions, rules of evidence, or professional adversaries, the court's dispute processing was constrained by lack of money and time, great social distance between the highly educated and professional judge and disputants, and limited power and authority. Scarcity of organizational resources was graphically evident when testimony was not only cut off after a few mintues but also often smothered by the din of clerks' typewriters, punctuated by interruptions (phone calls to the judge always seemed to receive higher priority, as did conferences with clerks), and overshadowed by the judge's nearly constant perusal of documents while the parties presented their cases.

Like other street-level bureaucrats bounded by lack of time and organizational resources (staff, money), the judge was forced to routinize: allowing roughly equal time periods per dispute, confining the dispute to familiar legal shorthands, and presenting formulistic agreements and standardized lectures on proper behavior (Lipsky, 1976: 202). Routinization can also be justified on other grounds: It is the ethos of public bureaucracies not to play favorites, to treat clients with similar problems equally. On the other hand, constricting the scope of the case and applying generally worded directives treated *unequal* cases equally by ignoring major aspects of the dispute.

Social distance between the professional judge and disputants also hampered consensual dispute resolution.[12] Though definitive socioeconomic information on all disputants could not be obtained, great differences between the judge and disputants in dress, manner of speech, levels of education, occupational status

[11]Through communications with Heleen Ietswaart and from her field notes I would conclude that two other judges processed claims similarly, though the styles differed somewhat. The "pro-Popular Audience judge" (see Note 9) seemed to exercise control over testimony and held somewhat longer hearings as a result. It was this court's practice, in some cases, to have one of the clerks draw up an agreement between the two parties, which they would then sign. Though this gave the appearance of consensual mediation, the agreements were fairly standard in content. They gave emphasis to the obligation of the parties to solve their own arguments, or suggested that they avoid one another, and relied upon generally phrased moral and patriotic precepts. The other judge seemed to cut off testimony quickly, complained of the demands on the court's time, and expressed amazement to the disputants (particularly in claims that did not concern property) that they could waste so much of their time in foolish bickering.

[12]For discussions of the social background of judges, see Schubert (1963), Danelski (1966), Grossman (1966), and Cook (1973).

and privilege, residential context, and income pervaded the Popular Audiences. The judge underscored these by his difficulty in relating to nonproperty aspects of disputes lacking familiar legal remedies. More than once the judge lamented to the observer that he was unable to understand "these people" or mentioned that they "lacked culture." This social distance contrasted sharply with ethnographic studies of third-party dispute practices in which the "judge" is fully integrated into the culture of the disputants. Combined with an apparent lack of training in mediation techniques, this social distance placed the judge at a disadvantage in finding a workable resolution to all aspects of the dispute.

The use of formal law to guide dispute outcomes is not only attributable to the social position of the judge but also a convenient routinizing tool useful in a structurally determined, time-bounded hearing process. The Popular Audiences program was, after all, an extension of the formal judicial power of the state to people who otherwise might not have had access to it. The judge had more formal authority than the *presidente* in the Brazilian squatter settlement Santos (1977) has analyzed but was constrained by his professional position in the judicial career structure to keep his decisions within the confines of formal law. This combined with a lack of organizational resources to truncate disputes, ignore claims, and leave unexplored remedies or consensual agreements.

Lack of organizational resources was compounded by lack of real power. Though the court exercised considerble power over disputants within the confines of the courtroom, the judge's ability to influence disputants outside the court was extremely limited (Lipsky, 1976: 199). The judge's elevated position in the courtroom (he did not go to the neighborhoods), control over testimony, and patterns of speech, as well as the deference accorded him, showed he was in command of the proceedings. Few disputants rebelled against this, though some expressed facial dissatisfaction with the frequent interruptions or with dispositions. To secure compliance with dispositions presented a larger dilemma. The court threatened to use the police, but their resources were already overextended by the requirements of the court's normal criminal jurisdiction. This lack of power also made it difficult to force reluctant defendants to attend court. Citations were backlogged, and knowledgeable defendants could take the chance that they would never be enforced. These limitations in the dispute process within Popular Audiences should not imply criticism of the judge. Indeed, he was to be admired for holding the hearings at all and for conducting them in a reasonable, civil manner, given the structural constraints.

Disputants may have seen the judge as a legitimate authority and may have followed his decision for this reason. Voluntary court appearances, expressions of deference, facial reactions to outcomes, and interviews with a subsample of disputants conducted in the courthouse immediately after the hearings sometimes suggested this respect. In some cases settlements appeared to have been reached, usually when material stakes dominated disputes. When both disputants came to court willingly, they sometimes appeared predisposed toward "letting someone else decide"; they had granted the court some measure of authority on the basis of its place in the Chilean legal structure. Open expressions of dissatisfaction or confusion when the judge considered only a portion of the dispute or made a vague disposition suggested that any authority initially conferred upon the judge was transient and of limited effectiveness.

This is not to suggest that Popular Audiences should be measured by the degree to which disputes were replaced with harmonious relations. Certain kinds of disputes might not be susceptible to friendly outcomes, even after long hearings conducted by less socially distant judges trained in mediation. Conceptions of justice might demand an outcome that displeased one or both disputants. Rather, one might argue that the Popular Audiences had been a success by the criterion of improved access shared by the DC and UP, since they generated a steady caseload and offered disputants some chance of having their dispute processed.

But this "market" standard has shortcomings. Given the size of their jurisdiction, the Popular Audiences heard a very small number of cases. The similarity of case types across three courts and the disputes disclosed by interviews in a neighborhood without either Popular Audiences or an indigenous court suggest that disputes abounded.

It might also be claimed that those disputes heard by the Popular Audiences represented the entire subsample of disputants who wanted judicial help. The evidence suggests, however, that few people knew of the Popular Audiences. Survey data from a sample of 400 residents of ten Santiago neighborhoods, and my own informal survey of 50 residents of neighborhoods within the court's jurisdiction, revealed that less than 1 percent had heard of the Popular Audience program (Cheetham et al., 1972: 347). The inconveniences experienced in getting a hearing and the likelihood that the disposition would be useless also diminished demand. On the other hand, the interviews from a neighborhood without a regular third-party dispute-processing agent indicated potential demand if access were easy and the court regarded as fair, effective, and legitimate. Residents testified to disputes degenerating into physical struggles or shouting matches or simply festering, sometimes without the offending party being aware of any problem.[13]

Low commitment of judicial resources, social distance between judge and disputants, and lack of power and authority hampered dispute resolution and institutionalization of the Popular Audiences. Perhaps their impact would have been greater had they been limited to disputes that fell within familiar legal categories but previously had not been heard because of the poverty of the

---

[13]Interviews with fifteen "knowledgeables" selected on a reputational basis in the neighborhood of José Maria Caro, January, February, March 1972 (Cheetham et al., 1972: 37).

disputants. It might be argued that other cases should have been left to the disputants to resolve. This strategy would have been consistent with the DC policy of seeking to extend material benefits and services to "marginal" sectors of the population rather than organizing the poorer classes to adapt institutional arrangements to their particular needs. But it would be erroneous to measure the potential impact of decentralized courts solely in terms of the existence of disputes that were not being resolved, for this implies that disputants would have flocked to the Popular Audiences had the judges been given more training and resources. Such a market analogy ignores the impact of social organization upon disputing (Felstiner, 1974) and other political and normative considerations explored later in the chapter.

THE SQUATTER SETTLEMENT COURTS

Campamento Political Structure and Strategy

During the squatter settlement movement marking the end of Frei's administration the MIR organized several *campamento* invasions. The MIR believed that socialist revolution would come through violence and that the left should organize people for militant, extraparliamentary political participation. Initially pursuing an urban guerrilla strategy, the MIR staged bank robberies and distributed the funds to squatter settlements. By the late 1960s it saw in the new squatter movement a chance to expand its political base. By organizing groups of families without homes to invade vacant urban lands, erect temporary houses, and establish defenses against police attack, the previously underground party became involved in mass-oriented work and gained territorial bases. Once identified with the MIR, however, these lands were more likely than other left *campamentos* to be targeted for police repression. The MIR's relatively small political base, its decision not to challenge the DC electorally, and its political position to the left of the UP parties made its squatter settlements especially vulnerable. Defense measures had to be prepared to give notice that the settlers meant to stand their ground. In three of these settlements, the neighborhood court system grew out of these initial security measures (Cuellar *et al.*, 1971: 158–159; Fiori, 1973: 84–85).

A squatter militia organized defense tactics and also performed internal police functions. Maintaining the security of the *campamentos* was its only goal. Militiamen kept an eye out for police infiltrators. They broke up fights and caught petty thieves whose activities not only caused personal loss but also threatened general morale and increased suspicion. In some cases they simply "beat up" the thief; in others they tried to fine or expel him. The militia served as police, judge, and jury.

Allende's election removed the external police threat, and general relaxation of militia activity marked the first postelection months. The three *campamentos* moved to new common land provided by the government. Construction of temporary housing dominated life in the *campamento*, dubbed Nueva Habana.

In early 1971, the *campamento* dissolved the militia in an effort to place judicial and police functions within a newly erected government framework. The political structure rested upon twenty-four elected block committees (about sixty-four families per block). The *campamento* formed work fronts, each having specific task areas (Health, Sports and Recreation, Construction, Mothers, Culture and Education, Vigilance). Each block and front elected one representative to the Directorate, the main legislative and governing body of the *campamento*. In addition, the *campamento* had a Steering Committee (*Jefatura*) of five, elected at large. The Vigilance Front, taking over the duties of the militia, had one representative selected by each block committee and other volunteers. Each block committee, in addition to making policy for the block and discussing issues to be decided by the Directorate, also performed judicial functions for disputes arising within the block. The Directorate judged more serious disputes and those crossing block lines. Thus, block committees and the Directorate had a blend of judicial, legislative, and executive functions (Grupo de Trabajo, 1972: 48–51).

This was a highly elaborate political structure compared with other Latin American shantytowns, in which a central committee attempts to establish patron–client relations with the central government or a political boss (*cacique*) governs (Powell, 1969: 211–212; Lutz, 1970: 140; Cornelius, 1975: Ch. 6). It reflected a MIR political strategy of encouraging residents to participate and to learn both political ideas and skills. It aimed to make this community a model of self-government, which came to imply, as events developed, notions that this unofficial government of Nueva Habana was legitimate—and that Chile's traditional institutional government arrangements, even those executive offices under the control of the UP, were not. To the MIR, the latter had been established by the ruling class, and their performance under the UP had to be judged by their responsiveness to the poor and working classes. Furthermore, the MIR did not intend to establish an isolated utopian commune but saw Nueva Habana as part of a larger effort to revolutionize national politics. The strategy of broad political participation and education, its interaction with national goals, and the way it developed in practice (for the MIR did not control this politically varied community of 9000 people, though it exercised strong influence) greatly affected the manner in which local disputes were processed by the new judicial system and other political bodies.

A brief illustration of two areas of activity will illuminate strategy and practice and set the stage for analysis of the development of dispute processing. The immediate problem facing the Health Front was to gain quick, tangible results that would promise solutions to the typical *campamento* problems of malnutrition, infant mortality, epidemics, and the general debilitation of widespread chronic bad health. The front gained volunteer doctors and nurses sympathetic to the goals of the *campamento*. But more professionals, supplies, a clinic, training, and education were also needed. The Health Front demanded supplies and construction materials from the government and doctors from local hospitals operating within the National Health Service. It also demanded that the National Health Service train residents in nutrition and relatively easy health skills—giving injections, taking temperatures, bandaging, administering medicine. *Demand* is the key word here, and it was expressed through petitions, demonstrations, and sit-ins.

If one of the goals was to improve health, another was to mobilize front members into political activity. Making demands was to be part of a process through which participants would learn the biases of Chilean private and public health care. The goals were interrelated. Participation in asserting political demands would secure the resources to improve health care. Success in improving health care encouraged broader participation and furthered political education. In this front, however, success posed the danger that those who possessed technical expertise (the doctors) might come to dominate decision making. Recognition of this problem was itself an element of political education. In addition, the front attacked the problem by treating doctors as equal members, not outside consultants, and therefore subject to political criticism.

In the Construction Front a different set of problems existed. The *campamento* needed permanent housing and had very high rates of unemployment. In the past, some squatter settlements had been able to gain government recognition of land title, and a few had won pledges of government assistance in home construction. When the government built homes, it contracted with private companies associated in the Chamber of Chilean Construction. Frei had also attempted a "sweat capital" program in which the government provided low-cost materials and the residents constructed their own homes. The Construction Front also demanded the pledge of homes but insisted that the UP government neither hire private contractors nor use "sweat capital." Rather, it should pay residents of the *campamento* to construct the new settlement. It won this demand, and work began. The front also debated the problem of organizing work structures and established work teams with elected leaders and collective decision making. Some 300 residents participated in this front.[14] This brief sketch simplifies a complicated process. Both fronts encountered delays and bottlenecks and protested bad materials and lack of government cooperation. Participation did not continually advance to higher levels. There were successful endeavors, but gains were not easily won.

Other fronts, such as Recreation, were more traditional and less militant in

[14]Interviews with Nueva Habana informants; see also Grupo de Trabajo (1972).

their approach or, as in the case of the Mothers Front, suffered from lack of clear-cut goals. This latter front did not openly challenge traditional sex-based political oppression, instances of which could be found within the *campamento*. Also, this squatter settlement was exceptional, even among the more militant, for its high level of sustained participation (Castells, 1977: 369–375). To some extent, the confrontational style sometimes practiced by Nueva Habana and other *campamentos* against the UP was facilitated by the latter, which was both reluctant and sympathetic—and did not want to lose political ground to the MIR. A similar style in a Mexican context, for example, might well have resulted in police repression (Cornelius, 1975: 39). Here the relatively open, nonrepressive character of the Allende government fostered political participation and education by yielding encouraging, if grudging, results without repression.

Neighborhood Dispute Processing

CRIMINAL CASES

These strategies were reflected in the new dispute-processing institutions, but they were less developed and less fully institutionalized there than in the activities of the Health and Construction fronts and the Directorate.[15]

Although the *campamento* arguably could have created tribunals to handle disputes between neighbors, the prosecution of acts defined as criminal by Chilean law and the punishment of behavior tolerated by that law was inconsistent with constitutional provisions for the establishment of courts (Constitución Chilena, Articles 80, 81, 82). The Vigilance Front had primary responsibility for detecting criminal activity. Block committees and the Directorate held trials of criminal cases. Reported cases came to the block committee (minor thefts or assaults) or the Directorate (recidivism, thefts, and assaults) by way of the Vigilance Front or other residents. In most reported criminal cases little doubt seemed to exist about the facts. Defendants might plead mitigating circumstances but not innocence. Merely suspicious activities were not prosecuted or were dealt with informally; the "courts" seemed to hear only cases of those caught, as Chileans say, "with their hands in the dough" (*con las manos en la masa*).

Sanctions initially had traditional overtones—confinement through a form of house arrest or fines. After a few months block committees criticized those as impractical (house arrest) or unfairly discriminatory against the poor. Fines were replaced by admonitions and different forms of required activities helpful to the community or victims and, if possible, related to the crime. For example, a

[15]Castells (1977: 365), viewing a number of squatter settlements in Chile, seems to regard the formation of local courts as being the most significant of all their activities.

drunk caught urinating in the streets would be required to spend a day cleaning streets. Someone caught stealing building materials would have to return them and donate several days' labor to the construction projects. The creativity of the sanctions also gave them a certain *ad hoc* quality. The most severe sanction was expulsion from the community, imposed for serious assaults, thefts, or recidivism. By the end of 1972, a half-dozen people had been banished. Given housing shortages, this was a serious hardship. It was also, perhaps, inconsistent with the goal of trying to create a model community for others to copy, in that it burdened other communities with its most troublesome cases.

The Vigilance Front and block committees relied upon the larger community to enforce these sanctions, to keep track of the execution of sentences, to spot banished offenders, and to recognize strangers, particularly after anti-UP economic sabotage escalated in late 1972. Though this cooperation and participation were not rare, we cannot know their precise extent in the community of 9000. As discussed later, the level of judicial activities varied from block to block. However, numerous residents testified that collective efforts had greatly reduced criminal activity by the end of 1972.[16]

The criminal-dispute-processing activities of Nueva Habana illustrate political themes important to my analysis. By handling matters clearly within the exclusive jurisdiction of the official court system, they challenged the legitimacy of established Chilean institutions more directly than did the activities of other fronts. Although initially substantive and procedural norms resembled those of the official legal system, political criticism eventually led to innovative alternatives. Finally, the settlement attempted to prevent crime and enforce court decisions by organizing its citizens to be vigilant. This effort, and the direct connection between block committees and the Vigilance Front, sought to avoid the development of a separate specialized police force wielding excessive or arbitrary power.

LEGISLATIVE DISPUTE PROCESSING

Two other types of cases intially came before block committees as individual complaints but eventually were processed as legislative issues affecting the entire *campamento*. Speakeasies (*clandestinos*) presented a problem common to poor neighborhoods. They often poured out raucous noise and drunks at all hours. Several cropped up in the *campamento*, one of which was the subject of a case demanding its removal. It is significant that the complaint arose at all, because in other neighborhoods residents testified that they were intimidated by *clandestino* customers. The issue was referred to the Directorate, which decided to convene a

---

[16]Interviews and correspondence with Nueva Habana informants; see also Grupo de Trabajo (1972), Fiori (1973), and *Chile Hoy* (February 9, 1973: 32).

Popular Assembly of the entire *campamento* to vote upon the issue. There, some argued in favor of the *clandestino*, noting the inconvenience of having to journey to a "real" bar and the money and red tape it took to gain a license. Others complained of the nuisance, the fighting and insults suffered by residents, and the burden upon the Vigilance Front. Still others placed the drinking problem in the broader context of Chile's heavily unemployed lower-class male population and saw the speakeasies as a refuge from family responsibilities, with politically debilitating effects. The Popular Assembly voted out all the *clandestinos*.

The outcome is less noteworthy than the procedure employed. Though the *clandestino* was quite illegal under Chilean law, airing the issue not only avoided the inconvenience of the official Chilean police bureaucracy but also declared the *campamento* independent from it. The Directorate itself could have "outlawed" speakeasies or could simply have had the Vigilance Front harass them out of the *campamento*. The Popular Assembly provided a forum for full discussion of an obviously controversial and pervasive problem, a forum in which it would be educational to analyze widespread drunkenness within a political, anticapitalist framework encompassing issues broader than speakeasy noisiness. Its decision would carry legitimacy.

A thornier problem involved black marketeering by local merchants. In 1971 Allende's wage–price policies dramatically increased purchasing power by holding down prices of officially regulated basic commodities. But by 1972, production could not keep pace with increased demand, and sabotage and organized hoarding by the opposition exacerbated commodity shortages. By late 1972, black marketeering had spread to many basic products.

The numerous small shops in Nueva Habana were tremendously tempted to sell goods secretly at inflated prices. Some citizens issued complaints against individual merchants. Again, black marketeering was illegal by Chilean law, but the Allende administration had insufficient resources to enforce it. The problem was confronted by the Directorate. Punishing black marketeering was not an easy decision. The merchants themselves were not well-to-do, rapacious business people gouging their customers but residents earning small sums from tiny shops. Relations with customers were not anonymous business matters but part of a social fabric. Moreover, moral issues were compounded by a cultural context in which gaining resources through "connections" (in this case to a wholesaler with goods) or patron–client relations was traditional and widespread. By 1972 merchants all over Santiago, and an even larger number of customers, were playing the market (DeVylder, 1976: Ch. 5; Roxborough et al., 1977: 115; Stallings, 1978: Ch. 6). It is difficult to ask someone to observe the rules of the game when everybody else is breaking them with abandon.

The Directorate approved severe sanctions against merchants who continued black market activities, not as a means of striking out against the local "capitalists" but because the merchants created potential divisiveness within the community. The black market motivated merchants to play favorites with scarce basic commodities, rewarding customers with the most money or closest relationship. The black market threatened to rend the collective, egalitarian social fabric of Nueva Habana and to do so along differences of wealth within a generally poor population and particularistic social connections. The Directorate's proposal was then discussed in block committees, where disturbing questions arose. Would it not be unfair to merchants in Nueva Habana, because residents with more money could simply buy on the black market outside the campamento? Merchants, or others able to get goods, might simply choose to market them outside the campamento, undetected and unpunished. These objections were overridden, and black marketeering was prohibited under pain of banishment. But the questions suggested the limits of "neighborhood control" in trying to achieve local, fair solutions for economic problems of national proportions.

By late 1972, however, as a result of systematic opposition efforts to shut down the economy, the problem of shortages of supplies had gone beyond the issue of black marketeering. The major tasks were to find sufficient food for the campamento population, avoid long lines, and ensure that all residents had sufficient clothing and other basic necessities. The campamento formed a popular market, centralizing collection of products from state-controlled distribution agencies (the state controlled only 28 percent of distribution) and dispensing basic quantities based on family size. Private merchants were more or less excluded unless they worked for the popular market, but even those who did experienced problems in getting foods for their shops and were increasingly relying on other sources of income.[17]

FAMILY AND NEIGHBOR DISPUTES

Block committees also processed intrafamilial and neighbor disputes similar to those that came before the professional Popular Audiences. They tended to hold hearings longer than the ten minutes typical of the Popular Audiences and sometimes went on for several hours and through several adjournments. The disputants had more time to air their grievances, and the block committees had more time to search for a solution agreeable to the parties.

In one case a woman complained to her block committee that her husband habitually mistreated their children, blaming them for everything that went

[17]The UP government established programs to monitor local market activity through formation of neighborhood price-regulation committees. The development of these began in mid-1972 but achieved a high level of activity during the truck owners' strike of October 1972. In 1973 the government began to provision some neighborhoods and families through a popular market basket program. See Chile Hoy (January 13, 1973: 31).

wrong, shouting at them, and beating them excessively. Two neighbors not only encouraged her to bring the matter to the block committee but also testified to hearing shouting and crying, thus corroborating her story. The husband agreed to speak to the block committee after two of its members talked with him privately. It emerged that he was around the house more after having been laid off from his job in a small factory. Because the block committee could discover nothing about the behavior of the children to provoke him so, it pointed out that his hostility might stem from frustration over his dismissal and subsequent unemployment, neither of which was his fault. The committee suggested he seek work in the Construction Front but also admonished him for his abusive behavior.

Here the block committee was intervening in a dispute that otherwise might not have come to the surface and been negotiated by the disputants and probably would not have been heard by any other third party. It entered into the previously private domain of the family. Of course, traditional Chilean law and courts deal with family issues and have jurisdiction in child abuse cases. But in practical terms the case would not have come before the courts even if the father had violated the law. It is significant that neighbors not only testified in the case but also had a hand in bringing it to the attention of the block committee. The committee, in turn, took cognizance of the case and summoned the husband with what seems to be more ease and less formal procedures than the Popular Audiences. Perhaps the committee also failed to probe deeply into the complexities of the marriage, but at least it was the disputants and not the law who defined the dispute. Testimony about the marriage did not raise other disputes and did not seem relevant to the treatment of the children. Evidence about employment, however, not only was a mitigating circumstance but also, more importantly, served as a basis for political education about the social causes of a seemingly private problem. This, in turn, could help to resolve other disputes by counseling parties to be less ready to cast blame. It could also absolve individuals of responsibility, but the committee, having taken heed of the husband's problem and suggested a solution, nonetheless admonished him.

In another instance, a husband complained that his wife was not fulfilling her obligations to the family because of excessive participation in the affairs of the campamento. It turned out that the wife was an active member of one of the work fronts and therefore was spending much less time in the house. She claimed, however, that she kept the house clean and procured and prepared food for the family. The husband was not unsympathetic to the goals of the front or her participation in it but complained about the extent of her involvement. On the other hand, he was not particularly enthusiastic about it and did not himself participate actively in the affairs of the campamento. The wife did not accept his complaint and evidently did not see the problem as capable of resolution by compromise. She simply did not have any more time to spend with him and was not, in any case, particularly enthusiastic about the marriage.

The block committee did not agree with the complaint and supported the woman's energetic participation. It suggested that the dispute went beyond the explicit conflict between participation and family obligations—but chose not to probe deeply into problems in the marriage. At the same time, the block committee did not examine the basic "bargain" involved in the case: the traditional family obligations of the woman balanced against her political participation. It did not suggest that she would have more time for participation in the front if she did not have sole responsibility for such things as buying food, though apparently the woman herself also did not bring up this point.

In yet another case, neighbors complained to a block committee about a drunk's behavior both on the street and inside his home. Their complaint was supported by a member of the Vigilance Front. Despite the expulsion of the *clandestinos*, the problem of alcoholism had not been eliminated, in part because new taverns had been established outside the *campamento*. The neighbors claimed that this particular person often behaved lewdly and had been loud and raucous in his own house in the middle of the night. The defendant did not deny that he drank on occasion but argued that those who brought the complaint simply did not like him and were using the complaint to harass him. He implied, in fact, that one reason for his drinking was his neighbors' unfriendliness, an argument that engendered some derision from his adversaries. He claimed that he had been a good citizen ever since the land invasion, worked hard at a low-paying job to support his family, and needed a chance to relax occasionally with a little wine.

The block committee took a hard line against public drunkenness and strongly admonished the defendant, warning him that it would be more strict in the future. But it also questioned the complainants about their behavior toward the man and asked the parties how they thought relations might be improved. After some discussion the man promised to behave himself, though not to stop drinking entirely, and the parties promised to try to be more friendly to the man, after the court suggested gently that they do so.

Here the block committee made an order about one aspect of the dispute— public drunkenness—but also attempted to get the parties to explore other areas of their relations and nudged them toward a consensual solution. Because the block committee was physically close to the disputants, and other neighbors supported its action, it was in a better position to monitor compliance with its dispositions than were the Popular Audiences.

These cases should not be taken to mean that the block committees resolved, or even heard, all disputes or that they engaged in the kind of continuous intervention characteristic of, say, marriage counseling. As will be shown, many block committees did not participate in dispute processing at all. But among those that did, one could detect approaches to dispute processing in cases within the family and between neighbors that differed in style and context from those of the Popular Audiences.

LEADERSHIP CASES

Finally, the *campamento*, on occasion, processed disputes about political participation and leadership. One elected member of a block committee habitually missed meetings, and he was asked to appear before the committee in a judicial proceeding for failure to fulfill his obligations. No punishment was involved, but he was asked to explain his absences and either fulfill his pledge or relinquish his post. Another case involved a well-known leader of the *campamento*. He had been elected to lead a number of residents in a land invasion to establish another *campamento*. Suddenly, shortly before the invasion was to be launched, the man suddenly lashed out at several of those on the invading committee, cursing and striking at them. The Directorate held a hearing about the matter. No provocation could explain the outbreak, but investigation indicated that the man had been greatly overworked in his political activities and had lost his job some time before, severely straining his ability to provide his family with basic necessities. The Directorate analyzed the attack in terms of this economic and political strain and tied it to inherent problems created by capitalist labor markets. The man was not punished, though he was removed from leadership of the planned activity.

Development of Neighborhood Courts

Although the *campamento* innovated in the area of criminal justice, responded to collective problems with legislative solutions, subjected leaders to criticism, and handled family and neighbor disputes, the development of regular judicial procedures and institutions was uneven. The activities of and participation in the Vigilance Front waxed and waned; block committees varied greatly in their attention to judicial issues, most never dealing with cases at all and others quite irregularly. Although the Directorate heard cases, primarily criminal matters, other issues occupied much more of its time. Moreover, it never was clear what was the proper forum for criminal matters. Although the socioeconomic background of disputes was frequently analyzed, the standards by which cases should be judged often were not agreed upon or understood. When the procedures were first set up there were complaints about self-help resolutions and rough summary treatment by some members of the Vigilance Front.[18]

How can we account for this stunted development? First, the goals were ambitious. The MIR sought to establish an alternative judicial system based on socialist principles in a newly formed squatter settlement of some 9000 residents, the great majority of whom were not members of the party, though perhaps were

[18] Interviews with Nueva Habana informants, and Fiori (1973).

sympathetic to its activities. Second, the neighborhood court was neither a familiar issue nor a particularly salient one for the residents. It was of primary concern to national political elites. A survey of some 400 residents of ten squatter settlements, including Nueva Habana, conducted six months after the demise of the UP neighborhood court proposal, indicated that only 33 percent had heard of it (Cheetham *et al.*, 1972: 189). In the same survey, *prior* to being asked about the UP plan, respondents were asked general questions about neighborhood courts, as well as about their attitudes toward the traditional system of justice. They revealed considerable alienation from the traditional system (74 percent thought the courts biased in favor of the rich) (*Ibid.*: 91) and notable enthusiasm for the *idea* of neighborhood courts (42 percent unconditionally in favor, 13 percent conditionally in favor) (*Ibid.*: 130). However, in a later section the survey informed respondents of the UP proposal in detail and a now more familiar issue elicited extremely high enthusiasm (78 percent unconditionally in favor, 10 percent conditionally in favor) (*Ibid.*: 310).

After the survey mentioned the UP neighborhood tribunal proposal, a shift of similar proportions occurred in the attitudes of respondents toward collectively resolving conflicts previously regarded as private or within the competence of external agencies (*Ibid.*: 116, 118, 119, 180, 301). For example, once the respondents knew about the UP proposal, 79 percent thought residents should bring serious family fights to the new tribunal. Before they had begun to think about neighborhood courts, 37 percent would have brought such fights to the attention of the police, 25 percent would have sought help from other neighbors or a neighborhood committee, and 37 percent would have done nothing (*Ibid.*: 116). Some of these opinion shifts could be attributed to the popularity of the UP among respondents, 74 percent of whom favored one or another left political grouping (*Ibid.*: 53). However, it seems clear that the survey itself educated respondents about the notion of neighborhood courts. Though enthusiasm was present, the whole idea was new, and Nueva Habana did not have a well-worked-out plan.

The community also lacked a general commitment to collective development. This was not a group of people so dissatisfied with society that they had decided to separate and form a utopian socialist commune. Nor was it a collective enterprise in farming. Most laborers worked outside the settlement, in a large number of different places. Thus, despite its origins in a collective land invasion, its ties to the MIR, and its support for the left, Nueva Habana was an urban neighborhood of several thousand residents living in single-family dwellings, being supported by privately earned incomes, and, until late 1972, privately consuming goods. Survey evidence suggested that residents, once informed about neighborhood courts, would gain enthusiasm for collectively processing some kinds of disputes previously regarded as being in the private domain. But only a handful of Nueva Habana residents had participated in the survey. Moreover, it is one thing to express a preference in answer to a survey and quite another to be the first to take a family quarrel to the local block committee. For example, respondents in the survey, before being presented with the idea of a neighborhood court, were asked what they would do about a noisy *clandestino*. The great majority said they would take the issue to one forum or another. If that had reflected reality, there would have been no *clandestino* problem in Santiago (*Ibid.*: 118).

The abstract goals of the neighborhood courts also contrasted sharply with the more concrete and vital needs represented by housing, work, and health problems. The Health and Construction fronts received greater attention and wider participation. The Recreation Front also had higher levels of participation, not because it was more important but because it presented more familiar organizing problems with more obvious solutions.

Their low salience and abstractness inhibited development of the neighborhood courts. The newness of collective processes and issues of justice posed additional obstacles. Collective decision making in hearings or meetings requires time, skill, and patience and can involve a participant in mysterious, confusing, or intimidating processes. These difficulties are exacerbated when both the means of solving the problem and the goals are abstract. Frustration sets in, leading to lower participation or "exit" from the process. For both block committees and disputants, problems of community cleanliness and public order were relatively easy to perceive (though finding a "socialist" process and solution was more complicated). Bringing previously "private" problems (such as child abuse or family quarreling) or new problems (such as uncooperative political participation) to a neighborhood court and processing them in a way that the rest of the population viewed as fair and just presented more intractable difficulties.

Nonetheless, one might argue that if the need for dispute processing had been great, popular demand would have involved more block committees in extensive judicial action. But demand is a political as well as an economic phenomenon. Increased participation by the residents would have contributed to changing their consciousness so that matters previously seen as private came to be seen as collective concerns, and residents gained confidence in the ability and legitimacy of the block committees in the performance of judicial functions. However, political education emphasized some issues more than others, in response to the concrete needs of the population, the sense of priorities of the political leadership, and the nature of class conflict in the tumultuous years of the Allende government. Dispute processing was not one of the issues emphasized.

National political conditions increasingly inhibited development of the neighborhood court system. First, Nueva Habana's courts came under attack by right-wing newspapers, resulting in an investigation by the official court system. In mid-1972 the community suffered its first really serious crime: A schoolteacher was raped. The victim and several of her friends in the settlement, said by some to have been members of a Trotskyist faction (Fiori, 1973: 96), convened the Popular Assembly, which held a trial and called for extreme physical punishment. The crowd agreed and began searching for the criminal. The political leadership of the neighborhood steering committee heard about the proceedings and called a second meeting, in which cooler heads prevailed. They criticized the unofficial status of the first meeting and proposed a more thorough exploration of the evidence and a chance for the accused to testify before the Directorate. This was accepted, but the accused had left the *campamento* and gone to the right-wing media. Seizing the opportunity to discredit the MIR and the left in general, opposition papers printed sensational stories of this example of "people's justice" and called for an investigation of the "illegal people's courts" (*El Mercurio*, May 3, 1972: 1; May 4, 1972: 3; May 5, 1972: 1; *La Tribuna*, May 3, 1972: 1; *Las Ultimas Noticias*, May 5, 1972: 5; May 10, 1972: 23). Given other *campamento* priorities, the attack and subsequent judicial investigation was sufficient to convince the *jefatura* to downplay the role of the neighborhood courts and express its willingness to cooperate with the official police, without giving them carte blanche to sweep through the neighborhoods or disavowing the right of residents to resolve some situations of internal order (*El Mercurio*, May 4, 1972: 1, 10).

As Chilean political conflict became more intense and the MIR grew in numbers and influence, it increasingly sent its experienced members into new areas now open to organizing. This drained leadership from Nueva Habana. The disruptive strategy of the right opposition in Chile created crises of provisioning within the *campamento*, beginning in October–November 1972 when truck owners, joined by factory owners and professional associations, closed down their enterprises in an effort to grind the economy to a halt (Roxborough, *et al.*, 1977: 116; Boorstein, 1977: 208; Sigmund, 1977: 184; Levenson, 1977: 59; Stallings, 1978: Ch. 6). Nueva Habana was compelled to concentrate all its energies on defense and the detection of mass hoarding, joining in *ad hoc* coordinating committees of *campamentos*, factories, and farms outside Santiago to coordinate production and distribution of vital goods. Economic and political survival was at stake and took precedence over the work of the *campamento's* neighborhood courts (Grupo de Trabajo, 1972: 136).

CONCLUSION

These two judicial experiments display striking similarities. Each emerged from the convergence of a squatter settlement movement and competition among center and left political parties, which led to critiques of the judicial system. Both suffered from the lack of clear, concrete goals and had an inadequate concept of the disputes they would process or the role they should play. Their development was retarded by a lack of organizational resources and the relatively low priority accorded their activities by the larger organizational context in which they were situated—the Popular Audiences in the traditional hierarchy of the Chilean judiciary, and the neighborhood courts in the political structure of the *campamento*. [19]

It can also be argued that similar legal outcomes sometimes emerged from these dispute resolution processes in the sense that they shared common perceptions of right and wrong activities in some kinds of disputes. Though the Popular Audiences did not formally hear criminal cases, the notion of wrongdoing in the neighborhood courts often was similar to the likely outcome in the official judicial system. Thefts were thefts; public drunkenness was frowned upon; wife beating was bad; *clandestinos* were against the law; and getting along with one's neighbors was a good thing.

Dispute processing in the two experiments was also marked by differences. The Popular Audiences spent a shorter amount of time on each dispute and tended to circumscribe the dispute within familiar legal categories or, failing that, within the amount of time available. Neighborhood courts seemed to give greater amounts of time and freer rein to disputants to define the boundaries of the dispute. They emphasized the role of social factors in order to advance political education, whereas the Popular Audiences tended to see disputes as the sole responsibility of the individual disputants. In essence, the Popular Audiences arbitrated while using forms that suggested consensual agreements. The judge had access to police power, and some disputants were willing to grant him limited authority as official representative of the state. The neighborhood courts sometimes used mediation and other times relied upon neighbors to ensure the decision would be carried out. Neither of these concepts was well developed. Given the uneven participation of block committees and the secondary importance of the courts, these mechanisms were only partially successful.

These differences in approach can partially be accounted for by the lay–professional distinction. The social distance of professional judges from disputants, their training in formal law, and the press of their normal duties all are consonant with shorter hearings, more arbitration, and reliance on formal law and enforcement. Closer ties with the community permitted block committees to take longer, use mediation, rely on the community, and adhere less to formal law.

The critical distinction between the two experiments lies in the underlying ideal of the relationships between the courts and their clients and the courts and the national polity. The judge in the Popular Audiences, and those DC sectors proposing expansion of the judiciary to meet the needs of the poor, wanted the new courts to deliver traditional services to a previously excluded marginal clien-

[19]For an analysis relating demand for judicial services to changes in the political economy of the state resulting in a decline in resources, see Heydebrand (1977).

tele. They had no fundamental objection to the current structural arrangements of Chile save that a large majority was excluded from participation.

A very different outlook inspired the neighborhood courts. The use of lay judges derived not only from a notion that peers might be more able than nonresident professionals to process neighborhood disputes but also from a sense that the traditional courts were illegitimate and that a professional structure violated egalitarian ideals. The purpose of the lay courts was more than just the maintenance of public order. It was to teach citizens that they had a right to form their own laws, that many disputes were shaped by the economic system, and that citizens should learn to make their own collective decisions, even about matters previously regarded as private. In a sense, the *campamentos'* neighborhood courts are more appropriately compared to other neighborhood institutions in Nueva Habana than to the Popular Audiences.

Tracing the role of ideology as a variable (distinct from modes of social organization and economic cooperation) in the formation and development of different modes of dispute processing can be a difficult, controversial task (Shapiro, 1976; Schwartz, 1976). Decisions affecting forms of social organization or the initiation of political structures are often intertwined, explicitly or implicitly, with ideological notions. Ideology is not easy to measure; it does not occur in clearly separable form. Nevertheless, it seems clear that the differences between the Popular Audiences and neighborhood courts cannot be explained without reference to their distinctive ideological sources.

The decentralization strategies that derived from these ideological differences were not developed in detail. In the case of the Popular Audiences (and the DC proposal for neighborhood courts), a strategy of decentralizing bureaucracy was chosen on the grounds that the problem to be solved was lack of access. But in shaping the service to be offered, the Popular Audiences paid little attention to the form of social organization, the nature of disputes, or alternative methods for handling (e.g., self-help, negotiation, avoidance) that already existed (Felstiner, 1974; Danzig and Lowy, 1975; Galanter, 1976). Rather, burdened by lack of support from the judicial hierarchy and a shortage of organizational resources, the court fashioned hearings as best it could.

The neighborhood courts of Nueva Habana also did not make a systematic assessment of the social organization they encountered. The goals went beyond efficiently resolving disputes and establishing a reputation for fairness. Courts were to be part of an effort to change the existing form of social organization so that resolution of problems previously regarded as private affairs or matters for the state would be handled by local collective means. To do this required encouraging political participation and engaging in political education.

The inadequacy of the decentralization strategies and the difficulty encountered in their implementation might be explained by the abstract and even controversial nature of the task, lack of organizational resources, and inexperience of the innovators (Yates, 1976: 151–158). But these variables are best understood within the broader organizational contexts of the innovations—the judiciary and the squatter settlement, each of which were the products of class conflict and state policies. The judiciary, under pressure from left political parties, themselves pushed by mounting class conflict, allowed a minor shift in priorities that would mitigate the conflict, but the concession was so grudging as to be ineffectual. Most judges did not participate. The one I studied did so under heavy constraints.

The squatter settlement courts emerged from a popular protest movement, a section of which wanted to go beyond the legal forms of political participation employed by the major left and center electoral parties. These neighborhood courts represented a conscious attempt to form what Santos (1977) calls legal pluralism, a legality distinct from and partially independent of the dominant and official legality of the state.

In Santos's study, the pluralistic dispute-processing institutions were limited to real property disputes and drew heavily upon the official ideology underlying Brazil's capitalist legal forms. They gained the compliance of litigants by using their expertise in local housing conditions and *threatening* to use state police power. The court would not carry through the threat because it did not wish to risk interference by state institutions that already encroached on local independence. But although the court made efforts to maintain some independence, it was avoiding rather than rebelling against the fascist repressive state of Brazil. Its leaders came from the upper stratum of the squatter settlement and sought upward mobility within the capitalist economy. Santos sees the limitations upon jurisdiction and independence and the lack of ideological rebellion as a reflection of the power of the fascist state and the low level of class struggle against these conditions.

The contrasting strategies—extension of the legal order through Popular Audiences and the displacement of traditional institutions in Nueva Habana—should be interpreted in light of the decreasing ability of the state to preserve the social order required by capitalism and the intensification of class conflict opposed to that order. The DC responded to these interrelated developments by seeking to ameliorate the conditions contributing to class conflict, and Popular Audiences were one such response. At the same time, class conflict and the diminished authority of the state created the conditions under which rebellious communities like Nueva Habana could explicitly reject traditional legality. Yet the very factors that allowed such experiments to occur prevented them from maturing. The intensity of class conflict and the (ultimately successful) resistance of the bourgeoisie forestalled the development of new forms of dispute resolution comparable to those found in societies where socialists have captured state power (Cohen, 1967; Berman, 1969).

These dramatic national developments suggest that just as differences in dispute processing cannot be attributed solely to the lay or professional qualifications of the judges and must be seen in terms of divergent ideologies, so the common underdevelopment of the two innovations cannot be reduced to their inadequate organizational resources and low organizational priorities. To consider only variables internal to the two court systems would obscure the critical differences in their organizational contexts—the historical priorities of the Chilean judiciary, formed as a result of class-based economic competition, and the development of political institutions in the brief history of Nueva Habana. Different as they were in many respects, the two experiments share one fundamental attribute. Each unfolded in the same historical space—the turbulent class conflict of Chile in the late 1960s and early 1970s. Each was shaped and ultimately destroyed by the mutations of Chilean society. Increasing popular mobilization by the urban lower class and the presence within these movements of political left-wing groups and parties created the necessary conditions for the rise of unofficial courts that directly challenged the legitimacy of the traditional judiciary. The judiciary responded with the Popular Audiences in an effort to quiet criticism and mediate the growing conflict. Nonetheless, the mobilizations were not able to accomplish the tasks confronting them, and judicial issues received lower priority than the pressing needs of housing, food, and self-defense. This blunted the challenge to the judiciary, which consequently failed to extend the reform to other courts. It also stunted the development of the unofficial neighborhood courts. This is not to suggest that had the mobilization been more powerful all problems encountered in the two experiments would have been solved. Indeed, I have argued that Popular Audiences with professional judges had inherent problems and that the goals of the neighborhood courts were very ambitious. Nor do I claim that other forms of neighborhood mediation are impossible without the level of popular mobilization found in Chile. But I do believe that such a level of class conflict is necessary to spawn an overt challenge to traditional legitimacy and force major changes in traditional priorities.

Judicial institutions are profoundly historical phenomena. Their developments are interlaced with the surrounding society, with its own particular character and past, and cannot be understood fully in the narrower framework of a few critical explanatory variables without careful examination of myriad relative activities and class-based forces involving judges, police, lawmakers, and political parties—not to speak of the many ordinary people whose disputes might provide both a rationale and a force leading to the establishment of new judicial institutions.

REFERENCES

Abel, Richard (1973) "A Comparative Theory of Dispute Institutions in Society," 8 *Law & Society Review* 217.

Altshuler, Alan (1970) *Community Control: The Black Demand for Participation in Large American Cities.* New York: Pegasus.

Berman, Jesse (1969) "The Cuban Popular Tribunals," 69 *Columbia Law Review* 1317.

Boorstein, Edward (1977) *Allende's Chile, An Inside View.* New York: International Publishers.

Castells, Manuel (1974) *La Lucha de clases in Chile.* Buenos Aires: Siglo Veintiuno.

———— (1977) *The Urban Question: A Marxist Approach.* London: Edward Arnold.

Cerroni, Umberto (1972) "La interpretación de clase del derecho burgués." 15 *Cuadernos de la realidad nacional* 85 (December).

Cheetham, Rosemond, Santiago Quevedo, Gaston, Roja, Eder Seder and Franz Vanderschueren (1972) *Pobladores: del legalismo a la justicia popular.* Santiago: Universidad Católica de Chile.

Cohen, Jerome Allen (1967) "Chinese Mediation on the Eve of Modernization," 2 *Journal of Asian and African Studies* 54.

Cook, Beverly B. (1973) "Sentencing Behavior of Federal Judges: Draft Cases—1972," 42 *Cincinnati Law Review* 597.

Constitución Chilena, Articles 80, 81, 82.

Cornelius, Wayne (1975) *Politics and the Migrant Poor in Mexico City.* Stanford, Calif.: Stanford University Press.

Cuellar, Oscar, Rosemond Cheetham, Santiago Quevedo, Jaime Rojas, and Franz Vanderschueren (1971) "Experiences de justicia popular en poblaciones," 8 *Cuadernos de la realidad nacional* 153.

Danelski, David J. (1966) "Values as Variables in Judicial Decision-Making: Notes toward a Theory," 19 *Vanderbilt Law Review* 721.

Danzig, Richard and Michael J. Lowy (1975) "Everyday Disputes and Mediation in the United States: A Reply to Professor Felstiner," 9 *Law & Society Review* 675.

Devylder, Stefan (1976) *Allende's Chile: The Political Economy of the Rise and Fall of the Unidad Popular.* Cambridge: Cambridge University Press.

Epsing-Anderson, Gosta, Robert Friedland and Erik Olin Wright (1976) "Modes of Class Struggle and the Capitalist State," 5 *Kapitalistate* 186.

Farias, Victor (1972) "El caracter fundamental de la legaldad burguesa," 15 *Cuadernos de la realidad nacional* 15 (December).

Felstiner, William L. F. (1974) "Influences of Social Organization on Dispute Processing," 9 *Law & Society Review* 63.

Fiori, Jorge (1973) "Campamento Nueva la Habana: Estudio de una experiencia de autoadministractión de justicia," 7 *Revista latinoamericana de estudios urbanos regionales* 84.

De la Fuente Moreno, Manuel (1973) "Hacia un enfoque autocfitico de la justicia," in M. Garreton (ed.) *Sobre la justicia en Chile.* Valpariso: Ediciones Universitarias.

Galanter, Marc (1976) "Delivering Legality: Some Proposals for the Direction of Research," 11 *Law & Society Review* 225.

Gil, Federico (1966) *The Political System of Chile.* Boston: Houghton-Mifflin.

Grossman, Joel B. (1966) "Social Backgrounds and Judicial Decision Making," 79 *Harvard Law Review* 1551.

Grupo de Trabajo Procesos Socio Politicos y Diseñso Urbana (1972) *Organización y lucha poblacional en el processo de cambios: La Experiencia del Campamento "Nueva Habana."* Facultad de Arquitectura y Urbanismo, Universidad de Chile.

Heydebrand, Wolf V. (1977) "The Context of Public Bureaucrcies: An Organizational Analysis of Federal District Courts," 11 *Law & Society Review* 759.

Horowitz, Irving Louis (1967) *Rise and Fall of Project Camelot: Studies in the Relationship between Social Science and Practical Politics.* Cambridge, Mass.: MIT Press.

Katznelson, Ira (1976) "The Crisis of the Capitalist City: Urban Politics and Social Control," in M. Lipsky and W. D. Hawley (eds.) *Theoretical Perspectives on Urban Politics.* Englewood Cliffs, N.J.: Prentice-Hall.

Kotler, Milton (1969) *Neighborhood Government: The Local Foundations of Political Life.* Indianapolis: Bobbs-Merrill.

Kristol, Irving (1968) "Decentralization for What?" 11 *The Public Interest* 17.

Levenson, Deborah (1977) *The Worker's Movement in Chile, 1970–1973.* M. A. Dissertation, Department of History, University of Massachusetts-Boston.

Lipsky, Michael (1976) "Toward a Theory of Street Level Bureaucracy," in W. Hawley and M. Lipsky (eds.) *Theoretical Perspectives on Urban Politics.* Englewood Cliffs, N.J.: Prentice-Hall.

Lutz, Thomas H. (1970) *Self-Help Neighborhood Organizations, Political Socialization, and the Developing Political Organization of Urban Squatters in Latin America.* Ph.D. Dissertation, Department of Political Science, Georgetown University.

Novoa, Eduardo (1964) "Los conceptos de estado y propriedad en el derecho positivo chilena," 6 *Revista de derecho economico* 36.

———— (1965) "La crisis del sistema legal chileno," 62 *Revista de derecho y jurisprudencia* 57.

———— (1972) "Hacia una nueva conceptualización jurídica," 15 *Cuadernos de la realidad nacional* 203.

O'Brien, David (1975) *Neighborhood Organization and Interest-Group Processes.* Princeton, N.J.: Princeton University Press.

Pastrana, Ernesto and Monica Threlfall (1974) *Pan, techo y poder.* Buenos Aires: Ediciones S.I.A.P.

Powell, Sandra (1969) "Political Participation in the Barriadas: A Case Study," 2 *Comparative Political Studies* 207.

Roxborough, Ian, Phil O'Brien, and Jackie Roddick (1977) *Chile: The State and Revolution.* New York: Holmes and Meir.

Santos, Boaventura de Sousa (1977) "The Law of the Oppressed: The Construction and Reproduction of Legality in Pasargada," 12 *Law & Society Review* 5.

Schubert, Glendon (1963) "Judicial Attitudes and Voting Behavior: The 1961 Term of the United States Supreme Court," 28 *Law and Contemporary Problems* 100.

Schwartz, Richard D. (1976) "Law in the Kibbutz: A Response to Professor Shapiro," 10 *Law & Society Review* 439.

Shapiro, Allan E. (1976) "Law in the Kibbutz: A Reappraisal," 10 *Law & Society Review* 415.

Sigmund, Paul (1977) *The Overthrow of Allende and the Politics of Chile, 1964–1976.* Pittsburgh: University of Pittsburgh Press.

Spence, Jack (1971) "Analysis of Judicial Structures," Deparment of Political Science, Massachusetts Institute of Technology.

———— (1973) "Analysis of Judicial Structures in Five Culturally Diverse Cases," Department of Political Science, Massachusetts Institute of Technology.

———— (1979) *Search for Justice: Neighborhood Courts in Allende's Chile.* Boulder: Westview Press.

Stallings, Barbara (1978) *Economic Development and Class Conflict in Chile, 1958–1973.* Stanford: Stanford University Press.

Useem, Michael (1974) *Protest Movements in America.* Indianapolis: Bobbs-Merrill.

Yates, Douglas (1976) "Political Innovation and Institution Building: The Experience of Decentralization Experiments," in W. Hawley and M. Lipsky (eds.) *Theoretical perspectives on Urban Politics.* Englewood Cliffs, N.J.: Prentice-Hall.

Yin, Robert K. and Douglas Yates (1975) *Street-Level Governments: Assessing Decentralization and Urban Services.* Lexington, Mass.: D. C. Heath and Company.

Yngvesson, Barbara and Patricia Hennessey (1975) "Small Claims, Complex Disputes: A Review of Small Claims Literature," 9 *Law & Society Review* 219.

9

Law and Revolution in Portugal: The Experiences of Popular Justice after the 25th of April 1974

BOAVENTURA DE SOUSA SANTOS

> Would it be wise to imagine that a social movement the causes of which lie so far back can be checked by the efforts of one generation? Can it be believed that the democracy which has overthrown the feudal system and vanquished kings will retreat before tradesmen and capitalists?
>
> (Tocqueville, 1954: ix)

INTRODUCTION

In 1974 and 1975 Portuguese society underwent a revolutionary crisis, in the course of which many popular movements emerged. They differed as to social objectives, strategy and tactics, organizational strength, degree of control by formal political organizations, etc. But they had a common class composition: The urban or rural working class (or occasionally the peasantry) allied themselves with radicalized sectors of the urban petty bourgeoisie. Because these movements arose in a revolutionary crisis, all of them questioned the legitimacy and challenged the hegemony of the capitalist state. They shared a more or less systematic critique of the mechanisms of social production and reproduction in the capitalist society and created social practices in which more or less radical alternatives were offered.

In a revolutionary crisis the question of legality becomes one of the most pervasive social questions. This is so, first, because the crisis itself originates through an action that is illegal from the point of view of the former regime, which is thereby partially or totally overthrown. Such "original" illegality be-

251

THE POLITICS OF INFORMAL JUSTICE
Volume 2

comes a basic political and ideological datum that structures the praxis of the classes and class fractions involved in different (and often opposing) ways. Furthermore, in a period of acutely intensified class struggle the several classes and class fractions will offer different, and sometimes antagonistic, conceptions of legality—such as democratic versus revolutionary legality—and no one class or class fraction is powerful enough to impose its own conception upon the others. These diverse conceptions of legality are not equally distributed across legal fields, nor do they preclude the existence of areas of legal consensus. The divided universe of law remains a common reference point for the social classes involved in the struggle.

Whenever the revolutionary crisis takes place in a capitalist society, the greater the antagonism among the different conceptions of legality, the lower the probability that social contradictions will be handled at the level of their surface structures (i.e., as social tensions) and hence the lower the probability that the negative dialectics of the state will function (see Santos, 1982: 251). To the extent that social contradictions cannot be dispersed through the mechanisms usually available to the capitalist state, the individual legal controversies whose insulation from class conflict had been made possible by the bourgeois legal forms and practices will be reevaluated in terms of their class content and location in the social struggles. As the state is deprived of its externality vis à vis social and economic relations, it is converted into just another center of social power among many (*Ibid.*). In such circumstances obedience to its laws and acceptance of its legal conceptions tends to become a question of tactics, not only for the revolutionary classes but also for all other classes. Depending on the intensity of the revolutionary crisis, the breakdown of the state monopoly of legal power may affect most of the state apparatus, in which case the situation may be described as one of dual power, in the sense that there are at least two conflicting centers of social power struggling for hegemony. Indeed, this situation has characterized the most important revolutionary crises of the modern age.[1] In less fundamental revolutionary crises, and in prerevolutionary crises, the breakdown of the state may touch only a portion of its apparatus, and even there it may be more or less profound. In this situation, dual power is restricted to the particular apparatus, and the consequent political impact depends upon the specific location of that apparatus in the structure of political domination. The several centers of social and political power in a situation of dual power generate different social and political practices in which divergent conceptions of legality are incorporated. These become the legitimating theories behind the exercise of power and

[1]For analyses of dual power in different revolutionary contexts, see for France, Soboul (1958); for Russia, Anweiler (1958), Ferro (1967: vol. 1, p. 89ff.; vol. 2, p. 22ff), Trotsky (1967: 251ff.), and Lenin (1970: 48ff., 55ff.); for Germany, Broué (1971: 161ff.); for Spain, Broué and Témime (1961: 103ff.); and for Latin America, Mercado (1974); for Portugal, Santos (1979: 151ff.). For a critical view of dual power strategy in the socialist movement, see Poulantzas (1978).

may perform other more "practical" functions, such as repression and facilitation. Conceptions of legality are never the exclusive feature of formal political organizations. Indeed, a situation of dual power is likely to occur to the extent that such conceptions are appropriated by the masses in the social movements they more or less spontaneously generate.

In the present chapter I will analyze the phenomenon of popular justice as it occurred in Portugal during the recent revolutionary crisis. It is legitimate to speak of a popular movement despite the small number of cases and the active participation of formal political organizations. Before I proceed, a conceptual clarification is needed. The concept of popular justice has been used in the most diverse social and political contexts. It has denominated all or part of the administration of justice in precapitalist societies, as in the Portuguese *ancien régime* in which three types of justice coexisted: royal justice, seigneurial justice, and popular justice. It has referred to the numerous forms of popular participation in the administration of justice in the democratic capitalist countries, such as neighborhood tribunals and juries. It has designated the "exceptional justice" established by fascist regimes to eliminate their political enemies, such as Hitler's *Volksjustiz*. It has been applied to all or part of the administration of justice in state socialist societies. Finally, the concept of popular justice has been used to characterize the initiatives taken by the masses in revolutionary or prerevolutionary crises in response to, and usually in conflict with, the official administration of justice, as in the French Revolution, the Paris Commune, the Russian Revolution, Chile in 1970–1973, and Portugal in 1974–1975.[2]

For the purposes of the present chapter I will limit the concept of popular justice to the last of these situations. Historical analysis of the most important revolutionary crises in modern times leads us to a concept of popular justice in which the following elements tend to be present. It is class justice; that is, it appears as justice exercised by the popular classes parallel to or in confrontation with the state administration of justice. It embodies alternative criteria of substantive legality or at least alternative criteria for the interpretation and enforcement of preexisting legality. It is based on a concrete notion of popular sovereignty (as opposed to the bourgeois theory of sovereignty) and thus on the idea of direct government by the people. Consequently, it requires that judges be democratically selected by the relevant communities and act as representative members of the masses, who are autonomously exercising social power. It operates at a minimum level of institutionalization and bureaucratization (a nonprofessionalized justice with very little division of legal labor and immune to systematic rationality). Rhetoric tends to dominate the structure of the discourse mobilized

---

[2]Indeed, it has been used in yet other contexts, and the quest for a "true" popular justice still stimulates much discussion; see the debate between Brady (1981a, 1981b) and Longmire (1981a, 1981b).

in the processing and settlement of conflicts. Formal coercive power may or may not exist, but when it does it tends to be used in interclass conflicts for the punishment of class enemies, whereas educative measures tend to be favored in intraclass conflicts. In sum, popular justice in a revolutionary crisis is a form of "revolutionary law in action," the embryo of a new power structure, though popular justice is less comprehensive than revolutionary legality since it is restricted to revolutionary actions that directly confront the judicial decision-making apparatus of the state.[3]

What have generally been considered instances of popular justice in Portugal do not satisfy that concept in the way it has been defined here. Even if the concept is thought of as an ideal type that concrete historical instances can only approximate more or less, some of the cases mentioned in this chapter barely meet the criteria. Nevertheless, I include them because they point in the direction of the appropriation of judicial justice by the popular classes. They also reflect the revolt of these classes against the official apparatus of justice, which, under cover of the separation of powers and the principle of legality, not only failed to keep pace with the revolutionary process but also tried to slow its advance, thus neutralizing the practical effects of the victories obtained by the revolutionary forces.

I will begin by describing the cases. I will then elaborate on the social and political conditions that made them possible. Finally, I will analyze their strategic and tactical value in light of the revolutionary objectives to which they more or less consciously pointed.

THE EXPERIENCES OF POPULAR JUSTICE

Popular justice in Portugal after the 25th of April 1974 involved a broad range of actions varying in political scope, in the degree and kind of popular mobilization and internal organization, and in the level of confrontation with official justice. As a descriptive strategy, the whole range of cases and situations may be grouped in two categories: the struggle for the redefinition of criminal justice and the struggle for the right to decent housing. Within each category I will begin with a brief narrative of those cases that relate more remotely to the concept of popular justice and will then concentrate my analysis on the most representative instances.

---

[3]The institutional forms of popular justice may not differ significantly between revolutionary and nonrevolutionary situations. Where they do differ is in their linkages to larger sociopolitical movements, the level of mass mobilization, their class composition, and their relationship to the state. Popular justice in a nonrevolutionary situation, though ultimately independent from the state, tends not to confront it directly but leads, at most, to what I call complementary or nonconfrontational dual power; see Santos (1979: 162).

The Struggle for the Redefinition of Criminal Justice

The cases described here display a profound distrust for the state administration of justice and its agents. Such an attitude is not rare among the popular classes in capitalist societies. But in a revolutionary crisis it tends to be dramatized through collective actions of a kind that in a nonrevolutionary situation (and certainly in Portugal prior to April 25, 1974) would lead to immediate repression. Furthermore, this negative attitude of distrust is accompanied by the positive collective energy to create an alternative production of justice, however embryonic, in a more or less open confrontation with the state administration of justice. Traces of such a social movement can be found in popular vigilance against crime, as in the case of a small town in the north of the country in July 1974 that decided to organize an armed militia with pickets on duty at night after concluding that the Republican National Guard (GNR),[4] had failed to protect the community against increasing property crime. The embryo of an alternative may also be found in popular autonomous investigations of crime. In one case, which took place in a small village in November 1975, the alleged crime had been committed in 1969 when a rural worker was found dead in a well. The villagers never accepted the explanation, offered by the police and the local doctor, that the man had committed suicide but believed, instead, that he had been killed by the GNR agent stationed in the village. In view of the passive attitude of the criminal court, the villagers started to organize and people began to point to the GNR agent as the murderer. A few months later the agent committed suicide. In a plenary assembly (*plenário*) of the village the people decided to create an investigating committee to uncover the whole truth.

In other cases the focus is on the dramatization of the attitude of mistrust toward bourgeois justice, and the alternative remains a mere slogan. In September 1975 a large group of industrial workers, shouting demands for popular justice, invaded and searched the police headquarters in Oporto in an attempt to seize a landlord who, the previous day, had murdered one of his tenants, another industrial worker, after the latter had refused to pay a rent increase. In June 1975, in the town where the anniversary of the GNR murder of the communist rural worker, Catarina Eufemia, was being celebrated, a rural worker, walking by the house of a large landowner (*latifundiário*), cried out several times: "Death to the PIDE," "Death to the Fascists," "Long live liberty." Feeling threatened, the landowner took the case to the local GNR headquarters, where he apparently had good friends, and the worker was indicted for the crime of threats and defamation. There were popular demonstrations on behalf of the defendant and against the GNR. Because of the "emotional climate" the case was transferred

---

[4]The Republican National Guard functioned as the police in rural areas and was much hated by the rural workers.

from the local court to the criminal court in Lisbon. On the date set for the trial dozens of supporters of the defendant filled the courtroom, crying, "Down with the fascist laws," "Popular Justice." Because the defendant and his witnesses were absent, the trial was postponed twice.

None of these cases, taken in isolation, represents revolutionary legality. But two attributes must be taken into account. First they were recurrent—a fact of particular significance in a country that for fifty years had been ruled by a fascist regime and thus by an authoritarian ideology that demanded unconditional reverence for and submission to the state apparatus. Second, the cases took place in a social context in which other more radical confrontations with bourgeois legality and justice were made possible.

The first popular tribunal ever organized in Portugal, and also the best known, was that in which José Diogo was tried. José Diogo Luis, a rural worker (tractor driver), thirty-six years old, married and the father of three children, born and still living in the municipality of Castro Verde (Alentejo), was arrested by the GNR on the afternoon of September 30, 1974, and charged with having stabbed a big landowner with a knife a few hours earlier. The victim, Columbano Libano Monteiro, age seventy-eight, also a resident of Castro Verde, was taken to the hospital and died twelve days later. According to the autopsy his death was caused by peritonitis resulting from the wound and by heart failure. After having been indicted for murder by the criminal court of Ourique, José Diogo had to await trial in the municipal jail of Beja since bail is denied in such cases according to Criminal Procedure Code article 291–2(a).

There were no eyewitnesses. Interrogated by the police, José Diogo declared that he had been working for Columbano for the past three months and had been fired the previous week. He had gone to Columbano's house that day with the sole intention of asking to be rehired because he badly needed money. A woman who lived in Columbano's house, when questioned by the police, declared that she had run upon hearing Columbano's cry for help and had seen him in José Diogo's arms; the victim told her right after the crime how the defendant had attacked him. The woman also declared that she had heard that after the crime the people of Castro Verde had collected 500 escudos and offered them to the defendant's wife, promising her another 500 in the event of Columbano's death.

In a letter written in prison and addressed to the Association of Ex-Political Anti-Fascist Prisoners (AEPPA), who had meanwhile selected three of their lawyers to defend the prisoner, José Diogo tells how it all happened. After stating that he has been a (Marxist-Leninist) communist for many years, and after denouncing both bourgeois official justice and those who had become communists only after the 25th of April, José Diogo describes the *latifundiário* Columbano as the "biggest enemy of the people in the region of Castro Verde."

He then goes on to list his accusations against the rich man, at length and in detail. Columbano is accused of a lifetime of despotic behavior, torturing the rural proletariat of the area both physically and psychologically, subjecting them for many years to forms of domination and exploitation so cruel that they can be compared only to slavery. Columbano is accused of beating his employees brutally—"Once the fascist hangman grabbed one of his servants by the ears and raised him in the air, making the poor wretch cry with pain and fear"—denouncing his workers as communists to the political police (PIDE-DGS), with whom he was on very good terms, forbidding his workers to drink water from the wells in his estates—"thus this hangman used to torture his poor slaves, compelling them to bring bottles of water from home"—and exacting from the people in general the utmost subservience, casually striking those whose behavior toward him he considered less than respectful, such as failing to take off their hats when he passed.

According to another of José Diogo's accusations, simply because one of his servants, who was also his tenant, resisted Columbano's order to move to another of his estates, the "hangman" had all the servant's things thrown out on the street in the middle of the night, heedless not only of the servant but also of his wife and three small children. Columbano was at his most tyrannical and cruel, José Diogo insists, during his fourteen years as mayor of Castro Verde. For example, when a municipal road was being built, Columbano assigned the workers in such a way that each would be working as far from his home as possible—"just to torture them."

After his accusatory portrayal of Columbano Libano Monteiro, José Diogo speaks of his own experiences leading to the crime:

I worked for that hangman as a tractor driver for three and a half months during threshing and haying time . . . from sunrise to sunset, including Sundays and holidays without any extra pay, on the contrary, he was paying me ten escudos less than the salary established by the union. . . . He was always watching us and telling his friends that we would do nothing if he were not there. . . . He even wanted to forbid me to smoke because, he said, I would then be wasting his time, but I didn't obey, I would have been a coward if I did, for it is completely unbearable for a man to be working all day for 12 or 14 hours without stopping every once in a while for five minutes to smoke a cigarette, after all that heat and dust, sitting on the thresher under the scorching sun with no shade, no nothing.

José Diogo goes on with his vivid description of the hard work in the fields, "the fascist always behind me, watching me, sneering at the slave from inside his car." The relations between employer and employee became still worse when José Diogo decided to remind Columbano of his rights, invoked the newly established collective bargaining contracts and other labor laws, and spoke of the overthrow of fascism by democracy.

Then the fascist beast would look at me as if he wanted to eat me and say: "a man respects the laws when he wants to, if he doesn't he shits on them." And he would say: "don't you know that democracy is shit?" And he would go on abusing the workers and the union and the new government and praising his friend Salazar.

As José Diogo says in his letter," this class struggle" went on until one day the landowner fired the tractor driver because he refused to obey an order that would have resulted in hours of overtime work. "That was his opportunity for revenge." José Diogo lost his job and his family's bread.

A week later need drove José Diogo back to Columbano who, he knew, needed a tractor driver.

> I walked up to his gate and asked his permission to talk to him and he allowed me to go into the garden. . . . As I was walking toward the hangman I didn't even think of taking off my cap. . . . The fascist hangman wouldn't even let me speak at all. . . . He called me stupid and worse names because I hadn't taken off my cap, though we were outside in the open air. He grabbed me, trying to throw me out forcefully, striking me, seizing me violently by the arms and making them bleed with his nails. . . . I then lost control of myself and stung the fascist with my pocket knife in self-defense against his claws.

I have reproduced José Diogo's account at length because Columbano's behavior toward the rural proletariat was not atypical and reveals the nature of the relations of production that were dominant in Alentejo before the 25th of April and the agrarian revolution. As will be seen later, José Diogo's description of Columbano was fully confirmed by many other rural workers of the area. Indeed, a spontaneous popular movement of solidarity with José Diogo soon began to take shape in Castro Verde. The first expression was the money that was immediately raised to help José Diogo's family, as mentioned earlier. These expressions of solidarity were responsible for what the state attorney would later call "the emotional climate around the case," which led him, a few days before the date of the trial (May 1975), to apply for change of venue from the court of Ourique (which had original jurisdiction).

The case was transferred to the criminal court in Lisbon and the trial rescheduled for July 8, while José Diogo remained in prison. In a public statement, the AEPPA condemned all this as revealing

> the class character of the bourgeois laws and courts that keep José Diogo in prison while the murderers of the PIDE and the Spinolist conspirators are set free. If in fact there is an "emotional climate" it is nothing more than the expression of the popular feelings about this story and trial: the peasants' hatred of the *latifundiário*, a close friend of the PIDEs' and their solidarity with a class brother.

The solidarity movement was being actively supported by a few political organizations of the revolutionary left, which tried to transform the Diogo case into a broad political movement against bourgeois legality and in support of the notions of popular democracy and popular power then under discussion in the Assembly of the delegates of the Armed Forces Movement (MFA)[5]. The radio,

[5]The Armed Forces Movement overthrew the Salazar regime in 1974.

the press, and television made the Diogo case known all over the country (a film was produced, but its exhibition was banned at the last minute).

Then the Supreme Court, again at the request of the state attorney general and upon the same grounds, granted an exceptional motion for another change of venue. The case was moved to the town of Tomar and the trial date rescheduled for July 25. The AEPPA denounced this, too, as a "deliberate political decision," since the process was being transferred to "a region of the country where the reactionary forces have lately been acting with increasing violence" and "where a climate hostile to the defense" could easily be created. Before the new trial date was set, José Diogo's lawyers contacted the MFA to suggest that the armed forces intervene in favor of a trial in Lisbon, or preferably in Ourique, and that José Diogo be granted bail.

In a petition to the Lisbon court the lawyer for Columbano's sister, in turn, asked that the trial be postponed. He denounced the political forces

> that transformed a common crime—committed without any ideological motivation, as can easily be seen by simply reading the charges and the defendant's own declarations—into a heroic act against the *latifúndio* and against fascism. . . . To legitimize Diogo's crime is, to our mind, a regression . . . back to vendetta. . . . The classless society, surely, cannot be reached by granting the citizens, or some citizens, the right to stab one another.

The lawyer concluded by requesting a trial by jury (recently reestablished after the overthrow of the Salazar regime), which he considered the only legitimate form of popular justice. And when the date of the trial was not changed, the lawyer declared, in another petition, that he would not be present at the trial. "A trial under the present circumstances will not be a trial but a theatrical farce. The result of such a farce can never be justice; it will necessarily be a *simulacrum* of justice."

A big rally, organized by the political forces that supported José Diogo, was held in Tomar on the date of the trial. According to the *Expresso* reporter, close to 1000 people, mostly rural workers from Alentejo and industrial workers from Lisbon, jammed the area in front of the courthouse. But the official trial did not take place for the simple reason that the defendant, although awaiting trial in prison and therefore "at the disposal of the judicial system," was not brought to court, and the judges ignored both his whereabouts and the reasons for his unavailability. Two hours later the presiding judge read the court's decision: The trial was postponed until October 1; considering that the defendant could not be held responsible for the situation, since he was in prison, he was granted bail, which was set at 50,000 escudos (about $1,000). Radio appeals were made to raise the bail. In three hours almost twice that amount had been collected through contributions by private citizens and workers' and residents' commissions.

At the same time, and while they were still in the courtroom, members of the AEPPA suggested an immediate trial of José Diogo by a popular court, i.e., a jury composed of twenty workers democratically elected by those present. The suggestion was accepted, and the jury was selected, composed of eight industrial workers representing eight workers' commissions, ten representatives of the people of Castro Verde, and two members of the AEPPA. During the trial, which took place on the steps of the official court building, the popular court heard the witnesses for the defendant, who fully confirmed José Diogo's description of Columbano, presented earlier in the chapter. Twice the court asked the audience if anybody wanted to testify in favor of Columbano; there was no response. The court then adjourned, and twenty minutes later the sentence was read to the hundreds of people assembled. The jury considered:

> that the constitution of this popular court, given the exceptional circumstances that surrounded this trial in Tomar, is entirely correct and just; [but taking into account] that the popular courts must assume the form of assemblies of popular masses so that all the people may participate in them, the popular jury will submit their decision to the popular assembly of Castro Verde for ratification.

The jury's sentence was:

> to condemn posthumously the *latifundiário* Columbano for the oppression and exploitation of the people of Castro Verde and to consider him an enemy of the people of Alentejo; to consider that José Diogo committed no crime though in the jury's opinion his act was an individual act, even if excused in view of the circumstances mentioned in the documents read and heard in this popular court.

Finally, the jury decided to send the text of the sentence to the Assembly of the MFA, meeting that day (July 25, 1975).

The Struggle for the Right to Decent Housing

Hundreds of thousands of families live in slums and squatter settlements in and around the two major cities of Portugal—Lisbon and Oporto—and are often at the mercy of unscrupulous landlords and subletting profiteers. As might be expected, the problem became much more serious with the intensified industrialization process of the 1960s.

The house occupation movement began right after the 25th of April 1974. Hundreds of families who lived in the slums around Lisbon (*bairros da lata*) occupied the newly built state and municipal apartment complexes, some of them still under construction. In the "normal times" of the overthrown regime those homes would have been distributed, through a slow and complicated bureaucratic process, to middle- or low-middle-income families. Though such apartments were considered to be "social housing" or "low cost public housing," the fixed rents were always too high for those who lived in the *bairros da lata*. Though the occupation movement started spontaneously and initially lacked organization, soon commissions of slum residents were created to structure the movement, to control and defend the occupations, and to fight against opportunism.

The movement was soon extended to include the occupation of vacant houses that were privately owned. In other instances, groups of tenants decided to stop paying rents that they considered to be exhorbitant. When eviction notices were received the tenants refused to leave the houses; when the police or the armed forces were called upon to intervene the residents offered resistance and sometimes managed to stay. The provisional government recognized the bad housing conditions of the working class but considered the occupations illegal. In September 1974 a decree was passed ordering all landlords to list their vacant houses within four months. Most landlords evaded the law.

Despite military and police repression, the occupation movement continued to expand. By the beginning of 1975 it had become a national movement. Some organizations of the revolutionary left started supporting it and even engaged in several occupations in order to set up popular clinics, cultural centers, nursery schools, etc. The major political parties, including the Socialist and the Communist parties, condemned the occupations as "anarchistic" and "adventurist."

In March 1975 some of the eviction proceedings were suspended. In April a new law was passed legalizing all the existing occupations (with certain conditions and exceptions) and forbidding any new ones. But this new law was not enforced, and the occupation movement continued to expand. The residents' commissions proliferated and took an increasingly active role in house occupations. Some commissions, however, were against the occupations because of their illegality. A similar divergence developed inside the law enforcement agencies. While the regular police continued to repress the occupants, the COPCON (Armed Forces Operational Command of the Continent, under the command of Otelo Saraiva de Carvalho) supported them and helped them to stay in the occupied houses.

In the meantime landlords sued the occupants, and there were many trials in October 1975, creating a direct confrontation between the popular movement and the official court system. The first occurred during the rally in front of the courthouse, organized by the secretariat of the revolutionary residents commissions of Lisbon, on the occasion of the first trial of an occupant. Dozens of demonstrators invaded the court building with cries of: "Popular courts yes, bourgeois courts no!" "This case belongs to the people!" "Only the people can try the people!" Although the occupant's lawyer maintained that the defendant had the right to remain in the house even under bourgeois law, the demonstrators refused to recognize the jurisdiction of the court and wanted the judges to sign a statement declaring their lack of authority to try similar cases. They demanded that the occupant's case be handed over to the secretariat of the revolutionary residents' commissions. When the court clerks refused, the demonstrators invaded the court offices and took the papers with them. The judge considered that the dossier had been stolen, and criminal proceedings against the demonstrators were initiated. In the opinion of the secretariat of the revolutionary residents' commissions, there had been no theft: "What happened was that the case was transferred from the bourgeois court to the popular court."

In October and November 1975 the secretariat of the revolutionary residents' commissions organized popular courts in Lisbon and its suburbs. I have selected the case of Maria Rodrigues, who was occupying a house illegally, in violation of the April law mentioned earlier. Her landlady sued, and she was to be tried early in November. Under the law she could be imprisoned for up to two years and, of course, evicted. In an attempt to halt the enforcement of the official law and prevent a great many other trials, evictions, and prison sentences, the secretariat of the revolutionary residents' commissions organized a boycott of the trial of Maria Rodrigues in the official court, calling for a rally in front of the courthouse on the trial date.

Although the judge had already decided not to conduct the trial under the circumstances, he sent for the defendant. Members of the residents' commission of the area where she lived showed up in her place and declared, "She will not be taken from among the people." The judge then decided to discontinue the proceedings and postpone the trial until December, whereupon the people's representatives announced their decision to try Maria Rodrigues before a popular court that same day, in the inner courtyard of the official building, and invited the judge, the lawyers, and all the other officials to attend it. But the magistrates preferred to watch the events from the windows of the building.

The popular jury was composed of twenty-eight delegates of several residents' commissions. For a couple of hours people spoke about the housing question, denouncing the landlords' parasitic greed for profit and calling for self-defense committees against the ruthless exploitation of such profiteers. Maria Rodrigues told of her own experience: "They beat me. I had to go to the hospital for treatment and then I had a miscarriage. They killed the twins I was bearing." She had been in the eighth month of her pregnancy.

Finally the sentence was read:

> The popular tribunal in session today, November 4, 1975, at the Lisbon courthouse, decides the following in accordance with the will of the people here present:
>
> 1. To consider the landlady a speculator, an exploiter, and an oppressor of the people and as such an enemy of the people.
> 2. To consider the landlady's friends as fascists and enemies of the people.
> 3. To have all these fascists submitted to a popular tribunal as soon as the workers seize power.
> 4. To consider Maria Rodrigues acquitted and fully entitled to the house she is now occupying.

POPULAR JUSTICE IN THE CONTEXT OF THE PORTUGUESE REVOLUTION

The events and situations described in the preceding discussion and considered as an embryonic social movement toward popular justice must be analyzed and evaluated in the light of the sociopolitical context in which they occurred—the Portuguese revolution.[6] This began as a military revolt led by a sizable group of democratic and antifascist young officers, who were eager to put an end to the colonial war. In relation to the political project at home the program of the MFA was straightforward despite its generalities: immediate destruction of the fascist features of the state apparatus, elections for a constitutional assembly where parliamentary democracy would be restored, political pluralism and autonomy for working-class organizations, and an antimonopolist economic policy aimed at a more equitable distribution of wealth. Concerning the colonial question, however, the program was rather ambiguous. It called for a political settlement in a large Portuguese space. Such ambiguity was the inevitable consequence of the fact that the young officers had felt compelled to compromise with Spinola who, aside from Costa Gomes, was the only general who had had conflicts with Caetano's regime. To compromise was then considered important, not only to minimize the possibility of resistance by some military units loyal to the old regime but also to avoid any attempt at a unilateral declaration of independence by the white population in the colonies, particularly in Angola.

Spinola clearly represented the interests of monopoly capital, whereas the young officers of the MFA, from the start, were granted a tremendous popular support by the working class and large sectors of the petty bourgeoisie. This popular mobilization (economic *and political* strikes broke out throughout the country) was instrumental in bringing about Spinola's total defeat, as well as the neutralization of the rightist elements inside the MFA and the political radicalization of its more leftist elements. This fact, plus the firm rejection by the leading liberation movements of any Spinola-type solution for the colonial question, were the main preconditions for what would become the most remarkable decolonization process of modern times—a decolonization process almost totally free from neocolonialist features.

The qualitative changes in the political process took place after March 1975 when Portuguese society underwent a revolutionary crisis: extensive nationalization of the industry, total nationalization of the banking and insurance system, land seizures in Alentejo, house occupations in large cities, workers' councils, self-management in industrial and commercial enterprises abandoned by their

[6]It is possible, even probable, that future historians will deny the Portuguese experience of 1974–1975 the status of a true revolution, as they have done with the German revolution of 1918.
In this and the following six paragraphs I draw upon my earlier account (1979: 156–158).

former owners, cooperatives in industry, commerce, and agriculture, neighborhood associations, people's clinics, and cultural dynamization in the most back-
ward parts of the country. None of these measures, taken individually, challenged the capitalist foundations of society or the class nature of state power.
However, all these measures taken together—along with the internal dynamics of
working-class mobilization and of popular initiative, the generalized paralysis of
the state apparatus, and the developing conflict within the armed forces—did
indeed bring about a revolutionary crisis. But on no occasion was there a situation of dual power conceived of as a situation of "global confrontation" between
"two dictatorships." Although a full analysis of this fact is still to be made, it
seems to me that one of the major causal factors lies in the very nature of the
events that led to the revolutionary crisis. It all started as a *military* revolt, that is,
a revolt from above, originating within the state apparatus itself. The aim was to
destroy "the fascist state power," but indeed only the most explicitly fascist
features of the state were destroyed, such as the political police, political courts
and prisons, the one-party system, and paramilitary fascist militias. The state
apparatus was otherwise kept intact, with its fifty-year heritage of authoritarian
ideology, recruitment, training, and practice. Though under popular pressure
there were some purges of personnel in public administration and industry, they
were rather limited in number, often opportunistic, and, in some crucial sectors
of the state apparatus, such as the administration of justice, virtually nonexistent.
In any case, purges were always restricted to personnel and never reached the
structures of state power. As to the two branches of the repressive state
apparatus—the police (PSP and GNR) and the armed forces—the situation was
even more striking. Since the police offered no resistance to the young officers of
the MFA, there was no need to dismantle or even restructure the organization;
only the top officers were replaced. As to the armed forces, they were shaken to
their roots, but precisely because the revolt originated in their ranks and the
political process was kept under military leadership, the armed forces felt globally
relegitimated and postponed any profound internal restructuring. This explains,
among other things, why the soldiers' committees appeared very late in the
process and without internal dynamics.

In sum, the state apparatus, once cleansed of its distinctly fascist features, did
not collapse but rather suffered a generalized paralysis. Because the political
events had started inside it, it was "relatively easy" to bring about the paralysis of
the bourgeois state power. In this sense there was no bourgeois rule. But neither,
and for similar reasons, was there proletarian rule. In this connection the role
played by the major working-class parties—Socialist (PS) and Communist
(PCP)—must be mentioned briefly. Having gained considerable influence in the
state apparatus and inside the armed forces after March 1975, the PCP, the only
political organization worth the name, looked suspiciously on the spontaneous
mobilization and creative organizations of the working class, both at the point of

production and at the point of reproduction. Under the mystifying argument that the enemy had already been destroyed by the nationalization of monopoly capital and that the sector of the MFA then in power would, if supported, carry out the class interests of the proletariat, the PCP always favored policies inside the state apparatus and rejected as adventurist the idea of revolutionary legality and popular power. The Socialist party, of recent formation and heterogeneous composition, resented the influence of the Communists in the state apparatus and rejected as authoritarian any political form but parliamentary democracy. Drawing its support from the bourgeoisie and sectors of the petty bourgeoisie and working class who resented the power politics and the arrogance of the Communists, the Socialist party soon became the opposition party *par excellence*. As in Germany in 1918, the Socialists became the leading party in a broad coalition of bourgeois and conservative political forces that, as the recent developments reveal, subsequently managed to subordinate them.

The same process that had rapidly achieved the suspension or neutralization of bourgeois rule had, at the same time, prevented proletarian rule from emerging in its own name. This was less a situation of dual power than a situation of dual powerlessness, a situation that was resolved in favor of bourgeois rule in November 1975. Indeed, one of the striking features of the Portuguese revolution was to demonstrate that the bourgeois state may undergo a generalized paralysis for an extended period of time without leading to a collapse. On the contrary, it remains intact as a kind of reserve state, only to be reactivated if, and as soon as, the relations of forces change in its favor.

Within the global situation of dual powerlessness I have just described, restricted forms of dual power emerged in specific areas of social life and in specific sectors of the state apparatus. One such situation occurred within the judicial apparatus and assumed the form of popular justice. It is hardly surprising that the most significant instances of popular justice took place in the period between March 11 and November 25, 1975. House occupation started right after the 25th of April 1974, but at the beginning it lacked both organization and political focus. It was a spontaneous, immediatist movement inspired by the desire to find decent housing without questioning the foundations of a society that had consistently denied the people the right to adequate living conditions.

After March 11 the residents' commissions increased in number, became more powerful and active, and began to think of themselves as political instruments, as the embryos of a radically new power structure—a power organized from the bottom up; a power at the service of the oppressed classes; in short, a popular power. This was possible because the now-radicalized revolutionary process had made the class nature of the state into a practical question.

Since the question was raised but not solved, however, the revolutionary residents' commissions and all other organizations of popular power (workers' commissions, soldiers' commissions, village councils, etc.) could aim no further than the creation of pockets of dual power, that is, counterpowers opposed to the state power. The José Diogo case and all the most significant instances of popular justice take place in this context. They frame the question of power in a specific way: as a question of legality. The class struggle in which they are involved manifests itself as a struggle for the definition of legality. And indeed one of the crucial discussions of the period centers around the dichotomy: democratic legality versus revolutionary legality.

In order to understand the scope and the precise terms of this discussion it is necessary to take into consideration the sociology of the legal structure and the legal profession prior to the 25th of April. The following analysis will sometimes contrast the Portuguese and the Chilean experiences, for two reasons. First, the question of legality was also important in Chile under President Allende (though it was posed in very different terms, as we will see later in the chapter). Second, the discussion of strategy and tactics among the different political organizations during the Portuguese revolutionary crisis often used the Chilean case as a reference point.

Whereas the Popular Unity (UP) coalition in Chile inherited a liberal democratic state and a democratic tradition, the movement of April 25 inherited a corrupt, fascist-type state and a tradition of brutal repression against the working class. This distinction is extremely important in understanding the differences between the class struggles in the two countries both before and after the political changes under analysis. In Chile the UP could invoke many progressive laws (concerning labor, land reform, state intervention in the economy, etc.), which were the result of years of successful pressure by the working class and its allies on the liberal democratic state. Though enforced only selectively, if at all, they produced contradictions inside the bourgeois legal order, and such contradictions, which had remained more or less dormant for many years, retained their explosive potential until a political agent emerged from the intensification of the class struggle.

The authoritarian legal order in Portugal was, in a sense, more coherent than the Chilean legal order since capitalist domination of the state demanded that no concessions be made to the working class and its allies. Corporatist labor legislation denied the existence of class struggle, and a highly complex and efficient repressive apparatus maintained social harmony. The working class was subjected to brutal repression both in industrial cities and in the countryside (particularly in Alentejo). Political police, military and paramilitary forces, shock police, special labor courts, political courts, political prisons, and a national legislative assembly totally controlled by the fascist party—these were some of the direct instruments of political repression under the Portuguese version of fascism.

In Portugal, as in Chile, the core liberal legal institutions—the courts—limited themselves to applying the laws, even unjust ones, as mandated by the theory of the separation of powers embedded in the civil code. In actual fact the judges had lost the limited independence granted them by the liberal state tradition. There were two main reasons for this, aside from the repressive environment that affected everyone except those who directly benefited from it. On the one hand, the judges often served in special courts subjected to strict political control and burdened with very low status. On the other, the system of promotion in the judiciary was partially based upon the judge's loyalty to the social and political institutions of the regime, as this was reflected in his decisions. The higher the judicial level, the more political the criteria for promotion became. Everything pushed the judge toward passivity and routinization. And indeed, with some exceptions, the judiciary tended to attract the less successful law graduates. The better students went into politics or teaching, or became lawyers or legal advisers in big companies.

Because they enjoyed professional autonomy, lawyers tended to become active in politics. The democratic opposition to the Salazar regime recruited some of its best leaders among lawyers. But in recent years, as the last Lawyers Congress (1972) fully demonstrated, the future of the profession had become a source of worry. According to some, its traditional autonomy was being eroded by the growing practice of seeking retainers from large corporations and some government departments. Though lawyers as a class favored the protection of civil and political rights, only a few were willing to defend people accused of political crimes and threatened with trial in the political court. Although it expressed a concern for equal access to justice, the bar association—whose internal democracy was strongly questioned for many years—never managed to organize the efficient delivery of free legal services.

Law school teaching was generally very conservative, providing the social and political institutions of the regime with intellectual support and scientific sophistication. Law professors, most of whom had never practiced law, cultivated highly theoretical discussions of legal dogmatics and legal philosophy, which were sometimes an alibi, whether or not conscious, for social aloofness and political passivity. This rendered law teaching irrelevant to the solution of the concrete legal problems that practitioners (lawyers and judges) confronted in their everyday professional lives.

Besides being responsible for the drafting of legal codes, law professors most often participated in the legal life of the nation by giving highly paid expert opinions on cases involving monopoly capital or wealthy families. Given this scientific–ideological environment, the few progressive law professors found it difficult to reconcile their professional skills with their political activities. It is no surprise that law schools never organized legal services for the poor, never promoted the sociological study of law, and never fought for an interpretation of the law more favorable to the interests of the oppressed classes.

This brief synopsis indicates why the question of legality was raised differently in Chile and in Portugal. In Chile under Allende, the question of legality centered around the struggle for the progressive enforcement of progressive laws already on the books. At this level the class conflict was fought as a conflict between rival and contradictory interpretations of the law. Prestigious lawyers, putting their professional skills at the service of the oppressed classes, explored all the minutiae of the bourgeois laws in order to build a convincing argument before the courts. This also explains why the official court system was widely used as an arena for class struggle: The possibility of new, revolutionary laws was virtually precluded because the legislature was controlled by the bourgeoisie.

In Portugal, on the contrary, the question of legality centered around the destruction of the fascist state, revocation of the laws that most directly "justified" the repression of workers and their allies, and the enactment of new laws that would pave the way toward the democratization of the state. This means not that inequality before the law was greater in Portugal because there were almost no progressive laws on the books, but rather that the principal question was the creation of a new legality and not the interpretation of existing legality. This explains why the courts played a very insignificant role in Portugal, aside from their decisive ideological function as a symbol of "civilized interaction." The struggle for a new legality was fought inside the MFA, inside the provisional government, inside the Constitutional Assembly after April 25, 1975, and on the streets. A situation such as I have described tended to unleash popular forces that could easily escape from the control of the new political leaders. In Portugal, unlike Chile, there was a rupture with the political system, a global rejection of a form of political domination. Such a broad political change was favorable to a process of social radicalization even if the *capitães* (captains') movement began as a democratic (not socialist) movement.

At first, the question of a new legality was conceived by the MFA as the question of respect for democratic legality. The argument for democratic legality went as follows: There was no reason to believe that all legislation in force during the fascist regime was fascist in nature and hence must be ignored by the people. On the contrary, once the fascist state had been dismantled and the legislation directly responsible for fascist repression revoked, all remaining legislation continued in force, to be applied by the courts and obeyed by the people. If not, the very foundations of harmonious civilized life would be undermined, and the end result would be anarchy. All necessary readjustments would occur through new legislation to be produced by the political organs legitimized by the people. One of the pillars of democratic legality was thus guaranteed. The other was respect for the courts and their agents. True, judges had been robbed of their independence under fascism, but they had also been its victims. Now that the special courts had been abolished, the conditions were created for "redignifying" the judicial system and the legal profession. A first and important step in this direction would be popular compliance with judicial decisions.

The idea of democratic legality had a definite appeal in a country that had suffered almost fifty years of dictatorial rule. But there were some problems. First, there were areas (labor, for example) where fascist legislation had been revoked but not replaced. A legal vacuum was created that could only be filled by popular initiative. In such cases the question was not one of legal or illegal behavior but rather of alegal behavior. Second, to resort to laws that, though not "directly fascist," reflected a period of latent class struggle in which the bourgeoisie exercised its powers with little restraint, and to apply them in a period of political liberation and intensifying class struggle, would require a degree of repression that was incompatible with the very democratic, antifascist nature of the 25th of April movement. Third, when new laws were actually passed they tended to lag behind the rhythm and the radicalization of the popular movement, as evidenced by the law on house occupations (April 1975). Consequently, such laws were not enforced.

All these factors taught the popular movement that both the old and the new legislation reflected class interests and that, in practice, the principle of respect for democratic legality deprived the oppressed classes of initiative in a class struggle that was being fought with increasing intensity. The radicalized sectors of the popular classes therefore started opposing the idea of democratic legality with the idea of revolutionary legality.

The growth of the idea of revolutionary legality was a long process that reached maturity only after March 11, 1975. Before that, the political aims of the popular movement were far from revolutionary. In the house occupation movement, for instance, the objective was decent housing, and it was precisely in the resistance to eviction orders that the movement became conscious of itself and underwent a process of radicalization. When eviction orders were met with resistance the police would be called, but whenever the popular movement was strong enough the police would retreat and avoid violence. In such cases the armed forces could be counted upon to support the police. But the military also would retreat, though probably for different reasons, if the popular resistance encountered were sufficient to require violent repression. The police, haunted by a past of ruthless brutality, suffered from a kind of "guilt complex" and were very sensitive to being reminded of the earlier times. They knew that they were being closely scrutinized by the public and carefully followed a strategy of minimum risk. Under the circumstances, nonintervention was more attractive to the highly bureaucratized police corps. The armed forces, on the other hand, had become the symbol of popular liberation, and the demonstrators frequently reminded them of that. At the time, this alone was powerful enough to prevent them from acting according to the rules they had learned in the barracks before the 25th of April. Moreover, the hierarchy of command was not as effective as it had been in "normal times," and the repressive orders of the high command were often ignored or circumvented by the operational officers. Thus, even though the repressive forces maintained their internal cohesion, they were uneven in their behavior, which depended on the strength of the popular movement. This was quite disturbing to the "normalcy" to which the court system aspired. The lack of predictability in the execution of court decisions was a destabilizing factor and made the judges defensive, to the point where they often avoided deciding (e.g., by postponing the trial).

After March 11, when bourgeois domination was questioned in practical terms, the situation changed qualitatively. The dialectical relation between the MFA and the popular movement led to a further radicalization of both, and the revolutionary process entered a new stage. Both the destruction of the old power structure and the idea of a radically new society left the ghetto of leftist theories and became part of the political struggle. The substantial radicalized sectors of the popular classes, both urban and rural, decided to take greater political initiative in the struggle for final liberation. In addition, whereas the MFA had previously assumed the role of a third party in the class struggle, important segments of it now sided with the popular classes.

The impact on official justice could not have been greater. Court decrees, such as evictions were consistently ignored. The COPCON troops, when asked to intervene, not only refused to enforce court orders but also protected the occupants against attack. In some instances the troops even participated actively in new house occupations. For the oppressed classes, this was revolutionary legality opposed to democratic legality.

Otelo Saraiva de Carvalho summarized the idea of revolutionary legality better than anyone else: "We, the COPCON, are almost an illegal organ because we ignore the Penal Code. We act according to good sense . . . we know nothing about the Penal Code. . . . We must put the Penal Code on the shelf and assume a purely revolutionary attitude." Contrasting revolutionary and democratic legality, he said: "There are no limits on revolutionary legality but those imposed by good sense and revolutionary coherence. . . . Experience tells us which are the good measures and which the bad. We then eliminate the bad ones and make new laws on the basis of the good ones." Asked about the criterion for the distinction between good measures and bad, Otelo answered: "The benefit for the workers. If the working class accepts our measures that means we are on the right path."

In order for any modern state system of justice to function adequately, it must be supported by a disciplined, subservient, cohesive, and efficient repressive structure. In Portugal after March 11 that structure collapsed. The contradictions leading to its collapse were found both between different law enforcement agencies and within each one. When the police were about to execute a court order the people would call the COPCON, which, invoking military precedence, would force the police to retreat. But the actions of the COPCON were themselves inconsistent. Given the increasing politicization of the troops, their manner of intervention often depended on the political ideology of the commanding officer.

The contradictions in the executive agencies of official justice were inevitably reflected in the courts and the legal profession. Similar cases received divergent legal treatment depending on the degree of popular pressure exerted. Even within a single case successive measures were often contradictory because of the amount of popular pressure at the time they were decided. For example, in the José Diogo case the Ourique judge refused to grant bail, but the Tomar judge reversed this decision in view of popular pressure and the exceptional circumstances surrounding the case.

The José Diogo case served to dramatize the "crisis of the legal system" and brought to a climax the discussion of the question of legality. The bar associations of both Lisbon and Oporto considered the events in Tomar to be the product of a delirious mob. They felt that irrational mass behavior and the vile insults directed against the judiciary sought to undermine democratic authority and thus create a climate of anarchy and open the way for a new dictatorship. The Tomar judge was criticized for having yielded to popular pressure.

Diogo's lawyers, on the other hand, thought that the judge's decision had been very progressive in giving full consideration to the exceptional circumstances of the case. And indeed it was rather unusual that the defendant, though in preventive detention and therefore at the disposal of the state, failed to appear, and even the judge did not know the reason. The breakdown of the legal order could be read in the judge's response when the press asked about the whereabouts of the accused: "I know as much as you do. We called the prison and were told that he would not come, but nobody knows who gave the order. . . . We know nothing else and are truly chagrined."

The Association of Judicial Magistrates drew the attention of the state to the urgent need to promulgate new laws. Judges had also been the victims of fascism, it said, and nothing was being done to restore their independence and dignity. Because no new laws had been passed, the judges were forced to apply the old legality with the well-known consequences. The state attorneys also challenged the state through their radical union, although with a different emphasis: "Either the courts are changed or we will serve as legal advisers in popular courts. We do not want to go on supporting the bourgeois legality through a structure that must be destroyed immediately."

The internal cohesion of the legal system was deeply shaken. State authority was in danger. For very different reasons the major political parties were concerned about the erosion of state authority. They favored either democratic legality or the new legality being produced by the organs of sovereignty established by the movement of the 25th of April. Respect for this legality was considered to be the only guarantee that the revolutionary forces would not be adulterated by adventurers and would reach their objectives. Their position was that the popular classes should avoid embarking upon anarchic behavior, such as the exercise of popular justice, which was thus stigmatized. The only acceptable form of popular justice was the jury system (recently reintroduced) or any other form of popular participation in the administration of justice, as long as it was integrated into the official institutional apparatus. Otherwise, in the words of the socialist leader in the Constitutional Assembly, popular justice would be a cloak for barbarism and the lynch law, as had happened during the Nazi regime in Germany. In the Constitutional Assembly only the UDP (Democratic Popular Unity, a Marxist–Leninist organization) applauded the cases of popular justice.

The José Diogo case was simply the tip of the iceberg. As already mentioned, the popular movement was being radicalized on different fronts: Workers took over factories that had been abandoned or neglected by their proprietors; land was occupied in Alentejo; houses were occupied in big cities. When the eviction cases brought by urban landlords reached trial, the revolutionary residents' commissions prepared a political response: an active boycott of the trial followed by popular justice. The dilatory tactics of the judges were also a political response. Legality was explicitly a political, not a legal, question. The confrontation between democratic legality and revolutionary legality (which generated complex, and even strange, class alliances on both sides) was, to a great extent, a class struggle and thus an important component of the revolutionary process itself.

AN EVALUATION OF POPULAR JUSTICE IN THE REVOLUTIONARY PROCESS

The experiences of popular justice can be evaluated not in the terms of the reactions of the official legal system and its agents, which were predictable, but only in the light of the revolutionary process as a whole. The most significant experiences of popular justice after March 11, 1975—the Diogo case and popular tribunals in the house occupation cases—were always understood by their participants as embryos of popular power that, in a transitional phase, would constitute a parallel power or counterpower. They therefore evaluated their experiences against these political objectives.

In the José Diogo case both the lawyers for the defendant and the popular jury were fully aware of the exceptional nature of the popular court, as shown in the text of the sentence reproduced earlier in the chapter. A regular popular court should have a jury democratically elected by the popular assembly of the relevant community, Castro Verde in this case. Since this procedure had not been followed, the popular jury of Tomar took responsibility for seeking ratification of their decision by the popular assembly of Castro Verde in the shortest possible time. The exceptional procedure was not the result of a whimsical, irrational decision made on the spur of the moment. One of Diogo's lawyers recognized and justified the exceptional character of the popular court in a press interview:

"When the bourgeoisie resorts to exceptional courts—trying the case in Tomar and not in Ourique where the events had occurred and the court had original jurisdiction—it is only just that the people also resort to exceptional forms of justice."

In order to respect the adversary principle that both parties are entitled to present and defend themselves in court, the popular jury had asked the audience, more than once, whether someone wanted to take on Columbano's defense. The "disrespect" shown for this basic principle was the main criticism leveled at the popular court by the lawyer for Columbano's sister. It was more a political than a legal criticism because the lawyer, from the beginning, had refused to participate in the "theatrical farce" of Tomar.

The popular court, on the other hand, viewed Diogo's conduct from a revolutionary point of view. His act was considered "an individual act," that is, a nonrevolutionary act, since revolution is characterized by collective, not individual, violence. His act was not fully justified; it was merely excused in view of extenuating circumstances in the case. Diogo had acted almost in self-defense, and if his behavior had been excessive, it was understandable once the personality and the prior conduct of the victim toward the workers were taken into consideration. José Diogo's violent act was nothing compared to the constant violence of Columbano.

In the Maria Rodrigues case, on the contrary, as in all the cases of house occupation, the defendant's conduct was entirely justified in the eyes of the popular court in terms of any progressive concept of social justice. As long as there were houses without people, it was unjust that there were people without houses. The occupant's action, though individual, was revolutionary collective action because it was part of a movement. The occupant's right to stay in the occupied house could be weighed only against comparable rights asserted by other members of the community. This balance of rights was possible only in the popular courts since the bourgeois courts had refused to recognize the occupant's rights.

Popular courts are thus revolutionary instruments, instances of parallel power or counterpower in a state undergoing a more or less generalized paralysis.[7] The

---

[7]A closer analysis reveals that the relationship between popular and official courts was not the same in the different instances of popular justice. Lawyers played a much more important role in the Diogo case than they did in the house occupation cases. In the former, they were active in both courts, participating in the popular proceedings but also asking the official court that the accused be granted bail. Nevertheless, both the Diogo and the Maria Rodrigues cases, however poorly organized as forms of popular justice, point toward a revolutionary legality and a revolutionary legal form. The general features of the concept of popular justice presented in the introductory section of this chapter are specified and made concrete in the embryonic alternative these cases offer to state justice. The normative boundaries of the cases are transformed so that the class content of the dispute—always mystified by bourgeois legality—becomes apparent. The object of the dispute is thus immensely

correct analysis of situations of parallel power or counterpowers requires that the strategies of each actor be considered. The revolutionary forces that supported popular justice chose a strategy of "direct confrontation with the bourgeoisie and bourgeois justice." To play by the rules of bourgeois legality would have meant class collaboration with all its trappings. If Diogo had been tried in the official court, it is conceivable that a good defense could have been made (using legal concepts such as self-defense, necessity, etc.). If he had not been acquitted, he would probably have gotten a light sentence. Similarly, before the popular jury was convened, Maria Rodrigues's lawyer had claimed that his client had the right to stay in the occupied house even under bourgeois law. His words met with the following answer by one of the demonstrators: "They grant us the right today but will take it away tomorrow."

In a strategy of confrontation there is no place for a "progressive interpretation" of bourgeois law. And indeed, during all these months, there was no significant effort by progressive lawyers to explore the contradictions between the old laws and the new and to put these contradictions at the service of the oppressed classes.

The revolutionary forces were probably aware of the risks of a strategy of confrontation but thought that the final collapse of the bourgeois state and the bourgeois legal order was imminent and that every effort should be aimed at accelerating that process. It was of particular interest in that it dramatized the capacity of popular organizations to disrupt what should have been one of the most stable state apparatuses, according to liberal political theory. It was widely known that an intense struggle was taking place inside the MFA, which was therefore sensitive to external pressure. Popular justice would strengthen the bargaining positions of those groups that favored a socialist program based on the structures of popular power.

---

expanded and the gap between the "real" dispute and the processed dispute—characteristic of bourgeois legal process—is eliminated. Moreover, the class relations in the dispute are inverted. The popular jury, organized on the basis of class position rather than abstract citizenship, assumes responsibility for doing justice on behalf of the oppressed classes; accordingly, the defendant in the state court becomes the plaintiff in the popular court and vice versa. The effect of isolation—also characteristic of bourgeois justice—disappears since both parties come to court not as abstract individuals but rather as class members. The trial form is retained; however, not only is the jury structure changed but the rules defining the relevant issues also are completely subverted. The actions of José Diogo and Maria Rodrigues are contextualized in the history of class struggle in Alentejo and in the urban ghetto, respectively, and are evaluated differently in the light of their different meanings in that struggle. There is no strict distinction between substantive and procedural issues; the question of the fairness of the trial is mediated by the recognition that the dispute as brought to court is the tip of the iceberg, a small detail of a much broader class struggle in which the class enemy can never be presumed not guilty. There is neither professional monopolization of the legal process nor technical expropriation of legal language and discourse.

The preceding discussion is taken from my earlier account (1979: 159).

On the other side, the bourgeoisie (or rather the state bureaucracy, which was the organic, but relatively autonomous, representative of a bourgeois rule that was temporarily paralyzed) and the other social forces momentarily allied to it in the defense of official legality followed a very different strategy: They avoided open confrontation and sought to minimize the practical effects of all attacks, keeping the legal system as intact as possible and ready for action in the better days they hoped would come. Not many progressive laws were passed. Cases were not solved; trials were merely postponed. Whereas the revolutionary forces saw the postponement of trials as the neutralization and paralysis of official justice, the state bureaucracy saw it as the best way to keep the cases under control in a period of intense (though probably short-lived) class struggle. This was a covert strategy, which could therefore go unnoticed and thus evade the vigilance and resistance of the enemy.

This strategy also involved some risks. If popular courts were to proliferate, they would become a "hangman's noose" around the neck of the official legal system. Persistent disrespect for the judges and excessive leniency in dealing with demonstrators could produce deep and irreversible traumas in the legal structure. But in fact, the attacks on the courts were restricted to the big cities, and popular courts were held only in Lisbon and its suburbs. Besides, there were signs that this stage of the class struggle would not last long and would soon be replaced by one more favorable to respect for democratic legality.

These were the strategies. Their success or failure depended upon their integration into the overall struggle, and thus on the correctness of their concrete analysis of social reality. Struggles around the judicial system tend to be considered "secondary" in view of the subordinate place that the legal structure occupies in the system of political domination of the capitalist state. But this is not the case when the "main" contradictions are fought through "secondary" contradictions. When such a "travesty" occurs, the judicial system is subjected to specific "vibrations" and "pressures," such as those resulting from important lawsuits involving either significant economic interests of the bourgeoisie or the activities of principal agencies of public administration.

In Portugal, during the period under analysis, the struggle around the court system was truly secondary since, as mentioned earlier, no important cases were brought to court. Lawyers were even known to have advised their clients to wait for better times. Given the specific characteristics of the revolutionary process, the main contradictions were fought through and within the armed forces. After a period of open confrontation the struggles reached a climax on November 25, 1975. The military group in support of popular power suffered a total defeat. The COPCON was dissolved, and Otelo Saraiva de Carvalho was arrested and sent to a military prison. Respect for democratic legality was easily and rapidly restored. The legal apparatus was at hand and ready to be used. Once the "emotional climate" surrounding the cases had disappeared they could be processed and tried "according to the law." In March 1976 Maria Rodrigues was found guilty and forced to leave the house she occupied and, on top of that, ordered to pay damages of 1500 escudos to the landlady, as well as all court costs. Early in June 1976, the criminal court of Lisbon ordered the police to hunt down José Diogo, who had failed to come to court on the trial date. Once the COPCON had been dismantled, the repressive forces recovered their internal cohesion and the police could become more "persuasive" in executing court orders.

In March 1976, a widely publicized conference of the bar association in Lisbon concluded that house occupation was a crime, through "convincing and subtle legal arguments." In the same month, lawyers who kept defending occupants in the courts were threatened with disciplinary action by the bar association. Eviction orders became more and more frequent. Organized resistance became increasingly difficult and only rarely successful. Pressure upon the government was fruitless. Responding through the press to the demands of a rally organized by house occupants, the minister for housing and urban affairs said, "We are governed by the rule of law and our democratic State respects the separation of powers. The Government cannot interfere with the judicial function."

Did popular justice arm or disarm the popular classes? Would it have been better to use the weapons of democratic legality? Post factum explanations are always too easy, which probably is why they constitute the bread and butter of "revolutionary theoreticians." It would be simple, for instance, to say that popular justice was always meant to be part of a larger program of popular power, and therefore the latter alone should be the object of evaluation. But this is a formal explanation and thus explains very little. It also neglects the fact that many revolutionary groups still held erroneous and dangerous conceptions of the relation of strategy and tactics, so that the most commendable strategic choices might have been ruined by ill-conceived tactical actions. I shall therefore focus my analysis on the experiences of popular justice and evaluate the strength of the revolutionary forces supporting them. The strategy of the revolutionary forces revealed a strength made out of weakness, whereas the strategy of official justice revealed a weakness made out of strength. The best evidence for this is the successive postponements of trials. The popular jury could force an entry into the official court *house* in a spectacular fashion, but popular intervention never managed to penetrate *inside* the official dossier and procedures.

But the weakness of the strategy is structural and (leaving aside the Diogo case for the moment[8]) its results clear when we contrast the land occupation movement in Alentejo with the house occupation movement in the major cities. I will discuss the following aspects: organization (leadership and mobilization), the enemy (class nature and relations), and the object of the struggle (land, housing). The land occupation in Alentejo almost from the very beginning had a more

---

[8]Diogo's case involved an isolated act; it was not a revolutionary action even for the popular court.

unified revolutionary leadership provided (for good and for bad) by the Portuguese Communist party. In contrast, house occupations began as a scattered movement and, though gradually organized, were never subordinated to a unified leadership.[9] As mentioned earlier, the movement split after March 11 into those residents' commissions that chose the path of democratic legality, looking for support from the traditional structures of local government, and the revolutionary residents' commisssions that dominated the movement in Lisbon. It should also be noted that the house occupation movement took place in large cities with a past of democratic opposition to fascism and where the ideological predominance of the petty bourgeoisie reinforced the appeal to democratic legality. This ideological factor generated resistance to the revolutionary activity even among the occupants themselves. But on the other hand, the ideological influence of the radicalized petty bourgeoisie was also responsible for the extreme radicalism of some of the decisions of the revolutionary commissions. I have already referred to the quixotic, almost clownish, demand that the court formally declare its incompetence to try occupation cases. In the Maria Rodrigues case, the popular decision was that the occupant should not only keep the room she had occupied but also be given the whole house, and the landlady herself should be evicted. When the residents' commission tried to enforce its decision the resistance of the community became apparent, and even some members of the commission felt that they were transforming "the aggressor into a victim" and recognized that a retreat would be sensible.

Popular mobilization faced additional difficulties related to the object of the struggle. In Alentejo the big estates and farms had brought the rural workers together in both their workplaces and their residences. They lived and socialized together in the same struggle against the landowners. These factors favored a rapid and strong popular mobilization. In the house occupation movement, by contrast, the people were scattered all over the city. Even if they lived in the same slum, they soon spread themselves out to different houses and areas. The greater the concentration of occupants in a given area, the easier the mobilization for struggle.

It should be added that whereas the popular classes fought for the right to work in land occupations, they fought for the right to a residence in house occupations. The former fight related to the very core of capitalist domination—the relations of production—whereas the latter related to the conditions for the

[9]I am far from thinking that a unified leadership can be achieved only through a party structure, much less one organized along Leninist lines. Such a structure is probably implied in Brady's call for "a strong, disciplined and revolutionary party" as the precondition for "the unification of popular justice action" (1981b: 184). The belief that unified leadership of the revolutionary movement was possible without bureaucratic centralism and party dictatorship was central to the thought of Rosa Luxemburg, and her reflections on this are still relevant today; see Kitschelt and Wiesenthal (1979).

reproduction of labor power. This difference played an important role in mobilization since the political consciousness of the land occupation movement (its causes and its objectives) was greater. Finally, the enemies confronted in the two cases had different class characteristics. In Alentejo the struggle was fought against the rural monopolistic bourgeoisie who, by their wealth, their style of life, and their repressive behavior toward the workers, had long ago been recognized by the people as their implacable enemies. On the other hand, the house occupation movement was directed against a much more complex and heterogeneous enemy—sometimes the state, sometimes middle levels of the bourgeoisie, and sometimes even the petty bourgeoisie. Under such conditions mobilization was much more difficult.

The relation sought to be established with the enemy was also very different. In the land occupation movement the enemy had to be destroyed, its power reduced to nothing: The land was expropriated, and the farms became cooperatives and collective units of production. In the house occupation movement there was no question of destroying the enemy but only of reducing his power: In most cases the houses were not expropriated; their owners were only compelled to rent them. A permanent relationship was to be established between the occupant and the landlord, one that was not necessarily conflictual.

In retrospect, and despite recent attacks on the agrarian reform, the land occupation movement was much more successful than the house occupation movement. But it would be intolerable self-righteousness to tell the house occupants post factum what they should have done. They could argue that the path of legality would not have led them very far either, as the experiences of democratic legality after November 25 prove. It is conceivable, however, that if pressure had been exerted toward enacting new laws and signing leases, it would have been more difficult subsequently to deprive the popular classes of the right to decent housing.

On the other hand, all false radicalism (the manifestation of which is triumphalism) is dangerous in any revolutionary process because it does not respect the rule of parsimony, which should always be applied in threatening the enemy. This danger was particularly great in the Portuguese case. Although (or precisely, because) the courts were not the arena for any important struggle during the crisis, they performed a decisive ideological function as the main guarantor of social stability and civilized interaction. The relevance of this function was symbolized by the reluctance of most of the political forces emerging from the 25th of April 1974 to intervene in the judiciary. (Indeed, as mentioned earlier, beyond the elimination of the political courts no political measures were taken, such as the purges common in other sectors of public administration.) Threats against such a sensitive area of political domination could easily have created panic, not only among the dominant classes but also among the less mobilized sectors of the popular classes, unless they had been backed by a credible, widely accepted, counter-hegemonic ideology and a set of political and organizational alternatives minimally structured around clearly defined strategic objectives. This, as we know, was not the case.

REFLECTIONS

This chapter is the condensation of a tension between social scientific analysis and political evaluation. The tension is anchored in the author's social practice as both a social scientist and an active political participant during the revolutionary crisis; it cannot be eradicated by any epistemological magic wand. Indeed, this tension permeates all social scientific work but tends to be particularly intense when (a) the social process analyzed is recent; (b) it constitutes a rupture with a previously established order; (c) it has involved an extremely high level of social participation; and (d) it tends to be evaluated by all intervening social and political forces in strategic terms, that is, in terms of future struggles.

In such conditions the scientific text is likely to be saturated by more or less explicit evaluations and therefore calls for a corresponding reading. The epistemological Gordian knot is that political evaluation is never a mere retrospective prediction, particularly when the social process under analysis and evaluation is a revolutionary crisis. Indeed, scientific prediction—which positivistic social science collapses into explanation—is always a prediction of possible alternatives within established and unquestioned structural limitations; in this sense it is always a prediction of the past. In this framework, a revolutionary crisis is an excluded alternative, and as such it cannot be predicted, though it can and must be explained. But once it has occurred, and as it develops, both the antirevolutionary *and* the revolutionary forces tend to analyze the revolutionary course in predictive rather than in explanatory terms, that is, they tend to analyze the revolution in nonrevolutionary terms. This has to do with the dominant conceptions of social revolution and social reform and of the distinction between them, which lead the revolutionary forces to struggle to seize the existing (authoritarian) power and forms of power rather than seek to transform such power and develop new forms of power in which the autonomous participation of the popular classes is guaranteed.

In this context the social scientist's struggle to explain is a political as much as a scientific struggle. Because explanation is always future oriented, hesitation in the analysis is in part, at least, the product of a perplexity about strategy. Such perplexity is not likely to be attenuated once the crisis is over. Revolutionary crises provide us, at the most, with negative knowledge: We know more about what is not to be done. But, contrary to commonsensical evidence, the more we know about what is *not* to be done, the less we know about what *is* to be done. Indeed, the only shred of positive knowledge about revolutions is that—to borrow from Catholic theology (appropriately in the case)—all revolutions are virgins, but none conceives without sin, even in the country of Our Lady of Fátima.

REFERENCES

Anweiler, O. (1958) *Die Rätebewegung in Russland 1905–1921*. Leiden: Brill.
Brady, James P. (1981a) "Sorting Out the Exile's Confusion: Or Dialogue on Popular Justice," 5 *Contemporary Crises* 31.
_____ (1981b) "Towards a Popular Justice in the United States: The Dialectics of Community Action," 5 *Contemporary Crises* 155.
Broué, P. (1971) *Révolution en Allemagne (1917–1923)*. Paris: Minuit.
Broué, P. and E. Témime (1961) *La révolution et la guerre d'Espagne*. Paris: Minuit.
Ferro, Marc (1967) *La Révolution de 1917*, 2 vols. Paris: Aubier.
Kitschelt, H. and H. Wiesenthal (1979) "Organization and Mass Action in the Political Works of Rosa Luxemburg," 9 *Politics and Society* 153.
Lenin, V. I. (1970) *Selected Works in Three Volumes*, vol. 2. Moscow: Progress Publishers.
Longmire, Dennis R. (1981a) "A Popular Justice System: A Radical Alternative to the Traditional Criminal Justice System," 5 *Contemporary Crises* 15.
_____ (1981b) "Cutting the *Gordian Knot*: Continuing the Dialogue on Popular Justice," 5 *Contemporary Crises* 39.
Mercado, Zavaleta (1974) *El Poder dual en America Latina*. Mexico: Siglo XXI.
Poulantzas, Nicos (1978) "Towards a Democratic Socialism," 109 *New Left Review* 75.
Santos, Boaventura de Sousa (1979) "Popular Justice, Dual Power and Socialist Strategy," in B. Fine *et al.* (eds.) *Capitalism and the Rule of Law*. London: Hutchinson.
_____ (1982) "Law and Community: The Changing Nature of State Power in Late Capitalism," in R. L. Abel (ed.) *The Politics of Informal Justice*, vol. 1: *The American Experience*. New York: Academic Press.
Soboul, Albert (1958) *Les Sans-Culottes Parisiens en l'An II. Mouvement populaire et gouvernement révolutionnaire, 2 Juin 1793–9 Thermidor An II*. Paris: Librarie Clavrueil.
Tocqueville, Alexis de (1954) *Democracy in America*, vol. 1. New York: Vintage Books.
Trotsky, Leon (1967) *L'histoire de la Révolution Russe*, vol. 1: *Fevrier*. Paris: Seuil.

10

A Socialist Legal System in the Making: Mozambique before and after Independence

BARBARA ISAACMAN
ALLEN ISAACMAN

On June 25, 1975, Mozambique gained its independence after ten years of armed struggle against Portuguese colonialism. The new government, led by FRELIMO (the Mozambican Liberation Front), was committed to dismantling the colonialist–capitalist system and starting the country on the long process of socialist transformation. Although the armed struggle was guided by a Marxist–Leninist theoretical framework, it also demonstrated that it was essential that the future socialist state be fundamentally Mozambican and reflect the unique historical and cultural experiences of its oppressed people.

Operating within the constraints imposed by the underdeveloped economic base, high rate of illiteracy, cumbersome and formalistic bureaucracy, and lack of familiarity with the principles of popular democracy, the Mozambican government began to implement its vision of a new society. The government recognized the need to construct a new legal system that would reflect and reinforce the aspirations of the popular classes—workers and peasants—although it assigned this task a lower priority than the economic transformation. It drew heavily on the experiences in the liberated zones—those areas governed by FRELIMO during the armed struggle—as it did in all the other sectors to be

281

transformed. In these liberated regions the legal process had been democratized and, through trial and error, an embryonic system of popular justice had evolved. A central principle is a commitment to involving the entire community in all aspects of the legal process in order to protect and promote the interests of workers and peasants and ensure their active participation in the process of creating a socialist state. In short, popular justice is a critical component of class struggle in Mozambique.

This chapter examines the development of popular justice and the tensions inherent in institutionalizing and formalizing it on a national scale. Both in the liberated zones and during the postindependence period this process has been characterized by a dialectic between experimentation and formalization, practice and theory, that ensures both popular input and adherence to revolutionary principles. Because the legacy of colonialism weighs so heavily, we have included a brief overview of the colonial–capitalist legal system, some of whose vestiges have not yet been destroyed.

THE COLONIAL LEGAL SYSTEM: AN OVERVIEW

Although Portugal maintained a nominal presence in Mozambique from the sixteenth century, it did not effectively occupy and administer the colony until the last years of the nineteenth century. From then until the early 1960s, when a combination of nationalist pressure and international protest necessitated a number of cosmetic reforms, the colonial regime maintained separate legal systems for the "civilized Europeans" and the "primitive native population." The former were regulated by a version of the metropolitan legal code, designed to maintain harmonious relations within the settler community, guarantee its privileged racial and class position, and protect the interests of both Portuguese and foreign capital. The indigenous societies were expected to continue to live according to the rules of their "traditional" legal systems, as interpreted and applied by the colonial administrators aided by those local chiefs who became part of the state apparatus. These customary regulations were necessarily subordinate to and modified by specific state legislation in order to meet the needs of the coloinal–capitalist system (see Mondlane, 1970; A. Isaacman and B. Isaacman, 1981a).

The formal legal system derived from metropolitan law. In most cases the Mozambican Provincial Assembly ratified legislation passed in Lisbon with only minor modifications. As one prominent white jurist recalled:

All the major decisions (and the tiny ones) which guided the life of the courts were taken in Lisbon. It was there that the main laws were worked out and it was in terms of those laws that the courts had to define their activities and within which they had to confine themselves. That is to say, the laws forged in the colonizing metropole were exported just like wine or cloth to the colonies and constituted a body of foreign norms [Balthazar, 1979: 9].

Even before the 1926 coup that ultimately brought Salazar to power and ushered in a half century of fascism, legislation had been enacted to enshrine conservative social values and, above all else, to defend the interests of the colonial bourgeoisie and the various factions of capital. An elaborate family code that guaranteed the primacy of patriarchal values, a criminal code that placed a priority on protecting property, and labor regulations that limited the efforts of white workers to strike—all reflected these concerns (Penvenne, 1979). The highly formalized legal system, firmly in the hands of the colonial bourgeoisie, emphasized procedures, rules, paperwork, litigation, and professional adjudication.

The Salazar regime added a veneer of corporatism and a new level of political repression. Although the corporatist ideology was never as firmly entrenched in Mozambique as it was in the metropole, the fascist regime dismantled the independent trade union movement and replaced it in 1937 with state-controlled corporate sindicalism, which became the sole legal representative of the workers (*Ibid.*; Smith, 1974). The Colonial Act of 1930 (modified in 1935 and again in 1947) (Smith, 1974) also served the interests of Portuguese capital by reserving Mozambique's human and natural resources for exploitation primarily by national investors (Ministério das Colonias, 1948: 105–116; Smith, 1974). For more than thirty years a variety of laws were passed that reinforced this principle by discriminating against foreign interests and, to a lesser degree, local capital (*Ibid.*; Minter, 1972).

To ensure the social harmony that corporatist ideology envisioned, the state employed numerous instruments of oppression. Informers, secret agents, police, the military, and the court system repressed any opposition that surfaced (see Anderson, 1962; Duffy, 1961; Mondlane, 1970; Henriksen, 1978; A. Isaacman and B. Isaacman, 1981a).

At the same time that the Salazar regime introduced aspects of corporatism into Mozambican society it also expanded and formalized the dualistic legal system.[1] Indeed, one of its first acts was to enact the *regime do indigenato*, which ensured that the overwhelming majority of Africans would be legally frozen into a subordinate racial, cultural, and class position (Diploma Legislativo No. 162, Boletim Oficial de Moçambique [B.O.M.], 1929, No. 22, 1ª serie, June 1,

---

[1]From the moment that particular societies in Mozambique were conquered, they were placed under the jurisdiction of the colonial administration or the concessionary companies, each of which had a complete monopoly of legal and judicial authority, which it exercised without reference to formal Portuguese law. The distinction between legal systems governing the European and African communities was formalized in the 1921 Native Assistance Code (Mondlane, 1970: 40).

1929).[2] Under this legislation, Africans and mulattoes were divided into two groups. The tiny minority who could read and write Portuguese, had rejected "tribal" customs, and were gainfully employed in the capitalist economy could be classified as *assimilados* or *não indígenas*, if they were able to prove this to the colonial administration. In theory they enjoyed all the rights and responsibilities of Portuguese citizens. Africans and mulattoes who could not satisfy these requirements had to carry identity cards, fulfill stringent labor requirements, and live outside the European residential areas. These persons, known as *indígenas*, were not considered citizens and remained subject to customary law (see Bender, 1978: Ch. 22).

Although it was theoretically possible for any African or mulatto to change his legal status, the constraints imposed by the colonial–capitalist system—including the lack of schools, the limited opportunities for paid employment, and the culturally arrogant and racist assumptions of the authorities—virtually precluded any assimilation. The colonial minister, Armindo Monteiro, speaking to a conference of administrators, was unequivocal on this point:

> We do not believe that a rapid passage from their African superstitions to our civilization is possible. For us to have arrived where we are presently, hundreds of generations before us fought, suffered and learned, minute by minute, the intimate secrets in the fountain of life. It is impossible for them to traverse this distance of centuries in a single jump [1935: 108–109].

As late as 1961 less than 1 percent of the African population was legally assimilated (Mondlane, 1970).

If 99 percent of the African population remained largely outside the formal Portuguese legal system, they were still subject to some of its most pernicious features. Their lives, and in many cases their very survival, were profoundly shaped by the regime's tax laws, labor laws, and criminal code. Above all else, this legislation was designed to create an abundant supply of cheap labor.

From the outset of the modern colonial period, the ability of Portugal to extract the resources of Mozambique depended on the mobilization and control of unfree labor because the Portuguese economy, archaic and on the verge of bankruptcy, lacked the capacity to export the fixed capital necessary for development.[3]

---

[2]This legislation was modified in certain respects by the Estatuto dos Indígenas Portuguesas das Provincias da Guinea, Angola e Moçambique, Decreto-Lei No. 39.666 (1954).

[3]The small amount of Portuguese capital exported at the end of the nineteenth and beginning of the twentieth centuries went to Brazil, Angola, and other more attractive markets. Thus, even in the capital city, Lourenço Marques, only 27 percent of the investment consisted of Portuguese capital in 1900. The city's electrical system, trolley system, and first modern wharf complex were all financed by foreign capital, primarily British—a situation not unlike that in Lisbon itself.

The state first attempted to attract national capital by offering massive concessionary grants of rich agricultural and mining lands, some in excess of 50,000 square miles. These efforts proved unsuccessful, and even the foreign firms that were attracted by such offers were generally undercapitalized

An 1899 government commission, charged with analyzing the prospects for development in Mozambique, stated explicitly:

> We need native labor, we need it in order to better the conditions of these laborers, we need it for the economy of Europe and for the progress of Africa. Our tropical Africa will not grow without the Africans. The capital needed to exploit it, and it so needs to be exploited, lies in the procurement of labor for exploitation. Abundant, cheap, solid, labor . . . and this labor, given the circumstances, will never be supplied by European immigrants [Reproduced in Silva Cunha, 1949: 144].

Even before this commission was established the state had introduced a series of tax laws designed to force many African agriculturalists off their land and create the beginnings of a semiproletariat.[4] Colonial officials anticipated that male members of the rural population who had to pay a hut or head tax in European currency would be compelled to seek employment, at least on a temporary basis, on European plantations, in the embryonic light-industrial sector, and in the port towns of Lourenço Marques and Beira.

Although the tax laws provided the state with a new source of revenue, they failed to generate a cheap labor force on the scale anticipated by the colonial regime. Many African peasants were able to circumvent the labor requirement by cultivating new or additional cash crops to pay their taxes (Carvalho, 1912; Young, 1977). Others chose to work in the mines and plantations of neighboring South Africa[5] or Rhodesia at salaries that were double what the undercapitalized Mozambican firms offered. By 1912, for example, 91,000 Mozambican men were working in the South African mines alone, and during the remainder of the colonial period the average was just over 100,000 (Centro de Estudos Africanos, 1977). Only a slightly smaller number were working in Rhodesia. Finally, during the twentieth century, well over a million Mozambicans clandestinely fled and permanently resettled in the neighboring British colonies, where taxes were appreciably lower and salaries somewhat higher.

---

and highly speculative (Vail, 1976; A. Isaacman and B. Isaacman, 1981a). Faced with this acute capital shortage, the colonial state offered additional inducements to prospective investors, including guaranteed government contracts, monopoly protection, reduced tariffs, and, above all else, a generous supply of cheap labor. This strategy proved unsuccessful, and only after Salazar came to power and imposed restrictions on foreign investment did Portuguese capital assume a relatively important position in Mozambique.

[4]In nominally controlled parts of the colony tax laws date back at least to 1878 (Arquivo Histórico de Moçambique [A.H.M.]; Fundo do século xix, Governo Geral, cx. 2: Governador de Quelimane to Secretário Geral do Governo, 4 February 1886).

[5]For the Portuguese colonial regime, which signed an export contract in 1901 with the South African mine owners (WNLA), the agreement provided a much needed source of capital. Lisbon received a progressively increasing amount of money for each laborer WNLA recruited plus a guarantee that South Africa would divert a specific percentage of imports and exports from the adjacent South African province of the Transvaal to the Mozambican port of Lourenço Marques.

Since the capitalist sectors in Mozambique were unable to attract workers, even with these tax "incentives," the colonial state had to resort to undisguised coercion. In 1899 a harsh native labor code was introduced (Duffy, 1967: 139). The legal basis for forced labor (*chibalo*), which continued under varying guises until 1961, was delineated in Article 1:

> All native inhabitants of the Portuguese overseas are subject to the moral and legal obligations to seek to acquire through work, those things which they lack to subsist and to improve their own social conditions. They have full liberty to choose the means through which to comply with this obligation, but if they do not comply in some way, the public authorities may force them to comply [Silva Cunha, 1949: 151].

And force them they did. Local administrators had complete discretion to determine who was "idle," and virtually all administrators supplemented their modest incomes through gifts and favors from European planters, merchants, and factory owners in return for African labor. As a result, the rural areas were transformed into a large labor reserve. It was not uncommon for men, captured and bound by African police (*sepais*), to be sent to distant areas to work on state or private projects for two or three years, despite that the theoretical limit for *chibalo* was six months (Mondlane, 1970; Penvenne, 1979; interviews[6] with Nhacatala, Macamo, Simba, and Tose). Women, though legally exempt from *chibalo*, often suffered a similar fate. An American sociologist who visited Mozambique in the early 1920s noted that "women, even pregnant or with a nursling, were taken for road work by the Cipaes" (Ross, 1925: 40).

Although supplying forced labor to the private sector was officially outlawed in 1928, it continued unabated. As late as 1947 a Mozambican government administrative circular confirmed the practice of contracting "idle" natives. Exemptions were limited to those *indígenas* who had been employed by the state or a private firm during the previous six months, had worked in South Africa during a similar period, were involved in large-scale commercial agriculture, or owned fifty head of cattle. Since there were only 600,000 head of African cattle in the entire country, only 12,000 Africans could possibly have been protected under this clause, and the number of registered commercial farmers was probably in the hundreds (Anderson, 1962: 89; Mondlane, 1970: 91).[7]

[6]Between 1976 and 1980 the authors interviewed more than 200 Mozambicans in Maputo, Gaza, Inhambane, Sofala, Tete, Nampula, Niassa, and Cabo Delgado provinces. Those interviews that were used in writing this chapter are listed following References.

[7]*Chibalo* laborers not only worked under grueling conditions, often subjected to physical abuses by African *sepais*, state officials, and European employees, but also received almost no remuneration for their labor. As late as the 1950s the fixed salary for six months of *chibalo* labor was $3.00 per month, and the workers were responsible for arranging their own food, clothing, and lodging during this period. Numerous accounts exist of sexual abuses by European and African overseers of the workers' wives and daughters who came to bring them their daily rations.

Because of the widespread availability of *chibalo* laborers, European employers were not com-

In addition to corvée labor, the Salazar regime introduced a law in 1938[8] compelling Mozambican peasants to cultivate cotton rather than food or other cash crops in order to aid Portugal's fledgling textile industry (Saraiva Bravo, 1963; A. Isaacman et al., 1980). By 1944 more than one million peasants had been forcibly integrated into this system and the colony was producing almost enough to meet the demands of the metropole.[9] On a somewhat smaller scale the state imposed a similar system of forced rice production. In 1957 the average yearly family income from cotton production in northern Mozambique was $11.00, which barely covered the family's annual taxes. This left most peasants without money to purchase the food they could no longer produce, causing widespread famine (A. Isaacman et al., 1980). As a result, Mozambican peasants were reluctant to cultivate cotton, and the state had to use a variety of brutal coercive tactics to terrorize the peasantry and secure their compliance (interviews with Nhacatala, Macamo, Simba, and Tose).

To the extent that the colonial legal system regulated the behavior of the African population, it reflected the need for cheap labor and the concern of the colonial bourgeoisie to protect its property interests. In the rural areas African chiefs and sepais received unlimited license to intimidate and abuse peasants who failed to pay taxes or satisfy labor requirements. Africans who remained intransigent were brought before the Portuguese administrator who, under colonial law, was both prosecutor and judge. He meted out punishments, ranging from public floggings to forced labor on the distant São Tomé cocoa plantations,

---

pelled to provide even the minimal amenities to their workers. When they were unable to get a sufficient supply of voluntary workers, factory owners, merchants, and planters had only to contact the local administrators, who sent their subordinate chiefs to round up the number requested. It was also common for employers to use chibalo labor as strikebreakers. In the major strike of stevedores in the port of Lourenço Marques in 1963, for example, chibalo labor employed by the Lourenço Marques railway was brought to the port to break the strike. Similarly, when workers engaged in slowdowns or demanded higher salaries, they were often informed that they would be sacked and conscripted as chibalo labor themselves. Thus, both directly and indirectly, the chibalo labor system weakened the bargaining position of the small, underpaid African working class and ensured the continuation of miserable working conditions and the maximization of profits for the various factions of capital and the colonial bourgeoisie in both the urban and rural areas.

[8]B.O.M., series 1, No. 27, July 6, 1938. The first legislation was passed in 1926 but was not rigorously enforced (ibid., No. 37, September 11, 1926, p. 22).

[9]The colonial state organized and controlled all aspects of cotton production. It issued concessions to twelve Portuguese companies, each of which had a buying monopoly within a specified part of the country. In each region the state established the minimum acreage that each family had to cultivate as well as a timetable for planting, the system of weeding, and quality control mechanisms and regulated inland marketing centers. The state-controlled Cotton Marketing Board also fixed the price paid for raw cotton at an artificially low level in order to maximize the profits of the concessionary companies and the Portuguese textile industry. In 1939 the average price per kilogram of first-class raw cotton paid to African cultivators was $0.02. The company then processed it and sold it to Portuguese textile firms for ten times that amount.

with an eye toward instilling fear and satisfying the labor requirements of his clients. One white lawyer recalled the unchecked and unlimited power of the administrator, master of thousands:

> At the local and district levels administrative and judicial functions were merged in the same official. . . . The colonial administration thus concentrated in his hands all the means necessary to safeguard and maintain colonial exploitation. The administrator supervised the conomic sectors, secured the recruitment of forced labor for the plantations, public works or works abroad, collected taxes, was the person responsible for security, distributed favors, and judged and punished at his discretion. It was hard to find an administration without the constant ritual of palmatorias [beatings with a wood-spiked club] [Balthazar, 1979: 9].

Numerous United Nations and International Labor Organization reports document this regime of capricious and excessive punishments (see International Labor Organization, 1962).

In the urban centers, the criminal code was used to protect the property rights of the settler population and to prevent any agitation for change. That theft of $300 was treated as a serious crime punishable by long-term imprisonment symbolized the settler community's preoccupation with crimes of property, since few Africans could amass such wealth. Conversely, robbery of goods valued at $70 or less, whose owners were primarily poor shantytown dwellers, was considered a minor offense. Political opposition of any form—strikes, protest writings, public rallies—was not tolerated, and dissidents, black as well as white, were apprehended by the notorious secret police and sent to Machava Prison, the penal camp at Ibo Island, and the cocoa plantations of São Tomé. Many never returned.

With the exception of tax, labor, and criminal laws, "traditional law," interpreted by the colonial administrator with the aid of the chiefs and a council of elders, governed the lives of most Africans. Traditional law was an assortment of customs carried over from the precolonial period but interpreted so as not to conflict with the colonial–capitalist system. Although the "traditional" system varied substantially among the patrilineal, polytheistic peoples of central and southern Mozambique and the matrilineal and Muslim groups of the north, all shared two common characteristics: Customary law defined normative behavior and legitimated and ensured the privileges of the ruling strata or class—elders and males (B. Isaacman and J. Stephen, 1980). Thus, the widely held belief that the royal family was the spiritual guardian of the land and could guarantee its fertility provided the ideological underpinning for that family's dominant economic and political position, just as ancestor worship formalized the gerontocracy and initiation rites, bride-price, polygyny, and widow inheritance ensured and enforced the subordinate position of women. These inequalities became more pronounced with the imposition of the dual legal system. The position of chiefs and elders who were willing to collaborate was strengthened, and the ideology of women's inferiority was reinforced by patriarchal colonial legislation and Christian doctrine (*Ibid.*; Chanock, 1978).

Colonial studies of the "traditional" legal system (Cabral, 1925; Rita-Ferreira, 1954; Junod, 1962; Mattos, 1965), as well as our own fieldwork, suggest that there were three or four recurring areas of conflict. Not surprisingly, given the level of rural impoverishment, disputes over scarce resources occurred with great frequency. Since virtually all Mozambican societies recognized rights of usufruct over the land, rather than absolute ownership, land litigation never figured prominently. The principal conflicts brought before the tribal courts were alleged thefts of livestock (which had important social as well as economic value) agricultural equipment and food. Control over the means of production and the allocation of foodstuffs were vital for survival in a relatively underdeveloped subsistence economy distorted by the labor and production needs of the capitalist sector. Desire for scarce consumer goods, such as bicycles, radios, cloth, and cigarettes (purchased in South Africa or from rural merchants) also precipitated petty theft, which was a problem in societies without locks and keys.

Intensive competition over control of women's productive and reproductive capacities was a second major source of litigation. This increased during the twentieth century as a result of the lengthy absences of men, which magnified the productive role of women and undermined marital stability. Competing claims between lineages were articulated in litigation over bride-price, adultery, divorce, and widow inheritance (B. Isaacman and J. Stephen, 1980).

The chief and his councillors also resolved cases of minor physical violence, alcoholism, and witchcraft accusations. The last, which reflected deep-seated tensions within the society, occurred most frequently during times of famine and intensified forced-labor recruitment. In such cases the chief, with the help of a diviner, would administer the poison ordeal (*muabvi*), which, although illegal, was allowed to flourish (*Ibid.*). This ritual generally required the accused witch to consume a potion that was both lethal and extremely difficult to ingest. If the person vomited, this proved his or her innocence, since the supernatural spirits would not permit someone to die unjustly. If the accused died, this was viewed as proof of guilt, and the death was seen as eliminating a social ill.

Thoughout the colonial period, judicial hearings were held publicly. Minor cases were brought before the chief who, as both the representative of the Portuguese regime and guardian and repository of the past, was the ultimate arbitrator. He was paid by both parties for his services. The chief was aided by a council of elders conversant with the traditional legal system. Since the law did not view women as persons, they could not appear before the courts but had to be represented by a male relative (B. Isaacman and J. Stephen, 1980). Once a decision was reached it was transmitted to the colonial administrator who, in theory, had to approve it. But except for those cases that explicitly violated colonial legislation or were considered to be either very complicated or potentially serious, most disputes were effectively decided by the chiefs, since a single administrator could not oversee the resolution of all controversies in a population of 50,000–100,000. The serious cases were either deferred until the administrator visited the village or the accused was sent to the district capital for trial (Bailey, 1969; Balthazar, 1979).

The broad outlines of this dual legal system operated unchanged until 1961. Growing international pressure and nationalist agitation compelled the Salazar regime to make a number of wide-ranging, although largely cosmetic, reforms. The Estatuto dos Indígenas, which divided the population into two legal categories, was abolished, and all indigenous inhabitants of Mozambique theoretically became Portuguese citizens. At the same time Mozambique and the other colonies acquired the status of "Overseas Provinces."

In reality, however, fundamental distinctions along racial and class lines persisted. Africans had to carry identity cards different from those of Europeans, and they continued to be subject to police harassment and abuse. Moreover *de jure* social and economic discrimination continued. Urban centers were reserved for whites, and Africans were compelled to live in the shantytowns that grew up haphazardly at their peripheries. Similarly, although forced labor was abolished in 1961, legislation permitted coercion in emergency situations, and peasants, though no longer compelled to grow cotton, often suffered harsh retaliation if they failed to do so (Mondlane, 1970: 91; A. Isaacman *et al.*, 1980).

More importantly, the Salazar regime refused to consider the possibility of independence for Mozambique. Intensified political repression, highlighted by the massacre of 600 unarmed men, women, and children at Mueda in 1961 (interview with Baquile; Mondlane, 1970) forced many Mozambicans to realize that the only way to end the abuses inherent in colonialism—including the oppressive legal system and supporting state apparatus—was through armed struggle.

FRELIMO, THE LIBERATED ZONES, AND THE BIRTH OF AN INFORMAL LEGAL SYSTEM

In June 1962 Mozambicans representing three different nationalist organizations in exile united to form the Mozambican Liberation Front, commonly known as FRELIMO. After two years of preparation, the movement initiated an armed struggle in the two northern provinces of Cabo Delgado and Niassa, and by 1966 it had driven the colonial regime out of several relatively small areas of those provinces (see Figure 10.1). These areas, which came to be called the liberated zones, were characterized by the collapse and withdrawal of colonial institutions and their gradual replacement, through a process of experimentation, with a new set of democratic political, economic, and social structures. In

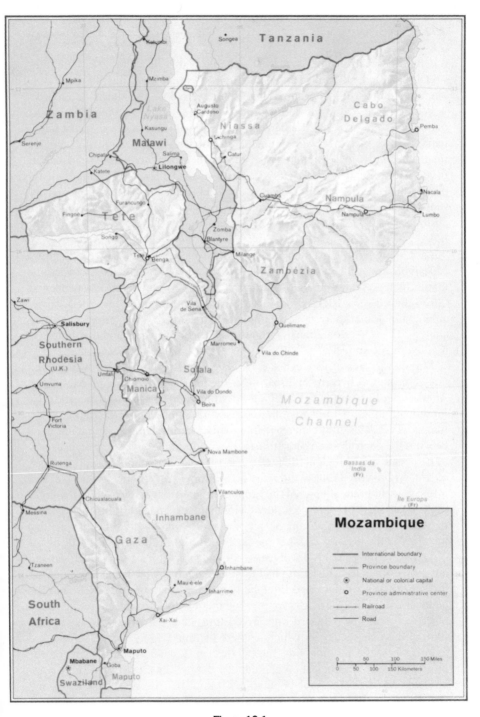

Figure 10.1

this fluid context, an informal legal system—highly decentralized, nonprofessional, based on substantive and procedural rules that were unwritten and flexible, and emphasizing education rather than coercion—also slowly developed.

When FRELIMO was formed in 1962, the bonds uniting the various nationalist factions were extremely weak. The organizations of exiles that joined hands to form FRELIMO did so reluctantly and largely at the urging of younger, unattached militants with more direct and recent experience of the harsh realities inside Mozambique. The factors that had divided these organizations in the past—tribalism, regionalism, and a lack of clear and detailed goals and strategies—persisted. All they shared was an opposition to Portuguese colonialism (Saul, 1973; Munslow, 1974; A. Isaacman, 1978; Alpers, 1978; Kruks, n.d.).

As a nationalist movement, FRELIMO welcomed and actively recruited Mozambicans of all social classes—peasants, workers, merchants, chiefs, and intellectuals—as long as they demonstrated a commitment to independence. Given their diverse backgrounds, it is hardly surprising that differences existed among the militants over such fundamental issues as the primacy of class analysis, the role of traditional authorities in the movement, and the strategy to be used in the struggle.

Despite this lack of ideological coherence, FRELIMO initiated its first military campaign in September 1964 under the leadership of Eduardo Mondlane. After a brief flirtation with Ché Guevara's theory of revolution, the nationalist movement chose to emphasize the primacy of politics and mobilization of the masses. Translated into concrete action, this meant forging a permanent bond between the guerrillas and peasants based on a comprehensive set of shared goals. "The people are to the guerrillas like water is to a fish," emphasized a military command bulletin. "Out of the water fish cannot live. Without the people, that is to say, without the support of the people, the guerrillas cannot survive" (quoted in A. Isaacman, 1978: 17). President Mondlane expanded on this theme when he stated: "The army leads the people, but more importantly yet is the fact that the army is the people, and it is the people who form the army" (1970: 149).

To ensure the peasants' involvement in and support for a protracted, dangerous armed struggle, FRELIMO had to protect them against retaliation, improve their material conditions and the quality of their lives, integrate them into the political and military struggle, and imbue them with hope for the future. Such objectives could be achieved only by creating liberated zones—an embryonic form of the new society for which all were fighting.

Integrating the peasants into the political process and institutionalizing the principles of mass participation and popular democracy proved to be quite complicated. Most of the rural population, intimidated by the colonial regime, initially were reluctant to participate actively in the weekly public meetings, or *reuniões*, which became the hallmark of FRELIMO's efforts to maintain its ties with the peasants. Marcelino dos Santos, a founding member of FRELIMO, noted this lack of confidence and political awareness in the early stages of the struggle. "Even now for us the basic problem is not guns; the Portuguese have guns, too, but that does not make a revolutionary, the problem is a political one. Political consciousness is at the base" (1973: 28). Gradually, as their confidence and consciousness increased, the peasants began to take a more active role in the meetings and to grapple with the perplexing problems and challenges posed by the armed struggle. The meetings, chaired by FRELIMO cadres who served as a vanguard, provided a forum for political education and a context for collective decision making. "A good number of hours are spent discussing problems and everybody has to have a go at a subject before an action can be taken," noted one Western journalist in 1969. Above all else, he concluded, "it was extremely important in a struggle of this nature to understand the goals and problems involved" (*Mozambique Revolution*, 1969).

Revitalizing and restructuring production in the liberated zones received the highest priority.[10] The flight of colonial administrators, European planters, and cotton concessionary companies facilitated the shift from a forced labor–cash crop economy to one based primarily on the production of the staples needed to feed both the peasants and the militants. But the departure of the Europeans did not resolve questions concerning the organization of labor or the ownership of property, which arose almost immediately as a number of chiefs, farmers, and petty traders—members of FRELIMO who had accumulated a modest amount of capital during the colonial period—began to replace the European landlords and merchants by organizing their own plantations and marketing schemes (Vieira, 1979: 13).

> The landowners in the province of Cape Delgado started in 1966 to put the people to work on their lands. They began to put people to work in the cashew plantations. And after working on the cashew harvest for a month, a person would receive only a shirt. Then, after having marched for eight days up to the Rovuma River with a sack of cashews, he would receive one *capulana* [a cloth]. Thus began the contradictions. And after he reached the Rovuma and took the piece of clothing which the landlord was going to use for sale, he received salt, he worked for a week on the landlord's fields, and received in payment salt and a tin of condensed milk [*Ibid*].

Such actions generated a groundswell of peasant opposition and reinforced the position of most members of the FRELIMO Central Committee that the collec-

---

[10]The liberation movement also attacked a number of other inequities institutionalized during the colonial–capitalist regime. In place of the private shops, notorious for their price gouging, a network of People's Stores was organized to distribute goods produced within the liberated zones or imported from Tanzania (interview with Barradas). FRELIMO discarded the colonial emphasis on curative medicine, which was both elitist and expensive, in favor of preventive medicine. In the first year alone, more than 100,000 peasants were inoculated against smallpox (A. Isaacman, 1978). Similarly, militants established a network of schools to attack the tyranny of illiteracy and the colonial mentality. By 1977, more than 10,000 students were enrolled in primary schools.

tivization of labor was an essential precondition for improving the material conditions of everyone in the liberated zones. FRELIMO's cadres held long meetings with the peasants in which they attempted to overcome peasant conerns about private rights of usufruct, demonstrate the advantages of collective labor and an equitable distribution of production, and discuss the threat posed by the nascent "black elite." By the end of 1966 FRELIMO had begun to experiment with a variety of agricultural cooperative systems,[11] some of which ultimately became the prevailing mode of production, although the rural population often continued to cultivate family plots as well. In addition to increasing production, collective labor created a sense of common purpose and identity among the peasants and between them and the army, many of whose members periodically worked side by side with the peasants in the fields. The shared work experience was an important source of new values and class consciousness and helped to shape FRELIMO's emerging ideology (group interview, Communal Village M'sawise; A. Isaacman, 1978: 19–20).

Creating a system of popular justice assumed a somewhat lower priority than the broader political tasks associated with mass mobilization and the critical issues of reorganizing relations of production, health, and education (cf. Spence, 1982). Nevertheless, it was essential for a state-in-the-making to establish general guidelines of sanctioned behavior, especially since the colonial legal system was both irrelevant and inoperative.[12] The need for a new legal system was dramatized by the efforts of chiefs and elders to utilize customary law as the basis of adjudication in the liberated zones. This sparked a sharp reaction from both the peasants who were being oppressed and the younger FRELIMO militants who saw this as an attempt to block any meaningful social transformation. One of the latter recalled:

> When speaking of the liberated zones, we must also speak of these structures, of the feudal power and the law flowing from such power, "customary law," and of the necessity for struggle against it, a struggle which at times took on violent forms. It was a question of abolishing the political law, the constitutional, feudal law, the whole system of feudal administration. . . . We had to struggle, then, against feudal customary law, we had chiefs who had power of life and death. One of them, for example, locked people up and burnt them alive; he burnt them and had the right to do so. It was necessary to embark upon a struggle against this power, which was both a political power and a religious power, since the two went together [Vieira, 1979: 12].

[11]The most common form of agricultural cooperative was one in which the peasants worked the land jointly and shared the produce and profits that, even after a portion was allocated to the guerrillas, was appreciably higher than what they had received from the concessionary companies and planters. In some areas peasants retained control over their own plots but worked two or three days a week on a communal plot growing food primarily for the army. Finally, there were also a number of FRELIMO farms located at military bases, schools, hospitals, and refugee centers, which were worked by militants and civilians together.

[12]Criminal law had vanished with the flight of the Portuguese administrators, and the old property, tax and labor codes had no meaning outside the colonial–capitalist context in which they developed.

Out of the concrete experiences of the liberated zones—the reverses and abuses of power as well as the achievements—new definitions of appropriate behavior, new values, and new ways of resolving problems gradually developed. These, in turn, were discussed and debated among FRELIMO militants and between militants and peasants. They were generalized subsequently and given a degree of coherence, structure, and theoretical importance.[13] Sergio Vieira, a member of FRELIMO's Central Committee, recounted this process at some length:

And so we began to pose the problem: we are fighting against whom? To establish what? The soldiers were giving their lives, the people were sacrificing themselves, they were carrying heavy loads, for what? Precisely what was the object of the struggle? What were we after? To achieve what? We were engaged in this battle to liberate the area, this land richly irrigated with blood. And now, this land, soaked with our blood, was it to be a land of exploitation?

Were we making these sacrifices to continue to be exploited? The people were to carry a mortar barrel for 5, 6, 7, 8 days, for what? What were we to say to the people? What were we struggling for? To accomplish what? Were these zones not ours, colonialism had left them, and now what? What were we about?

We posed this question, and a new property law began, and the collective fields started. With a new system of distribution in operation, we began to give to each person according to his work and not according to his ownership. The cashew groves of absentee owners were expropriated, they passed to the ownership of the people. In the second stage: "you have the cashews which are yours and which you are able to handle," otherwise they passed to the circle unit, the locality, structure or the district organization.

And so a new property law arose as well as a new fiscal law. The colonial taxes had disappeared, but there was a contribution toward our power—the part of the product collected that was for the Popular Forces, for the schools, for the Kindergartens, for the hospitals. It was reinvested in the fields of the circle, and the whole product was then returned to the popular power. It fed the bases, it fed the kindergartens, it fed the hospitals, it fed the people who transported materials, it was marketed through the Department of Production and Commerce. A new concept for finance arose, a new revenue law. That much we certainly managed to do.

... A new commerical law arose, all internal commerce became the monopoly of the cooperatives, which were the basis of People's Stores. In that period they were known as cooperatives. In reality they were not really cooperative, they were People's Shops, they were State Shops. All internal commerce fell within their monopoly. No one could trade internally, our point of departure being the struggle against speculation, when people had been put to work in the fields for a scrap of cloth.

Foreign trade also became a monopoly. There was a Department of Production and Commerce that totally controlled external trade, all of which passed through the hands of this department. The people sold to the cooperative their sesame, their rice, their nuts, their cereal, their honey, their ivory, their fish and other articles. And the Department of Production and Commerce organized the export and sale of these products. And every single item imported was imported

[13]The influence of Marxism on this process of theorizing and generalizing prior to 1969 is unclear. Thereafter, as the movement became radicalized, Marxism figured even more prominently (see Saul, 1979; Bragança, 1980).

through this department—the cloth, the milk, everything that came, the matches, the candles, the crockery, the tools [*Ibid:* 13].

Vieira's account, presented to the faculty and students of the university law school in 1977, is necessarily telescoped. It collapsed into a moment a dialectical process that took several years and was, as he acknowledged, highly contentious and linked to fundamental class divisions within FRELIMO that only began to be addressed explicitly in 1969.

Although the translated version of Vieira's presentation specifically refers to "laws," these were, in fact, little more than principles of justice consistent with FRELIMO's broad vision of a just society and the demands of war (Comité Central, 1976: 48–49). Indeed, one of the defining characteristics of the informal legal system that grew up in the liberated zone was that the legal principles were neither formally developed nor codified. FRELIMO lacked the state structure to do either. Rather, those principles were disseminated orally through mass meetings and modified to fit the changing realities of the liberated zones.

On occasion these new legal principles met stiff resistance from the local populace. The attack against polygyny, for example, which reflected FRELIMO's commitment to women's rights, generated heated debate both within the ranks of the militants and at the popular meetings. The formation of the women's military detachment in 1966 represented the movement's effort to demonstrate that women were capable of assuming the same roles and responsibilities as men. Nevertheless, resistance to this proposition remained strong within both the civilian and the military population, and an intensive educational campaign was necessary before significant inroads could be made (B. Isaacman and J. Stephen, 1980).

Although the generalization of concrete experience from the liberated zones provided the source from which new substantive legal principles were forged, the twin concepts of popular democracy and mass participation determined the form and operation of the disciplinary committees, one of whose tasks was to serve as informal tribunals. Although varying in detail from one area to another, they shared a common set of organizing principles: (*a*) all people living in the liberated zones had the right to legal protection; (*b*) all tribunals should be composed of lay judges popularly elected from the local community; (*c*) all members of the community should participate in the judicial process; (*d*) tribunals should not only adjudicate but also educate; and (*e*) traditional practices that did not conflict with FRELIMO's vision of social and economic justice should still be used to resolve legal problems in order to ensure that the new, developing system was rooted in the people's history.

To achieve these objectives, disciplinary committees were established throughout the liberated zones, along with vigilance groups of peasants and soldiers, to protect the interests of the community. In some densely populated regions each village had its own committee and informal police force. In other areas a number of smaller or scattered communities were aggregated into a larger administrative unit, known as a circle, which then established a tribunal and vigilance group. The informal courts usually had four to six lay judges, all of whom were selected at public meetings. When a court was being formed, FRE-LIMO cadres first outlined its broad responsibilities and the qualities judges should exhibit (group interview M'sawise), after which there would be an election. In general, the individuals chosen had publicly demonstrated their commitment to the armed struggle and often held important local positions, such as being "responsible" for production or distribution. To further the emancipation of women, FRELIMO cadres urged that they be elected to the courts as well. Such intervention generally resulted in some token involvement, but the overwhelming majority of elected members were males. FRELIMO cadres were more successful in thwarting the efforts of traditional authorities, who often sought to acquire positions in the courts so as to manipulate them to their own advantage.

The high degree of popular participation and the simplified legal proceedings reflected FRELIMO's commitment to the democratization of justice. Courts generally met at regular intervals when there was no planned collective activity—commonly Saturday afternoon and Sunday. All adult members were expected to attend the proceedings and were encouraged to provide relevant information. All hearings were held in the local dialect without any reference to the colonial legal code. Discussions were often nondirected and rambling, and disagreements were intense, as one might expect in conflicts among neighbors and within families. The most frequent cases involved domestic crises (divorce, adultery, and inheritance) and conflicts over property claims of limited value. Disciplinary cases, including unwillingness to participate in collective labor, and assaults were also resolved within the informal court structure.

The legal process, as well as the decisions, tended to reflect FRELIMO's commitment to incorporate those customary practices that were consonant with the principles of popular democracy and therefore considered "progressive." This was extremely difficult to operationalize because the traditional legal system was inextricably linked to the system of "feudal inequality" that FRELIMO was simultaneously seeking to destroy. (Debates and discussions on this complex issue continue to this day.) Nevertheless, the movement was sensitive to the need for new institutions and policies to be deeply rooted in the peasants' past. Thus, holding the hearing in the center of the village in the presence of all adults was an obvious carryover from earlier times, although the participation of women was clearly an innovation imposed by FRELIMO. The decision not to transcribe the proceedings and the explicit references to how cases had been resolved in the past served similar ends.

The involvement of the entire adult community also revealed the important educational function performed by the new court system. Mass participation and public discussions helped to define and clarify what was and was not permissible in the new society, as well as the responsibilities of every member. Similarly, if in a very crude and tentative way, the tribunals often located both the cause and the resolution of a problem in its broader social context. Witchcraft accusations, for example, precipitated discussion about the tyranny of superstition and the material benefits diviners secured by reinforcing obscurantism. Similarly, complaints over bride-price payments provided the occasion for discussion of the need to emancipate women (group interview M'sawise; Vieira, 1979; B. Isaacman and J. Stephen, 1980).

In much the same way punishments served to educate. Thieves who stole from the community or people who shirked their responsibilities were not sent to jail or beaten, as they had been during the colonial period; instead, they were required to do extra work in a communal field or on a collective project. The object of such a penalty was to instill an appreciation of the dignity of labor and a sense of community responsibility (group interview M'sawise; Vieira, 1979). Those convicted of more serious crimes, such as murder, treason, or desertion, either at public regional meetings or by the Party Regional or Central Committee, were sent to formal reeducation camps (interviews with Macore and Hunguana; Vieira, 1979: 13). There, in a highly regimented environment that emphasized both extensive political education and intensive collective labor, an attempt was made to rehabilitate the offender so that he or she could later be reintegrated into society. Given this emphasis on rehabilitation, it is not surprising that capital punishment did not figure prominently in the evolving legal system. Even those FRELIMO members found guilty of participating in the 1969 assassination of President Mondlane were sent to reeducation centers rather than executed.

Mondlane's death highlighted the growing conflict within FRELIMO over the future of the liberation struggle. Even before his assassination the divergent ideological tendencies inside the nationalist movement had coalesced into two competing factions on the Central Committee. One group adopted a narrow nationalist posture with racist overtones. Its ultimate goal was to create an independent, black nation governed by an educated black elite that would replace the white colonists. The other group contained a majority of the senior militants led by President Eduardo Mondlane, Samora Machel, and Marcelino dos Santos. It argued that independence would mark only the first step in the process of creating a new society. Rejecting the notion that an educated, nationalist elite should guide the country and benefit from its wealth, and bitterly attacking the racism of the other faction, it insisted on the primacy of class. These progressive forces prevailed, and at the Second Party Congress in 1968 and at a subsequent meeting of the Central Committee FRELIMO explicitly redefined its long-term goals to be "both national independence and ending the exploitation of man by man" (FRELIMO, 1976: 92–96).

Although a gap remained between the commitment to eliminate human exploitation and the application of Marxist theory to that end, FRELIMO was clearly moving toward the latter position after 1969. Reflecting on this period, Samora Machel, who became president after the assassination of Mondlane, recently noted: "We evolved a theory out of our practice and then we found that this theory of ours evolving out of our practice had already acquired a theorization under different circumstances. This theory and theorization is Marxism–Leninism" (quoted in Davidson, 1980:77–78). In a conversation with us, he was particularly emphatic about the importance of FRELIMO's experiences in the liberated zones during the armed struggle:

> Marxism–Leninism did not appear in our country as an imported product. Mark this well, we want to combat this idea. Is it a policy foreign to our country? Is it an imported product or merely the result of reading the classics? No. Our party is not a study group of scientists specializing in the reading of Marx, Engels and Lenin. . . . In the process of the struggle we synthesized our experiences and heightened our theoretical knowledge. It's different from first studying the theory of how to wage a war and then going out to do it. We did it and we synthesized [interview with Machel].

This radicalization process had far-reaching implications for the developing legal system. The proposition that "laws do not arise spontaneously but to defend the interests of certain social classes" became an important part of FRELIMO's theorizing and generalizing (*Ibid.*). Thus, the emerging legal system had to become an instrument to protect the interests of the oppressed peasants and workers.

Between 1969 and the defeat of the colonial regime in 1974 there was a consolidation and, in some respects, a formalization of the principles and practices developed in the liberated zone. FRELIMO's clearer ideological stance facilitated the destruction of the last vestiges of traditional authority. It also highlighted the potential danger of a black bourgeoisie that if left unchallenged could co-opt and ultimately destroy the revolution. The need to emancipate women also received greater emphasis. In December 1972 the Central Committee of FRELIMO established the Organization of Mozambican Women (OMM) in order to involve all women in the revolutionary process and protect their legal rights in the new society (Saul, 1973; A. Isaacman, 1978; B. Isaacman and J. Stephen, 1980).[14]

During this five-year period the system of informal justice was extended and

---

[14]In his opening address to the first OMM Conference in March 1973, Samora Machel laid out FRELIMO's ideological position on the subordination of women in traditional society and the proper form for the struggle against it:

1. It is the private ownership of the means of production that is the basis for the exploitation of both men and women.
2. Women are doubly oppressed because of their special role as reproducers of workers, and their

somewhat formalized. Military victories enabled FRELIMO to expand the frontiers of the liberated zones in the northern provinces and to open up new regions in the central provinces of Tete, Manica, and Sofala. In these areas the legal principles and procedures previously developed, although still not codified, were adopted *in toto.* Cadres organized meetings, democratically elected tribunals began to adjudicate, and popular vigilance groups protected the communities. Although there were some local initiative and experimentation and continuing efforts to incorporate progressive aspects of the local customary law, a tendency to transpose the legal system from one region to another, thereby creating a unified system, marked a new degree of formalization.

THE TRANSITIONAL PHASE AND
THE ROLE OF THE "DYNAMIZING GROUPS" IN
EXTENDING POPULAR JUSTICE

A coup in Portugal in April 1974, partly precipitated by the increasingly successful efforts of FRELIMO and its counterparts in Angola and Guinea-Bissau, brought down the fascist regime. The new government in Portugal initially attempted to manipulate the decolonization process to ensure a neocolonial solution. FRELIMO, however, rejected its overtures and intensified the armed struggle. In September Lisbon capitulated and signed the Lusaka Accord, which permitted a transitional government led by FRELIMO to take power for a ten-month period to be followed by independence on June 25, 1975.

---

subordination to men is based on the need of feudal society to establish who controls their productive and procreative functions.
3. The contradiction is not between men and women but between both of them and the exploitative system of private property (1974: 20–24).

Thus the struggle would have to be against both the system that maintained private property and the ideological and cultural mechanisms that maintained women in subordinate positions and taught them to be content with their subordination.

The antagonistic contradiction is not between women and men, but between women and the social order, between all exploited people, both women and men, and the social order. The fact that they are exploited explains why they are not involved in all planning and decision-making tasks in society, why they are excluded from working out the concepts which govern economic, social, cultural and political life, even when their interests are directly affected. This is the main feature of the contradiction: their exclusion from the sphere of decision-making in society. This contradiction can only be solved by revolution, because only revolution destroys the foundations of exploitative society and rebuilds society on new foundations, freeing the initiative of women, integrating them in society as responsible members and involving them in decision-making [*Ibid.*: 24].

The prospect of independence required FRELIMO to shift its emphasis from consolidating and formalizing the gains made in the liberated zones to the more difficult task of extending its political presence throughout the entire country. This was not easy. Despite ten years of armed struggle, about three-quarters of the countryside and all of the major cities, located primarily in the south, remained under colonial domination. Not only did FRELIMO lack experience in organizing the urban centers, but workers and peasants outside the liberated zones lacked a clear understanding of the movement's objectives, as well as practice and self-confidence in the decision-making process—all necessary prerequisites for popular democracy and popular justice. The problem confronting FRELIMO was whether it could mobilize the majority of the people who had not experienced the challenges, setbacks, and victories of the liberated zones.

To meet this challenge FRELIMO had to do more than merely reproduce and extend the institutions of the liberated zones, since the objective conditions in the rest of the country were so radically different. This new situation, like the original armed resistance, demanded a greater degree of flexibility and experimentation—informed, to be sure, by ten years of struggle and Marxist theory.

The central integrating institution in this process was the "dynamizing group" (*grupo dinimizador*). The dynamizing group, a committee of eight to twelve "responsibles," had three broad tasks: first, to raise the political consciousness of the workers and peasants; second, to lay the basis for the collectivization of labor; and third, to attack the social ills that afflicted their communities. Translated into concrete actions, the dynamizing group had to stimulate and organize such disparate activities as health campaigns, literacy programs, political education meetings, and community development plans. Although based on the principles of mass mobilization developed in the liberated zones, its particular form and broad mandate was a response to the unique needs of this period of Mozambican history (interviews with Machay, Nduvane, Sumaili, Mondlana, and dos Santos; joint interview with Vasco Cubai and Elias Cubai).

The dynamizing group was composed of individuals chosen by local residents and fellow workers for their understanding of FRELIMO's policies and their militancy. In rural communities, urban shantytowns, industrial centers, state offices, hospitals, and schools, Mozambicans gathered during the transitional period to select their representatives. At these meetings, as in the liberated zones, FRELIMO cadres explained the tasks of the dynamizing group and described the attributes its members should have. One local official in Gaza province explained the process in the following way:

Members of the dynamizing groups were chosen in general assemblies of all the people. Members of the party arrived to hold a meeting and encourage people to organize and select dynamizing group members. They explained what was necessary, what the role of the dynamizing group was, what its fundamental characteristics would be. They indicated that each dynamizing group should have a secretary and adjunct, and should emphasize the mobilization of the peasants. And that the people themselves must choose their representatives. . . . Some of the dynamizing group members were chosen because they have good comportment, know how to speak to the people, and how to resolve problems. They distinguished themselves by acting out the political line of FRELIMO [interview with Machay].

Although some members of the colonial petty bourgeoisie, both black and white, combined their educational and other advantages with public avowals of FRE-LIMO rhetoric in order to get elected, most dynamizing groups chose responsible citizens who represented the interests of the workers and peasants (A. Isaacman, 1978: 36–42). For all their potential abuses, these elections represented the first time that Mozambicans living outside the liberated zones had been able to participate in the democratic process, and they constituted grass-roots structures linking FRELIMO to the people.

Initially, the dynamizing groups had responsibility for a wide range of activities. Of particular concern for this chapter was their informal legal role. At a time when the colonial administration and police were paralyzed, colonial legal codes were discredited in the eyes of the oppressed, and FRELIMO lacked sufficient cadres and troops to carry out either the legal or the police function, the dynamizing groups assumed major importance. In their somewhat unstructured way, and with varying success, they helped to explain and disseminate new values and definitions of normative behavior, adjudicated minor disputes between constituents, and protected the integrity of the community and the work place.

As part of the process of political education, dynamizing groups held weekly mass meetings focusing on such issues as how the "new Mozambican" should conduct himself or herself so as to be free from both colonial bourgeois values and the traditional feudal mentality. These discussions, often lengthy and diffuse, explored the critical questions facing Mozambicans during these confusing and unsettling times and sometimes turned into heated debates. They often had obvious legal ramifications. Does a man have a right to several wives? What are the evils of alcoholism and prostitution? Should workers be allowed to strike? Who is the enemy? How did the previous laws reflect the interests of the colonialists and the chiefs? (interviews with Machay, Nduvane, Sumaili, Mondlana, and dos Santos; joint interview with Vasco Cubai and Elias Cubai).

Dynamizing groups also served as informal courts to resolve minor disputes. Women brought complaints about abusive husbands or adultery to the OMM, which, together with the dynamizing group, sought to resolve these and other domestic problems. Similarly, individuals were chided by the dynamizing groups for refusing to participate in cooperative activities, failing to do their share of the work, alcoholism, prostitution, profiteering, polygyny, and other antisocial activities that threatened the community or work place. After hearing the charges, the accused had the opportunity to respond and to indicate what actions he would take to remedy the situation. Most punishments required attendance at meetings and political education classes, supplemented on occasion with work on collective projects (group interviews, Communal Village 25 de Setembro and Vidreira Factory).

Dynamizing groups also organized vigilance committees to protect the work place and the community against enemy infiltration and sabotage, believing that defense of the revolution was the responsibility of all citizens. During the transitional period and in the uncertain year after independence Portuguese emigrants took advantage of the confusion and the lack of state surveillance to liquidate their assets for illegal transfer abroad, and what they could not take with them the planters and factory owners often destroyed. To prevent the sabotage of estates, industrial equipment, and trucks, as well as the theft of raw materials and valuable records, vigilance groups were organized in factories and on plantations. Although workers and peasants often lacked the knowledge necessary to prevent many of these acts of sabotage, their collective actions heightened political consciousness and began to take on a class character.

At the same time, the cities were plagued by a crime wave as police functions faltered. Neighborhood vigilance groups, working primarily at night, combated robberies, burglaries, attempted murder, and rapes. To be sure, there were excesses, such as the beating of suspected criminals by irate members of the community, but these were rare. Vigilance committees also guarded against the distribution of subversive literature and terrorist acts committed by departing Portuguese: Bombs and smaller explosives were discovered, and neighborhood groups helped to capture a number of reputed enemy agents (Sachs, 1979: 37–38).

As informal institutions of justice, independent of the transitional state apparatus, the dynamizing groups and vigilance committees lacked any real punitive power. Although they resolved minor civil disputes and opposed antisocial behavior through moral suasion and political education, they had no recourse to punitive measures, unlike the disciplinary committees in the liberated zones. Moreover, the old colonial laws with their built-in biases remained in effect. Thus, a robber apprehended while stealing several chickens or a blanket was immediately freed by the police or magistrate because thefts involving less than $70 were not punishable as crimes despite the substantial hardship they might cause to poor Mozambicans (*Ibid.*).

Despite this, the dynamizing groups and their vigilance committees did provide an important new framework through which the broad principles and procedures of popular justice were extended. Reflecting on their ambiguous role, Marcelino dos Santos, then vice-president of FRELIMO, noted that "they created a new sense of confidence among the oppressed masses and convinced them that they had the capacity to transform Mozambique." He concluded that "this was the very essence of People's Power" (interview with dos Santos). Although the principal political functions of the dynamizing groups have since been assumed by FRELIMO party cells and their legal functions by the newly established people's tribunals, those groups still perform important educational and mobilizational functions within the local urban communities.

INDEPENDENCE AND THE INSTITUTIONALIZATION OF A FORMAL LEGAL SYSTEM

Formal independence held out the prospect that FRELIMO could continue the societal transformation begun in the liberated zones. But in the legal sphere, as in all sectors of society, there were powerful obstacles that had to be overcome. Not the least of these was the absence of lawyers, judges, and other trained personnel who could draft new legal codes. Indeed, during the short transitional period there was not a single Mozambican appointed to judicial or prosecutorial office, and at independence the country had only some twenty-five lawyers, not all of whom had made a definite commitment to remain (Balthazar, 1979: 50–51). That the Portuguese codes were cumbersome, procedurally complicated, and extremely legalistic further hindered initial efforts to rewrite them.

Almost immediately after it assumed power, the new government took three important steps to reduce the effects of the abuses inherent in the colonial codes. Five days before independence the Central Committee of FRELIMO approved a new constitution,[15] which automatically revoked all colonial laws in conflict with either the fundamental objectives of the new state or the broad socialist principles laid out in the constitution. Article 4 identified the principal goals of the new Mozambican state:

- The elimination of colonial and traditional structures of oppression and exploitation
- The extension and strengthening of people's democratic power
- The building of an independent economy and the promotion of cultural and social progress
- The building of people's democracy and the construction of the material and ideological foundations of a socialist society
- The pursuit of the struggle against colonialism and imperialism

The constitution also recognized work as the criterion for the distribution of national wealth (Article 7), committed the state to the battle against illiteracy (Article 15) and to the emancipation of women (Article 17), and outlawed all acts

---

[15]For an official English translation, see Sachs (1979). The constitution was amended in 1978 to reflect the greater formalization of state structures, primarily the people's tribunals, and it is this version that has been translated.

creating divisions or privileged positions based on color, race, sex, ethnic origin, place of birth, religion, level of education, social position, or occupation (Article 26).

In one fell swoop the legal basis of race, tribe, class, and sex discrimination was eliminated. Rights of citizenship were unqualified by origin or skin color. There was no attempt to provide guarantees for minorities because all citizens were equal under the law and were to be treated uniformly.

The constitution generally embodied and codified the practices of the liberated zones, modified to meet the needs of a sovereign government. In this respect, it was substantially different from the constitutions of most new African states, which were modeled on those of the former colonial governments and written by the colonizers prior to granting independence. The constitution, as one eminent legal scholar noted, posed questions that reflected the realities of a Mozambican society in transformation.

> Whereas other constitutions consisted largely of a network of intricate institutional arrangements, nearly half the articles of the constitution are affirmative and educational in character. Similarly, where other constitutions place the emphasis on procedural rights for individuals and minorities, this constitution lays stress on social rights and societal duties for all citizens. The Mozambican constitution is not regarded as simply a Mozambique version of some ideal document embodying principles arrived at by a consensus of juristic wisdom, valid for all time and place. Rather, it is viewed as a specific product of a struggle for sovereignty and for social liberation, and, as such, the foundation of the new society [Sachs, n.d.].

Two months after independence, the government nationalized the legal profession, which had served the interests of the colonial bourgeoisie (Decreto Lei 4/75, August 16, 1975). Thereafter, legal representation would be equally available to all citizens, regardless of race or class.[16] This decision further accelerated the emigration of the remaining lawyers, which, in turn, exacerbated the shortage of trained personnel and created longer delays in the legal process.

In addition to taking these two steps the government moved swiftly to end the legal exploitation of workers. Given their oppressed position and their central role in the ongoing Mozambican revolution, it was natural that colonial labor relations would be one of the first objects of reform. During the colonial period the labor courts had been used to stifle worker discontent (which periodically surfaced despite state-controlled unions) and protect the privileged position of employers. The judicial machinery was cumbersome and unable to respond efficiently to workers' complaints even if a particular judge was sympathetic. Furthermore, both the complexity of the procedures and the fact that only

---

[16]At approximately the same time the health (Decreto Lei 5/75, August 19, 1975) and educational systems (Decreto Lei 12/75, September 6, 1975) were nationalized, creating another reason for many lawyers to flee.

employers could afford lawyers virtually guaranteed that the claims of unrepre-
sented workers would be dismissed on technicalities. Only unionized workers
had access to these courts, and only European workers could belong to unions.

To eliminate these abuses the government abolished the labor courts and
established labor commissions unequivocally committed to "defend the interests
of the working class and achieve justice in the work place" (Decreto Lei 14/75,
September 11, 1975). Staffed by lay persons appointed by the Ministry of Labor,
the commissions were instructed to rely on common sense and the principles of
popular justice outlined in the constitution and "not to be slaves to the letter of
the law many of which [sic] were passed during the colonial period" (Ibid.). The
labor commissions have thereby been able to counteract many of the inequities
built into the colonial codes, which still have not been repealed. All workers
have the right to bring complaints to the commission, as do dynamizing groups
and production councils, the embryonic unions founded in 1976 (Articles 12,
25). During the five years since their creation the commissions have resolved
numerous cases involving occupational disease, work accidents, and job discrimination and have ordered enterprises to eliminate the conditions giving rise
to these abuses. They have the right to impose fines up to $700—an appreciable
sum of money in Mozambique (Article 26). The labor commissions represented
the first formal attempt to transfer structures and procedures developed in the
liberated zones to the new situations facing the independent government. Operating with lay judges and using commonsense principles, they were merely a
modification of the disciplinary committees of the liberated zones.

The government also gave a high priority to restructuring the family and
ending the exploitation of women. The OMM, aided by dynamizing groups,
began a national campaign against polygyny, child marriage, initiation rites, and
bride-price—all of which reinforced women's sense of inferiority and ensured
their continued subordination within the family (B. Isaacman and J. Stephen,
1980). Public meetings were held, and the women's movement organized regular discussion groups; dynamizing groups confronted the guilty parties, exerted
pressure on them, and, on rare occasions, even had recalcitrant individuals
arrested and sent to prison or reeducation centers (Ibid.; interview with Amati).
To consolidate these tentative gains and to enshrine in law the concept of
marriage as a partnership of equals, it was necessary to rewrite entirely the
colonial family code, which reflected Portuguese patriarchal attitudes and the
reactionary ideology of the Portuguese Catholic church.

Despite its archaic nature the colonial family code, like the colonial labor
code, was not abolished. The failure to introduce new legislation was partly a
consequence of the severe lack of trained personnel, but it was also a strategic
decision. On the basis of its experiences in the liberated zones, FRELIMO
believed that the democratization of justice required substantial popular input
and discussion as well as a study of indigenous legal traditions, whose progressive

aspects should be retained. Moreover, in the first instance it was more important to create new, more accessible legal institutions, such as the labor commissions, than to worry about "the letter of the law," which could be, and often was, ignored by the new, untrained judges.

The absence of new codes and legal structures meant that the practices of informal justice developed in the liberated zones and modified during the transitional period continued to operate, though now they were formal adjuncts of the state and the party. Dynamizing groups spread throughout the country to places where they had never before functioned. From 1975 until the end of 1977 they assumed most of the local political and legal functions in areas that had not been part of the liberated zones. Only in 1978, after a vigorous campaign to create new FRELIMO party cells[17] and to establish both a national legislative system and an embryonic network of local courts, was the authority of the dynamizing groups gradually reduced. Similarly, the number of vigilance groups increased substantially during this period, and they assumed greater responsibility for combating crime. In the northern province of Cabo Delgado, for example, more than 1000 committees patrolled their communities and work places by 1979 (*Notícias*, October 10, 1979). The vigilance committees were instrumental in dramatically reducing the number of murders, assaults, and robberies.[18] The OMM also expanded throughout the country and intensified its campaign against bride-price, polygyny, wife abuse, initiation rites, widow inheritance, and job discrimination (B. Isaacman and J. Stephen, 1980).

The most controversial informal legal institutions that continued to operate were the reeducation centers. Rumors have periodically been circulated by the Western press that the centers were characterized by harsh conditions and brutality similar to those prevailing in Siberian labor camps. What we actually saw at M'sawise, a reeducation center housing former secret police and colonial collaborators, was completely unexpected. The sentries at the rope gate were detainees, and the only weapon we noticed throughout our visit was in the hands of a camp resident going off to hunt for the center's food. The center had no armed guards, no dogs, no barbed-wire fences, and no cells. The thirty-three-year-old commandant and his eight assistants mingled easily with the detainees and expressed no concern that their families lived less than 300 yards from the prisoners' barracks. When we pressed him about the lax security, he acknowledged that when the center had first opened in 1977 there had been a number of unsuccessful escapes. The remoteness of the center and the speed with which neighboring peasants reported fugitives to authorities soon convinced the

[17]The decision to broaden FRELIMO from the original group of militants was part of a larger transformation of FRELIMO into a Marxist–Leninist vanguard party, which occurred in 1977.

[18]Homicides declined from an average of 1500 a year at the end of the colonial period to 88 in 1979. Robberies and assaults also declined substantially, though not on the same scale (interview with Machel).

residents of the futility of such attempts (interviews with Director of M'sawise Reeducation Center, Faducurane, Balate, Weisman, Nyantumbo, and Bitole).

The political background of the prisoners at M'sawise makes it unique. When we spoke with detainees who had been held at other centers, we learned that most had been arrested for theft or related crimes committed since independence. Ramon Sainda, a merchant caught selling stolen property, and Ricardo Mungey, accused of embezzling $12,000 from the factory he managed, were typical of the residents at the Chibutu Center, whereas most of those at Inhassune were "marginals"—unemployed petty criminals—detained for theft and vagrancy (interview with Mungey and Sainda).

Nevertheless, conditions at the various centers are remarkably similar.[19] Inmates are organized into brigades whose members live and work together and are responsible for one another's health and welfare. They also decide how to discipline fellow members who violate the camp's code of behavior.

The most startling aspect of all the reeducation centers is the lack of coercion.[20] None has barbed wire, high walls, or even gates, and all the detainees with whom we spoke indicated that they had never suffered or witnessed corporal punishment (interviews with Faducurane, Balate, Weisman, Nyantumbo, Bitole, Mungey, Sainda, Abdul, Macore, and Chimo). When we expressed our skepticism, Mario Balate, a resident and veteran of several camps, angrily interrupted, "I am describing what happened. I am not trying to defend the government. If they hit us I would say so" (interview with Balate). Problems such as petty thefts, fights, and laziness are resolved at weekly brigade meetings, where members recommend appropriate action to the commandant, who makes the

[19]According to interviews with thirty residents from seven centers, a typical day begins at 4:30 A.M. After an hour of exercise, followed by breakfast, detainees working in brigades start their assigned tasks. Most residents farm, but we observed smaller groups constructing houses, forging hoes, weaving, and repairing roads. All the brigades, including those clearing fields a few kilometers from the camp, are unsupervised, although each had a "responsible" elected from among its members. The two hours before lunch are devoted to literacy classes and political education. The afternoon includes a discussion of the day's national and international news, a work stint, showers, and supper. After dinner there are sports and cultural activities until 9:00 P.M. This schedule is repeated without variation Monday through Saturday morning.

Living conditions are harsh. The food, primarily corn porridge and relish, is not terribly interesting by Western standards, but it is no worse than the diet of most rural Mozambicans. Similarly, housing and health facilities are rudimentary but comparable to those we observed in rural communities throughout the country.

[20]Ministry of Justice officials concede that there were occasional abuses during the unsettled period following independence, when local vigilance groups, police, soldiers, and rural administrators sometimes overstepped their authority. An indeterminant, but small, number of Mozambicans were arbitrarily arrested and incarcerated in reeducation centers for an indefinite period, without trial. These abuses ended in 1978 with the formal establishment of popular tribunals (interviews with Amaral and Hunguana).

final decision. Extra work on Saturday afternoon or Sunday is the typical punishment (*Ibid.*).

According to the staff, the goal of the centers is rehabilitation of the detainees with the aim of reintegrating them into Mozambican society. The twin mechanisms are literacy training and political education. The daily literacy classes offer many residents of the camps their first opportunity for formal education.[21] Political education consists of classes, informal discussions, daily news announcements, and cultural events. FRELIMO officials believe that the experience of working together, developing self-reliance, and participating in collective decision making within the brigades reinforces and adds meaning to the new values instilled in the classroom.

Although exact statistics are unavailable, high-level Justice Ministry officials indicated that the reeducation centers are in the process of being phased out. They emphasized that the centers were expanded as a temporary measure to fill the vacuum created by the paralysis of the colonial legal system[22] and the flight of almost all judges at independence. In 1979 and 1980 at least three centers were closed and 2600 inmates, including several hundred political offenders, reintegrated into Mozambican society—approximately half of all detainees (interviews with Amaral and Hunguana).

During the three years after independence, at the same time that the institutions of informal popular justice gradually assumed greater importance, the Justice Ministry began to grapple with the problems of establishing a new legal system to replace the colonial residue. The new system needed to incorporate and rationalize the imprecisely defined institutions and practices developed in the liberated zones and expanded during the transitional phase. Replacing the colonial courts with a network of popular tribunals received the highest priority (*Ibid.*). Study groups within the ministry also began to formulate new family, criminal, and procedural codes, and to examine the complex issues of penal reform (*Ibid.*).

To ensure that both the future codes and the new court system would be rooted in Mozambican history and culture and reflect the experiences of the liberated zones, ministry brigades spent several months in 1978 meeting with members of the rural population in all ten of the country's provinces. The brigades, composed primarily of third- and fourth-year law students who were to be the future provincial judges, collected ethnographic material on traditional law, examined the operation of the disciplinary committees during the armed struggle, and explained to the people in nontechnical language the broad juridical foundations of the new legal system (*Ibid.*; Sachs, 1979: 55).

[21]At the time of independence it was estimated that 95 percent of the population was illiterate.
[22]Until the end of 1978 the colonial court system continued to operate and to reinterpret the old codes to accommodate the changed reality, but they were merely the vestiges of another era.

Armed with these insights, the Justice Ministry created a national court system at the end of 1978 to replace the moribund and dysfunctional colonial apparatus (Decreto Lei 12/78, December 2, 1978). The jurisdiction of the popular tribunals correspond to the administrative structures established in the constitution—provinces, districts, and localities (Article 10). The provincial courts handle the more serious crimes and larger civil disputes (Articles 23, 25), whereas the district courts handle crimes that carry a penalty of two years or less and civil disputes involving smaller amounts (Articles 32, 33). The tribunals at the locality and communal village level deal only with minor offenses and disputes (Article 38).

This new system offered the overwhelming majority of Mozambicans their first opportunity to have cases tried in a court of their peers rather than by capricious colonial administrators or collaborating chiefs. In the last two years more than 200 popular tribunals have been established in the major urban centers, and in some district seats, localities, and communal villages in each province (interviews with Amaral and Hunguana).

The broad principles of popular justice first formulated in the liberated zones guide the new court system. Every court includes some lay judges elected by their fellow workers and neighbors. The formalistic procedures of the colonial past have been drastically simplified because the lay judges could not comprehend them and because there are no private attorneys to capitalize on procedural errors. Thus, procedures have become more intelligible even without a new procedural code. Like the labor commissions, the judges reach decisions based on common sense and general notions of justice outlined in the constitution.

Similarly, much of the formalism and paperwork has disappeared. Litigants do not know what paper must be filed by what date or in what form. The president of the court, a trained jurist or, at the district level, a person with a few months of legal training, assists the litigants with some of this and ignores the remainder.

Substantive changes have also occurred without code revision. According to the senior judge of Maputo province, for example, there has been a substantial reduction in the penalty imposed for property crimes unaccompanied by personal injury (interview with Amaral); in Tete province the courts have acted vigorously to punish people who engage in the lethal practice of using the poison ordeal to identify witches—something the colonial courts generally ignored (interview with the president of the Niassa Provincial Court). Although it is still illegal to perform or to have an abortion, since independence the police, the medical profession, and the judges have exercised discretion in deciding which perpetrators to prosecute (interview with Honwana). The courts are also committed to rehabilitating convicted criminals through work programs and political education rather than merely incarcerating them. As of August 1980, there were only 8000 Mozambicans in jail out of a population of more than 12 million (interview with Amaral).

Other substantive changes have also been introduced informally. Although divorce is not permitted in the Family Code inherited from the Portuguese, divorces are regularly granted by the provincial people's tribunals. This means, of course, that the section of the Family Code prohibiting divorce has informally been found to violate certain constitutionally protected rights (Constitution, Article 79). Although the government does not want to encourage divorce, the courts will permit the parties to end their marriage if the OMM, the party, or the dynamizing group fail to reconcile them.

At the local level and in the communal villages the tribunals are composed entirely of lay judges selected by either the local legislative assembly, if it has already been established, or the community at large (Law on Judicial Organization, Articles 36, 52). Orientation sessions, organized by the FRELIMO party cell, resemble those that occurred in the liberated zones. They continue to stress the importance of electing women judges, and most courts appear to have at least one woman member. At the communal village Agostinho Neto in Inhambane province, four of the eight judges were women (interview at Communal Village Agostinho Neto). Although women remain a minority, their presence on the courts is part of a long-standing FRELIMO commitment to give women a legal personality, to guarantee equality before the law, and to ensure that the perspective of women is considered in judicial deliberations.

Whatever the sexual composition of the local courts, almost all the judges were initially illiterate, like those at Lumbo in Nampula province (*Notícias*, June 16, 1979). Their inability to read and write obviously hindered their efforts to understand the laws and to produce court records, which were to be used to help formulate future legislation. To overcome this problem, national literacy campaigns have given special priority to court members (interview with Laisse). These programs, together with periodic visits by mobile judicial brigades who explain new legislation and provide a broader political orientation, help the local courts to work relatively smoothly.

The local tribunals sit once a week and are open to the public. Indeed, in many communal villages all the adults attend. The tribunals hear a wide range of minor disputes and petty crimes. Despite substantial regional variation in the mix of cases, which reflects both local cultural traditions and contemporary social and economic realities, interviews conducted throughout the country suggest that domestic issues predominate. Of the twenty-six cases adjudicated at communal village Musira in Cabo Delgado province during the second half of 1979, for example, thirteen dealt with divorce and the related issue of polygyny, five with robbery, and the remaining eight included accusations of witchcraft, prostitution, conflict over property, and claims of debt (Tribunal Popular). At two communal villages in Inhambane province in the south, where men generally still spend most of their working lives in the South African gold mines, adultery was the single most important issue (group interviews, Communal Village Agostinho Neto and Communal Village 25 de Setembro), whereas in Lumbo, to the north, the more varied court docket included problems of premature marriage, inheritance, and theft (*Notícias*, June 16, 1979).

As might be expected, similar cases are not necessarily resolved uniformly despite acceptance by the judges of the broad principles of popular justice outlined in the constitution and the common orientation they receive from the justice brigades. In the Muslim north where traditional values remain strong, for example, there is a tendency to exonerate or to punish only minimally men who commit polygyny, purchase wives, or abuse their spouses. Moreover, even within a particular region or community, extenuating circumstances profoundly influence the decisions.

Consider the resolution of five family disputes in Mauria in Cabo Delgado—one of the few tribunals in which written records were kept from its inception—in which FRELIMO's unequivocal opposition to polygyny and its strong commitment to the sanctity of the family came into conflict. In the first case a husband demanded restitution of 300 escudos ($10) in bride-price because his wife did not want to remain married. The judges, who were required to attempt a reconciliation (Law on Judicial Organization, Article 38), asked the young woman why she sought a divorce so soon after her marriage. She explained that when she had married she was unaware that her husband already had a wife and that she did not want to be exploited in a polygynous relationship. Moreover, she could not return the money since she had used it to feed her family. The court sustained her position and dissolved the marriage.

In the second case the husband wanted a divorce because his wife did not respect him. The court refused to grant it, despite the fact that the man was also polygynous. In making their decision the judges noted that FRELIMO was opposed to divorce, that the couple had been married for a long time, and that they had several children. After hearing testimony from a number of witnesses, the court observed that the marital problems were largely due to the man's drinking. It ordered the vigilance committee to confiscate his homemade distillery and to prohibit him from drinking. He was also required to work for three months in the collective fields and to receive political education in the FRELIMO party cell.

A month later the tribunal dissolved a new marriage at the request of the wife, who denied knowing that her husband already had several wives. But because other witnesses convinced the court that both parties knew of the polygyny, it sentenced them both to work in the communal fields—the man for sixty days and the woman for twenty.

In the fourth case a husband sought a divorce because his wife was having an affair and had contracted gonorrhea. She acknowledged the transgression but said it had only occurred once. Other members of the communal village indicated that she had been involved in a number of extramarital relationships. Despite that the couple had been married for several years, the court ordered a divorce and required the woman to attend political education classes held by the OMM.

There was one domestic problem the tribunal had great difficulty resolving. One of the "responsibles" of the communal village, who had already been divorced twice, sought a third divorce on the ground that her husband did not love her. The judges acknowledged that this was a serious problem but also criticized her comportment. As a FRELIMO member and a "responsible" she was obligated to combat divorce; if she were awarded a third divorce, the practice would be legitimated. After agonizing deliberations, the court decided that it lacked the competence to decide and sent the case to the district tribunal.

The five cases are interesting on a number of levels. They illustrate the court's attempt to reconcile two potentially conflicting positions—the attack on polygyny and support for the integrity of the family. They also demonstrate the important role played by the larger community in the judicial process. In the public hearings, which were well attended, independent testimony by communal village members was decisive in at least three of the five cases. The judges appear to follow two principles relatively consistently: They seek to reconcile the couple whenever possible, especially in established marriages with children, but they will dissolve those marriages where extreme abuse has occurred. Finally, both the punishments and the lengthy perorations by the presiding judge concerning the evils of polygyny, wife abuse, divorce, and alcoholism reveal the important educational function these local courts perform.

More serious crimes and complicated civil matters are resolved at the district and provincial levels, where the presiding judge, appointed by the state, must have some higher education and formal legal training. At the district level the appointed judge is required to have a sixth-grade education and to have completed a six-month legal course (interviews with Amaral, Hunguana, and João). Orlando João is typical of the young district court judges. Twenty-five years of age, he worked as a clerk in the bureaucracy at the end of the colonial period. Because of his education and because he had not been compromised by the colonial regime, he was selected in 1979 to attend a legal training program where he studied FRELIMO ideology and Mozambican history, as well as the colonial legal codes. He then went home to preside over the Inharrime district court in Inhambane province, all of whose other members were elected by the legislative assembly (interview with João). Refresher courses are planned for him and other district court presiding judges, but the training of new judges has a much higher priority since, as of 1980, most provinces had only one or two district courts in operation (interview with Amaral).

The provincial people's tribunals, currently the nation's highest,[23] are more specialized and more professional. In Maputo province, for example, the court is

[23]The Law on Judicial Organization (Decreto Lei 12/78, December 2, 1978) calls for the establishment of the Supreme People's Tribunal, "composed of at least six judges appointed by the Minister of Justice from full law graduates over the age of twenty-five, and at least eighteen elected judges, half of whom act as substitutes" (Article 14). For a translation of this law, see Sachs (1979:

divided into three civil sections, five criminal sections, a children's section, and a police section dealing primarily with road accidents. Each section is composed of one appointed judge and at least five judges elected by the provincial assembly (interview with Amaral). Before the election, justice brigades and FRELIMO party officials go to each candidate's work place and neighborhood to solicit information from those who know him or her best. The elected judges are drawn from all sectors—factory workers, clerks, teachers, nurses, and peasants. Table 10.1 indicates their diversity.

Of the 118 elected judges, the overwhelming majority are workers in factories, state farms, hospitals, and schools. Although a few are highly educated professionals, such as teachers and doctors, most are ordinary Mozambican citizens with only a minimal formal education. The thirty representatives of mass democratic organizations come from the Mozambican Women's Movement, the Youth Movement founded after independence, and the Production Councils located at all work places.

Whatever their backgrounds, all the elected judges have other full-time jobs and take two-month annual paid leaves of absence to sit on the court. Each year they serve in a different section of the court in order to obtain the widest possible exposure (interview with Amaral).

At both the district and provincial levels lay judges act more like jurors—making findings of fact—whereas the trained judges draw conclusions of law. This role differentiation is expressly prescribed by the Law on Judicial Organization (Articles 15, 22). In part, this division of labor reflects the gulf in education and legal training that divides appointed and elected judges. There is also a tendency for many of the latter to defer to the presiding judges—although this seems to vary from court to court and to depend on the personalities and self-confidence of the various judges.

All trials at the district and provincial levels are open to the public, and the accused has the right to be represented by either a public defender or a layperson of his choice (Constitution, Article 35). The public defenders must have at least a sixth-grade education and have completed a six-month training program similar to that of a district judge, although law students or trained lawyers occasionally perform this function (interview with Amaral). The trials we observed were characterized by a presumption of innocence, vigorous questioning of the witnesses by several of the judges, and intense debate between the public defender and the state prosecutor.

The purpose of these criminal proceedings is not just to try the defendant for an isolated act but to locate the social and economic context within which the

---

57). Plans for the Supreme People's Tribunal are not yet final because of the extreme shortage of qualified personnel. There is also a temporary Supreme Military Tribunal that resolves cases of alleged security violations.

TABLE 10.1
Composition of the Elected Judges of the Provincial Court of Maputo

	Men	Women
State functionaries	5	1
Members of Mass Democratic Organizations	5	25
Workers	70	12
Total	80	38

SOURCE: Ministry of Justice, 1980.

crime occurred, evaluate its seriousness, prevent it from recurring, and determine how best to reeducate and reintegrate the accused. Two sets of criminal cases illustrate the pursuit of these objectives. In the first, a man found guilty of killing his grandmother received a sentence of twelve-years imprisonment; a month earlier a son found guilty of murdering his mother was punished with twenty-years imprisonment (*Notícias*, October 20, December 24, 1980). The lighter sentence imposed in the former case reflected the unusual extenuating circumstances. In a long, emotionally charged, and sometimes rambling presentation, the accused revealed that ever since he reached sexual maturity his grandmother had forced him to have sexual intercourse with her. After he became impotent, he went to a diviner who told him that his grandmother was a witch who had captured his sexuality. His only recourse was to kill her.[24] In the latter case the judges concluded that the killing was premeditated after hearing a number of witnesses testify about the lengthy history of conflict between mother and son.

In a similar vein, two embezzlement cases resulted in substantially different penalties despite that the amounts of money involved were almost identical (*Notícias*, November 1, 20, 1980). In the first, a bookkeeper at a state cashew factory stole $2000, for which he was given a thirty-month sentence. In the other, an employee in a government ministry falsified documents, using an official stamp he had previously stolen, and absconded with $2200. In his trial several of the judges noted that the accused was a member of FRELIMO and that membership in the party carried with it special obligations. Instead of being a model of the "new Mozambican," he had abused his position and betrayed the trust of the people. As a result, he was stripped of his party membership and received a sentence of seven-years imprisonment.

The fragmentary court records, our own observations, and discussions with various officials in the Ministry of Justice, including the minister, make it clear

[24]According to Justice Ministry authorities, the diviner will also be subsequently tried.

that the rigid and severe punishments enshrined in the colonial penal code, although still officially authorized, have uniformly, if informally, been modified by the decisions of the provincial and district courts. Periodic meetings between Justice Ministry officials, their provincial counterparts, and judges have produced a consensus that adapts the range of penalties for each crime to the new priorities and values of the socialist society in the making (interviews with Amaral, Honwana, and Hunguana). It is also the result of periodic meetings between Justice Ministry officials, their provincial counterparts, and the judges. Mitigating and aggravating factors, including the motivation of the guilty party, recidivism, physical violence, restitution, cooperation by the accused, and confession are given considerable weight. Although it is estimated that confessions occur in about 75 percent of the cases, that alone is not sufficient to prove guilt (Guild Notes, 1980). As one of the previous cases illustrates, a member of the party or a person in a position of authority who commits a crime is likely to be punished more severely—a tradition that originated in the liberated zones.

The provincial courts, and to a lesser degree those at the district level, also play an important educational function. By situating the particular crime in its broad social context the judges, especially the presiding judge, frequently use the proceeding as a vehicle for addressing evils inherited from the traditional or the colonial society. In the children's court long discussions about the evils of brideprice, initiation rites, and polygyny regularly take place. Similarly, one proceeding we attended, involving charges of misappropriation of funds by an OMM "responsible," became a forum for an attack on the abuse of power by officials of Mass Democratic Organizations, the party, and the state. Cases raising broader issues appear twice a week in a column in Notícias, the country's largest newspaper, and in several daily radio news broadcasts.

Notwithstanding the considerable achievements of the people's tribunals in democratizing justice, they continue to be plagued by the legacy of colonialism. That most Mozambicans are illiterate and have varying degrees of competence in Portuguese obviously complicates the judicial process. Both parties and witnesses often have difficulty comprehending questions from the bench and responding coherently. Moreover, their demeanor and reticence clearly reflect the anxiety associated with memories of the colonial courtroom. Because the substantial educational gap between presiding and lay judges confers too much authority on the former, it further distorts the judicial process and frustrates the real meaning of popular justice.[25] Finally, the small number of trained judges, public defenders, and prosecutors delays trials. As of August 1980, more than two-thirds of the 3800 people held in Mozambican jails were still awaiting trial (interview with Mangage). The minister of justice acknowledged this problem but expressed the

[25]In order to increase the confidence of the elected judges and reduce the influence of the presiding judge the former are encouraged to ask questions first and vote first on the decision (Guild Notes, 1980).

hope that the combination of the six-month training courses and a new genera-tion of university-trained lawyers would alleviate it within the next few years (interview with Hunguana).

One of the most important dimensions of the evolving legal system has been penal reform. In several highly publicized incidents, guards and other officials have been removed, even imprisoned, for abusing prisoners. In the most cele-brated case, the director of Machava Prison, the country's largest, was removed from his position in response to prisoner complaints that they were being mis-treated (A. Isaacman and B. Isaacman, 1981b: 21; see also Sachs, 1979: 32–36). Of greater significance was the decision to close down the antiquated colonial jails and move the prisoners to rural penal centers that emphasize rehabilitation through education and collective labor, both of which are difficult to pursue in prisons. Between 1978 and 1980 eleven centers were established, and two more are presently under construction. Approximately 1000 inmates have already been transferred, and several of the worst jails have closed (interview with Mangage). It is anticipated that the transfer of most prisoners will be completed within a few years, although those considered particularly dangerous are likely to be kept in traditional prison settings.

These centers exhibit many of the characteristics of the reeducation centers. The major difference is that the institutionalization of the new legal system mandates that all residents sent to the centers must have been convicted of crimes and given determinate sentences. Rural penal centers also have no cells, no barbed wire, and no dogs to confine or intimidate the prisoners. Each has only a handful of guards, none of whom is normally armed: The penal center in Sofala, with more than 1000 prisoners, has four; the one in Manica, with slightly fewer inmates, has two (*Ibid.*). The prisoners divide their day between collective labor, often in fields outside the formal confines of the center,[26] and classes in which they receive literacy training and study Mozambican history and FRELIMO ideology. They also have discussion groups in which they analyze each person's past and present behavior. Plans are underway to construct workshops at these centers so prisoners can acquire basic skills as carpenters and tailors and in other trades (*Ibid.*).

Another major innovation in the penal system is the plan to resettle the families of prisoners and incorporate them into the rural penal centers. This experiment was begun in Zambézia province in 1980. According to Justice Ministry officials, similar arrangements will be made in all the centers, each of which eventually will be transformed into a communal village (interviews with Hunguana and Mangage).

The writing of new codes is also an important part of the legal transformation,

---

[26]As in the case of the reeducation centers, some prisoners initially attempted to escape but were either frustrated by the remoteness of the center or captured by vigilance groups (interview with Mangage).

although it has progressed somewhat more slowly. As of 1980, draft Family and Legal Assistance codes have been completed. The experience of creating a new Family Code reveals both the problems posed by the vestiges of colonial and traditional law and the importance of involving the people in the reconstruction of their legal system. When Mozambique became independent, it inherited a Portuguese Family Code that was hopelessly out of date and that governed the family relations of only those members of the Portuguese and assimilated communities whose marriages had been celebrated in a Catholic church or registered by the state; it thus excluded the vast majority of Africans who married according to "traditional" law or lived in de facto unions of varying degrees of stability. Some of its contents had already been discarded in Portugal, such as the prohibition of divorce, and much of the remainder had implicitly been repealed by the constitutional guarantee of gender equality because those provisions reflected patriarchal principles of family organization. Moreover, since many of the numerous "traditional" practices that governed family relations among the African population inculcated and reinforced the concept of the inferiority of women and permitted their exploitation, the new government was committed to eradicating them. The party, the state, the OMM, and the OJM (the Youth Movement) had already begun to struggle against initiation rites, premature marriage, the payment of bride-price, and polygyny.[27]

The major questions to be resolved in creating a new, uniform Family Code are how to make it relevant to the varied experiences of the Mozambican people and how to use it against reactionary ways of thinking and behaving. The government has attempted to respond to both questions simultaneously by making the Family Code a subject of study throughout the country. The first draft of a new Family Code was completed in 1977 and was immediately subjected to intense debate in every residential area and work place in Mozambique. The knowledge of traditional practices thereby acquired was analyzed at a meeting of the Ministry of Justice in 1978, after which the code was redrafted and disseminated for further discussion. This process will continue until the code is considered ready for passage by the People's Assembly, the national legislature of Mozambique.

Both the contents of the draft code and the process by which it is being formulated have great educational value. The code starts from the proposition that marriage is a consensual union between a man and a woman with equal rights and duties (Articles 1, 2, 4). This concept is foreign to the Portuguese code and to traditional law, both of which recognized the superior position of the

---

[27]Other African countries have chosen not to tamper with their pluralistic systems of justice in this sphere (see, e.g., Stibich, 1969). They recognize traditional, Muslim, Christian, and Hindu practices that regulate family relationships. Mozambique is unique in recognizing the need for a uniform family law.

husband. It also establishes the minimum age for marriage at eighteen for women and twenty-one for men to ensure that the parties have the necessary physical and psychological maturity for married life (Article 5). Though it declares the importance of preserving the family unit (Article 33), divorce is permitted. But dissolution of the marriage does not terminate the responsibilities of both parties to their children (Article 35)—another principle that is foreign to traditional law and not recognized by the partners of de facto unions. Single mothers can compel the fathers of their children to pay support (Article 53), and the courts can legitimate de facto unions (Article 20). The code also establishes norms of behavior between parents and children (Articles 44–45) and between the family and the state (Article 3).

One of the major issues to be resolved by those who drafted the code was how severely to punish reactionary practices that are still important to large segments of the population. Their uncertainty is visible in the end product. Although the code disapproves of the payment of bride-price (Article 4), it is not penalized, nor is polygyny outlawed. In order to discourage immature unions, marriage is prohibited for females under age sixteen and males under eighteen, and parental consent required for females under eighteen and males under twenty-one (Article 5). The government hopes that these reactionary practices will disappear with time and that children growing up in the new Mozambique will abide by the provisions of the Family Code even where it does not compel conformity. In this sense, the code is as much a program for the future as a mechanism for regulating existing relationships.

The creation of a national system of legal assistance has proceeded more slowly. Although the constitution expressly guarantees that all persons accused of crime have the right to representation (Article 35), and the private practice of law was abolished so that all citizens would have equal access to legal representation regardless of their economic circumstances, the extreme shortage of trained legal personnel has made it impossible to achieve these goals. A recently completed draft law attempts to further them by establishing a National Institute of Legal Assistance to take the place of the private bar that existed during colonial times. It is composed of lawyers with graduate law training, judicial technicians with bachelor of law degrees, and defenders who generally lack university degrees (Articles 8–9). Only members of the institute can represent persons in criminal and civil matters and be consulted on legal questions (Article 7). The draft statute recognizes a duty of confidentiality to the client (Article 13), and the institute, like a bar association, is responsbile for disciplining its members and maintaining the standards of the profession (Article 17). The fundamental difference, however, is that members of the institute are salaried employees. They get paid according to their rank and the size and complexity of their caseload (Article 15), whereas the fees charged are determined according to the economic situation of the client and the complexity and social value of the matter (Article 14).

Although this statute is central to the administration of the judicial system, it has less educational value than the Law on Judicial Organization or the Family Code and therefore has received less public exposure and discussion. Nevertheless, it is extremely significant that it is among the first major changes in the legal system. When it is passed by the People's Assembly, the initial phase of restructuring and formalizing the judicial system will be complete and the era of informalism will be over, for there is really no need for the equivalent of a bar association in an informal system of legal service delivery.

CONCLUSION

Increased formalization of the system of popular justice has characterized the first five years of Mozambican independence. The state and the informal system of justice are no longer antagonistic, as they were during the armed struggle. Both now promote and protect the interests of workers and peasants. Toward this end the state has absorbed and adopted many of the premises, procedures, practices, and institutions first developed in the liberated zones—witness the labor commissions, the popular tribunals, the struggle for women's emancipation, and the emphasis on rehabilitation and reintegration in the criminal justice system. FRELIMO remains committed to incorporating progressive aspects of "traditional law" and to rooting the new legal system in the Mozambican reality. Finally, the dialectic between theory and practice, experimentation and formalization, retains its centrality in the process of attacking and transforming other vestiges of the colonial–capitalist legal system.

REFERENCES

Alpers, Edward (1978) "The Struggle for Socialism in Mozambique," in C. Rosberg and T. Callaghy (eds.) *Socialism in Sub-Saharan Africa*. Berkeley: University of California, Institute of International Studies.

Anderson, Perry (1962) "Portugal and the End of Ultra-Colonialism," 16 *New Left Review* 88.

Bailey, Norman (1969) "Government and Administration," in D. Abshire and M. Samuels (eds.) *Portuguese Africa: A Handbook*. New York: Praeger.

Balthazar, Rui (1979) "The Judicial Machinery under Colonialism," in A. Sachs (ed.) *Principles of Revolutionary Justice*. London: Magic.

Bender, Gerald (1978) *Angola under the Portuguese*. Berkeley: University of California Press.

Bragança, Aquino de (1980) "Le Marxisme de Samora," 217 *Afrique–Asie* 19.

Cabral, A. A. P. (1925) *Raças, usos e costumes dos indigenas provincia de Moçambique*. Lorenço Marques: Imprensa Nacional.

Carvalho, F. (1912) *Distrito de Quelimane: relatório do Governador, 1911–1921*. Lorenço Marques: Imprensa Nacional.

Centro de Estudos Africanos (1977) *The Mozambican Miner*. Maputo: Universidade Eduardo Mondlane.

Chanock, Martin (1978) "Neo Traditionalism and the Customary Law in Malawi," 16 *African Law Studies* 80.

Comité Central de FRELIMO (1976) "Relatório do Comite Central de FRELIMO," 293 *TEMPO* 48.

Davidson, Basil (1980) "The Revolution of People's Power," 32 *Monthly Review* 75.

Dos Santos, Marcelino (1973) "FRELIMO Faces the Future," 55 *African Communist* 28.

Duffy, James (1961) *Portuguese Africa.* Cambridge, Mass.: Harvard University Press.

_____ (1967) A *Question of Slavery.* Cambridge, Mass.: Harvard University Press.

FRELIMO (1976) *Documentos Base de FRELIMO.* Maputo: FRELIMO. Guild Notes (1980) "Report from Mozambique," *Guild Notes* 5, 20 (November–December).

Henricksen, Thomas (1978) *Mazambique.* London: Rex Collins.

International Labor Organization (1962) "Report of the Commission Appointed under Article 26 of the Constitution of the ILO to Examine the Complaint Filed by the Government of Ghana Concerning the Observance by the Government of Portugal of the Abolition of Forced Labour Convention," 45 *Official Bulletin* 149 (Number 2, Supplement 11).

Isaacman, Allen (1978) A *Luta Continua—Creating a New Society in Mozambique.* Binghamton, N.Y.: Fernand Braudel Center for the Study of Economics, Historical Systems, and Civilizations.

Isaacman, Allen and Barbara Isaacman (1981a) "Mozambique during the Colonial Period," 6 *Tarikh* (forthcoming).

_____ (1981b) "Creating a New Legal System," 26 *Africa Report* 19.

Isaacman, Allen, M. Stephen, Y. Adam, M. J. Homen, E. Macamo, and A. Pillilao (1980) "Cotton Is the Mother of Poverty," 13 *International Journal of African Historical Studies* (forthcoming).

Isaacman, Barbara and June Stephen (1980) *Women, the Law and Agrarian Reform in Mozambique.* Addis Ababa: Economic Commission on Africa.

Junod, Henri (1962) *The Life of a South African Tribe.* New York: University Books.

Kruks, Sonia (n.d.) "From Nationalism to Marxism: The Ideological History of FRELIMO, 1962–1977." Unpublished.

Machel, Samora (1974) A libertação da mulher e uma necessidade da revolução, garantia da sua continuidade, condição do seu triunfo. Maputo.

Mattos, Maria Leonor Correiade (1965) "Notas sobre o direito de propriedade de terra do Povos Angoni, Acheua e Ajaua da Provincia de Moçambique," 7 *Memorias do Instituto de Investigação Cientifica de Moçambique* 3.

Ministerio das Colonias (1948) *Colectânea de legislação colonial.* Lisbon: Agência Geral das Colonias.

Minter, William (1972) *Portuguese Africa and the West.* New York: Monthly Review Press.

Mondlane, Eduardo (1970) *The Struggle for Mozambique.* Baltimore: Penguin.

Monteiro, Armindo (1935) *Da governação de Angola.* Lisbon: Agência Geral das Colonias.

Mozambique Revolution (1969) 38 *Mozambique Revolution.*

Munslow, Barry (1974) "Leadership in the Front for the Liberation of Mozambique," in R. Hill and P. Warwick (eds.) *Southern African Research in Progress.* New York: Center for Southern African Studies.

Penvenne, Jeanne (1979) "Forced Labor and the Origin of an African Working Class: Lorenço Marques, 1870–1962," 13 *Boston University African Studies Center Working Papers* 1.

Rita-Ferreira, Antonio (1954) "Os Azimbas," 24 *Boletim da Sociedade de Estudos Moçambicans* 47.

Ross, Edward A. (1925) *Report on Employment of Native Labor in Portuguese Africa.* New York.

Sachs, Albie (ed.) (1979) *Principles of Revolutionary Justice.* London: Magic.

_____ (n.d.) "Mozambican Legal System." Unpublished.

Saraiva Bravo, N. (1963) A *cultural Algodoeira na economia do norte de Mocambique.* Lisbon: Junta de Investigações do Ultramar.

Saul, John (1973) "FRELIMO and the Mozambique Revolution," in G. Arrighi and J. Saul (eds.) *Essays on the Political Economy of Africa.* New York: Monthly Review Press.

——— (1979) *The State and Revolution in East Africa.* New York: Monthly Review Press.

Silva Cunha, J. M. da (1949) *O trabalho indigena: estudo do direito colonial.* Lisbon: Agência Geral das Colonias.

Smith, Ian (1974) "Antonio Salazar and the Reversal of Portuguese Colonial Policy," 15 *Journal of African History* 653.

Spence, Jack (1982) "Institutionalizing Neighborhood Courts: Two Chilean Experiences," in R. L. Abel (ed.) *The Politics of Informal Justice,* vol. 2: *Comparative Studies.* New York: Academic Press.

Stibich, Robert (1969) "Family Law in Some English-SPeaking African States," 2 *African Law Studies* 49.

Tomlinson, Barry (1977) "The Nyasa Chartered Company," 18 *Journal of African History* 109.

Tribunal Popular de Aldeia Communal de Muaria (1979) "Registos de Actas." Unpublished.

Vail, L. (1976) "Mozambique's Chartered Company: The Rule of the Feeble," 17 *Journal of African History* 389.

Vieira, Sergio (1979) "Law in the Liberated Zones," in A. Sachs (ed.) *Principles of Revolutionary Justice.* London: Magic.

Young, S. (1977) "Fertility and Famine: Women's Agricultural History in Southern Mozambique," in R. Palmer and N. Parsons (eds.) *The Roots of Rural Poverty in Central and Southern Africa.* Berkeley: University of California Press.

Interviews

Abdul, Masan (August 15, 1980), Unango, Niassa Province.

Amaral, Aires de (August 8, 1980), Maputo, Maputo Province (senior judge of the Provincial Court).

Amati, Sarifa (August 21, 1977), Chai-Chai, Gaza Province.

Balate, Marjo Matsambo (August 18, 1980), M'sawise, Niassa Province.

Baquile, Jacinto (July 21, 1979), Montequez, Cabo Delgado Province.

Barradas, Armindo (August 30, 1977), Maputo, Maputo Province.

Bitole, Jose Victor (August 18, 1980), M'sawise, Niassa Province.

Chimo, Gilberto Chambino Banana (August 19, 1980), M'sawise, Niassa Province.

Communal Village Augostinho Neto, group interview (August 4, 1980), Inharrime, Inhambane Province.

Communal Village 25 de Setembro, group interview (August 27, 1977), Nampula Province.

Communal Village 25 de Setembro, group interview (August 27, 1977), Nampula Province.

Cubai, Elias, and Cubai Vasco (August 22, 1977), Gaza, Gaza Province.

Director, Reeducation Center at M'sawise (August 18, 1980, M'sawise, Niassa Province.

Dos Santos, Marcelino (September 22, 1977), Maputo, Maputo Province (a founding member and vice-president of FRELIMO; currently secretary of the Central Committee for Economic Policy).

Faducurane, Sebastia Nacala (August 18, 1980), M'sawise, Niassa Province.

Honwana, Gita (February 1, 1980), Maputo, Maputo Province (presiding judge of one of the criminal sections of the Maputo Provincial People's Tribunal).

Hunguana, Teodato (August 12, 1980), Maputo, Maputo Province (minister of justice).

João, Orlando (August 5, 1980), Inhambane, Inhambane Province.

Laisse, Carlos Candido (August 11, 1980), Maputo, Maputo Province (national director of the literacy program).

Macamo, Salamao (February 16, 1979), Guija, Gaza Province.

Machay, Manuel Armando (August 21, 1977), Gaza, Gaza Province.

Machel, Samora (May 3, 1979), Maputo, Maputo Province (president of FRELIMO and the president of the People's Republic of Mozambique). Portions of this interview were published in 24(4) *Africa Report* and 12 *Southern Africa* 6.

Macore, Eduardo Jose (August 19, 1980), M'sawise, Niassa Province.

Mangage, Mario Fumo Bartolomeu (August 22, 1980), Maputo, Maputo Province (national inspector for prison services).

Mondlana, Rodrigues (August 15, 1977), Maputo, Maputo Province.

Mungey, Ricard (August 15, 1980), Unango, Niassa Province.

Nduvane, João (August 20, 1977), Gaza, Gaza Province.

Nhacatala (July 28, 1979), Chai, Cabo Delgado Province.

Nyantumbo, Azaria Jose (August 18, 1980), M'sawise, Niassa Province.

Presiding Judge, Provincial Court of Niassa Province (August 18, 1980), Lichinga, Niassa Province.

Sainda, Raymond (August 15, 1980), Unango, Niassa Province.

Simba, Makwati (February 13, 1979), Chibuto, Gaza Province.

Sumaili, Francisco (August 22, 1977), Gaza, Gaza Province.

Tose, Rafael (August 4, 1980), Inharrime, Inhambane Province.

Vidreira Glass Factory, group interview (August 17, 1977), Maputo, Maputo Province.

Weisman, Fiedeles (August 18, 1980), M'sawise, Niassa Province.

About the Authors

RICHARD L. ABEL is Professor of Law at the University of California, Los Angeles. He has been editor of *African Law Studies* and of the *Law & Society Rieview* and has written on African legal systems, dispute institutions, and the sociology of family law, of American and British lawyers, and of the legal protection of health and safety. He is currently working on the comparative sociology of lawyers.

MARC GALANTER is Professor of Law and of South Asian Studies at the University of Wisconsin–Madison. He has written extensively about the development of the modern Indian legal system and the relation of law to caste and religion in India, his most recent publication being *Competing Equalities: The Indian Experience with Compensatory Discrimination*. He has also written on litigation, lawyers, and courts in American society. His current research interests include the settlement of civil cases and the changing role of the judge, the impact of large-scale lawyering, and the development of innovative styles of delivering legal services in the Indian setting.

BRYANT GARTH is Assistant Professor at Indiana University School of Law (Bloomington). He has worked with Professor Mauro Cappelletti in Florence on the Access-to-Justice Project sponsored by the Ford Foundation, coauthored the project's general report, and coedited two of the volumes: *Access to Justice: A World Survey* and *Access to Justice: Emerging Issues and Perspectives*. His most recent book is *Neighborhood Law Firms for the Poor: A Comparative Study of Recent Developments in Legal Aid and in the Legal Profession*.

JOHN O. HALEY is Professor of Law at the University of Washington. He was a Fulbright Research Scholar at Kyoto University in 1971–1972 and practiced law in Tokyo from 1972–1974. His principal interests are the Japanese legal process, contract, antitrust, and administrative law. He is an editor of *Law in Japan: An Annual*.

HELEEN F. P. IETSWAART received her J.S.D. from Yale Law School in 1977; her dissertation was a socio-legal study of the handling of worker dismissal grievances in Chile. She spent 4 years (1974–1978) engaged in teaching and research on law and sociology of law in Africa and Latin America, under the auspices of UNESCO. She is now a consultant to the French Ministry of Justice, conducting research on the American and British experience with delegalization, and is also studying (with Werner Ackermann) the social responses to political repression.

ALLEN ISAACMAN is Professor of History and Adjunct Professor of Afro-American and African Studies at the University of Minnesota and has been Professor of Mozambican History at the University Eduardo Mondlane in Mozambique. His first book, *Mozambique: The Africanization of a European Institution, The Zambesi Prazos 1750–1902*, won the 1973 Melville J. Herskowitz Award as the most distinguished publication in African studies. He has also published *The Tradition of Resistance in Mozambique 1850–1921*, and *A Luta Continua—Creating a New Society in Mozambique*, plus numerous articles examining historical and contemporary aspects of Mozambique and Zimbabwe. In addition, he has written shorter journalistic pieces in the *Los Angeles Times*, the *Christian Science Monitor*, *In These Times*, *Afrique-Asie*, and *Africa Report*.

BARBARA ISAACMAN is an attorney working for the Central Minnesota Legal Aid Association. She was formerly Professor of Law at the University Eduardo Mondlane. She coauthored *Women, The Law and Agrarian Reform in Mozambique* and collaborated on *The Tradition of Resistance in Mozambique*. She has published articles in both Africanist journals and law journals, and has coauthored several interpretative pieces on contemporary southern Africa which appeared in the *Los Angeles Times*, *Christian Science Monitor*, *In These Times*, *Afrique-Asie*, and *Africa Report*.

SALLY ENGLE MERRY is a legal anthropologist specializing in the role of law in urban societies. She is currently Assistant Professor of Anthropology at

Wellesley College. She has published an ethnography on crime and social organization in an urban neighborhood, *Urban Danger: Life in a Neighborhood of Strangers*, as well as articles on court use in urban neighborhoods, legal levels and legal spheres, racial integration, and the role of gossip and scandal in social control. She is now beginning a study on the role of mediation in patterns of disputing in American urban neighborhoods.

CATHERINE S. MESCHIEVITZ received an M.A. (History, 1973) and a J.D. (1979) from the University of Wisconsin–Madison, where she is presently a Ph.D. candidate in Modern South Asian History. She spent 1977–1978 in India on a grant from the University of California-Berkeley Professional Studies Program, as a Fellow at Delhi University Law College and the Indian Law Institute. She is now in Madras, India, working on her dissertation topic—litigation in the courts of the Madras Presidency in the early nineteenth century—sponsored by grants from the Fulbright-Hays Program, the American Institute of Indian Studies, and the Social Science Research Council.

UDO REIFNER is Assistant Professor of Law at the Free University in West Berlin. His major work concerns consumer credit problems and consumer-oriented legal reasoning in civil law. From 1976–1980 he worked with Erhard Blankenburg at the Wissenschaftszentrum Berlin on an empirical study of legal aid for people of moderate means. The historical background for that study led to research on the legal institutions of German fascism, and he has edited a collection of essays on that subject. He is beginning a theoretical and empirical inquiry into the collective use of the legal system.

BOAVENTURA DE SOUSA SANTOS is Professor of Sociology at the School of Economics, University of Coimbra, where he also teaches sociology of law at the Law School. He received a law degree from that institution, studied criminal law and philosophy of law in West Germany, and earned a J.S.D. at Yale Law School. His primary interests are popular justice, legal pluralism, and the theory of the state, and he has conducted field research in Rio de Janeiro and Recife (Brazil) and Angola, as well as in Portugal.

JACK SPENCE, Associate Professor of Political Science at the University of Massachusetts–Boston, received his J.D. degree from Harvard University and his Ph.D. from Massachusetts Institute of Technology. He is currently studying U.S. and Cuban court decentralization innovations and legal intervention into urban-housing crises.

Subject Index